Studien aus dem Max-Planck-Institut
für Sozialrecht und Sozialpolitik

Band 74

Ulrich Becker | Olga Chesalina (eds.)

Social Law 4.0

New Approaches for Ensuring and Financing Social Security in the Digital Age

Nomos

The Deutsche Nationalbibliothek lists this publication in the Deutsche Nationalbibliografie; detailed bibliographic data are available on the Internet at http://dnb.d-nb.de

ISBN 978-3-8487-7149-3 (Print)
978-3-7489-1200-2(ePDF)

British Library Cataloguing-in-Publication Data
A catalogue record for this book is available from the British Library.

ISBN 978-3-8487-7149-3 (Print)
978-3-7489-1200-2 (ePDF)

Library of Congress Cataloging-in-Publication Data
Becker, Ulrich / Chesalina, Olga
Social Law 4.0
New Approaches for Ensuring and Financing Social Security in the Digital Age
Ulrich Becker / Olga Chesalina (eds.)
393 pp.
Includes bibliographic references.

ISBN 978-3-8487-7149-3 (Print)
978-3-7489-1200-2 (ePDF)

1st Edition 2021

Published by
Nomos Verlagsgesellschaft mbH & Co. KG
Waldseestraße 3-5 | 76530 Baden-Baden
www.nomos.de

Production of the printed version:
Nomos Verlagsgesellschaft mbH & Co. KG
Waldseestraße 3-5 | 76530 Baden-Baden

ISBN (Print): 978-3-8487-7149-3
ISBN (ePDF): 978-3-7489-1200-2

DOI: https://doi.org/10.5771/9783748912002

Onlineversion
Nomos eLibrary

Preface

The contributions to this book are based on presentations at a two-day conference held at the Max Planck Institute for Social Law and Social Policy in Munich on 12 and 13 December 2019. The revised papers consist of five "general" contributions and nine "case studies" covering Belgium, Italy, the United Kingdom, the Netherlands, Denmark, Sweden, Spain, France and Estonia.

We would like to thank the authors for taking part in our project and their great commitment. Our meeting in Munich was not only a very fruitful but also a very enjoyable event. We look back to it now with even more fond memories, in times in which Europe is caught in the midst of a raging pandemic and measures like lockdowns and travel restrictions are making personal encounters impossible.

We would particularly like to thank *Fritz Thyssen Stiftung* for their generous financial support of our conference. We are also grateful for the help from many colleagues at our Institute with various matters regarding organisation and publication. Last but not least, we would like to thank Christina McAllister for her proofreading and corrections.

Munich, November 2020

Ulrich Becker
Olga Chesalina

Table of Contents

List of Authors 11

Part I: Starting Points: The Changing World of Work as a Challenge for Social Security

Chapter 1
Social Law 4.0: Challenges and Opportunities in Social Protection 15
Ulrich Becker and Olga Chesalina

Chapter 2
Platform Work: Critical Assessment of Empirical Findings and its Implications for Social Security 39
Olga Chesalina

Part II: Ensuring Social Security: Employment Status Classification and Innovative Solutions

Chapter 3
The Sharing Economy in Belgium: Status due to Taxation or Non-Status? 75
Yves Jorens

Chapter 4
Is the Classification of Work Relationships Still a Relevant Issue for Social Security? An Italian Point of View in the Era of Platform Work 97
Edoardo Ales

Chapter 5
Relationship between Employment Status and Scope of Social Security Protection: The United Kingdom Example 117
Philip Larkin

Chapter 6
Extending Social Insurance Schemes to "Non-Employees": The Dutch Example 147
Gijsbert Vonk

Chapter 7
Collective Agreements and Social Security Protection for Non-Standard Workers and Particularly for Platform Workers: The Danish Experience 171
Natalie Videbæk Munkholm

Chapter 8
Looking for the (Fictitious) Employer – Umbrella Companies: The Swedish Example 203
Annamaria Westregård

Part III: Financing of Social Security: Experiences and New Approaches

Chapter 9
The Influence of the Platform Economy on the Financing of Social Security: the Spanish Case 231
Borja Suárez Corujo

Chapter 10
Social Security in the Platform Economy: The French Example – New Actors, New Regulations, Old Problems? 257
Francis Kessler

Chapter 11
New Forms of Employment and Innovative Ways for the Collection of Social Security Contributions: The Example of Estonia 281
Gaabriel Tavits

Part IV: Transborder Perspective: The Future Role of the European Union

Chapter 12
Building Up and Implementing the European Standards for Platform Workers 309
Paul Schoukens

Chapter 13
Social Law 4.0 and the Future of Social Security Coordination 335
Grega Strban

Chapter 14
Taxation of the Platform Economy: Challenges and Lessons for Social Security 363
Katerina Pantazatou

List of Authors

Edoardo Ales, Dr., Professor at the University of Naples "Parthenope"

Ulrich Becker, Dr., Director at the Max Planck Institute for Social Law and Social Policy and Professor at the Law Faculty of LMU, Munich

Olga Chesalina, PhD., Senior Researcher at the Max Planck Institute for Social Law and Social Policy, Munich

Borja Suárez Corujo, Dr., Professor at the Autonomous University of Madrid

Yves Jorens, Dr., Professor at Ghent University

Francis Kessler, Dr., Professor at the Sorbonne Law School, University of Paris I Pantheon-Sorbonne

Philip Larkin, Dr., Senior Lecturer at the University of Bedfordshire

Natalie Videbæk Munkholm, PhD., Associate Professor at Aarhus University

Katerina Pantazatou, PhD., Associate Professor at the University of Luxembourg

Paul Schoukens, Dr., Professor at KU Leuven

Grega Strban, Dr., Professor at and Dean of the Law Faculty at the University of Ljubljana

Gaabriel Tavits, Dr., Professor at and Director of the School of Law at the University of Tartu

Gijsbert Vonk, Dr., Professor at the University of Groningen

Annamaria Westregård, Dr., Associate Professor at Lund University

Part I:
Starting Points: The Changing World of Work as a Challenge for Social Security

Chapter 1
Social Law 4.0: Challenges and Opportunities in Social Protection

Ulrich Becker and Olga Chesalina

I. Starting Points

1. Digitalisation, Industrial Relations and Social Protection

Digitalisation has a strong impact on our societies. It intensifies the societal process of individualisation in general, and it influences a specific type of social relationships, namely industrial relations, in particular. Those relations are already changing. The term "non-standard work" which is being used both by the ILO[1] and the OECD[2] indicates such changes – although the main part of the workforce is still working under full-time labour contracts,[3] and although it is questionable whether temporary contracts and part-time work can be regarded as non-standard at all as they have not only formed part of the labour markets for a long time, but also do not pose any difficulties with a view to identifying a legal relationship between employees and employers which follows the rules of labour law and leads to the inclusion in traditional social security systems. Nevertheless, there is no doubt that new forms of work are arising, both within industrial relations as well as outside, especially in the form of self-employment. The keywords here are short-term labour contracts and labour contracts with a marginal number of working hours (like mini-jobs, zero-hours contracts, on-call work and other forms of casual work), hybrid and

1 International Labour Organization, Non-Standard Forms of Employment, 2020, https://www.ilo.org/global/topics/non-standard-employment/lang--en/index.htm. Accessed 14 September 2020.

2 Non-Standard Work, Job Polarisation and Inequality, in: OECD, It Together: Why Less Inequality Benefits All, OECD Publishing, Paris, 2015, pp. 135-208, https://www.oecd-ilibrary.org/employment/in-it-together-why-less-inequality-benefits-all_9789264235120-en. Accessed 14 September 2020.

3 See also *Schoukens, Paul/Barrio, Alberto,* The Changing Concept of Work: When does Typical Work Become Atypical?, in: European Labour Law Journal, 8 (2017) 4, pp. 1-28, doi:10.1177/2031952517743871.

multiple employment, proliferation of self-employment and bogus self-employment, triangular relationships with more than one person on the employees' or employers' side (like employee-sharing or temporary agency work). The outcome is an increasingly fragmented labour market, a rise in precarious and informal work, a shifting of risks from the employer to the employee, and a growing grey zone between dependent employment and self-employment.

Digitalisation is a catalyst for respective changes. It allows for new ways of communication, for more flexibility and more mobility; it enhances informality, and it enforces globalisation as territorial boundaries of human interactions lose their relevance. New employment patterns are emerging, and the most prominent one is platform work including crowdwork[4] and work on demand via apps[5].

Those changes in the labour market pose, in turn, challenges to social protection, in particular if social protection is organised via traditional forms of social security. Social security aims at protecting against the vicissitudes of life, at securing against social risks. It is, through its specific function, closely linked to societal structures. These structures are currently experiencing changes for two other reasons: the ageing of our societies leads to a change in the age structure of populations; individualisation, pluralisation and shifts of role models lead to a change of household structures. Together with changing labour markets, these different processes make it necessary to adapt the existing social security systems. While this necessity is, generally speaking, nothing new and rather forms a typical feature of institutions that are established in order to react to societal needs, the multitude of ongoing changes and their magnitude make the reform-

4 Crowdwork is a new form of employment that "uses an online platform to enable organisations or individuals to access an indefinite and unknown group of other organisations or individuals to solve specific problems or to provide specific services or products in exchange for payment", see: Eurofound, New Forms of Employment, Luxembourg: Publications Office of the European Union 2015, doi:10.2806/937385, https://www.eurofound.europa.eu/sites/default/files/ef_publication/field_ef_document/ef1461en.pdf. Accessed 14 September 2020.

5 In the case of work on demand via apps the execution of specific services, such as transport, cleaning and running errands etc. is offered to an indefinite number of individuals by means of electronic platforms (app companies), see: *De Stefano, Valerio*, The Rise of the "Just-in-Time Workforce": On-Demand Work, Crowdwork and Labour Protection in the "Gig-Economy", in: Conditions of Work and Employment Series, International Labour Office, Geneva, 71 (2016), https://www.ilo.org/travail/whatwedo/publications/WCMS_443267/lang--en/index.htm. Accessed 14 September 2020.

ing of social security a particularly difficult task. Necessary reforms concern all relevant features of social security, namely coverage, the definition of an appropriate level of benefits, and the financing.[6]

2. *Core Questions*

This project concentrates on the two most important questions in the context of social protection in a digitalised world, and on the two most urgent problems raised by the consequences of digitalisation for the labour market: (a) access to social protection and (b) its future financing.

a) Access to Social Protection

Social security in its traditional form is based on two binary distinctions at two different levels. The first concerns the distinction between economic and non-economic activities. Social insurance as a cornerstone of both social security and social protection is, in a certain way, a consequence of the former activities: it covers those who are economically active, which also allows for its financing through contributions – independent of whether social insurance is being organised in the shape of the so-called Bismarckian insurance scheme or following the Beveridgean model. It is a longstanding debate whether social protection should overcome this basic binary distinction or not, and this debate always pops up when changes on the labour markets occur – which is why it is no surprise that it is on the agenda again in these times of digitalisation. There are good reasons in favour of decoupling social protection from economic activities, although better reasons are still against it. In the end, it is a question of how to organise the coexistence of people in a stable, freedom-based political community. First, if we want to base our communities on individual freedoms and solidarity, and if we want to keep these fundaments, we will have to organise our communities accordingly; in this context, it is advisable to put emphasis on self-responsibility and to establish institutions which re-

6 See *Becker, Ulrich*, New Forms of Social Security? A Comment on Needs and Options for Reform in a National and Supranational Perspective, in: Pichrt, Jan/ Koldinská, Kristina (eds.), Labour Law and Social Protection in a Globalized World: Changing Realities in Selected Areas of Law and Policy, Alphen aan den Rijn: Wolters Kluwer 2018, pp. 205-211.

mind us that this is one basis of our life together. Second, companies should not be excluded from assuming social responsibility. They profit from market economies, and they thus must also take on their share of responsibility – which means that they should have the obligation to financially support institutions which are necessary in order to reconcile individual freedom and markets with human dignity and participation in an open society.

It is not necessary to go further into this debate here as our project takes into account the interdependencies between both binary distinctions, but concentrates at least in its starting points on the second binary distinction at a second level, i.e. a rather operational one. Traditional social protection in the form of social security as it still forms a fundament of all European welfare states, is not only based on economic activities, but also draws a distinction between dependent and independent work. The reason for this categorical distinction at the level of constructing concrete schemes is rooted in the 19th century and the times of industrialisation. Dependent work became a new form of economic activity, and those who had to rely on it became those in need of social protection as the traditional societal safety nets lost their protective role.

Nowadays, new forms of work are those brought about by the digitalisation of the labour market. Most welfare states are, for good reasons, convinced that "digital workers" are also in need of social protection. As with all forms of "new" economic activities, there are two different strategies of how to deal with them and how to include them into existing social security systems.[7] The first is a "doctrinal" solution: every distinction between dependent and independent work has to be based on a respective legal term (like "employed earner", or "Beschäftigung"), and the interpretation of this term as exercised by administrative authorities and courts might be flexible enough in order to cover "new forms" of work. The second solution is a political one that may be pursued in two different ways: a legislator can try to define new categories of persons and to make them part of an existing social protection system, be it one for dependent workers, be it one for the self-employed; or it can set up a new social protection system for a newly defined group – which will in most cases be an (re-)assemblage

7 For more details *Becker, Ulrich*, Die soziale Sicherung Selbständiger in Europa, in: Zeitschrift für europäisches Sozial- und Arbeitsrecht (ZESAR), (2018) 8, pp. 307, 315 et seq.

of already well-known social security tools.[8] All this is anything but new: in many countries, so-called "homeworkers" are a legally defined group of economically active persons explicitly covered by social protection – not so much as a reaction to changes in the labour market but as a reaction to a too narrow definition of employed earners in the initial phase of social insurances. It is not by chance that a modernised understanding of homeworkers may also cover a vast range of new digital work. Yet, the extent to which solutions actually open up possibilities in order to rearrange access to social protection, and what solutions are appropriate, depends very much on the institutional pathways that exist in a given country. If, for example, social protection for the self-employed does not exist or is of a rather rudimentary nature, this naturally restricts options for including digital workers into social protection. In many countries, the weaknesses and gaps in social protection for the self-employed have become visible through the COVID-19 crisis, which functions like a magnifying glass in this respect.[9] That efforts have to be taken to improve access to social protection is obvious. Within the EU, a respective (political) obligation follows from the Council Recommendation on access to social protection for workers and the self-employed of 8 November 2019[10] (see also below, Section II.4.) according to which member states are recommended to "provide access to adequate social protection to all workers and self-employed persons" (1.1.) – in the sense of not only formal, but also effective coverage (pt. 9. of the Recommendation).

b) Financing of Social Protection

Financing social protection has already become a major challenge due to demographic processes such as the aging of our societies. Digitalisation will pose additional problems. This does not hold true in the first place be-

8 *Chesalina, Olga*, Extending Social Security Schemes for "Non-Employees": A Comparative Perspective, in: Zeitschrift für ausländisches und internationales Arbeits- und Sozialrecht, (2020) 1, pp. 3-12.

9 See *Becker, Ulrich/He, Linxin/Hohnerlein, Eva Maria/Seemann, Anika/Wilman, Nikola*, Protecting Livelihoods in the COVID-19 Crisis: Legal Comparison of Measures to Maintain Employment, the Economy and Social Protection, MPISoc Working Paper 7/2020, https://www.mpisoc.mpg.de/fileadmin/user_upload/data/Sozialrecht/Publikationen/Schriftenreihen/Working_Papers_Law/MPISoc_WP_7_2020_Corona_Livelihood_Nov.pdf. Accessed 6 November 2020.

10 OJ C 387/1, 15 November 2019.

cause digital work is often seen as being rather "informal" – although it is often being carried out without written contracts and formal registration. Yet, this does not necessarily mean that the collection of contributions would have to experience additional difficulties. Rather to the contrary: if contributions were based on the revenue from the rendering of services, or on the expenses for these revenues respectively, the underlying transactions will already be existent in digital form and thus easily traceable. In this regard, digitalisation also opens up opportunities for social protection – given that the relevant data will be made available: it enables, and it will also urge, the administration involved to make use of digital technologies.

Nevertheless, digitalisation may lead to a reduction of social security contributions as more economic activities will be performed in form of self-employment and as employer's contribution will be missing. This hints to a well-known problem of social security regarding the self-employed: it is comparatively costly for the insured. As a consequence, state subsidies may seem to be an unavoidable remedy, or else the level of social protection will remain rather low.[11] A general solution to these problems is to open up new sources for financing. The most prominent example is certainly the French general contribution (*contribution sociale généralisée* – CSG).[12] It is questionable, and has even been qualified differently by the highest French and European courts, whether the CSG is a tax or a social security contribution.[13] In any case, it shifts financing into the direction of taxes – which might be suitable for those branches of social security that aim at providing a certain infrastructure such as health insurance, but also leads back to the question of how to organise social security in general and to the role of financial sources in particular.

If one wants to maintain a contributory financial basis of social security, at least for a major part, other and more targeted solutions should be found. There is an interesting example in Germany that comes from the social insurance for artists (*Künstlersozialversicherung*) introduced by the Artists' Social Insurance Act[14] in 1983. Artists and publicists have to pay

11 See for example *Becker*, ZESAR 2018 (fn. 7), pp. 307, 314.

12 See for the CSG and the *contribution au remboursement de la dette sociale* (CRDS) information of the French Treasury, https://www.economie.gouv.fr/particuliers/contribution-sociale-generalisee-csg. Accessed 7 November 2020.

13 See for a qualification as contribution: ECJ of 15 February 2000, C-169/98 (Commission/France), ECR 2000, I-1049, recit. 34 et seq.; *Cour de Cassation* of 31 May 2012, 11-10,762; *Conseil d'Etat* of 27 July 2015, n° 334551. Arguing for a specific tax *Conseil Constitutionnel* of 19 December 2000, Déc. n° 2000-437.

14 Act of 27 July 1981 (BGBl. I, 705).

their own contributions which amount – like in other traditional insurance schemes – to 50 percent of the overall financial sources of the insurance system. For the other half, a third is paid from the state budget (as a state subsidy). The remaining two-thirds have to be paid through a specific fee or levy. This levy is imposed on the remunerations paid by a "marketer" to the independent artists and publicists in a calendar year, irrespective of whether the recipient is insured under the Artists' Social Insurance Act or not. Of course, this legal construction led to the question whether such an obligation of every marketer was in line with the constitution, in particular with the right to equal treatment: why would marketers have to pay for insurance, but others not, although the artists work independently? In this respect, the German Federal Constitutional Court made the remarkable statement[15] that it would be inappropriate "to deny that artists and publicists are in need of social protection and that marketers have a social responsibility simply because there is no formal employer-employee relationship"; it put emphasis on the fact that this relationship might be the most important case of a "social responsibility" as a justification for the obligation to contribute to a social insurance scheme which protects third persons, but that it is not exclusive; more generally, it follows that laws have to take social facts into account, that they should react to these facts and establish institutions fitting the particularities of a given economic activity "instead of making it a condition in advance that this form of existence be dissolved and transferred to a formal employment relationship".[16]

Today, laws have to answer how to organise social protection for digital workers. The reality of working conditions of many platform workers is comparable to the case made by the German Federal Constitutional Court.

---

15 Decision of 8 April 1987, 2 BvR 909, 934, 935, 936, 938, 941, 942, 947/82, 64/83 and 142/84, BVerfGE 75, 108.

16 BVerfGE 75, 108, 159 et seq.: „Es würde die Eigenart künstlerischen und publizistischen Schaffens verkennen und wäre daher sachwidrig, eine soziale Schutzbedürftigkeit der Künstler und Publizisten und eine soziale Verantwortung der Vermarkter ungeachtet dessen nur darum zu verneinen, weil rechtsförmlich kein Arbeitgeber-Arbeitnehmer-Verhältnis vorliegt. Denn dieses ist, wie dargelegt, zwar der hauptsächliche und weithin typische, aber nicht der ausschließliche Fall einer sozialen Verantwortlichkeit, die die Heranziehung zu fremdnützigen Sozialversicherungsbeiträgen rechtfertigt. Das Recht findet die Eigenart der Existenzform als Künstler oder Publizist vor, die mit dem Sachgehalt dieser Tätigkeit in Zusammenhang steht. Es ist dann sachgerecht, bestehender sozialer Schutzbedürftigkeit in einer Weise Form und Gestalt zu geben, die dieser Eigenart Rechnung trägt, anstatt vorab zur Bedingung zu machen, daß diese Existenzform sich auflöst und in ein förmliches Arbeitnehmerverhältnis übergeht."

Platform providers can, and may be urged to, take over financial responsibility as a consequence of their social responsibility. Under what conditions that could and should be realised, and how to implement such an obligation to pay social security contributions has to be discussed further. In this context, the technical problems are of secondary importance. The questions of how to impose which obligation and how to enforce it, must first of all be answered from a legal perspective. And this answer becomes especially challenging as many platform activities cross at least one national border. This is why coordination, and, to some degree, also harmonisation will be needed, both at the EU and the international level. That is one reason why a potential remedy for the challenges to social protection in the age of digitalisation must always take the transnational perspective into account.

3. *Aim of the Project and State of Research*

a) Insights from Innovations in Social Protection

Our book undertakes an analysis of the impact of labour market changes in the digital age on social security law and addresses the challenges to social security which arise through these changes by putting emphasis on platform work. It seeks to examine innovations: solutions and mechanisms for ensuring social security on the one hand, and those for financing social security on the other. In this regard, different national approaches – ones that have already been implemented (through legislation, collective agreements or private actors) or are presently under discussion (in the literature or draft laws) – are analysed in a comparative perspective. Although it is first and foremost the task of states to adjust their social protection systems, transborder issues will – as stated above – become even more important in the digital age. Therefore, we include the present and future role of the European Union: on the one hand, new coordination problems may arise; on the other, new forms of financing will also have an impact on the basic freedoms and basic rights, and we will have to ask whether it is possible or necessary to opt for new regulatory approaches at European level.

The overall aim of the book is to provide new insights on what a "Social Law 4.0" should look like. With respect to methods and the question of how to find these insights, we base our analysis on a systematic legal comparison which takes account of the existing empirical (social science) evidence, but also focus on case studies in order to give concrete and detailed examples of the different ways of adapting social security systems to the present challenges.

b) Innovations in Research

Although research on the impact of digitalisation on industrial relations is anything but new, contents and methods of our book are based on two innovative points.

First, we concentrate on a *social law perspective*. While labour law classification, working conditions and labour law protection for platform workers have already been the subject of numerous sociological, economic and political studies[17] and other legal publications,[18] so far only few studies

---

17 E.g. Digital Labour Platforms and the Future of Work: Towards Decent Work in the Online World, International Labour Office – Geneva, ILO, 2018, https://www.ilo.org/global/publications/books/WCMS_645337/lang--en/index.htm; Employment and Working Conditions of Selected Types of Platform Work, Luxembourg: Publications Office of the European Union, 2018, https://www.eurofound.europa.eu/publications/report/2018/employment-and-working-conditions-of-selected-types-of-platform-work; *Zachary, Kilhoffer/De Groen, Willem Pieter/Lenaerts, Karolien/Smits, Ine/Hauben, Harald/Waeyaert, Willem/Giacumacatos, Elisa/Lhernould, Jean-Philippe/Robin-Olivier, Sophie*, Study to Gather Evidence on the Working Conditions of Platform Workers, VT/2018/032, Final Report, 13 March 2020, European Commission, 2020; *Pesole, Annarosa/Urzí Brancati, Maria Cesira/Fernández-Macías, Enrique/Biagi, Federico/González Vázquez, Ignacio*, Platform Workers in Europe, EUR 29275 EN, Publications Office of the European Union, Luxembourg, 2018, ISBN 978-92-79-87996-8, doi:10.2760/742789, JRC112157, https://publications.jrc.ec.europa.eu/repository/bitstream/JRC112157/jrc112157_pubsy_platform_workers_in_europe_science_for_policy.pdf; *Forde, Chris/Stuart, Mark/Simon, Joyce/Oliver, Liz/Valizade, Danat/Alberti, Gabriella/Hardy, Kate/Trappmann, Vera/Umney, Charles/Carson, Calum*, The Social Protection of Workers in the Platform Economy, Study for the EMPL Committee, European Union, Brussels, 2017, http://www.europarl.europa.eu/RegData/etudes/STUD/2017/614184/IPOL_STU(2017)614184_EN.pdf. All accessed 14 September 2020.

18 Blanpain, Roger/Hendrickx, Frank/Waas, Bernd (eds.), New Forms of Employment in Europe, Alphen aan den Rijn: Wolters Kluwer 2016; *Prassl, Jeremias*, Humans as a Service, Oxford: Oxford University Press 2018; Meil, Pamela/Kirov, Vassil (eds.), Policy Implications of Virtual Work, Cham: Palgrave Macmillan 2017. The chapter by *Wynn, Michael/Paz-Fuchs, Amir*, Flexicurity Outside the Employment Relationship? Re-engineering Social Security for the New Economy, in: Westerveld, Mies/Olivier, Marius (eds.), Social Security Outside the Realm of the Employment Contract" (Cheltenham: Edward Elgar Publishing 2018), focuses "rather on changes in the labour market than on welfare institutions" (p. 32), whereas we analyse the interrelationship between employment and social policy.

and publications have been conducted on the social protection of platform workers from a legal perspective.

Second, this book does not want to merely add another study to the already existing publications that reflect specific single aspects of social protection in the changing world of work[19]; rather, it takes a holistic approach that systematises new insights concerning the future of social protection in the digital age. As this approach is based on a legal comparison and includes transnational perspectives, our study is at the same time a contribution to the more general topic of how welfare states develop, and it sheds light on a common European core of the concept of welfare state.

---

between labour law and social law from the social law perspective. The volume Casale, Guiseppe/Treu, Tiziano (eds.), Transformation of Work. Challenges for the Institutions and Social Actors (Alphen aan den Rijn: Wolters Kluwer 2019), addresses the changes affecting the world of work in national systems of labour law and social security. The main research themes of this volume and our undertaking overlap only insignificantly (e.g. concerning new forms of social security, required interrelationship (closer link) between social security and employment policies). The other six research themes of this volume – informal workers; migrant workers; global trade and labour; organisation, productivity, well-being at work; transnational collective agreements; the role of state and industrial relations – are mostly related to labour law and are not subject of our research project. The book by *Tiraboschi, Michele*, Labour Law and Welfare Systems in an Era of Demographic, Technological, and Environmental Changes, (Adapt University Press 2019) also focuses on labour law, in particular on the impact of the "Fourth Industrial Revolution" in Italian labour law and policy, and addresses the demographical challenges for welfare systems.

19 E.g. the contributions in: Pichrt, Jan/Koldinská, Kristina (eds.), Labour Law and Social Protection in a Globalized World: Changing Realities in Selected Areas of Law and Policy, Alphen aan den Rijn: Wolters Kluwer 2018, by: *Hajdú, József*, Social Security and the Modern and Post-Modern Forms of Work, (pp. 191-203); *Laborde, Jean-Pierre*, Social Security: A New Idea for the Twenty-First Century (pp. 183-190); *Martin Štefko,* Guaranteed Minimum Income for All? Task for the ILO" (pp. 213-220) and *Jorens, Yves*, Migrant Workers and European Social Law: Of a Respectable Age or Time for a Rebirth? (pp. 233-246). See also *Schoukens, Paul/ Barrio, Alberto/Montebovi, Saskia*, Social Protection of Non-Standard Workers: The Case of Platform Work (pp. 227-258) and *Stevens, Yves*, Social Security and the Platform Economy in Belgium: Dilemma and Paradox (pp. 259-286), both in: Devolder, Bram (ed.), The Platform Economy. Unravelling the Legal Status of Online Intermediaries (Cambridge – Antwerp – Chicago: Intersentia, 2019).

II. Structure and Contents

1. Background

The following chapters of this book start with a background paper on "*Platform Work: Critical Assessment of Empirical Findings and its Implications for Social Security*" (*Olga Chesalina*).

The main goal of this chapter is to find out implications for social security from empirical findings and practical evidence. The author stresses that careful attention must be paid when interpreting the figures and trends from such empirical research on platform work due to its numerous shortcomings. The chapter discusses the novelty of platform work in comparison to other forms of non-standard employment and the specifics of the business model of online labour platforms, the motivation of platform workers and their access to social protection, as well as dependence patterns. In the author's opinion, the category of financial dependence on platform work as explored in empirical studies is not suitable for justifying the classification of platform workers as employees and for justifying a social responsibility of platforms for workers; it is only a socio-economic characteristic of platform workers that reflects labour fragmentation, which is characteristic also of other types of non-standard work. It concludes that even if many challenges related to platform work are similar to the challenges of non-standard employment, the heterogeneity of platform workers and the fact that platform work is chiefly carried out as a side job – which is not typical for self-employment – should be taken into account. Numerous issues for future investigations are offered in the chapter (e.g. concerning changes of the platform operator's policy in relation to extending or reducing its social insurance responsibility; insurance schemes dedicated to platform workers; research questions for interviews with platform workers that can help to estimate and prevent fraud through the receipt of social assistance benefits etc.).

2. Ensuring Social Security: Employment Status Classification and Innovative Solutions

Access to social protection is related to a set of different conditions and to the pre-existing institutional setting. It depends on:

- the architecture of the existing social protection schemes and whether they are employment-based like the traditional social insurance, whether they include the self-employed, and if so, to what extent;
- the status of the worker, and in particular the assessment of the work performed following the traditional distinction between the employed and the self-employed, with special emphasis on the role of the courts;
- approaches concerning the employment status classification in labour, social security and tax law used in the respective country;
- the introduction of either new forms of social protection or new approaches within the existing schemes.

Even if many countries have already undertaken social law reforms widening the access to social security for self-employed persons and non-standard workers, there are still huge accessibility gaps[20] and difficulties concerning the calculation of social benefits, as social security systems had originally been designed for standard labour relationships and are still linked to a certain employment status. As dependent employment is associated with social contributions, many employers deliberately misclassify workers.

With the emergence of platform work it has become more difficult to clarify whether platform workers are employees or self-employed persons, and whether the platform provider or the requester (client) fulfils any employer functions. Platforms describe themselves as an intermediary or a market-place. The first decisions of national courts concerning the classification of platform workers for labour and social law purposes have been controversial. Whereas in many cases, for example in the case of Deliveroo riders in Spain,[21] the employee status was recognised, in other cases platform workers were classified as self-employed persons[22]. Therefore, Chapters 3 to 8 of this book also concern the employment status classification of platform workers for labour and social law purposes. They analyse court

20 European Commission, Access to Social Protection for All Forms of Employment – Assessing the Options for a Possible EU, Initiative Publications Office of the European Union, Luxembourg, 2018, pp. 295 ff., http://ec.europa.eu/social/main.jsp?catId=738&langId=en&pubId=8067&furtherPubs=yes. Accessed 18 October 2020.

21 See for an overview on case law of different courts *Beltrán de Heredia Ruiz, Ignasi*, Employment Status of Platform Workers, https://ignasibeltran.com/2018/12/09/employment-status-of-platform-workers-national-courts-decisions-overview-australia-brazil-chile-france-italy-united-kingdom-united-states-spain/#spa2. Accessed 7 November 2020.

22 Decision of the Labour Court of Second Instance of Munich of 4 December 2019 – 8 Sa146/19.

decisions related to this subject, look at the outcomes of these decisions and their relevance for social law issues, and examine whether the traditional criteria have undergone changes, or whether they have to be changed in order to tackle the challenges of platform work.

Chapter 3 deals with "*The Sharing Economy in Belgium: Status due to Taxation or Non-Status?*" (*Yves Jorens*). It describes a model introduced in 2016 which is based on separate fiscal and social regulations and a separate category for certain providers within the sharing economy aimed to encourage self-employment and to combat the grey economy. In 2018 the Belgian legislator went one step further, providing instead of a reduced tax burden rate a total tax and social security contribution exemption for income from certain forms of gainful activities. The author addresses issues concerning the nature of these activities and the transfer of certain forms of labour into the sphere of spare-time work. Furthermore, problems arising from the special treatment of these activities within the framework of Belgian social security legislation are dealt with. The author reflects on the decision of the Constitutional Court whether such a treatment can be objectively and reasonably justified and articulates the need for a new vision of social security that should "also be opened up for activities that do not or not always follow the normal scope of employment".[23]

In Chapter 4, the question "*Is the Classification of Work Relationships Still a Relevant Issue for Social Security?*" is asked from "*An Italian Point of View in the Era of Platform Work*" (*Edoardo Ales*). The chapter aims at "analysing the connection between the classifications of work activities in labour law and the protective statute they enjoy in social security".[24] It describes the new approach of the Italian legislator based on a political assessment of the weaknesses of specific groups of workers (which is not necessarily associated with assessing the social needs of a certain category of workers), taking into account the new forms of integration into the organisation. The author investigates the new category of "hetero-organised" collaborations and riders as bright examples of a continuous tendency to move away from a "tailor-made protective statute" towards "a new frontier of subordination". He describes different modalities of platform work in Italian legislation: subordinate work (smart working); hetero-organised collaboration and finally (false) autonomous work. The author identifies contradictions and gaps concerning the social protection of "hetero-organised" collaborators and autonomous riders; this means riders who are classified as au-

23 Chapter 3, Section IV, p. 96.
24 Chapter 4, Section I, p. 97.

tonomous workers and entitled to a wage, set by collective agreements, but who are simultaneously excluded from the scope of the general social insurance scheme for employees as they fall within the scope of application of the social insurance scheme for the self-employed.

Chapter 5 is entitled "*Relationship between Employment Status and Scope of Social Security Protection: The United Kingdom Example*" (*Philip Larkin*). The United Kingdom labour market has experienced the proliferation of non-standard forms of employment, in particular "zero-hours" contracts and "gig" work. The chapter examines the entitlement to social security benefits in the modern UK labour market and analyses difficulties resulting from employment status (self-employment or non-standard employment in combination with an irregularity of earnings and their precarious financial position) in the access to various social security benefits. Hereby, the author pays particular attention to Universal Credit, but also includes other benefits (e.g. Employment and Support Allowance). Furthermore, the question is analysed of whether, and how, the Welfare Reform Act can be made effective through legislative and technological reform. The author suggests that "the optimum solution to maintaining regular and stable payments of Universal Credit to gig workers in particular also lies in technology, with some form of integration of revenue authorities and digital platform software, so that gig workers have taxes automatically deducted from their earnings, relieving them of the burden of calculating this for themselves, and these calculations could be reported to the Department for Work and Pensions".[25]

Chapter 6 on "*Extending Social Insurance Schemes to 'Non-Employees': The Dutch Example*" (*Gijsbert Vonk*) presents a broad overview of the Netherlands' state of protection of non-standard employees and self-employed persons under social security law. The contribution is devoted to new approaches which have been taken into consideration in order to fill protective gaps for these persons. The author provides an analysis of policy objectives, legislative change and proposals for change made by successive governments in the Netherlands and by official advisory agencies since 2010 and an overview of lessons that may (not) be learned from the Dutch experience.

Chapter 7 reports on "*Collective Agreements and Social Security Protection for Non-Standard Workers and Particularly for Platform Workers: The Danish Experience*" (*Natalie Videbæk Munkholm*). It shows the implications of the uncertain employment status of non-standard workers on access to social

25 Chapter 5, Section VII, pp. 145 et seq.

protection with special attention on platform workers. Denmark is famous for the important role of collective agreements in the provision of additional social benefits and extending the scope of social protection. Denmark was the first country where, in 2018, a collective agreement for platform workers was concluded as a pilot project.[26] The contribution analyses the role of the social partners in developing the regulatory measures in tripartite negotiations and in negotiating supplementary social security measures in collective agreements for non-standard workers. Therefore, the author discusses the role of the social partners and demonstrates the strengths and weaknesses of the Danish experiences of providing platform workers with access to the social security systems. Special emphasis is put on the reform of the unemployment insurance system in 2017, changing this system to a more universal approach by taking into account income from all types of work. The author concludes that even if platform companies represent a new form of company and the employment status of these workers is often uncertain, these persons are still in need of social security.

Chapter 8 "*Looking for the (Fictitious) Employer – Umbrella Companies: The Swedish Example*" (*Annamaria Westregård*) provides an analysis of social security implications of the Swedish umbrella companies' business model which has been adopted in Sweden in the 1990s but became widespread with the growing of the collaborative economy. The author shows particular gaps and problems in the social security system and unemployment insurances for umbrella company workers, and she emphasises the importance of supplemental social security benefits in industry-wide collective agreements. The author seeks to answer whether or not umbrella companies are a possible way of extending social security protection to include this group of vulnerable employees and the self-employed. The contribution concludes that the different approaches concerning the concept of employment in Swedish labour, social security and tax law have resulted in a situation in which an umbrella company, from a social security point of view, pays taxes and social security contributions for its fixed-term workers who are employees according to labour legislation, while at the same time the umbrella company workers, when it comes to unemployment insu-

26 *Munkholm, Natalie Videbæk/Schjøler, Christian Højer*, Platform Work and the Danish Model: Legal Perspectives, in: Nordic Journal of Commercial Law, (2018) 1 pp. 116-145, https://journals.aau.dk/index.php/NJCL/article/view/2487. Accessed 18 October 2020.

rance, will be regarded as self-employed persons without current assignments and, therefore, will not be entitled to unemployment benefits.

3. *Financing Social Security: Experiences and New Approaches*

The rise of the platform economy, the proliferation of self-employment and non-standard forms of employment are starting to erode the contribution base of social protection systems, threatening the sustainability of the social security systems.[27] Traditional social security systems allow for risk-sharing among employers and employees. New forms of employment, combined with a lack of obligatory contributions paid, undermine the foundations of collective solidarity and the current institutional forms of social security. Companies profit from the proliferation of self-employment and the gig economy (cheap labour, without social insurance obligations and contributions), a fragmentation of labour and a shifting of risks to the weaker contractual party (employees or self-employed workers).

The question arises whether platforms providers / clients should assume their share of (financial) responsibility towards individuals and / or towards the state (and public institutions). And if this is so, further questions concern the conditions under which contributions should be paid: in which cases are persons who provide services via digital platforms and service contracts (to a certain degree) dependent on third persons (e.g. platform providers or clients) who control their activity, and does this make the latter responsible and justify the participation of the platform providers in the financing of social protection for the service providers? Does a shift in the structure of financing and the inclusion of new sources of financing comply with the principles of social insurance systems (in particular, the principle of solidarity)? And if this is the case, which institutional changes are necessary? Those were the background considerations for the contributions of Part III of the book and its Chapters 9 to 11.

Chapter 9 deals with "*The Influence of the Platform Economy on the Financing of Social Security: The Spanish Case*" (*Borja Suárez Corujo*). In Europe, Spain is the country with the second largest number of platform workers and probably with the highest number of court decisions concerning

27 *Chesalina, Olga*, Access to Social Security for Digital Platform Workers in Germany and in Russia: A Comparative Study, in: Spanish Labour Law and Employment Relations Journal, (2018) 1, pp. 17-28.

the classification of platform workers.[28] The aim of this chapter is to reflect on how this major technological shift could modify the financing structure of Bismarckian social security systems. The author emphasises that the financial balance of a social security model based on financing through social contributions could seriously be harmed once the platform economy gains greater weight. In the author's opinion, a progressive redesign of social security financial resources or a reconfiguration of benefits is required. The author investigates different options concerning future financing of social security in Spain in order to address the challenges posed by the rise of the platform economy.

Chapter 10 expands on the question "*Social Security in the Platform Economy: The French Example – New Actors, New Regulations, Old Problems?*" (*Francis Kessler*). While other countries are still discussing the possible options with regard to involving platforms in the financing of social security, imposing on them obligations in the field of social security and taxation and granting platform workers social security rights, France was the first country that has already introduced such regulations. In 2016, regulations concerning a social responsibility of platforms were introduced in the French Labour Code; they are applicable to self-employed persons who have access to one or more platforms offering electronic networking for their professional activities.[29] Among other things, this chapter of the Labour Code provides for social responsibility on the part of platforms for occupational accidents of platform workers. Furthermore, issues concerning the classification of platform workers in France are addressed; there are first cases where litigation has been resorted to. Classification of a worker as an employee means an obligation of platforms to pay social contributions for platform workers (e.g. Uber drivers). Furthermore, the author investigates various legislation novelties adapted until 2019: concerning the new sources of financing of social security in the gig economy, with the example of rental of furnished accommodation for short periods; anti-fraud measures concerning tax and social security obligations of online platform operators. He also provides an analysis of different legislative initiatives. The chapter concludes that – concerning the financing of social

28 *Royo Rodríguez-Piñero, Miguel*, Spain, in: Daugareilh, Isabelle/Degryse, Christophe/Pochet, Philippe (eds.), The Platform Economy and Social Law: Key Issues in Comparative Perspective, ETUI Working Paper 2019.10, Brussels, 2019, p. 92 f., https://www.etui.org/Publications2/Working-Papers/The-platform-economy-and-social-law-Key-issues-in-comparative-perspective. Accessed 14 September 2020.

29 Articles L. 7341-1 to Art. L. 7342-6 Code du Travail.

protection – the French legislator preferred to only marginally modify the existing rules rather than to implement comprehensive reforms.

Chapter 11 reports on "*New Forms of Employment and Innovative Ways for the Collection of Social Security Contributions: The Example of Estonia*" (*Gaabriel Tavits*). The author starts by describing the Estonian social security system and the role of social taxes and contributions for its financing. He continues with the general tendencies of development of social protection and its financing. The most significant shortcoming of the social security system is the Estonian health insurance system that excludes approximately 14 percent of the whole working age population due to the discontinuity of their income and employment. The author concludes that only fundamental changes in the financing of health care and in the state tax system would allow to address this challenge. Nevertheless, Estonia is often seen as the most excellent example of e-government and digitalisation in Eastern Europe (ranking 2nd out of the 28 EU Member States concerning digital public services in the Digital Economy and Society Index 2020[30]). It has already implemented some innovative mechanisms of administering social security and taxes, and of simplifying the taxation of services. The entrepreneur account, on the one hand, represents a new way of simplifying tax liability (including social taxes) and, on the other hand, enables access to social security, in particular health insurance. However, in order to get benefits from health insurance, a social tax of at least the minimum rate (540 euros per month) should be paid, which means that working for the minimum wage does not guarantee the minimum level of social protection.

4. *Transborder Perspective: The Future Role of the European Union*

The final Part IV of the book is dedicated to the transborder perspective. As the challenges of the changing world of work in many cases go beyond the national borders, the future role of the European Union, of international organisations, and of agreements of public international law needs to be addressed. In this context, we concentrate on the role of the European Union which is currently working on a renewal of its social policy programmes and trying to set up a common agenda. The so-called Euro-

30 Digital Economy and Society Index Report 2020 – Digital Public Services, https://ec.europa.eu/digital-single-market/en/digital-public-services-scoreboard. Accessed 14 September 2020.

pean Pillar of Social Rights shall serve as a general basis.[31] Contrary to the wording of its title, it does not contain individual entitlements but general principles that should guide both national and European policies of social protection.[32] One of these principles (No. 12) reads as follows: "Regardless of the type and duration of their employment relationship, workers, and, under comparable conditions, the self-employed, have the right to adequate social protection."

As part of the implementation of the European Pillar of Social Rights and based on Article 292 in conjunction with Articles 153 and 352 TFEU, the Council of the EU adopted its Recommendation "On access to social protection for workers and the self-employed" on 8 November 2019.[33] The Recommendation addresses the problem that up to half of the people in non-standard work and self-employment across the EU are at risk of not having sufficient access to social protection and/or employment services, which is a growing impediment to the sustainability of social protection systems and to the welfare of an increasing proportion of the workforce.[34] The main objective of the Recommendation is to provide access to adequate social protection to all workers and the self-employed and to establish minimum standards in the field of social protection of workers and the self-employed.

In this context, Chapter 12 on "*Building Up and Implementing European Standards for Platform Workers*" (*Paul Schoukens*) focuses on how the EU institutions address the challenge of organising social security for platform workers. The contribution examines the question to what extent the Recommendation responds to the challenges for the organisation of social security that arise from the emergence and proliferation of platform work. For this reason, the typical features of platform work that present challenges to traditional social security are assessed based on the provisions

---

31 https://ec.europa.eu/commission/priorities/deeper-and-fairer-economic-and-monetary-union/european-pillar-social-rights/european-pillar-social-rights-20-principles_en. Accessed 14 September 2020.

32 See for its character and its possible indirect legal impact *Becker, Ulrich*, Die Europäische Säule sozialer Rechte, in: Zeitschrift für öffentliches Recht, (2018) 73, pp. 525-558.

33 Fn. 10.

34 European Commission, Commission Staff Working Document, Analytical Document accompanying the Consultation Document "Second Phase Consultation of Social Partners under Article 154 TFEU on a Possible Action Addressing the Challenges of Access to Social Protection for People in All Forms of Employment in the Framework of the European Pillar of Social Rights", Brussels, 20 November 2017, p. 25.

outlined in the Recommendation. Finally, the author analyses the shortcomings of the Recommendation (and its underlying EU vision on access to social protection), and what kind of EU legal action in the field of social security could still be relevant. Analysing the question whether the legal standards developed by the Recommendation are sufficient, the author comes to the result that common standards at EU level are needed. The chapter concludes that since income is generated no longer only mainly from standard employment but also from other non-standard activities and returns from goods, the traditional elements of social security systems (sources of financing, social security risks as well as eligibility conditions and calculation of benefits) should be reconsidered. At the EU level, a broad approach seems to be required: apart from the protection through social benefits, fair competition rules on the internal market should be elaborated.

Chapter 13 on "*Social Law 4.0 and the Future of Social Security Coordination*" (*Grega Strban*) changes the perspective and deals with the questions of cross-border movement. Due to digital technologies in a changing world of work many kinds of dependent and independent work can be carried out from any place in the world linked to the internet; there are diverse patterns of mobility. At the same time, EU provisions on the coordination of social security systems (Regulations 883/2004, 987/2009) and rulings of the Court of Justice of the European Union (e.g. case C-137/11 "Partena") still suppose primarily stable working arrangements and a fixed physical location.[35] The author seeks to answer how the coordination of national social security systems should be modified in order to follow the development of non-standard forms of employment and self-employment. He outlines that solutions to contemporary challenges of social security coordination lie in a more inclusive approach: not only freedom of movement of standard, but also of non-standard workers should be promoted. In order to achieve this goal, a targeted modification of the coordination regulations is required. Also, technical achievements should be used in order to provide for the exchange of information in relation to the movement of non-standard workers.

Although we can identify completely different rules on social contributions and taxes in all jurisdictions, a common problem of both types of

35 European Commission, Analytical Report 2018: Social Security Coordination and Non-Standard Forms of Employment and Self-Employment: Interrelation, Challenges and Prospects. Written by *Strban, Grega/Bermejo, Dolores Carrascosa/Schoukens, Paul/Vukorepa, Ivana*, Brussels, 2020.

public charges is that they are based on the physical presence of taxpayers and assets. The current rules are not fit for taxing in a digital economy characterised by online or virtual companies whose location is hard to determine. This may result in legal uncertainty, tax and social contribution evasion, or enforcement problems regarding the collection of tax and social contributions. Furthermore, the division between contributions and taxes is not always clear. Many different initiatives were launched at the national and supranational levels in order to tackle the challenges concerning the taxation of the platform economy. This is taken up in the final Chapter 14 on "*Taxation of the Platform Economy: Challenges and Lessons for Social Security*" (*Katerina Pantazatou*). It provides an analysis of the main problems concerning the taxation of the platform economy. The prime aim of the chapter is to try to answer "whether there is anything for social law to learn from tax law and whether taxation, one of the main sources of financing social protection, is adequately prepared to deal with the platform economy challenges"[36]. One of the outcomes of the chapter is that a coordinated approach in social and tax law in relation to employment classification would prevent resorting to circular arguments, such as using the platform worker's tax treatment for labour law classification purposes, which may lead to contradictory results. Another point concerns anti-fraud measures: the author highlights that incentives to encourage platform workers to declare their income together with a simplified reporting system would promote the appropriate payment of social contributions and the fight against false self-employment.

III. Conclusions and Perspectives

1. As can be seen from the brief summary of the chapters provided above, they contain an overview on a variety of approaches in order to meet the challenges posed to social protection in the digital age. The contributions cover a broad range of different topics such as the legal qualification of economic activities including both legal and practical issues concerning the inclusion of digital workers, the role of different systems of social protection including the relation between contributory-based and tax-financed schemes as well as the relation between basic and supplementary security, or the difficulties to secure a stable financial basis for social security.

36 Chapter 14, Section I, p. 364.

The contributions in this book do not only give evidence of the fact that despite recent amendments in the legislation, there are still a lot of obstacles to effective access to social protection for non-standard workers and self-employed persons. They also analyse new approaches for ensuring and financing social security, they put these approaches into the context of the overall social protection structure, discuss their pros and cons, and provide the reader with a critical assessment of whether, and to what extent, novel approaches can help to effectively meet current and actual challenges.

2. What can be learned from those different approaches presented in this book? Two points merit particular attention.

a) First, it is clear that many national solutions – or rather: the initial steps to meet challenges in the digital age at a national level – remain embedded in the national architectures of social protection institutions. There are sometimes structures of single national schemes which either open up specific gaps in social protection on the one hand, or allow for coverage without any classification of persons on the other. And also the actors involved, those playing a decisive role in shaping social protection systems, differ: where trade unions and employers' associations have a specific responsibility in this respect, they have to be actively involved in reforming social protection. Having said this, it is nevertheless rather more remarkable that not only few of the approaches described in this book might easily being transferred from one jurisdiction to another, or that such transferral would be possible with minor adjustments only. That holds especially true for rather technical approaches like making the enrolment of digital workers easier and providing economic incentives in this regard. Yet, the same transfer would be feasible when it comes to more fundamental aspects like putting certain social responsibilities on platforms and thus integrating these enterprises more closely into the systems of social protection.

b) Second, and if one wants to sum up the different approaches in reacting to digitalisation, we can observe a patchwork of single measures. Governments, and societies as a whole, not only have to deal with many details in order to maintain effectively functioning social protection. There also seems to be a certain lack of overall strategies and a certain tendency towards special solutions which often remain controversial and fragmented, or more generally speaking, a tendency towards modifications or extensions of existing social protection schemes in the light of specific developments.

This does not only call for more exchange and dialogue at EU level in order to establish a common social policy basis. It also leads to the question whether such "construction works" aimed at repairing the existing "buildings" of social protection suffice in order to meet future challenges or whether these should be scheduled for demolition and be rebuilt following new plans. Or, in other words: are new, and specific forms of social security necessary for digital workers? To what extent does digitalisation urge us to change (and not only further develop) the traditional structures of existing social security systems? These questions are even more urgent if one considers digitalisation as being one of a plurality of challenges, and in a way also as a phenomenon of more general societal changes. This leads to a reconsideration of the structural fundaments of social security and the coordination of different social protection schemes within every state[37], including the question of how to share which tasks between these schemes. It also requires the reconsideration of fundamental aspects of transnational social security coordination at EU level, especially the respective roles of places of employment and of residence[38].

3. Although these questions will have to be answered, we propose to take intermediate steps and to react in two steps to the challenges posed by digitalisation. The first concerns better knowledge of the factual developments: there is still the need for empirical analysis of the impact of digitalisation on the existing social protection systems, which is an endeavour that calls for interdisciplinary research as social science methods have to be applied while, at the same time, knowing which circumstances are taken into account for the application of social protection law.

In a second step, the existing law will have to undergo changes. These changes will certainly differ from one jurisdiction and one state to the next, depending on the national social protection architecture, the actors involved, and also the legal instruments available with regard to the administrative and constitutional law background. They may lead to a more universal, and at the same time more restricted, role of social security, leaving room for more variety as regards supplemental protection.

Yet, three aspects will be of universal importance in order to realise a Social (Protection) Law 4.0 – and going beyond the fact that protection systems themselves have to become (much more) "digitalised":

- where still existent, restrictive conditions for the access to social security have to be abolished even, and in particular, within employment-based systems, namely as regards requirements of a certain amount of economic activities or their regular form;

37 See Chapter 12, Section VI, pp. 328-333.
38 See Chapter 13, Section VIII, pp. 360-361.

- social protection for the self-employed needs to be improved, both with a view to the social risks covered and the level of protection;
- the financial basis of social security needs to be broadened, not only through subsidies from the general state budget but also through novel forms of public charges and the redefinition of social responsibilities;
- coordination has to be improved both between different types of social protection schemes and with other financial transaction systems, in particular the tax system – as social spending and levying taxes and other contributions are the core activities of welfare states in order to define access to and participation in our societies, sharing responsibilities between their members and laying a fundament for societal life.

Chapter 2
Platform Work: Critical Assessment of Empirical Findings and its Implications for Social Security

Olga Chesalina

I. Introduction

The platform economy is characterised by platform work as a new form of employment. So far, no uniform definition of platform work has been established in the literature, in empirical studies or across European and international organisations. Nevertheless, there is a consensus concerning the division of platform work into two main types. Valerio de Stefano has proposed to distinguish between crowdwork and work on demand.[1] Eurofound also follows this divison.[2] Crowdwork is a form of employment that "uses an online platform to enable organizations or individuals to access an indefinite and unknown group of other organizations or individuals to solve specific problems or to provide specific services or products in exchange for payment".[3] In the case of work on demand via apps the execution of specific services, such as transport, cleaning and running errands etc. is offered to an indefinite number of individuals by means of electronic platforms (app companies).[4] Other terms for crowdwork are "location-

1 *De Stefano, Valerio*, The Rise of the "Just-in-Time Workforce": On-Demand Work, Crowdwork and Labour Protection in the "Gig-Economy", in: Conditions of Work and Employment Series, International Labour Office, Geneva, 71 (2016), https://www.ilo.org/travail/whatwedo/publications/WCMS_443267/lang--en/index.htm. Accessed 12 September 2020.

2 Eurofound, Work on Demand: Recurrence, Effects and Challenges, Luxembourg: Publications Office of the European Union, 2018, doi:10.2806/463459, https://www.eurofound.europa.eu/publications/report/2018/work-on-demand-recurrence-effects-and-challenges. Accessed 12 September 2020.

3 Eurofound, New Forms of Employment, Luxembourg: Publications Office of the European Union, 2015, doi:10.2806/937385, https://www.eurofound.europa.eu/sites/default/files/ef_publication/field_ef_document/ef1461en.pdf. Accessed 12 September 2020.

4 *De Stefano, Valerio*, The Rise of the "Just-in-Time Workforce": On-Demand Work, Crowdwork and Labour Protection in the "Gig-Economy" (fn. 1).

independent", web-based,[5] online work, remote platform work[6]; other terms for work on demand are offline work, on-location platform work (location-based).[7]

Labour law classification, working conditions and labour law protection for platform workers have already been the subject of numerous studies and publications,[8] whereas social law research in this field is still in its infancy. Platform work has already been addressed in a wide range of sociological, economic and political studies. Nevertheless, questions regarding the social security of platform workers represent a very young field of research dealt with only in recent studies.

In studies, two approaches are used concerning the issue of access of platform workers to social protection: Firstly, there are various studies that exclusively target platform workers.[9] An excellent example worth mentioning is the study for the EMPL Committee entitled "*The Social Protection of*

---

5 *Pesole, Annarosa/Urzí Brancati, Maria Cesira/Fernández-Macías, Enrique/Biagi, Federico/González Vázquez, Ignacio*, Platform Workers in Europe, EUR 29275 EN, Publications Office of the European Union, Luxembourg, 2018, ISBN 978-92-79-87996-8, doi:10.2760/742789, JRC112157, p. 14, https://publications.jrc.ec.europa.eu/repository/bitstream/JRC112157/jrc112157_pubsy_platform_workers_in_europe_science_for_policy.pdf. Accessed 12 September 2020.

6 *Piasna, Agnieszka*, Counting Gigs. How Can we Measure the Scale of Online Platform Work? Working Paper 2020.06, ETUI, Brussels: ETUI aisbl, 2020, p. 11, https://www.etui.org/sites/default/files/2020-09/Counting%20gigs_2020_web.pdf. Accessed 12 September 2020.

7 Ibid.

8 Blanpain, Roger/Hendrickx, Frank/Waas, Bernd (eds.), New Forms of Employment in Europe, Alphen aan den Rijn: Wolters Kluwer 2016; *Prassl, Jeremias*, Humans as a Service, Oxford: Oxford University Press 2018; Meil, Pamela/Kirov, Vassil (eds.), Policy Implications of Virtual Work, Cham: Palgrave Macmillan 2017. In the handbook of Davidson, Nestor M./Finck, Michèle/Infranca, John J. (eds.), Cambridge Handbook of the Law of the Sharing Economy, Cambridge: Cambridge University Press 2018, the sharing economy is addressed from different legal perspectives, i. a. from the labour law perspective, but not from the social law perspective. Platform work as a kind of precarious work from the labour law perspective is devoted some contributions in Kenner, Jeff/Florczak, Izabela/Otto, Marta (eds.), Precarious Work. The Challenge for Labour Law in Europe, Cheltenham: Edward Elgar Publishing 2019.

9 *Berg, Janine*, Income Security in the On-Demand Economy: Findings and Policy Lessons from a Survey of Crowdworkers, in: Conditions of Work and Employment Series, International Labour Office, Geneva, 74 (2016); Digital Labour Platforms and the Future of Work: Towards Decent Work in the Online World, International Labour Office – Geneva, ILO, 2018, https://www.ilo.org/wcmsp5/groups/public/---dgreports/---dcomm/---publ/documents/publication/wcms_645337.pdf. Accessed 12 September 2020; Eurofound, Employment and Working Conditions of

Workers in the Platform Economy"[10], which provides comprehensive research findings on the social protection of platform workers. Secondly to be mentioned are studies that analyse the situation of platform workers among a larger category of persons in non-standard forms of employment,[11] new forms of work[12] or among self-employed persons.[13] The studies of the second group provide, in large part, insights from a social policy point of view rather than from empirical evidence. Many studies mention social security issues only briefly.[14] A mix between the first and the second approach is the study of the European Social Insurance Platform entitled

---

Selected Types of Platform Work, Luxembourg: Publications Office of the European Union, 2018, https://www.eurofound.europa.eu/sites/default/files/ef_publication/field_ef_document/ef18001en.pdf. Accessed 12 September 2020; *Pesole, Annarosa/Urzí Brancati, Maria Cesira/Fernández-Macías, Enrique/Biagi, Federico/González Vázquez, Ignacio*, Platform Workers in Europe (fn. 5); *Zachary, Kilhoffer/De Groen, Willem Pieter/Lenaerts, Karolien/Smits, Ine/Hauben, Harald/Waeyaert, Willem/Giacumacatos, Elisa/Lhernould, Jean-Philippe/Robin-Olivier, Sophie*, Study to Gather Evidence on the Working Conditions of Platform Workers, VT/2018/032, Final Report, 13 March 2020, European Commission, 2020.

10 *Forde, Chris/Stuart, Mark/Simon, Joyce/Oliver, Liz/Valizade, Danat/Alberti, Gabriella/Hardy, Kate/Trappmann, Vera/Umney, Charles/Carson, Calum*, The Social Protection of Workers in the Platform Economy, Study for the EMPL Committee, European Union, Brussels, 2017, http://www.europarl.europa.eu/RegData/etudes/STUD/2017/614184/IPOL_STU(2017)614184_EN.pdf. Accessed 12 September 2020.

11 *Spasova, Slavina/Bouget, Denis/Ghailani, Dalila/Vanhercke, Bart*, Access to Social Protection for People Working on Non-Standard Contracts and as Self-Employed in Europe. A Study of National Policies. European Social Policy Network (ESPN), Brussels: European Commission, 2017; OECD, The Future of Social Protection: What Works for Non-Standard Workers?, OECD Publishing, Paris, 2018, https://doi.org/10.1787/9789264306943-en. Accessed 12 September 2020.

12 OECD, New Forms of Work in the Digital Economy, OECD Digital Economy Papers, No. 260, OECD Publishing, Paris, 2016, https://doi.org/10.1787/5jlwnklt820x-en. Accessed 12 September 2020; OECD, Policy Responses to New Forms of Work, OECD Publishing, Paris, 2019, https://doi.org/10.1787/0763f1b7-en. Accessed 12 September 2020.

13 ILO/OECD, Ensuring Better Social Protection for Self-Employed Workers, paper prepared for the 2nd Meeting of the G20 Employment Working Group under Saudi Arabia's presidency, 8 April 2020, https://www.ilo.org/wcmsp5/groups/public/---dgreports/---ddg_p/documents/publication/wcms_742290.pdf. Accessed 12 September 2020.

14 *Pesole, Annarosa/Urzí Brancati, Maria Cesira/Fernández-Macías, Enrique/Biagi, Federico/González Vázquez, Ignacio*, Platform Workers in Europe (fn. 5); *Zachary, Kilhoffer/De Groen, Willem Pieter/Lenaerts, Karolien /Smits, Ine/Hauben, Harald/Waeyaert, Willem/Giacumacatos, Elisa/Lhernould, Jean-Philippe/Robin-Olivier, Sophie*, Study to Gather Evidence on the Working Conditions of Platform Workers (fn. 9); Digital Labour Platforms and the Future of Work: Towards Decent Work

"Are Social Security Systems Adapted to New Forms of Work Created by Digital Platforms?"[15]. It is mainly based on a questionnaire sent out to social security institutions that made it possible "to provide a state-of-the-art view on the situation of platform workers and social security in certain countries"[16]. This study covers two main types of platform work (online delivered platform work and locally delivered work).

This chapter provides a critical assessment of empirical studies and practical findings. In this context, we would like to focus rather on cross-national studies (European or international perspective) than on national studies (however, in some cases we shall also refer to those). With this understanding, the author seeks to elaborate the implications for social security and some proposals for future investigations. The chapter is organised as follows: The following, second Section discusses the novelty of platform work in comparison to other forms of non-standard employment and the specifics of the business model of online labour platforms. The third Section considers the size of platform work and issues concerning cross-border labour flows in platform work, reflecting the shortcomings of empirical studies. Implications for social security resulting from empirical findings are examined in the fourth Section. Hereby, the motivation of platform workers and their access to social protection as well as dependence patterns are analysed. Special attention is paid to comparing the situation of platform workers concerning access to social protection to that of non-standard workers and self-employed persons. The implications for social security from practical evidence are discussed in the fifth Section. Finally, and important from a social security point of view, shortcomings of empirical and practical evidence are summarised and proposals for future investigations are offered.

---

in the Online World (fn. 9); Eurofound, Employment and Working Conditions of Selected Types of Platform Work (fn. 9); *Florisson, Rebecca/Mandl, Irene*, Platform Work: Types and Implications for Work and Employment – Literature Review, Working Paper WPEF18004, Eurofound, Dublin, 2018, https://www.eurofound.europa.eu/sites/default/files/wpef18004.pdf. Accessed 12 September 2020.

15 ESIP, Are Social Security Systems Adapted to New Forms of Work Created by Digital Platforms?, 30 January 2019, https://esip.eu/images/pdf_docs/ESIP_Study_Platform_Work.pdf. Accessed 12 September 2020.

16 Ibid., p. 4.

II. Platform Work: What is Really New?

There is an ongoing discussion on whether platform work is something entirely new or rather a result of the evolutionary development of work organisation.[17] The supporters of the first approach consider platform work as the "most relevant manifestation of new forms of employment generated by technological change"[18], "a new way to share and exchange goods, services and knowledge"[19]. This group (which includes platform providers themselves) considers technology to be a driving force.[20] However, numerous researchers are sceptical about the leading role of technology behind the growth of the platform economy. Research has shown that it is not technology, but taxes, social contributions and other cost-savings that are key drivers of the expansion of platform work. Some research sees an interrelationship between the decline of standard employment relationships and the emergence and proliferation of platform work.[21]

Platform work reflects a number of different trends on the labour market over several decades[22]: fragmentation, segmentation and precariousness of work,[23] commodification of labour, control mechanisms of economic partners via telecommunication tools, disruption of the concept of firm, bogus self-employment, shift of risks from the employer to the employee

17 *Stanford, Jim*, The Resurgence of Gig Work: Historical and Theoretical Perspectives, in: Economic and Labour Relations Review, 28 (2017) 3, pp. 382-401, https://doi.org/10.1177/1035304617724303. Accessed 12 September 2020.

18 *Royo, Miguel Rodríguez-Piñero*, Spain, in: Daugareilh, Isabelle/Degryse, Christophe/Pochet, Philippe (eds.), The Platform Economy and Social Law: Key Issues in Comparative Perspective, ETUI Working Paper 2019.10, Brussels, 2019, p. 92 f., https://www.etui.org/Publications2/Working-Papers/The-platform-economy-and-social-law-Key-issues-in-comparative-perspective. Accessed 12 September 2020.

19 *Semenza, Renata/Mori, Anna*, New Self-Employment as a Theoretical Matter, in: Semenza, Renata/Pichault, François (eds.), The Challenges of Self-Employment in Europe. Status, Social Protection and Collective Representation, Cheltenham: Edward Elgar 2019, p. 27.

20 *Joyce, Simon/Stuart, Mark/Forde, Chris/Valizade, Danat*, Work and Social Protection in the Platform Economy in Europe, p. 14, http://eprints.whiterose.ac.uk/148824/. Accessed 12 September 2020.

21 Ibid., p. 3.

22 *Huws, Ursula*, Where did Online Platforms Come From? The Virtualization of Work Organization and the New Policy Challenges it Raises, in: Meil, Pamela/Kirov, Vassil (eds.), Policy Implications of Virtual Work, Cham: Palgrave Macmillan 2017, pp. 30-31.

23 *Joyce, Simon/Stuart, Mark/Forde, Chris/Valizade, Danat*, Work and Social Protection in the Platform Economy in Europe (fn. 20), p. 14.

and spread of self-employment and informal work. For this reason, some research does not consider the challenges presented by platform employment as something new in comparison to challenges posed by non-standard employment and self-employment.[24] This has been confirmed by a recent study of the European Commission.[25]

Digital technologies are one of the factors that contributed to the emergence of platform work. At the same time, digital technologies have significant consequences for the development of platform work: they enable virtual[26] connections between all participants of this business construction ("digital intermediation"[27]), they allow platforms to control platform workers permanently and to avoid employment law classification. These digital mechanisms were not known and used before. The proliferation of crowdwork in a certain country depends on the respective level of internet availability. Summarising all the above, we consider that all mentioned factors together called platform work as a new form of employment into existence.

Platform work is the outcome of a business model of labour platform companies. Natalie Munkholm argues in this book that platform companies represent a new form of company model rather than new forms of work.[28] In our opinion, we cannot separate a new form of business model from a new form of employment: they are both new as they are interconnected. Even if there is a variety of labour platforms, the assessment of academic literature and empirical findings allows us to highlight the following distinctive features of this business model:

---

24 *Garben, Sacha*, Tackling Social Disruption in the Online Platform Economy. Shifting the Narrative to the Benefits of (EU) Regulation, FEPS Policy Paper, July 2019, p. 7, https://www.feps-europe.eu/attachments/publications/feps%20paper%20-%20garben%20-%20clean%20final.pdf. Accessed 12 September 2020.

25 *Zachary, Kilhoffer/Pieter De Groen, Willem/Lenaerts, Karolien/Smits, Ine/Hauben, Harald/ Waeyaert, Willem/Giacumacatos, Elisa/Lhernould, Jean-Philippe/Robin-Olivier, Sophie*, Study to Gather Evidence on the Working Conditions of Platform Workers (fn. 9), p. 226.

26 Ursula Huws speaks about the "virtualization of work and virtualization of work organization", cf. *Huws, Ursula*, Where did Online Platforms Come From? The Virtualization of Work Organization and the New Policy Challenges it Raises (fn. 22), pp. 30-31.

27 *Stanford, Jim*, The Resurgence of Gig Work: Historical and Theoretical Perspectives (fn. 17), p. 384.

28 *Munkholm,Natalie Videbæk*, Collective Agreements and Social Security Protection for Non-Standard Workers and Particularly for Platform Workers: The Danish Experience, Chapter 7, Section IV, p. 200 in this book.

- There is a remarkable change in the structure of firms. Whereas the managerial firm is organised as an entity, platforms establish "hybrid governance structures".[29] As market organisations they outsource work and shift risks to platform workers.[30] While platforms try to possess few assets,[31] the "new" class of the self-employed[32] that has emerged through this business model often possesses some capital (e.g. car, flat) and are, at the same time, deprived of entrepreneurial freedom.[33]
- Platform companies pretend to be a mere marketplace and an intermediary, with the result that platform workers are considered to be self-employed.
- Platform companies (and also clients) try to avoid or limit labour and social responsibility[34] as well as a classification of platform workers as employees or as employee-like persons.[35]
- Digital and informational technologies are an integral part of this business model.
- Platforms advertise this form of employment with workers' autonomy and flexible working arrangements. In fact, they are "controlling autonomy"[36] in the way that platform workers are controlled through algorithms and also human management.

29 *Acquier, Aurélien*, Uberization Meets Organizational Theory. Platform Capitalism and the Rebirth of the Putting-Out System, in: Davidson, Nestor M./Finck, Michèle/Infranca, John J. (eds.), Cambridge Handbook of the Law of the Sharing Economy, Cambridge: Cambridge University Press 2018, p. 15.

30 Ibid., pp. 15, 19.

31 Nick Srnicek has proposed to call "Uber's business model" a "lean platform", cf. *Sniercek, Nick,* Two Myths About the Future of the Economy, in: Skidelsky, Robert/Craig, Nan (eds.), Work in the Future. The Automation Revolution, Cham: Springer VS 2020, p. 134.

32 *Lobel, Orly*, Coase and the Platform Economy, in: Davidson, Nestor M./Finck, Michèle, Infranca, John J. (eds.), Cambridge Handbook of the Law of the Sharing Economy, Cambridge: Cambridge University Press 2018, p. 72.

33 *Acquier, Aurélien*, Uberization Meets Organizational Theory. Platform Capitalism and the Rebirth of the Putting-Out System (fn. 29), pp. 15, 19.

34 *Desbarats, Isabelle*, Workers in Legally Constituted Online Platforms in France Should the Courts Determine Their Professional Categorization?, in: Revue de Droit Comparé du Travail et de la Sécurité Sociale – English Electronic Edition (2019) 4, p. 165.

35 *Hotvedt, Marianne*, The Contract-of-Employment Test Renewed. A Scandinavian Approach to Platform Work, in: Spanish Labour Law and Employment Relations Journal, 7 (2018) 1-2, p. 59, doi: https://doi.org/10.20318/sllerj.2018.4436.

36 *Ivanova, Mirela/Bronowicka, Joanna/Kocher, Eva/Degner, Anne*, The App as a Boss? Control and Autonomy in Application-Based Management. Arbeit/Grenze/Fluss – Work in Progress interdisziplinärer Arbeitsforschung No. 2, Frankfurt (Oder):

- Control through algorithmic methods (including rating systems) and financial incentives prevail over control through "classical labour law tools". Nevertheless, there is a covert subordination.
- The relationship between the platform and the platform worker is characterised by information asymmetries.[37] Platforms gather a huge amount of data concerning platform workers and, simultaneously, this information is withheld from platform workers.[38] This gives labour platforms greater power over workers.
- Platforms introduce recommendation systems based on data collected from workers in order to encourage them to adopt a certain targeted behaviour.
- Platforms purposely use the "overstaffing" strategy: regarding work via platforms, the number of active drivers, couriers or other platform workers registered with the platform is many times higher than would be necessary for the fulfilment of all orders during a certain period of time or during a shift.[39]

  Platform workers are highly substitutable and impersonalised. An extreme commodification of labour is happening.

While some courts have already recognised the new forms of control and monitoring mechanisms (and in particularly, geolocation) as features of employment relationship,[40] others have refused to do so. For example, in the first German labour law judgement concerning the employment classification of a platform worker, the courts of first and of second instance have refused to recognise his employee status.[41] It remains to be seen whether the Federal Labour Court[42] will recognise that the platform worker was practically, economically and personally dependent on the platform, including through the use of its monitoring mechanisms.

Viadrina, 2018, doi: 10.11584/Arbeit-Grenze-Fluss.2.; *Schönefeld, Daniel*, Kontrollierte Autonomie. Einblick in die Praxis des Crowdworking, in: Hensel, Isabell/Schönefeld, Daniel/Kocher, Eva/Schwarz, Anna/Koch, Jochen (eds.), Selbständige Unselbständigkeit, Baden-Baden: Nomos 2019, p. 76.

37 *Ivanova, Mirela/Bronowicka, Joanna/Kocher, Eva/Degner, Anne*, The App as a Boss? Control and Autonomy in Application-Based Management (fn. 36), p. 16.

38 Ibid., p. 16.

39 Ibid., p. 7.

40 E. g. in France the decision of the Labour Chamber of the Supreme Court of 28 November No. 17-20.079.

41 Decision of the Labour Court of Second Instance of Munich of 4 December 2019 – 8 Sa146/19.

42 The proceeding is scheduled for 1 December 2020.

The business model of labour platforms is highly changeable. The numerous court decisions in favour of the employee or worker status of platform workers prompt platforms to change their initial strategy and find new ways to avoid the application of compulsory labour and social law regulations.[43]

In fact, platform work is a highly heterogeneous category. Some platform workers are genuinely self-employed persons, i.e. professional self-employed workers. This group is the main beneficiary and sees platform work as an opportunity.[44] Simultaneously, the situation of other platform workers is even more precarious than that of workers in other non-standard forms of employment.[45]

III. *Empirical Evidence*

1. *Situation at a Glance*

Since the emergence of platform-mediated work, there have been a lot of attempts to estimate and evaluate this phenomenon. Today, there are already a number of studies and surveys that give insights into platform work. The estimations on the size of the platform economy vary significantly across the studies because of different research methodologies and different definitions of platform work used.[46] Different studies indicate

---

43 The most recent example being Uber, which has changed its app after the law "AB5" came into effect in order to avoid drivers operating as contractors to be classified as employees. In particular, it allowed drivers to set their own rates. Cf. *Paul, Kari*, Uber and Lyft must classify drivers as employees, judge rules, in blow to gig economy, The Guardian, 10 August 2020, https://www.theguardian.com/technology/2020/aug/10/uber-lyft-ruling-california-judge. Accessed 12 September 2020; other examples are mentioned by *Zachary, Kilhoffer/De Groen, Willem Pieter/Lenaerts, Karolien/Smits, Ine/Hauben, Harald/ Waeyaert, Willem/Giacumacatos, Elisa/Lhernould, Jean-Philippe/Robin-Olivier, Sophie*, Study to Gather Evidence on the Working Conditions of Platform Workers (fn. 9), p. 122.

44 *Semenza, Renata/Mori, Anna*, New Self-Employment as a Theoretical Matter (fn. 19), p. 28.

45 Some scholars consider platform work as a last stage of precariousness. See *Cavallini, Gionata/Avogaro, Matteo*, "Digital Work" in the "Platform Economy": The Last (but not Least) Stage of Precariousness in Labour Relationships, in: Kenner, Jeff/Florczak, Izabela/Otto, Marta (eds.), Precarious Work. The Challenge for Labour Law in Europe, Cheltenham: Edward Elgar Publishing 2019, p. 176.

46 *Zachary, Kilhoffer/De Groen, Willem Pieter/Lenaerts, Karolien/Smits, Ine/Hauben, Harald/Waeyaert, Willem/Giacumacatos, Elisa/Lhernould, Jean-Philippe/Robin-Olivi-*

that between one and five percent of the working age population are somehow engaged in platform work.[47] While one group of studies shows that the rise of work on demand (offline platform work) is significantly higher than that of crowdwork,[48] other studies come to the opposite result.[49]

Many studies demonstrate that platform work is "an emerging phenomenon of increasing importance but still modest in size"[50]. There are different scenarios and estimations concerning the growth of platform work, as to whether it has already peaked or continues to extend. According to one approach, confirmed in some more recent studies, the number of platform workers has dropped.[51] According to a different approach,

---

er, Sophie, Study to Gather Evidence on the Working Conditions of Platform Workers (fn. 9), pp. 44-45.

47 ESIP, Are Social Security Systems Adapted to New Forms of Work Created by Digital Platforms? (fn. 15), p. 4; *Forde, Chris/Stuart, Mark/Simon, Joyce/Oliver, Liz/Valizade, Danat/Alberti, Gabriella/Hardy, Kate/Trappmann, Vera/Umney, Charles/Carson, Calum*, The Social Protection of Workers in the Platform Economy (fn. 10); OECD, Measuring Platform Mediated Workers, OECD Digital Economy Papers, No. 282, OECD Publishing, Paris, 2019, pp. 8-12, https://doi.org/10.1787/170a14d9-en. Accessed 12 September 2020; *Zachary, Kilhoffer/De Groen, Willem Pieter/Lenaerts, Karolien /Smits, Ine/Hauben, Harald/ Waeyaert, Willem/Giacumacatos, Elisa/Lhernould, Jean-Philippe/Robin-Olivier, Sophie*, Study to Gather Evidence on the Working Conditions of Platform Workers (fn. 9), p. 44; *Freudenberg, Christoph*, Rising Platform Work. Scope, Insurance Coverage and Good Practices among ISSA Countries, German Federal Pension Insurance/Technical Commission on Old-Age, Invalidity and Survivors Insurance, World Social Security Forum, Brussels, 14-18 October 2019, p. 1.

48 *Drahokoupil, Jan/Fabo, Brian*, The Platform Economy and the Disruption of the Employment Relationship. ETUI Policy Brief, Brussels, 2016, http://www.etui.org/Publications2/Policy-Briefs/European-Economic-Employment-and-Social-Policy/Collective-labour-law-under-attack-how-anti-crisis-measures-dismantle-workers-collective-rights. Accessed 12 September 2020.

49 *Zachary, Kilhoffer/De Groen, Willem Pieter/Lenaerts, Karolien/Smits, Ine/Hauben, Harald/ Waeyaert, Willem/Giacumacatos, Elisa/Lhernould, Jean-Philippe/Robin-Olivier, Sophie*, Study to Gather Evidence on the Working Conditions of Platform Workers (fn. 9), p. 228; ILO/OECD, Ensuring Better Social Protection for Self-Employed Workers (fn. 13), p. 4.

50 *Pesole, Annarosa/Urzí Brancati, Maria Cesira/Fernández-Macías, Enrique/Biagi, Federico/González Vázquez, Ignacio*, Platform Workers in Europe (fn. 5), p. 5.

51 ILO/OECD, Ensuring Better Social Protection for Self-Employed Workers (fn. 13); *Urzí Brancati, Maria Cesira/Pesole, Annarosa/Fernandez Macias, Enrique*, New Evidence on Platform Workers in Europe, EUR 29958 EN, Publications Office of the European Union, Luxembourg, 2020, ISBN 978-92-76-12949-3 (online), doi:10.2760/459278 (online), JRC118570, p. 4.

platform work will continue to extend.[52] It is important to recall that platform work and labour platforms like TaskRabbit and Uber emerged and have grown after the global financial crisis of 2007.[53] The global coronavirus crisis of 2020, which is accompanied by job losses and a deep economic recession, will most likely contribute to the further growth of certain types of platform work and the emergence of new, as yet unknown forms of non-standard work. There is first evidence of such a development, e.g. the number of new registrations on the freelancer platform PeoplePerHour increased in March 2020: in the UK, registrations rose by 300 percent, in Spain by 329 percent and in Japan by as much as 513 percent.[54]

2. *Shortcomings of Empirical Studies*

The studies available up to now provide a lot of information about the socio-demographic characteristics of platform workers, their working conditions, access to labour and social protection. However, there are considerable limitations to the studies and the data:

(1) There is a lack of reliable data on platform work.[55] Official data is almost non-existent. Until 2016/2017, there was no official statistical data on the total number of platform workers at all, and until now only some countries have such data. One of the first large-scale official statistical data concerning electronically mediated employment (in-person, offline tasks and online task) was presented in the survey of the American Bureau of Labor Statistics (BLS) of May 2017.[56] It was found that one percent of the total employed population in the US were en-

52 *Huws, Ursula*, Where did Online Platforms Come From? The Virtualization of Work Organization and the New Policy Challenges it Raises (fn. 22).

53 Ibid., p. 29.

54 The Coronavirus Crisis is Shining a Light on the Difficult Situation Many Gig Workers Face, 8 April 2020, https://www.rolandberger.com/en/Point-of-View/The-future-of-the-gig-economy.html. Accessed 12 September 2020; *Achleitner, Ranjana Andrea*, Plattformbasierte Arbeit als Herausforderung der EU – Handlungsperspektiven und aktuelle Initiativen der Union, in: ZESAR, (2020) 9, p. 363.

55 *Zachary, Kilhoffer/De Groen, Willem Pieter/Lenaerts, Karolien/Smits, Ine/Hauben, Harald/ Waeyaert, Willem/Giacumacatos, Elisa/Lhernould, Jean-Philippe/Robin-Olivier, Sophie*, Study to Gather Evidence on the Working Conditions of Platform Workers (fn. 9), p. 229.

56 U. S. Bureau of Labor Statistics, Labor Force Statistics from the Current Population Survey, Electronically Mediated Employment, https://www.bls.gov/cps/electronically-mediated-employment.htm. Accessed 12 September 2020.

gaged in this form of employment. More recently, some official statistical agencies of OECD member states have formulated questions on platform work in labour force surveys[57] and Internet usage surveys.[58]

(2) There are more studies on crowdwork than on work on demand, as crowdworkers can be reached more easily by online surveys.[59] Also problematic is the fact that the earliest research is based mostly on an analysis of the Amazon Mechanical Turk (AMT) platform, which means that a significant part of the current scientific knowledge refers to US-American employees.[60]

(3) Often the samples sizes of empirical studies are too small to make clear conclusions about platform workers' characteristics.[61]

(4) Some studies do not differentiate between types of platform work (online and offline platform work), or between work for one platform or work for many platforms.

(5) Studies show that there are considerable differences in the numbers of platform workers both across countries and across studies for the same country.[62] Different factors may explain this situation:
- the high volatility of platform workers should be taken into account;
- some studies include – apart from activities on labour platforms – also activities on capital platforms like Airbnb;
- some studies count all registered users[63] while other studies count only active users,[64] giving a more accurate picture of this phenomenon;

---

57 E.g. Finland extended the Labour Force Survey with questions on platform work in 2017, cf. *Piasna, Agnieszka*, Counting Gigs. How Can we Measure the Scale of Online Platform Work? (fn. 6), p. 12.

58 OECD, Measuring the Digital Transformation: A Roadmap for the Future, OECD Publishing, Paris, 2019, p. 176, https://doi.org/10.1787/9789264311992-en. Accessed 12 September 2020.

59 *Joyce, Simon/Stuart, Mark/Forde, Chris/Valizade, Danat*, Work and Social Protection in the Platform Economy in Europe (fn. 20), pp. 5, 14.

60 BMAS, Plattformbasierte Erwerbsarbeit: Stand der empirischen Forschung, Forschungsbericht No. 498, 2017, p. 44.

61 OECD, Measuring Platform Mediated Workers (fn. 47), p. 4.

62 OECD, Measuring Platform Mediated Workers (fn. 47), pp. 8-11; OECD, Measuring the Digital Transformation: A Roadmap for the Future (fn. 58), p. 176.

63 ESIP, Are Social Security Systems Adapted to New Forms of Work Created by Digital Platforms? (fn. 15), p. 21.

64 *Piasna, Agnieszka*, Counting Gigs. How Can we Measure the Scale of Online Platform Work? (fn. 6), p. 6.

- there is no consistency in the definitions of platform work used in studies: while some studies use a broad definition of platform work, others use a rather narrow definition;
- many studies are not comparable as they cover different countries, use different definitions of platform work or online platforms, and examine different reference periods.[65]

(6) There are concerns in relation to the reliability of the studies. Relying on the outcome of studies concerning the classification of platform workers may lead to an inaccurate picture when the studies are based on the subjective opinion of the respondents. Many respondents misunderstand the questions and misinterpret the definitions of platform work[66] and "online platforms"[67] used in a survey. For example, in the COLLEEM I survey, the majority of platform workers (68.1 percent) define themselves as employees, but de facto they are self-employed.[68] There were different reasons for misinterpretations in this study, be it that the main activity of one respondent was in dependent employment, or that one respondent considered himself as an employee, or simply due to poor answer content.[69]

(7) While some studies cover platform work as a main job only when a substantial part of income is generated from it, others use a broader definition of platform work including cases where platform work is performed as a secondary job.[70] Also some of the existing official labour statistics of the OECD member states (e.g. France)[71] focus on a worker's primary job and can be unreliable in their coverage of secondary jobs and self-employment.[72] Researchers stress that official labour market statistics are generally not suited for capturing sporadic or secondary employment.[73] Using a longer reference period increases

---

65 *Urzí Brancati, Maria Cesira/Pesole, Annarosa/Fernandez Macias, Enrique*, New Evidence on Platform Workers in Europe (fn. 51), p. 11.

66 OECD, Measuring the Digital Transformation: A Roadmap for the Future (fn. 58), p. 176.

67 *Piasna, Agnieszka*, Counting Gigs. How Can we Measure the Scale of Online Platform Work? (fn. 6), p. 10.

68 *Pesole, Annarosa/ Urzí Brancati, Maria Cesira/Fernández-Macías, Enrique/Biagi, Federico/González Vázquez, Ignacio*, Platform Workers in Europe (fn. 5), p. 31.

69 Ibid.

70 OECD, Measuring Platform Mediated Workers (fn. 47), p. 8.

71 Ibid., p. 19.

72 Ibid., p. 14.

73 *Piasna, Agnieszka*, Counting Gigs. How Can we Measure the Scale of Online Platform Work? (fn. 6), p. 5.

the share of occasional platform workers in the estimated number of platform workers.[74]

(8) Platform work is often informal or not precisely regulated, which might lead to an underestimation of the real dimension of the platform economy.[75] However, there is a lack of statistical and empirical data on the prevalence of undeclared platform work.[76]

3. *Cross-Border Labour Flows in Platform Work*

The use of online labour platforms to access the global market is historically older than national labour platforms. For example, AMT was founded already in 2005.[77] Online crowdsourcing platforms can be seen as a further step in the development of "global sourcing" of value chains.[78]

There are different forms of cross-border online platform work. A platform worker can perform work in one (home or other) country or more countries – while the client, platform or both can be located in another (EU or third) country or countries. The more platforms and/or clients, the more complicated constellations are possible.[79] In the case of crowdwork, platforms and clients can always select a country which does not provide for any limitations or obstacles to platform work or which has not established any labour and social guarantees for platform workers. Mark Graham and Mohammad Amir Anwar write about a so-called "planetary labour market" in digital work[80], where "clients can choose who they work

---

74 OECD, Measuring Platform Mediated Workers (fn. 47), p. 19.

75 *Zachary, Kilhoffer/De Groen, Willem Pieter/Lenaerts, Karolien/Smits, Ine/Hauben, Harald/Waeyaert, Willem/Giacumacatos, Elisa/Lhernould, Jean-Philippe/Robin-Olivier, Sophie*, Study to Gather Evidence on the Working Conditions of Platform Workers (fn. 9), p. 93.

76 Ibid.

77 *Huws, Ursula*, Where did Online Platforms Come From? The Virtualization of Work Organization and the New Policy Challenges it Raises (fn. 22), p. 30.

78 Ibid., p. 34.

79 *Zachary, Kilhoffer/De Groen, Willem Pieter/Lenaerts, Karolien/Smits, Ine/Hauben, Harald/Waeyaert, Willem/Giacumacatos, Elisa/Lhernould, Jean-Philippe/Robin-Olivier, Sophie*, Study to Gather Evidence on the Working Conditions of Platform Workers (fn. 9), p. 94.

80 *Graham, Mark/Anwar, Mohammad Amir*, The Global Gig Economy: Towards a Planetary Labour Market?, in: First Monday, 24 (2019) 4, DOI: https://doi.org/10.5210/fm.v24i4.9913. Accessed 12 September 2020.

with, among a larger pool of people from around the globe".[81] According to Mark Graham and Mohammad Amir Anwar, a planetary market does not eliminate geography, but rather takes advantage of it.[82] Furthermore, platforms profit from the huge over-supply of labour that pushes down labour costs and restricts the ability of workers to bargain for better conditions,[83] including social security benefits. Klaus Schwab stresses that in these cases, the relocation of work to foreign countries happens invisibly.[84] Researchers speak of "virtual migration", which occurs without the spatial movement of the body across borders but facilitates new forms of the global division of labour.[85]

In order to properly assess the need for transnational regulation and coordination of social security and the required level and type of regulation (e.g. at the international, European or regional level; in bilateral or international agreements; or with a view to recommendations or directives at the European level), it is necessary to have a clear picture about online platform labour flows, where clients (customers), platforms and platform workers are located in different countries respectively. At the moment, we only have a fragmented picture about cross-border labour flows related to on-demand platforms ("real migration") as well as to crowdwork (referred to as "virtual migration"). Furthermore, there is only limited data available on the prevalence of cross-border platform work.[86]

Despite the huge gaps in information about cross-border labour flows, we can note several trends. First, the younger a platform, the more local is its character (local clients, local platform workers). The longer-established platforms have a broader spread of nationalities. Among the platform workers registered with the German platform "Clickworker", for instance, about one third are from Germany, one third are from other European

81 Ibid.

82 Ibid.

83 *Graham, Mark/Anwar, Mohammad Amir*, Labour, in: Ash, James/Kitchin, Rob/ Leszczynski, Agnieszka (eds.), Digital Geographies, Los Angeles: Sage 2018.

84 *Schwab, Klaus*, Die Vierte Industrielle Revolution, München: Pantheon Verlag 2016, p. 75.

85 Website of the project Digitalisation of Labour and Migration. Berliner Institut für empirische Integrations- und Migrationsforschung, http://www.platform-mob ilities.net/en/konzepte-notizen. Accessed 12 September 2020.

86 *Zachary, Kilhoffer/De Groen, Willem Pieter /Lenaerts, Karolien /Smits, Ine/Hauben, Harald/Waeyaert, Willem/Giacumacatos, Elisa/Lhernould, Jean-Philippe/Robin-Olivier, Sophie*, Study to Gather Evidence on the Working Conditions of Platform Workers (fn. 9), p. 94.

countries, and the remaining third are from the Americas.[87] According to its own figures, the platform "Upwork" counts eight million crowdworkers from 180 countries.[88] Second, language constraints dictate regional boundaries; for example, clients and platform workers speaking German are distributed, in addition to Germany, also across Switzerland and Austria. At the same time, access to certain global work platforms for non-native language speakers is likely to be associated with higher levels of educational attainment, even if the work carried out does not itself require high levels of education.[89]

IV. Implications for Social Security in Empirical Studies

1. Platform Work as a Main Job and as a Side Job, and Motivation of Platform Workers

There is interesting evidence that studies consider as a "main job" not work for one single platform, but platform work as a kind of work/job itself. Such an approach is typical of studies exploring self-employment, which demonstrate the distribution of the self-employed across economic sectors.

All existing studies devoted to platform work come to the result that platform work is mainly (to an extent of approximately 70 percent) carried out as a side job in addition to a second or multiple jobs. This confirms studies covering only crowdwork which have shown that for about one third of crowdworkers, platform work was the main source of income. For example, the ILO study of 2018 shows that for 32 percent of crowdworkers platform work was the main source of income.[90] The majority of platform

87 Eurofound, New Forms of Employment, Publications Office of the European Union (fn. 3), pp. 112-113.

88 *Däubler, Wolfgang*, Herausforderungen für das Arbeitsrecht – Deregulierung, Globalisierung, Digitalisierung, in: Arbeit und Recht, (2016) 8-9, p. 333.

89 *Forde, Chris/Stuart, Mark/Simon, Joyce/Oliver, Liz/Valizade, Danat/Alberti, Gabriella/Hardy, Kate/Trappmann, Vera/Umney, Charles/Carson, Calum*, The Social Protection of Workers in the Platform Economy (fn. 10), p. 31.

90 Digital Labour Platforms and the Future of Work: Towards Decent Work in the Online World (fn. 9), p. 41.

workers provide more than one type of service and are active on two or more platforms.[91]

In order to analyse the need for social protection, it is important to consider the reasons for working in the platform economy, and whether such activity is chosen voluntarily or due to insufficient alternatives on the labour market. Numerous studies have shown the following:

(1) The most common reason for being a platform worker is the flexibility in working arrangements, working time and location.[92]
(2) Another important reason is the opportunity to earn an additional income.[93]
(3) For some categories of workers, it is the only option on the labour market, e.g. for foreign workers. The studies confirm that foreign-born workers are significantly more likely to provide services via digital labour platforms than native workers.[94] For example, a study of 2017 on Finland states that 70-80 percent of all food couriers were immigrants.[95] The first large-scale statistical data on the share of migrant workers was presented in the survey of the BLS of May 2017 concerning electronically mediated employment.[96]
(4) Other categories who are interested in platform work are persons with disabilities and women with family obligations as they can only work

91 *Pesole, Annarosa/Urzí Brancati, Maria Cesira/Fernández-Macías, Enrique/Biagi, Federico/González Vázquez, Ignacio*, Platform Workers in Europe (fn. 5), p. 4.

92 *Forde, Chris/Stuart, Mark/Simon, Joyce/Oliver, Liz/Valizade, Danat/Alberti, Gabriella/Hardy, Kate/Trappmann, Vera/Umney, Charles/Carson, Calum*, The Social Protection of Workers in the Platform Economy (fn. 10), p. 44; OECD, The Future of Social Protection: What Works for Non-Standard Workers? (fn. 11), p. 33.

93 *Zachary, Kilhoffer/De Groen, Willem Pieter/Lenaerts, Karolien/Smits, Ine/Hauben, Harald/Waeyaert, Willem/Giacumacatos, Elisa/Lhernould, Jean-Philippe/Robin-Olivier, Sophie*, Study to Gather Evidence on the Working Conditions of Platform Workers (fn. 9), p. 72.

94 *Urzí Brancati, Maria Cesira/Pesole, Annarosa/Fernandez Macias, Enrique*, New Evidence on Platform Workers in Europe (fn. 51), pp. 4, 26-27.

95 Does the Worker have a Say in the Platform Economy? The Time of Opportunities project, SAK, Autumn 2017, p. 8, https://www.ituc-csi.org/IMG/pdf/sak_finland_report_does-the-worker-have-a-say-in-the-platform-economy.pdf. Accessed 12 September 2020.

96 U. S. Bureau of Labor Statistics, Labor Force Statistics from the Current Population Survey, Electronically Mediated Employment (fn. 56).

from home.[97] A “strong difference by gender for those who could only ‘work from home’” in favour of women has been shown.[98]

(5) Platform work could be a stepping stone into a labour relationship, e.g. for the long-time unemployed.[99] Nearly half of those for whom platform work is a main source of income were unemployed for more than one year in the past five years.[100]

Researchers point out that, at the moment, there is a lack of knowledge as to whether there are any differences in motivation between those for whom platform work is a side job and those that generate their main income from platform work.[101] Data contradicts the myth of student platform workers. The study by Huws et al.[102] demonstrates that the proportion of students among crowdworkers is not higher than their general distribution in the labour force. In Berg's survey[103] students make up 14.5 percent, and according to Serfling[104] nine percent.

There are different reasons and factors that determine the choice of platform work as a main activity: type of platforms and platform work (e.g. high-skilled workers[105]), the relative difference between average incomes in the country of the client and the country of the worker. Berg discloses

---

97 Weißbuch “Arbeiten 4.0” – Antworten der BA auf die Herausforderungen der Digitalisierung, p. 13, https://www.bmas.de/SharedDocs/Downloads/DE/Thema-Arbeitsmarkt/Arbeiten-4-0/stellungnahme-ba.pdf?__blob=publicationFile&v=2. Accessed 12 September 2020; *Joyce, Simon/Stuart, Mark/Forde, Chris/Valizade, Danat*, Work and Social Protection in the Platform Economy in Europe (fn. 20), p. 21.

98 Digital Labour Platforms and the Future of Work: Towards Decent Work in the Online World (fn. 9), p. 38.

99 *Forde, Chris/Stuart, Mark/Simon, Joyce/Oliver, Liz/Valizade, Danat/Alberti, Gabriella/Hardy, Kate/Trappmann, Vera/Umney, Charles/Carson, Calum*, The Social Protection of Workers in the Platform Economy (fn. 10), p. 56 f.

100 *Joyce, Simon/Stuart, Mark/Forde, Chris/Valizade, Danat*, Work and Social Protection in the Platform Economy in Europe (fn. 20), p. 21.

101 Ibid., p. 20.

102 *Huws, Ursula/Spencer, Neil H./Syrdal, Dag S./Holts, Kaire*, Work in the European Gig Economy, FEPS/Uni Europa/Hertfordshire University, 2017, p. 37, https://uhra.herts.ac.uk/bitstream/handle/2299/19922/Huws_U._Spencer_N.H._Syrdal_D.S._Holt_K._2017_.pdf?sequence=2. Accessed 12 September 2020.

103 *Berg, Janine*, Income Security in the On-Demand Economy: Findings and Policy Lessons from a Survey of Crowdworkers (fn. 9), p. 5.

104 *Serfling, Oliver*, Crowdworking Monitor No. 1, in: Discussion Papers in Behavioral Sciences and Economics (2018) 4.

105 *Freudenberg, Christoph*, Rising Platform Work. Scope, Insurance Coverage and Good Practices among ISSA Countries (fn. 47), pp. 10-11.

that motivations for platform work depend on the country of origin, e.g. Indian workers are more likely to rely on it as a source of main income while US workers consider it as secondary income.[106]

2. *Characteristics of Dependence*

a) Dependence as a Legal Category

From the social law perspective, the issue of "dependence" of platform workers is relevant for the employment classification for social law purposes, for the determination of the need for social protection as well as for the justification of the social responsibility of third persons who are not parties to the employment relationship.

Many researchers have referred to elements of dependence[107] of platform workers. According to the prevalent opinion in the literature, platform workers are at least economically dependent. This dependence is often evidenced through new control and monitoring mechanisms on the part of platform providers. However, it has not been conclusively clarified whether a new manifestation of personal dependence or of economic dependence has emerged, or whether these are cases of a completely new dimension of dependence. Wiebke Brose, for example, speaks of a new form of dependence on the platform provider – which she describes as a subtype of economic dependence which is taking on a new quality due to digital control mechanisms.[108]

Because of the heterogeneity of platform workers and the various kinds of platform work and platforms, as well as because of different strategies concerning the allocation of tasks (allocated by the platform, by the client

---

106 *Berg, Janine*, Income Security in the On-Demand Economy: Findings and Policy Lessons from a Survey of Crowdworkers (fn. 9), p. 11.

107 *Selzer, Dirk*, Crowdworking – Arbeitsrecht zwischen Theorie und Praxis, in: Husemann, Tim/Wietfeld, Anne (eds.), Zwischen Theorie und Praxis – Herausforderungen des Arbeitsrechts. Dokumentation der 5. Assistententagung im Arbeitsrecht vom 16. - 17.07.2015, Bochum 2015, Baden-Baden: Nomos 2015, pp. 27-48; *Waas, Bernd*, Crowdwork in Germany, in: Waas, Bernd/Liebman, Wilma B./Lyubarsky Andrew/Katsutoshi, Kezuka (eds.), Crowdwork. A Comparative Law Perspective, Frankfurt am Main: Bund Verlag 2017, pp. 142-186.

108 *Brose, Wiebke*, Von Bismarck zu Crowdwork: Über die Reichweite der Sozialversicherungspflicht in der digitalen Arbeitswelt, in: Neue Zeitschrift für Sozialrecht, (2017) 1, p. 14.

or by the worker),[109] it is not possible to define one single pattern of dependence for either the platform provider or client(s). While platform workers are often similar to employees or economically dependent self-employed persons in some aspects, there are also aspects in which they are different. In my opinion, the new business model of platform work brings about a new type of dependence for the workers involved. When we try to identify the most salient features that characterise this new type of dependence in relation to platform workers, the following aspects are to be highlighted:

(1) Traditionally, economically dependent self-employed persons are dependent on a *client*. Platform workers can be dependent on a client as well as on the platform or on both. In the case of work on demand, economic and personal dependence exists predominantly in relation to the platform and not to certain clients. However, through rating and evaluation mechanisms clients are also involved in the exercise of control. It seems that in the case of crowdwork, sometimes the dependence on a client is higher than on a platform and not limited to ratings. There are findings that "clients often give detailed instructions on how to complete the work or directly supervise work execution and control the work processes"[110].

(2) According to an assumption common until now in social law legislation, economically dependent self-employed persons typically work for *one client* or chiefly for one client. The idea behind the "one client criterion" was that if somebody works predominantly for one person, he or she cannot freely operate on the market given the extensive time commitment. The studies indicate that the majority of crowdworkers work for several clients. The abovementioned ILO study shows that eleven percent of freelancers have only one main client; 56 percent of them work with two to five different clients per month.[111] Workers on demand have numerous clients.

---

109 *Zachary, Kilhoffer/De Groen, Willem Pieter/Lenaerts, Karolien/Smits, Ine/Hauben, Harald/Waeyaert, Willem/Giacumacatos, Elisa/Lhernould, Jean-Philippe/Robin-Olivier, Sophie*, Study to Gather Evidence on the Working Conditions of Platform Workers (fn. 9), p. 55.

110 *Aleksynska, Mariya/Bastrakova, Anastasia/Kharchenko, Natalia*, Work on Digital Labour Platforms in Ukraine: Issues and Policy Perspectives, International Labour Office – Geneva, ILO, 2018, p. 33.

111 Ibid., pp. 32-33.

(3) A *long-lasting relationship* with a client serves as an indicator of economic dependence.[112] Studies demonstrate the high volatility of platform workers. The relation with a client is rather short (especially in the case of micro tasks and work on demand) and the fluctuation rate of clients is high. However, the relation with a platform can be of long duration. During the course of such relationships platforms can influence participation in other platforms by high or low multihoming costs, or through dependence on ratings or reputation systems.

(4) Many platform workers participate in *more than one platform*.[113]

b) Dependence Explored in Empirical Studies

As has already been mentioned, many empirical studies consider "*platform work*" as a *main job*. Furthermore, they refer to "*financial dependence on platform work*". Some researchers differentiate between those platform workers who exclusively work on platforms and call them *work-dependent platform workers*, and those who have one or more jobs in addition to platform work and term the latter *non-dependent platform workers*.[114] Other researchers use the term *financial dependence* to describe how much income is generated from platform work,[115] and this term is also used in the study for the EMPL Committee.[116] According to this study, 16 percent of the respondents – who were online platform workers (crowdworkers) – were *heavily* (more than 70 percent of their income comes from platform work) financially dependent on the platform economy, nine percent were *highly* (50-69 percent of income) and 13 percent were *moderately* (26-49 percent of income) financially dependent on platform work. Hereby, 68 percent of the respondents had one or multiple other jobs outside of the platform

---

112 *Willemsen, Heinz Josef/Müntefering, Michael*, Begriff und Rechtsstellung arbeitnehmerähnlicher Personen: Versuch einer Präzisierung, in: Neue Zeitschrift für Arbeitsrecht (NZA), 4 (2018), pp. 193-201, 195.

113 *Leimeister, Jan Marco/Durward, David/Zogaj, Shkodran*, Crowd Worker in Deutschland. Eine empirische Studie zum Arbeitsumfeld auf externen Crowdsourcing-Plattformen, Study 323, Hans Böckler Stiftung, p. 31, https://www.boeckler.de/pdf/p_study_hbs_323.pdf. Accessed 12 September 2020.

114 *Joyce, Simon/Stuart, Mark/Forde, Chris/Valizade, Danat*, Work and Social Protection in the Platform Economy in Europe (fn. 20), p. 20.

115 *Forde, Chris/Stuart, Mark/Simon, Joyce/Oliver, Liz/Valizade, Danat/Alberti, Gabriella/Hardy, Kate/Trappmann, Vera/Umney, Charles/Carson, Calum*, The Social Protection of Workers in the Platform Economy (fn. 10), p. 48.

116 Ibid.

economy.[117] The COLLEEM I study came to the result that 2.3 percent of the European working-age population in 14 Member States earned 50 or more percent of their income via platforms (both crowdwork and work on demand).[118] However, the recent COLLEEM II study showed a decline of the number of such persons to 1.4 percent (a drop of 0.9 percent).[119] Simultaneously, this study indicates a small increase of platform work as a side job.[120]

Workers with a stable job outside the platform economy have higher income security than those who rely on their platform earnings.[121] High-skilled workers may use platform work to supplement their income. Low-skilled workers without a permanent job are likely to become more dependent on platform work as their primary source of income.[122] For these groups of platform workers also organisational and algorithmic dependency on platforms has been demonstrated and their need for social protection is comparable with that of employees. Studies show an interrelation between dependencies on platform work or on platforms and the need for social protection coverage of platform workers. The study for the European Commission outlines that "those who depend the most on platform work are covered the least"[123].

---

117 Ibid.

118 *Pesole, Annarosa/Urzí Brancati, Maria Cesira/Fernández-Macías, Enrique/Biagi, Federico/González Vázquez, Ignacio*, Platform Workers in Europe (fn. 5), p. 3.

119 *Urzí Brancati, Maria Cesira/Pesole, Annarosa/Fernandez Macias, Enrique*, New Evidence on Platform Workers in Europe (fn. 51), p. 3.

120 Ibid.

121 *Zachary, Kilhoffer/De Groen, Willem Pieter/Lenaerts, Karolien/Smits, Ine/Hauben, Harald/ Waeyaert, Willem/Giacumacatos, Elisa/Lhernould, Jean-Philippe/Robin-Olivier, Sophie*, Study to Gather Evidence on the Working Conditions of Platform Workers (fn. 9), p. 75.

122 *Forde, Chris/Stuart, Mark/Simon, Joyce/Oliver, Liz/Valizade, Danat/Alberti, Gabriella/Hardy, Kate/Trappmann, Vera/Umney, Charles/Carson, Calum*, The Social Protection of Workers in the Platform Economy (fn. 10), p. 48; *Zachary, Kilhoffer/De Groen, Willem Pieter/Lenaerts, Karolien /Smits, Ine/Hauben, Harald/ Waeyaert, Willem/Giacumacatos, Elisa/Lhernould, Jean-Philippe/Robin-Olivier, Sophie*, Study to Gather Evidence on the Working Conditions of Platform Workers (fn. 9), p. 72; *Conen, Wieteke/Schippers, Joop*, Self-Employment: Between Freedom and Insecurity, in: *Conen, Wieteke/Schippers, Joop*, Self-Employment as Precarious Work. A European Perspective, Cheltenham: Edward Elgar Publishing 2019, p. 7.

123 *Zachary, Kilhoffer/De Groen, Willem Pieter/Lenaerts, Karolien/Smits, Ine/Hauben, Harald/Waeyaert, Willem/Giacumacatos, Elisa/Lhernould, Jean-Philippe/Robin-Olivier, Sophie*, Study to Gather Evidence on the Working Conditions of Platform Workers (fn. 9), p. 72.

We can assume that *financial dependency on platform work* might indicate a *new pattern of dependence* in comparison to the well-known legal construction of economic dependency of dependent self-employed workers on the principal/(main) client. However, this is rather a sign of the vulnerability of workers and a reflection of the labour fragmentation which is characteristic also for other types of non-standard work (e.g. on-call work, zero-hours contracts). Workers just struggle to accumulate orders from different platforms in order to make ends meet, especially if such a kind of employment is their main activity. The category of financial dependence on platform work explored in empirical studies is not suitable to justify the classification of platform workers as employees and to justify social responsibility of platforms over workers; it is only a socio-economic characteristic of platform workers.

Interestingly, this study simultaneously outlines that "self-employed platform workers who are economically dependent on a single platform [...] appear to be the most vulnerable and least protected by [...] social protection legislation at both national and EU level"[124]. It confirms the rationale and legitimacy of the already existing strategy of imposing social insurance responsibility on the (main) client for dependent self-employed contractors as this is provided for in the social legislation of some European countries.[125]

3. *Access of Platform Workers to Social Protection*

The general outcome of the different studies is evidence of a low level of access to social protection of platform workers, especially those for whom it is a main job. Insurance coverage differs significantly if platform work is carried out as a side job. Those for whom platform work is a side activity rely on social protection from salaried employment.[126]

---

124 Ibid.

125 *Chesalina, Olga*, Extending Social Security Schemes for "Non-Employees": A Comparative Perspective, in: Zeitschrift für ausländisches und internationales Arbeits- und Sozialrecht, (2020) 1, pp. 3-12.

126 *Zachary, Kilhoffer/De Groen, Willem Pieter/Lenaerts, Karolien /Smits, Ine/Hauben, Harald/ Waeyaert, Willem/Giacumacatos, Elisa/Lhernould, Jean-Philippe/Robin-Olivier, Sophie*, Study to Gather Evidence on the Working Conditions of Platform Workers (fn. 9), p. 26 and p. 72; *Garben, Sacha*, Protecting Workers in the Online Platform Economy: An Overview of Regulatory and Policy Developments in the EU, European Agency for Safety and Health at Work, Luxembourg: Publications Office of the European Union, 2017, https://osha.europa.eu/fr/publi

The study by Joyce et al. demonstrates that between 68 percent and 82 percent of micro task platform workers (for whom it is a main job) had no access to the different branches of social protection with the exception of healthcare.[127] Berg's study of 2016 indicates that 90.6 percent of crowdworkers (AMT workers in the US) did not contribute to social security[128] (in the US reality this is equivalent to not having access to social protection). This situation calls forth concerns among platform workers about their social security and accident insurance in particular.[129]

Those who carry out platform work as a main job are much less likely to be saving towards a pension – being the case for less than one in five – than those that carry out platform work as a side activity.[130] The study for the EMPL Committee (without specification as to which kind of platform work is considered – main or side job) reveals that only just over a third of micro task platform workers (35.5 percent) were paying into a personal pension.[131] Concerning access to different social benefits, this study reported that 22.6 percent of all platform workers have no access to healthcare, 47 percent – to sickness benefits, 60.6 – disability, 58.1 percent – old age, 69.5 – pregnancy, 63.1 percent – unemployment benefits.[132] This is a very interesting outcome which shows that "workers who were relatively heavily dependent on platform work were only marginally disadvantaged in

cations/protecting-workers-online-platform-economy-overview-regulatory-and-policy-developments; *Berg, Janine*, Income Security in the On-Demand Economy: Findings and Policy Lessons from a Survey of Crowdworkers (fn. 9), p. 16; Eurofound, Employment and Working Conditions of Selected Types of Platform Work (fn. 9), p. 19; *Pesole, Annarosa/Urzí Brancati, Maria Cesira/Fernández-Macías, Enrique/Biagi, Federico/González Vázquez, Ignacio*, Platform Workers in Europe (fn. 5).

127 *Joyce, Simon/Stuart, Mark/Forde, Chris/Valizade, Danat*, Work and Social Protection in the Platform Economy in Europe (fn. 20), p. 25.

128 *Berg, Janine*, Income Security in the On-Demand Economy: Findings and Policy Lessons from a Survey of Crowdworkers (fn. 9).

129 *Zachary, Kilhoffer/De Groen, Willem Pieter/Lenaerts, Karolien/Smits, Ine/Hauben, Harald/Waeyaert, Willem/Giacumacatos, Elisa/Lhernould, Jean-Philippe/Robin-Olivier, Sophie*, Study to Gather Evidence on the Working Conditions of Platform Workers (fn. 9), p. 72.

130 *Joyce, Simon/Stuart, Mark/Forde, Chris/Valizade, Danat*, Work and Social Protection in the Platform Economy in Europe (fn. 20), pp. 22, 25.

131 *Forde, Chris/Stuart, Mark/Simon, Joyce/Oliver, Liz/Valizade, Danat/Alberti, Gabriella/Hardy, Kate/Trappmann, Vera/Umney, Charles/Carson, Calum*, The Social Protection of Workers in the Platform Economy (fn. 10), p. 57.

132 Ibid.; *Florisson, Rebecca/Mandl, Irene*, Platform Work: Types and Implications for Work and Employment – Literature Review (fn. 14), p. 99.

terms of access to social protection, compared with occasional platform workers".[133] This means that for a significant number of workers who have another source of income, their other source(s) may come from other forms of insecure, non-standard employment or self-employed work,[134] which would also explain their limited access to social protection, especially to unemployment benefits and sickness benefits.[135] The ILO study of 2018 confirms that of crowdworkers engaged in other paid jobs, 33 percent were in non-standard employment, including part-time and casual work, and 25 percent were freelancers.[136] However, we have to keep in mind that many studies first of all represent the situation of micro task platform workers,[137] who are mostly unskilled or low-skilled, and we cannot transfer these results to the entirety of platform workers. Taking the German example, the study by Leimeister has shown that more than 50 percent of workers who carry out mostly unskilled and low-skilled "micro tasks" (which proved to be particularly precarious) are not insured in a pension scheme at all.[138]

However, platform workers differ significantly from each other in terms of income; dependence on platform work and their access to social protection. For instance, the study by Bertscheck et al.[139] has shown that in Germany, in 2016, about 44 percent of crowdworkers were included in a private pension scheme; 85 percent were insured in statutory health insurance, eight percent got social benefits in terms of unemployment benefits, social assistance and social welfare benefits.

A very important outcome of the research by Freudenberg is that in two thirds of the 30 ISSA members, additional income from platform work as a

---

133 *Forde, Chris/Stuart, Mark/Simon, Joyce/Oliver, Liz/Valizade, Danat/Alberti, Gabriella/Hardy, Kate/Trappmann, Vera/Umney, Charles/Carson, Calum*, The Social Protection of Workers in the Platform Economy (fn. 10), p. 64.

134 Ibid., p. 55.

135 Ibid., p. 65.

136 Digital Labour Platforms and the Future of Work: Towards Decent Work in the Online World (fn. 9), p. 42.

137 E.g. the study by Forde et al. (fn. 10), p. 11 is based on an original survey of 1,200 micro task platform workers across four established platforms: AMT, Clickworker, CrowdFlower and Microworkers.

138 *Leimeister, Jan Marco/Durward, David/Zogaj, Shkodran*, Crowd Worker in Deutschland. Eine empirische Studie zum Arbeitsumfeld auf externen Crowdsourcing-Plattformen (fn. 113).

139 BMAS, Befragung zum sozioökonomischen Hintergrund und zu den Motiven von Crowdworkern, Forschungsbericht 462, 2016, http://www.bmas.de/SharedDocs/Downloads/DE/PDF-Publikationen/Forschungsberichte/fb-462-endbericht-crowdworker.pdf?__blob=publicationFile&v=4. Accessed 12 September 2020.

side job is not taken into consideration for social security purposes.[140] This can be explained by different reasons: legislation does not provide for the coverage of extra income at all or merely below a certain threshold; platform work is carried out informally.[141]

4. *Comparison of the Situation concerning Access to Social Protection of Platform Workers and Non-Standard Workers, and that of Self-Employed Persons*

As already indicated in the Introduction, studies that analyse the situation of platform workers are divided into two main groups: One group of research is dedicated exclusively to platform workers. The other group of studies investigates the situation of platform workers within the broader categories of "non-standard employed" or "self-employed". Many studies point out that one of the most important factors that explains the limited access of platform workers to social protection is their classification as self-employed workers.[142] The challenges for the social protection of platform workers are regarded to be the same as the challenges for persons in other non-standard forms of employment and self-employed persons. Therefore, it has been proposed to improve the social protection of self-employed and non-standard workers in general, not only that of platform workers.[143]

Despite the fact that there are many similar challenges concerning access to social protection among these groups, caution is advised concerning the automatic transfer of the outcomes. Research points out that in order to answer whether we need a special tailor-made solution for platform workers or rather solutions for all atypical employees or self-employed workers in total, it is necessary to compare the coverage of social security

140 *Freudenberg, Christoph,* Rising Platform Work. Scope, Insurance Coverage and Good Practices among ISSA Countries (fn. 47), p. 18.

141 Ibid.

142 *Zachary, Kilhoffer/De Groen, Willem Pieter/Lenaerts, Karolien/Smits, Ine/Hauben, Harald/Waeyaert, Willem/Giacumacatos, Elisa/Lhernould, Jean-Philippe/Robin-Olivier, Sophie,* Study to Gather Evidence on the Working Conditions of Platform Workers (fn. 9), p. 71.

143 Ibid., p. 71. *Piasna, Agnieszka,* Counting Gigs. How Can we Measure the Scale of Online Platform Work? (fn. 6), p. 17; *Aleksynska, Mariya/Bastrakova, Anastasia/Kharchenko, Natalia,* Work on Digital Labour Platforms in Ukraine: Issues and Policy Perspectives (fn. 110); *Berg, Janine,* Income Security in the On-Demand Economy: Findings and Policy Lessons from a Survey of Crowdworkers (fn. 9).

in the entire working population at the same time.[144] This is the only way to assess whether they have particular deficiencies in access to social security and in the financing of social security.[145]

While platform work is mostly considered *de jure* as self-employment, it is interesting to compare the development of platform work with the development of self-employment in the appropriate country. On the one hand, official statistics and studies do not show an increase of self-employment taking place in general.[146] The studies show a steady decrease in the share of self-employed persons in Bulgaria, Ireland, Italy, Lithuania, Poland, Romania, Switzerland, Hungry and Portugal. On the contrary, in the UK, Netherlands and Slovakia, a substantial increase of self-employment can be observed.[147] Nevertheless, there are some new tendencies concerning self-employment: firstly, the number of self-employed persons with employees has fallen;[148] secondly, there are changes in motivation among the self-employed – for every fifth, this form of employment is involuntary;[149] thirdly, there is a rise in part-time self-employment while historically this form of self-employment has been the exception.[150]

On the other hand, it remains unclear whether platform workers are to be counted among the self-employed.[151] While the classification of "self-employed" should be the result of a legal review, in some studies, for example in the labour force studies, the employment classification is based on the subjective view of the interviewed person[152] with the result that –

144 Cf. BMAS, Plattformbasierte Erwerbsarbeit: Stand der empirischen Forschung (fn. 62), p. 22.

145 Ibid.

146 There are different reasons that can explain an increase or decrease in self-employment. For example, the fall in numbers of self-employed workers in the UK in the late 1990s was the result of a reclassification of some workers in the construction industry. See *Choonara, Joseph*, Insecurity, Precarious Work and Labour Markets, Cham: Palgrave Macmillan 2019, p. 113.

147 *Schippers, Joop*, Labour Market Flexibility, Self-Employment and Precariousness, in: *Conen, Wieteke/Schippers, Joop*, Self-Employment as Precarious Work. A European Perspective, Cheltenham: Edward Elgar Publishing 2019, p. 30.

148 *Joyce, Simon/Stuart, Mark/Forde, Chris/Valizade, Danat*, Work and Social Protection in the Platform Economy in Europe (fn. 20), p. 18.

149 Ibid.

150 *Choonara, Joseph*, Insecurity, Precarious Work and Labour Markets (fn. 146), p. 113.

151 *Joyce, Simon/Stuart, Mark/Forde, Chris/Valizade, Danat*, Work and Social Protection in the Platform Economy in Europe (fn. 20), p. 18.

152 *Choonara, Joseph*, Insecurity, Precarious Work and Labour Markets (fn. 146), p. 113.

for example in the study of Pesole et al. – 68.1 percent of platform workers claimed to be employees.[153]

Taking into account the result that platform work is carried out as a side job, it would be very important to compare the access to social protection of side platform workers with workers in other forms of non-standard work and self-employment also carried out as a secondary job. However, until now little is known about non-standard employment and self-employment as a side job as studies and labour force surveys predominantly focus on a main occupation. This information is easier to find in the national reports than in cross-national studies. According to one opinion, having a side job can indicate a reduction in standard employment.[154] However, the rate of persons with a second job in the EU is rather low (about four percent) and stable.[155] Eurofound demonstrates that according to data from the sixth European Working Conditions Survey nine percent of the self-employed without employees have another job.[156] However, these studies probably do not reflect the situation in certain European countries. For example, in France at the end of 2016, 23 percent of self-employed persons were also employees or used to be employees during the year. These averages reveal very different situations: half of the persons involved in pluriactivity have a main activity, whether as employees or self-employed persons, from which they earn a large income as compared to other self-employed persons with a less lucrative additional activity. The other persons involved in pluriactivity have both quite low self-employed incomes and wages: they often have intermittent activities or have just launched their business.[157] For example, the German study concerning self-employed gainful activity demonstrates that almost one third of all self-employed in Germany are working part-time; hereby, the share of self-employed persons with a side job is only 6 percent.[158] On the contrary, the

153 *Pesole, Annarosa/Urzí Brancati, Maria Cesira/Fernández-Macías, Enrique/Biagi, Federico/González Vázquez, Ignacio*, Platform Workers in Europe (fn. 5), p. 4.

154 *Joyce, Simon/Stuart, Mark/Forde, Chris/Valizade, Danat*, Work and Social Protection in the Platform Economy in Europe (fn. 20), p. 17.

155 Ibid.

156 Eurofound, Exploring Self-Employment in the European Union, Publications Office of the European Union, Luxembourg, 2017, p. 9.

157 One in four self-employed people also works as an employee. Cf. *Guilhem, Théron*, The French National Institute for Statistics (Insee), https://www.insee.fr/en/statistiques/4280464. Accessed 12 September 2020.

158 *Conen, Wieteke/Schippers, Joop/Schulze Buschoff, Karin*, Self-Employed without Personnel between Freedom and Insecurity, Hans-Boeckler-Foundation, Study No. 5, August 2016, pp. 30-31.

study of Bertelsmann Stiftung shows that 99 percent of platform workers in Germany carry out such an activity as a side job, and at the same time have better social protection.[159]

First insights demonstrate that platform workers differ significantly from each other in terms of income and that the spread of the household income among digital self-employed workers is even greater than among the "classic" self-employed.[160] Furthermore, some research and studies show that online platform work also poses new (and worse) health and safety risks and that offline platform work goes along with higher injury rates than other non-standard arrangements.[161]

V. *Implications for Social Security from Practical Evidence*

Concerning the social responsibility of platform operators, practice demonstrates a deep contradiction between their alleged position as an intermediary and their factual reaction to the social risks of platform workers, which demonstrates that platforms acknowledge their responsibility for some social risks.[162]

The study of the European Social Insurance Platform demonstrates that "Uber gives drivers and couriers across Europe a one-off childbirth allowance of 1,000 euros. The benefit is granted under the following conditions: Uber drivers must have completed 150 trips and Uber Eats couriers 30 deliveries in the two months prior to the birth of the child. In addition, Uber gives drivers and couriers across Europe a sickness or injury compensation for a maximum of 30 days on-trip and 15 days off-trip of varying amounts according to the country [...] The same conditions apply to this benefit as to the maternity or paternity benefit. In case of accidents while

159 *Baethge, Catherine Bettina/Boberach, Michael/Hoffmann, Anke/Wintermann, Ole*, Plattformarbeit in Deutschland, Bertelsmann Stiftung, 2019, https://www.bertelsmann-stiftung.de/fileadmin/files/BSt/Publikationen/GrauePublikationen/Plattform_07lay.pdf, p. 6, Accessed 12 September 2020.

160 *Leimeister, Jan Marco/Durward, David/Zogaj, Shkodran*, Crowd Worker in Deutschland. Eine empirische Studie zum Arbeitsumfeld auf externen Crowdsourcing-Plattformen (fn. 113), p. 43.

161 *Garben, Sacha*, Tackling Social Disruption in the Online Platform Economy. Shifting the Narrative to the Benefits of (EU) Regulation (fn. 24), p. 5.

162 Fairwork, The Gig Economy and Covid-19: Looking Ahead, Oxford, United Kingdom, 2020, p. 3.

working causing permanent disability Uber gives drivers and couriers across Europe a compensation. All of the above is provided by AXA"[163].

Also, other platform operators have insured their workers on demand (couriers, drivers) against accidents at work. For example, Yandex.Taxi in Russia has insured all rides from 1 January 2017. According to the information on the Yandex.Taxi website, in case of a car accident during transportation the client and the driver can claim damages for harm caused to life and health. The maximum amount of compensation is two million roubles.[164] Deliveroo offers its couriers "a scheme through private insurers that gives its riders accident insurance against medical expenses and loss of earnings".[165]

The COVID-19 pandemic has imposed on workers on demand (couriers, drivers etc.) immense risks to health and life. At the beginning of the pandemic, platforms refused to provide any social benefits to platform workers due to their status of "self-employed"/"independent contractors".[166] The strong pressure from regulators, driver's advocates and the media has forced platforms to respond to the health risk caused by COVID-19. Many platforms, especially those that provide ride-hailing services, have introduced regulations concerning sickness payments for platform workers e.g. Uber, on 7 March 2020, launched a global financial assistance policy for drivers diagnosed with COVID-19; on 15 March 2020 and on 17 April 2020, the scope of the regulation was extended to drivers required to self-isolate.[167] In fact, the conditions for individual payment are similar to the conditions for payment on the part of an employer to an employee of continued remuneration in case of temporary incapacity to work – cf. the eligibility conditions (waiting period) – at least one trip in the 30 days before the application for assistance; calculation of payment – average

---

163 ESIP, Are Social Security Systems Adapted to New Forms of Work Created by Digital Platforms? (fn. 15), p. 27.

164 Yandex homepage, https://yandex.ru/support/taxi/insurance.html. Accessed 12 September 2020.

165 ESIP, Are Social Security Systems Adapted to New Forms of Work Created by Digital Platforms? (fn. 15), p. 28, also *Zachary, Kilhoffer/De Groen, Willem Pieter/ Lenaerts, Karolien /Smits, Ine/Hauben, Harald/ Waeyaert, Willem/Giacumacatos, Elisa/Lhernould, Jean-Philippe/Robin-Olivier, Sophie*, Study to Gather Evidence on the Working Conditions of Platform Workers (fn. 9), p. 122.

166 Fairwork, The Gig Economy and Covid-19: Looking Ahead (fn. 162), p. 13.

167 *Katta, Srujana/Badger, Adam/Graham, Mark/Howson, Kelle/Ustek-Spilda, Funda/ Bertolini, Alessio*, (Dis)embeddedness and (De)commodification: COVID-19, Uber, and the Unravelling Logics of the Gig Economy, in: Dialogues in Human Geography, 10 (2020) 2, p. 205.

weekly earnings over the three months before the application; the maximum amount of payment – for up to 14 days.[168]

If platform companies, in fact, act only as a marketplace, there is no reason to provide for insurance against accidents at work, sickness payments or maternity benefits. They did indeed, *de facto*, admit responsibility for different social risks. It does not matter whether they decided in favour of such regulations voluntarily or rather involuntary as, for example, a reaction to the COVID-19 crisis.

VI. Conclusion

Numerous studies have already been dedicated to the measuring of platform work and its characteristics. The issues of social security of platform workers is still quite a young research field both in empirical studies and social law research. The main goal of this chapter is to find out implications for social security from empirical findings and practical evidence. Great insights have already been gained from empirical studies concerning the social protection of platform workers. The most important finding confirmed in all existing studies is that platform work is mainly carried out as a side job in addition to one or several other jobs. However, those who carry out low-qualified platform work as a main job, and especially for one single platform, are protected the least against social risks. To conclude, the following outcomes shall be stressed and proposals for future investigations be made.

1. The empirical studies provide a lot of information about the socio-demographical characteristics of platform workers, their working conditions, access to labour and social protection. However, careful attention must be paid when interpreting the figures and trends from such empirical research on platform work due to its numerous shortcomings.
2. The problem is that a large part of cross-national studies[169] represent the situation of crowdworkers and especially low-skilled micro taskers,

168 https://www.uber.com/en-BH/blog/update-covid-19-financial/. Accessed 12 September 2020.

169 *Berg, Janine*, Income Security in the On-Demand Economy: Findings and Policy Lessons from a Survey of Crowdworkers (fn. 9); Digital Labour Platforms and the Future of Work: Towards Decent Work in the Online World (fn. 9); *Forde, Chris/Stuart, Mark/Simon, Joyce/Oliver, Liz/Valizade, Danat/Alberti, Gabriella/Hardy, Kate/Trappmann, Vera/Umney, Charles/Carson, Calum*, The Social Protection of Workers in the Platform Economy (fn. 10).

who can be more easily captured by online research than workers on demand. Hereby, a significant part of the studies is based on research (surveys and interviews) of the American platform AMT. Caution is advised as regards the extrapolation of outcomes in relation to dependence patterns and access to social security from crowdworkers to other groups of platform workers (e.g. workers on demand, high-skilled workers) and to other countries with differing systems of social security.

3. We share the opinion[170] that for answering the question of how to address the challenges of social protection for platform workers – whether through a special tailor-made solution for platform workers (or even special groups of platform workers) or rather through solutions that address all non-standard workers – it is necessary to compare the formal and effective coverage of social security in the entire working population at the same time, and to find out whether there are special problems and gaps in access to social protection for platform workers.
4. Even if many challenges related to platform work are similar to the challenges of non-standard employment and self-employment, the heterogeneity of platform workers and the fact that platform work is chiefly carried out as a side job – which is not typical for the self-employed – should be taken into account. Further investigation concerning the "main" job situation of side platform workers is welcomed. In particular, it would be interesting whether the main job is carried out in self-employment or salaried employment and, if the latter is the case, what kind of salaried employment it is.
5. It is interesting that studies consider as a "main job" of platform workers not work for one single platform, but platform work as a kind of work what is typical for empirical studies exploring self-employment.
6. The category of financial dependence on platform work as explored in empirical studies is not suitable for justifying the classification of platform workers as employees and for justifying social responsibility of platforms for workers; it is only a socio-economic characteristic of platform workers that reflects labour fragmentation, which is characteristic also of other types of non-standard work.
7. The patterns of personal and economic dependence of persons who provide services via online labour platforms of platform providers or clients should be further investigated. This research can assist the inves-

170 BMAS. Plattformbasierte Erwerbsarbeit: Stand der empirischen Forschung (fn. 60), p. 22.

tigations as to who controls the activity of platform workers and whether platform providers are responsible for the service providers and, hence, whether their participation in the financing of social protection for the service providers would be justified.

8. In the past years, it has become a matter of scientific debate whether platform providers – or clients respectively – have to bear their share of social (financial) responsibility towards contractors (whose labour force might even be used to dump prices) and towards the state. To date, and especially since the coronavirus crisis, many examples are known from practice demonstrating that platforms are taking on responsibility for social risks (work accident, sickness, childbirth) of workers on demand concluding agreements with private insurance companies for the benefit of such workers. This demonstrates a deep contradiction between the alleged position of platforms as intermediaries and their factual reaction to the social risks of workers on demand. On the one hand, the assumption of responsibility by platforms – both voluntarily and undertaken under public pressure – should be explored in further research. Hereby, the changes of the platform operator's policy (extending or reducing its social insurance responsibility) in the course of time should be investigated. A very interesting case is presented in the form of insurance schemes dedicated to platform workers by AXA insurance company.
9. In some countries, social responsibility on the part of platforms in relation to platform workers has already been established in the legislation (e.g. in France). Many platforms in France have launched partnerships with private insurance companies for accident and liability protection of platform workers.[171] In other countries, some platforms have undertaken such steps voluntarily. It would be very interesting to get more empirical evidence in relation to enforcement aspects, the level of protection guaranteed and the allocation of costs between platforms and platform workers.
10. Up to date, there is a lack of statistical and empirical data concerning the share of informal (undeclared) platform work. This information is very important not only for the correct estimation of the real size of the platform economy. From the point of view of social security, this information can help to prevent fraud related to the receipt of social assis-

171 See *Kessler, Francis*, Social Security in the Platform Economy: The French Example – New Actors, New Regulations, Old Problems, Chapter 11, Section III, p. 270 in this book.

tance benefits from the state (e.g. in cases where a worker pretends to be unemployed, as platform work is not exactly regulated and often is not seen as "work"). The reviewed persons should be asked whether they are unemployed and whether they are receiving unemployment benefits and social assistance benefits.

Part II:
Ensuring Social Security: Employment Status Classification and Innovative Solutions

Chapter 3
The Sharing Economy in Belgium: Status due to Taxation or Non-Status?

Yves Jorens

I. Introduction

During the last couple of decades, the motto was a flexible labour market. The technological development, also known as the Industrial Revolution 4.0, contributed largely to this credo. It gave clients an extreme form of flexibility. The platform economy constitutes a great example of this evolution. With this new technology, it is possible to pay a person a small fee and "get rid" of him/her when they are no longer needed.[1] Clients can use platform workers' services only when needed and pay when the workers carry out a certain activity for them. By setting up a platform, the employer – or rather, the consumer (?) – aims to keep a high level of flexibility and to eliminate downtime to the greatest extent possible, while at the same time trying to control as much as possible the entire process in order to minimise transaction costs.[2] Thanks to his labour (?), the platform worker himself earns an additional reward, which may be low but not always insignificant for the person concerned. Nevertheless, this evolution within the flexible labour market presents the legislator with enormous challenges, both for the economy and for social law. Is it possible to consider the sharing economy as a complement or a substitution to the current economy? Does it give rise to unfair competition? How shall we, incidentally, describe these activities? Is it work? Furthermore, it is noteworthy that the activities carried out via electronic platforms are not described as work but rather as a service rendered, a task, a gig or a ride in the case of transport. Often, terms like work and employee are not used at all. It is as

1 *Marvit, Moshe Z.*, How Crowdworkers Became the Ghosts in the Digital Machine, The Nation, 5 February 2014, https://www.thenation.com/article/archive/how-crowdworkers-became-ghosts-digital-machine/. Accessed 30 July 2020.

2 *Prassl, Jeremias/Risak, Martin*, Uber, TaskRabbit, & Co: Platforms as Employers? Rethinking the Legal Analysis of Crowdwork, in: Comparative Labour Law and Policy Journal, 37 (2016), p. 625.

if one tried to indicate that it concerns a very special form of activities, which do not fit within the traditional way of thinking about work and the associated labour and social security protection. The persons carrying out these activities are often not known to their client, who calls on them through a click on a computer or an app.[3] Likewise, the persons concerned often have no idea at all who they are working for and if their clients are, for instance, a private person or a company.[4] However, it is exactly these questions that come with certain risks, because labour law and social security law do assume that work is carried out.

In social security law, contributions are often calculated on the basis of the income from work. And can it be said at all times that the income these persons earn is income from work? Can we therefore consider these activities as work-related activities within the meaning of the social security systems and, if not, is there not a risk that the financial basis of our systems will be compromised? It is, of course, exceptional not to qualify certain activities as work just because they would take place through a platform. If activities are considered to be work in the case of contracted work, they must, of course, also be seen as such if mediated through an app.[5] This chapter describes the reaction of the Belgian legislator to the sharing economy, the reaction of the Constitutional Court and reflects on a new vision for social security.

II. The Sharing Economy under Belgian Social Law

Any work carried out in Belgium takes on one of three forms: work performed in a subordinate capacity for remuneration on the basis of an employment contract (as an employee), work performed in execution of a status determined unilaterally by the public authorities (as a civil servant), and work performed in the context of a self-employed professional activity (as a self-employed person). A person who carries out an activity in Belgium comes under one of these three social statuses. In social security law,

---

3 See also *De Stefano, Valerio,* The Rise of the "Just-in-Time Workforce": On-Demand Work, Crowdwork and Labour Protection in the "Gig-Economy", in: Conditions of Work and Employment Series, International Labour Office, Geneva, 71 (2016), p. 5, https://www.ilo.org/wcmsp5/groups/public/---ed_protect/---protrav/---travail/documents/publication/wcms_443267.pdf. Accessed 30 July 2020.

4 *Warter, Johannes,* Crowdwork, Wien: OGB Verlag 2016, p. 297.

5 Clearly, this does not imply that some activities could not be excluded from social law as a voluntary activity under national law.

self-employed persons are all persons carrying out an activity which excludes them from social security for employees or from the status of civil servant.[6] The self-employed person follows the concept of (non-)employee, so that employment contracts are seen under the exact same terms for both groups in labour law and with regard to the status of self-employed persons. In the end, the Belgian Employment Relationship Act, which cites criteria on the basis of which a judgement is made as to whether there is an employment contract,[7] will establish if someone is an employee or a self-employed person. Whether one is an employee or a self-employed person will ultimately have to be judged by the court. Just as in many other countries, the answer to this question is not always unequivocal.[8] However, the impact of the answer to this question is not insignificant. The protection of the platform worker is much more limited under the self-employed status than under the employee status. However, this question is not always considered with the same attention by the platform worker in question. Platform workers are often unaware of their status or of its consequences in the short and long term. They often see platform work as an ancillary activity, a side job which can sometimes lead to the start of their own independent activity.

Therefore, every activity automatically falls under one single social status. That is no different for a platform worker. Activities within the sharing economy consequently fall under the traditional social and fiscal regime. The platform worker will therefore, like any other active person, be covered either by the social security system for employees or by that of the self-employed. In most cases, however, the person concerned will be considered to be self-employed.[9] This is partly due to the self-employed status being a residual category and also to the special tax presumption contained in the social status of self-employed persons. Under this scheme, there is a presumption – albeit a rebuttable one – on the basis of which a person who declares profits, income, remuneration from professional activities for tax purposes is presumed to be engaged in an independent activ-

6 Article 3 (1) of Royal Decree No. 38 of 27 July 1967 establishing the social status of self-employed persons.

7 Article 328-342 of the Programme Law of 27 December 2006.

8 See CAR (Belgian Labour Relations Commission) and tribunal discussions on Deliveroo.

9 See also *Stevens, Yves*, Social Security and Platform Work in Belgium: Dilemma and Paradox, in: Devolder, Bram (ed.), The Platform Economy, Unravelling the Legal Status of Online Intermediaries, Cambridge-Antwerp-Chicago: Intersentia 2019, pp. 262-263.

ity. Only miscellaneous income that is occasional and falls outside a professional context is not included. If a platform worker declares professional income, he will have to join a social security scheme as a self-employed person. If he declares the income from the sharing economy as miscellaneous income on his tax declaration form, this will be reclassified as professional income as soon as this is done on a regular basis and thus, the suspicion of a self-employed (secondary) activity arises.

1. *Indirect Legal Status*

Faced with an increasing number of private individuals offering services to other private individuals as mini-entrepreneurs, the Government wanted to strengthen this form of sharing economy and at the same time remove it from the grey zone in order to combat fraud. Therefore, it was decided to establish a special regulation. Through the Programme Law of 1 July 2016, a separate fiscal and social regulation was introduced for certain providers within the sharing economy.[10] Based on the realisation that the sharing economy could constitute an important growth engine for the economy, which therefore needed to be promoted, the legislator considered it important for workers to be able to carry out a limited activity with minimal administrative formalities in the context of the sharing economy.[11] The system consisted of introducing a separate category within miscellaneous income for income generated in the context of the sharing economy. However, the income from occasional services as miscellaneous income was in principle taxable at 33 percent but was often not declared. The Government's aim with the new regulation was not only to take out of its grey zone income that had previously often escaped taxation, but also to encourage entrepreneurship by giving people the opportunity to carry out a limited activity with a minimum of formalities.[12] If a number of condi-

10 Programme Law of 1 July 2016, Articles 35-39, https://www.ejustice.just.fgov.be/cgi_loi/change_lg.pl?language=nl&la=N&table_name=wet&cn=2016070101. Accessed 20 August 2020.

11 Explanatory memorandum of the Programme Law of 2 June 2016, Parliamentary Acts of the Belgian House of Representatives 2015-2016, No. 54-1875/001, p. 23.

12 Ibid. It must be mentioned that, in principle, someone who performs with a minimum of regularity or continuity a self-employed activity in addition to the job as employee (self-employed persons in secondary employment) must pay social security contributions to the social insurance fund he/she is affiliated with. The contributions (20.5 percent) are calculated annually on the basis of the net professional income.

tions were met, this income would henceforth be taxed at a net tax rate of 10 percent. The condition was that this income may not exceed a certain threshold amount (EUR 5,210).[13] In addition, the activities carried out under this regulation could not be closely linked to an activity carried out as a self-employed person or to the activity of the company of which he/she is the manager.[14] Nevertheless, closeness to the activities carried out as an employee did not pose a problem. The reason for this distinction stemmed from its objective. The aim of the regulation was, on the one hand, to encourage employees to try out self-employment and, on the other hand, to give the self-employed the opportunity to try out another professional activity.[15] It would, of course, be a different case if a self-employed person were to bring part of his activities under the cheaper status. In a nutshell, the Government simply aimed to encourage self-employment. Of course, it remains a delicate matter to determine which activities are closely related. Does a sectoral approach suffice?

Another condition is that the sharing platform had to be recognised. Through the recognition, the Federal Public Service Finances is not only able to assess whether the services are eligible for the regulation, but also ensures that the platforms provide the necessary cooperation in the deduction of the tax withheld on professional income and in the reporting of income. This way, income from grey labour can be made visible. The service provider must mention the gross amount of the income in its personal income tax declaration. This is the amount actually paid or granted by or through the platform, plus all amounts withheld by the platform or through its intervention. At the end of the year, the sharing economy platforms report this gross amount to the Federal Public Service Finances, which checks that the exempted limit has not been exceeded.

This tax section was also linked to a social section. Both sections had to be read together.[16] In accordance with the social status regulations for self-employed persons, income from platform work is not subject to Royal Decree No. 38[17] for the activity related to this income, as long as platform work-related income does not exceed the maximum amount provided for in the Income Tax Code. No one can deny that the importance of the shar-

13 Income threshold to be indexed of EUR 3,255, which is set at EUR 5,210 for the tax year 2019.

14 Explanatory memorandum of the Programme Law of 2 June 2016 (fn. 11), p. 24.

15 Ibid., p. 24.

16 Ibid., p. 12.

17 Royal Decree No. 38 of 27 July 1967 establishing the social status of self-employed persons.

ing economy is increasing. In fact, the Belgian Government set up this regulation to not "miss the boat". Moreover, the system of exemption from fiscal and parafiscal contributions indirectly subsidises the entire sharing economy. If one earns less than the threshold, the income is seen as miscellaneous income that does not give rise to the fiscal presumption of self-employment.[18] Thus, the legislator intervened through an ingenious system of fiscal and parafiscal exemption of income from platform work and regulated aspects of platform work.

With the adoption of the Act on Economic Recovery and the Strengthening of Social Cohesion on 18 July 2018, the legislator went even one step further.[19] Indeed, instead of a reduced rate of 10 percent net tax burden, there is now a total tax and social security contribution exemption for income from certain forms of employment. Natural persons can now carry out activities untaxed and exempt from contributions for a certain amount of income limited to EUR 6,000 per year. This limit is higher than the one set in the law of 2016.[20] Also, the activities are not limited to the sharing economy. There are three possibilities: association work, services from citizen to citizen, and the sharing economy. For the first two categories, a system has been set up that is in line with the existing tax system of the sharing economy through a recognised platform and has also been linked to it (in terms of maximum income limit). The law aimed to support association work which is by its very nature based on voluntary cooperation between citizens without a traditional subordinate relationship and possibly carried out at a legally limited fee.[21] For a specific list of activities,[22] natural persons may provide support to persons organising an activity. In addition,

---

18 This is on condition that (a) the services are provided exclusively to natural persons who are not acting in the course of their professional activity; (b) the services are provided solely under contracts established by means of an approved electronic platform; (c) the fees for the services are paid or granted to the service provider solely by the platform referred to or through that platform (Article 36 of the Programme Law).

19 Act on Economic Recovery and the Strengthening of Social Cohesion of 18 July 2018, https://www.ejustice.just.fgov.be/cgi_loi/change_lg.pl?language=nl&la=N&cn=2018071803&table_name=wet. Accessed 20 August 2020.

20 However, it should be noted that the income from the sharing economy is now added to the income from associations and occasional services between citizens.

21 Explanatory memorandum of the Government Bill on Economic Recovery and the Strengthening of Social Cohesion of 11 December 2017, Parliamentary Acts of the Belgian House of Representatives 2017-2018, No. 54-2839/001, p. 152.

22 As an animator, youth leader or coordinator providing sports initiation and/or sports activities; sports trainer, sports instructor, sports coach, youth sports coordinator; caretaker of youth, sports, cultural and artistic infrastructure; carer in

and by extension, the legislator also wanted to take into account the limited services performed by citizens among themselves. After all, these services are similar to association work, since they are also primarily carried out during leisure time, but on the other hand, the difference lies in the fact that the services are not performed through an organisation, but directly between citizens. Activities of this sort are occasional and are therefore not carried out on a regular basis. They are also described as a "favour for a friend". Finally, the system of the sharing economy is also mentioned, whereby the system of an untaxed sideline will also be made applicable to additional earnings from the sharing economy through recognised platforms. The difference with the occasional services between citizens is that in the sharing economy, the work is done through a recognised platform.[23] Since an association or citizen does not work through a recognised platform and in order to allow effective control, the performance of the association's work and the occasional performance between citizens must be declared in advance.[24] The application of this law is framed by a number of conditions which are, however, much less stringent as far as the sharing economy is concerned. Nevertheless, the law did not include a separate social section for the sharing economy.

As soon as a person earns more than the maximum threshold, that person cannot be considered as an occasional service provider and the services are by law irrefutably presumed to have been provided under the social status of self-employment.[25] In this sense, activities performed for remuneration but outside the framework of the sharing economy or outside the framework of occasional services will not be covered by this exemption. Therefore, one performs work that falls under the status of either employee or of a self-employed person. This applies both if one exceeds the threshold and if one does not comply with the application conditions. The inten-

childcare before, during and/or after school hours organised at school or during school holidays, as well as during transport to and from the school; providing help and support on an occasional or small-scale basis in the field of administration, management, the organisation of archives or the assumption of logistical responsibility for activities in the socio-cultural, sports, cultural, art education and education sectors. (Article 3 of the Act on Economic Recovery and the Strengthening of Social Cohesion of 18 July 2018).

23 Explanatory memorandum of the Government Bill on Economic Recovery and the Strengthening of Social Cohesion of 11 December 2017 (fn. 21), p. 158.

24 Articles 19 and 25 of the Act on Economic Recovery and the Strengthening of Social Cohesion of 18 July 2018.

25 Article 41 of the Act on Economic Recovery and the Strengthening of Social Cohesion of 18 July 2018.

tions of the legislator varied in this regard: to create an accessible, comprehensible and easily applicable legal framework with a focus on legal certainty for the provider (in terms of liability and in social, fiscal and administrative terms) and with fair compensation; to avoid the unbridled application of social legislation (fines, criminal liability of directors, etc.); to encourage ancillary activities in leisure time and to discourage and reduce undeclared or illicit work.[26]

The law is known as the "sideline" law or the "untaxed moonlighting" law. As the word itself already indicates, it involves activities carried out "on the side". Furthermore, in Dutch, the word for this phenomenon refers to chores which do not exactly correspond to labour or a secondary profession, precisely in order to highlight the very essence of these activities, namely that they are activities that rather take place in leisure time and as a hobby. Certain restrictions and conditions had to ensure that there was no competition with commercial activities and that an outflow from the professional labour market was avoided. For instance, activities that may be carried out in the context of association work and occasional services between citizens are limited to a defined list of activities. According to the legislator, these activities are of a special nature, which is the very reason for them to be given separate social and fiscal treatment and status. These are activities that mainly have an added social and societal value and therefore have a different purpose. Unlike an employee who wants to earn a living through work, or a self-employed person who wants to make a profit, these activities are purely ancillary and non-remunerative in nature and are therefore limited in their amount and fulfil a social interest.[27] However, this list is long. For example, activities from citizen to citizen can include: childcare, babysitting, family support services, tutoring, music/drawing/craft/technique lessons in the private home of the teacher or in the home of the client, small maintenance works to or around the home, help with administration and punctual help with small IT problems, with the exclusion of professional accounting, supporting persons with occasional or small household tasks in the home of the user, with the exception of regular cleaning.[28]

---

26 Explanatory memorandum of the Government Bill on Economic Recovery and the Strengthening of Social Cohesion of 11 December 2017 (fn. 21), p. 156.

27 Ibid., pp. 151-152.

28 Article 20 of the Act on Economic Recovery and the Strengthening of Social Cohesion of 18 July 2018.

The problem, however, is that all these activities can also be provided for in the regular labour market[29] and are not simply regarded as non-committal by those involved. To what extent can one still say that this is only about favours for a friend? These are activities that can also be perfectly carried out by the self-employed or companies. As a result, there is a competitive position vis-à-vis the regular labour market. Precisely in order to avoid this risk of competition, the legislator imposed a number of conditions for the application of this favourable financial and social system. In addition to the nature of the activity (limited list), it should also concern occasional services. These are additional services among other activities performed. The system is only accessible to persons who are already engaged in a main professional activity (i.e. working four-fifths) and who derive a social security status from it.[30] It surely seems that certain forms of labour are being transferred to the sphere of spare-time work. An employee who works four fifths as an IT specialist for an employer could, for instance, easily offer similar work the other day of the week, untaxed and exempt from contributions. A full-time worker could certainly consider this option with a view to part-time employment. In certain cases, the Belgian legislation provides for an allowance for a person who reduces his/her employment by 1/5 to 4/5, with a view to thematic leave (e.g. bringing up young children) or a career break, end-of-career jobs, time credit, etc.[31] The person involved then receives an allowance for unemployment and can still supplement this with an untaxed amount of income via the sideline law.

For a self-employed person, however, the condition applies that the activity must be different from the normally exercised professional activity.[32] But the requirement that it should be an additional activity is not entirely correct. Whereas this requirement does apply to the regulation of associations and occasional services between citizens, it does not apply to the sharing economy. In the latter case, it is not required to perform another main activity. Furthermore, the nature of activities does not play any role in the case of the sharing economy. All possible services may be performed. It should not necessarily be activities with added value for society. Only services that are an extension of the professional activity are excluded.

29 These activities can also be carried out by a (non-remunerated) volunteer.

30 Articles 4 and 21 of the Act on Economic Recovery and the Strengthening of Social Cohesion of 18 July 2018.

31 CLA No. 103 of 27 June 2012 introducing a scheme for time credit, career reductions and end-of-career jobs and the Royal Decree of 12 December 2001.

32 Article 20 of the Act on Economic Recovery and the Strengthening of Social Cohesion of 18 July 2018.

For the legislator, the individual purpose of these activities was the reason to proceed with a separate treatment of these activities with a complete exemption of fiscal and parafiscal contributions. Activities of this sort are not seen to constitute productive labour, which is the very basis of the social security system. It is not professional work, but more like a compensated favour for a friend. Therefore, these activities do not constitute labour and are excluded from the scope of the Belgian social security system. The solution the legislator had in mind was ambivalent, because although this labour became visible, the legislator did not consider it to be labour. The difficulty of making the traditional distinction between employees and self-employed persons, necessary within a professional social security system, enticed the legislator to look for a third "non-status" somewhere between professional work and voluntary work. The Government introduced, as it were, a new category of "reimbursed spare-time work" that moves between pure volunteering and work within the regular labour market as an employee, a civil servant or a self-employed person. Thus, although the person concerned may carry out these activities in a professional capacity, he/she is given the possibility to carry out the same activity under the status of an "untaxed side job". Therefore, as long as one stays below the foreseen threshold, the status does not play a role. As these persons are engaged in activities which do not constitute employment within the meaning of social law, they therefore do not enjoy protection under social legislation (e.g. no maximum working hours, no social security protection).

2. *Non-Status*

However, one may question whether this far-reaching fiscal and parafiscal exemption of income associated with the mentioned activities can be objectively and reasonably justified. Both legislations on the sharing economy demonstrate that for the legislator, different objectives were central to provide for a separate status: to make a major part of "grey" or "black labour" visible again; to find a solution to the difficulty of making the traditional distinction between employees and the self-employed, necessary within a professional social security system; to promote free enterprise and encourage additional activities without too many administrative formalities, not least because these activities are often of a marginal and ancillary nature and seek to offer added social value.[33]

The big fear was of course that this regulation would lead to unfair competition with the regular labour market. For example, the Belgian National Labour Council (CNT), which brings together the social partners in its opinion on this law, pointed out that it should not be the aim to discourage activities through recognised platforms, but that this activity should either generate additional income or be seen as a stepping stone to regular self-employment. However, such an activity should not aim to circumvent social legislation and thus create unfair competition between sectors or workers.[34]

The CNT points out that the introduction of the tax and social security contributions exemption for sharing platforms would have the consequence that, depending on the way in which these services are offered, the respective exemptions would apply purely and exclusively in function of the way in which the services are made known to the public and the way in which supply and demand are brought into contact with each other.[35] Therefore, the CNT was extremely critical of this law. For many, this law could therefore lead to new systems, in which regular entrepreneurs would have to compete with very cheap temporary labour. Consequently, the law quickly gave rise to joint action by many interest groups and trade unions before the Constitutional Court for annulment of this law.[36]

3. *Is the Sharing Economy not Labour?*

Before examining the various arguments put forward before the Constitutional Court, we should first examine which labour is covered by the Belgian social security system and which labour is excluded from it. After all, this is what the whole discussion is about. There is no doubt about activities carried out within the sharing economy being labour. Of course, this is

---

33 Explanatory memorandum of the Programme Law of 2 June 2016 (fn. 11), pp. 12-13; Explanatory Memorandum of the Government Bill on Economic Recovery and the Strengthening of Social Cohesion of 11 December 2017 (fn. 21), pp. 180-181.

34 National Labour Council (CNT), Opinion No. 2065, 29 November 2017, p. 22, http://www.cnt-nar.be/ADVIES/advies-2065.pdf. Accessed 20 August 2020.

35 Ibid., p. 23.

36 See Constitutional Court, Judgement No. 53/2020 of 23 April 2020, https://www.const-court.be/public/n/2020/2020-053n.pdf. Accessed 20 August 2020.

labour, it is simply not professional labour in the sense of social security legislation. The social security legislation in Belgium, as a professional system, is based on the requirement to exercise a professional activity. This is literally a consequence of the social status of self-employed persons: a self-employed person is any natural person who carries out a professional activity in Belgium by virtue of which he is not bound by an employment contract or by a status.[37]

In the self-employed professions, there is a special scheme for those who "in addition to the activity giving rise to submission to this Royal Decree, habitually and principally – that is to say, a person whose working hours are at least equal to those of a full-time employed worker" – so simultaneously – are employed as employees or civil servants. This is better known as self-employment in secondary activity.[38] In order to be self-employed, one must be engaged in a professional activity, which means an activity that is usually carried out and with the aim of making a profit. Thus, on the one hand, a minimum of regularity or continuity is required and, on the other hand, occasional work does not constitute a professional activity.[39] The requirement for a certain regularity often gives rise to interpretation problems and discussions, whereas in the past it was claimed that this required at least 18 days of activity per year. As early as 1976, this 18-day rule was abolished as the minimum threshold for work requiring insurance[40] and was replaced by the requirement of a certain regularity and continuity. Indeed, it was unfair that persons with significant professional income from a single occupation of less than 18 days would be treated more favourably than persons who, although working over a longer period of time, acquired a lower income.[41] On the other hand, a self-employed worker has to strive for profit even if he might not actually make any profit.[42] The profit motive excludes voluntary help from family members or

---

37 Article 3 (1) of Royal Decree No. 38 of 27 July 1967 establishing the social status of self-employed persons.

38 Article 12 of Royal Decree No. 38 of 27 July 1967 establishing the social status of self-employed persons.

39 Labour Court Brussels, 22 June 1984, TSR, 1985, 228; Labour Court Brussels, 13 January 2012, JTT, 2012, 462.

40 By law of 6 February 1976.

41 *Reyniers, Kelly/Van Regenmortel, Anne*, Bijklussen in de sociale zekerheid: de juridische omkadering kritisch belicht?, in: Janvier, Ria/Van Regenmortel, Anne/Vervliet, Valérie (eds.), Actuele problemen van het socialezekerheidsrecht, Bruges: die Keure 2011, p. 340.

42 Court of Cassation of 2 June 1980, JTT, 1982, 76; Court of Cassation of 26 January 1987, JTT, 1987, 254.

friends.[43] It is quite remarkable, however, that every self-employed person whose business is his/her primary occupation is expected to pay a contribution anyway, even when no profits are made. Indeed, the calculation of the contributions is based on the fiction that a certain minimum amount of professional income is reached, even if this is not the case. Therefore, this income is not exempted from contributions. It is only in the system of self-employment as a secondary occupation that contributions are only due if the professional income has reached a certain minimum amount, which is approximately 1/4 of the threshold amount in the sideline law. It is important in this context that self-employed persons in secondary employment also pay contributions under their self-employed status – with an exemption if the reference income is below a certain amount – even if no profits have been made and without this granting them additional benefits. This is, therefore, a form of solidarity: contributions paid must support the balance of the scheme for self-employed workers, while enabling them to enjoy the social advantages of the scheme to which they are subject due to their main activity.

In the employee system, it is somewhat less clear whether a professional activity is also required, but this is an indirect consequence of the fact that the National Social Security Office (NSSO) Law applies to employees and employers who are bound by an employment contract.[44] Labour law further defines what an employment contract is. In addition, this requirement also stems from the notion of solidarity that only those who pay contributions and wish to belong to the system and to a particular professional category[45] can have access to benefits. The concept of employment contract refers to an agreement under which work is carried out under the authority of an employer in return for remuneration. This is the basis for the obligation to contribute. Does this also require a professional activity? Or does every work we do, including e.g. babysitting and garden work, give rise to insurance if this were done through an agreement and under the authority of someone? The answer is not always clear. Legal doctrine points out that

43 Labour Court Brussels, 6 April 1981, TSR, 1981, 577.

44 Article 1 of the Law of 27 June 1969 revising the Legislative Decree of 28 December 1944 on social security for workers; Articles 1 and 2 of the Law of 29 June 1981 defining the general principles of social security for employees.

45 *Reyniers, Kelly/Van Regenmortel, Anne*, Bijklussen in de sociale zekerheid: de juridische omkadering kritisch belicht? (fn. 41), p. 351.

labour can be approached in two ways[46]: the first way examines whether the labour is for the benefit of the employer and whether the labour is the object of the performance or whether it can only be regarded as incidental to the main purpose of the contract. A typical example of this is a traineeship contract. If the sole purpose of the labour is to acquire the necessary professional skills and it forms part of a training programme, it will not be considered as work. On the other hand, labour can be considered as the objective to obtain an income to provide for living. This vision is also cited by the legislator as an objective in the sideline law. Labour means activities taking place on the paid labour market.

But this means that any activity, even if it is occasional, can be a professional activity as long as it provides a living.[47] Similarly, the limited fee obtained or the time or amount spent on such an activity does not constitute a criterion. The specificity of labour is not the nature of the activity, but rather the objective with which it is carried out, i.e. the acquisition of income.[48] What is a leisure activity for one person (e.g. football, working in the garden) is professional work for somebody else (professional footballer, gardener). Therefore, remunerated leisure activities can also constitute work performances. It is precisely due to the fact that remuneration is paid which exceeds the real costs and that it is not generosity that it can be considered to be a wage and therefore, in principle, the one receiving it is also subject to social security. Thus, everything one does to earn money is professional labour, even if it is a rather everyday activity. However, the legislation provides that certain work may be excluded from the scope of social security legislation (NSSO legislation).

It is of interest to us to know in which cases and for what reasons certain work is excluded from the scope of social security. Labour is only excluded if it is too marginal to be liable for insurance. The legislator hereby provides that the King (Government) may, under the conditions he determines, exclude from the application of this law those categories of workers who are employed in a job which is ancillary to their employment or which is essentially of short duration.[49] This confirms that, in principle,

---

46 *De Vos, Marc,* Loon naar Belgisch Arbeidsovereenkomstenrecht, Antwerp: Maklu 2001, p. 62; *Reyniers, Kelly/Van Regenmortel, Anne*, Bijklussen in de sociale zekerheid: de juridische omkadering kritisch belicht? (fn. 41), p. 353.

47 *Van Langendonck, Jef/Jorens, Yves/Louckx, Freek/Stevens, Yves*, Handboek Socialezekerheidsrecht, Antwerp: Intersentia 2020, pp. 139-140.

48 Ibid., pp. 138-139.

49 Point 4 of Article 2 (1) of the Law of 27 June 1969 revising the Legislative Decree of 28 December 1944 on social security for workers.

any work can be subject to insurance. The King has made use of this by excluding a number of categories. Nevertheless, the reason for the exclusion is not always explained.[50] Short-term work as a ground for exclusion is rare today, especially since the past rules excluding workers who did not normally work more than two hours a day have been abolished and replaced by the concept of occasional work.[51] Nonetheless, the latter notion is interpreted in a very restrictive way as an activity or several activities carried out for the household of the employer or his/her family, with the exception of manual household activities – think of intellectual labour such as performed by a governess, private teacher, babysitter – and manual non-household activities (driver, gardener), insofar as the employee does not perform these occasional activities in the household professionally and regularly and insofar as the activities do not exceed eight hours a week for one or several employers.[52] In this, the nature of the activities occupies centre stage. Whether 8 hours is still essentially of short duration is doubtful.

In addition, there are some activities that are excluded because they are ancillary to the job. But what is ancillary?[53] This includes in the first place, for example, a number of people who provide services for public services or activities of public utility, such as sports camps. It could be argued that "ancillary" implies that it is complementary to a job considered to be principal. This was also the original wording, but it was subsequently changed to an activity carried out for a maximum of 25 days. As a result, the exclusion refers more to short-term than secondary jobs. In addition, the following are also excluded: students for a particular number of hours (475 hours), some temporary workers in agriculture and horticulture as long as they do not work more than 25 days, temporary workers engaged by organisers of sports events for the day of those events. In essence, all these exceptions concern people who are exempted on the basis of the number of days' work and for a specific type of activity. One might, however, wonder if these are all services of a short duration. Moreover, "ancillary" does not indicate that the person concerned works in addition to a main activity. There are, furthermore, a few special arrangements for categories of

---

50 Articles 16 and 17 of the Royal Decree of 28 November 1969 implementing the Law of 27 June 1969.

51 Article 16 of the Royal Decree of 28 November 1969 implementing the Law of 27 June 1969 as modified by Royal Decree of 24 August 1987.

52 Ibid.

53 See Article 17c of the Royal Decree of 28 November 1969 implementing the Law of 27 June1969 and see also *Van Langendonck, Jef/Jorens, Yves/Louckx, Freek/Stevens, Yves*, Handboek Socialezekerheidsrecht (fn. 47), pp. 171-175.

staff who actually already pay full contributions in another system.[54] It is only exceptional that it is not an hour or day limit that is considered, but the "income" earned. This is the case for volunteer firefighters and the context of the "untaxed moonlighting" law that we are discussing here.

But even if we do not subject persons involved to social security, they are certainly not completely excluded from social protection. For example, most of them are covered by industrial accidents and occupational illness schemes[55]; or a solidarity contribution is paid by the employer, as is done for students (and by themselves) and in the case of flexi-jobs, so these workers also build up rights for e.g. unemployment and pensions.

4. Back to the Drawing Board

Consequently, the total exclusion of side jobs from the social legislation gave rise to a situation in which persons who carry out the same activities as self-employed persons or as service providers through a recognised electronic platform are treated differently. Is this therefore a breach of the principle of equal treatment or are there grounds for justification, and is this distinction based on an objective criterion which is reasonably justified? Discrimination occurs when equal categories are treated differently or different categories of persons are treated equally. Is there a difference in treatment?

To what extent are service providers through recognised electronic platforms comparable to employees and self-employed persons? According to the Belgian legislator, these groups are not comparable. After all, this law does not aim to replace the employment type of employee or self-employed person by a new employment type, but rather to avoid undeclared work. The same persons may fall within both categories. It is therefore not a comparison between groups of persons, but a comparison between different types of activities. The Constitutional Court does not follow this

54 It concerns doctors employed in hospitals who have a practice outside the hospital and pay full contributions on a self-employed basis. But in fact, it is not so much a question of short-term work or a secondary job, but of finding a solution to the difficulty of distinguishing between doctors who work in an institution as self-employed persons or as employees, or with regard to flexi-jobs in the catering industry: persons who, in addition to a main occupation for which they pay contributions, work to a limited extent in the catering industry.

55 With the exception of doctors, temporary support staff at sports events and civil servants providing performances during sports camps.

position at all. The Court points out that the introduction of the new status aimed, among other things, to remedy the lack of clarity about the classification as employee or as self-employed person. This lack of clarity was caused precisely by the fact that it is possible to carry out these activities both as an employee and as a self-employed person, depending on the concrete circumstances. Therefore, the compared categories are indeed comparable.[56] Are there any justifications for the different treatment?

One of the main objectives for the Government to establish this regime was to combat undeclared work. This objective is certainly pertinent, but is this the right way to go? Will this objective be attained by completely exempting someone from all contributions? Is it not aberrant to note that a measure aimed at avoiding undeclared work now, on the contrary, makes it possible to switch from a status subject to social security and tax obligations to a status exempting the person concerned from all those obligations?[57] It is almost as if the legislator wanted to encourage people to try another professional activity. Avoiding undeclared work through an exemption and by giving someone no status seems like values turned upside down. The name of the law in which this legislation was included speaks volumes: Act on Economic Recovery and the Strengthening of Social Cohesion. Social cohesion is thus "strengthened" by not granting a social security status!

For the legislator, the activities referred to are activities that take place in leisure time and are therefore carried out on an occasional basis. They are thus considered as ancillary activities. After all, their purpose is not so much to make a living. Of course, "ancillary" is a relative and very subjective notion. Moreover, in the sharing economy, there is no limited monthly amount, only a maximum annual threshold amount. Supposing that someone earns, for example, EUR 1,000 a month, it can hardly be said that this is incidental. This looks more and more like an alternative to part-time employment. It is not even required that the person concerned has a main activity in addition. Furthermore, the Constitutional Court points out that there is a contradiction between this assumption and the legislator's objective of stimulating entrepreneurship and providing a stepping stone to self-

56 See Constitutional Court, Judgement No. 53/2020 of 23 April 2020, recital A.12 and B.7.3, https://www.const-court.be/public/n/2020/2020-053n.pdf. Accessed 20 August 2020.

57 See Constitutional Court, Judgement No. 53/2020 of 23 April 2020, recital B. 6.10 and 7.5, https://www.const-court.be/public/n/2020/2020-053n.pdf. Accessed 20 August 2020.

employment through the creation of this status.[58] And rightly so! For many people it is more than a marginal activity, but it is an important, if not a necessary, addition to their income that supports them in their daily needs and intentions. For some, this work is necessary, not only in order to earn a living, but even to survive.

The idea is that this work is often carried out for reasons other than profit-seeking and at the service of others or of society.[59] But can professional work not also be carried out at the service of others or society? Moreover, if the same activities are carried out by an employee or a self-employed person, do they no longer have any special added social value? Quite rightly, the Constitutional Court also points out that the fact that it would concern a limited number of activities offering particular added value for society, whereas there is no such restriction in terms of permitted activities under the status of employee or self-employed person, does not justify the significant difference in treatment where identical activities are involved. Moreover, it does not appear that the activities listed in the law would all have a greater social added value than other possible activities.[60] Furthermore, the nature of the activities does not play any role in the sharing economy and therefore, the argument of the special added social value does not hold true.[61] Consequently, it has not been demonstrated that the difference in treatment has the objective of supporting activities with an added social value.[62]

The various arguments put forward by the Government are, to say the least, highly debatable and it should therefore come as no surprise that the Constitutional Court – more than rightly so – has overturned this regulation. At the same time, however, this also shows that the approach adopted to regulate platform work is debatable. Nevertheless, the potential im-

58 See Constitutional Court, Judgement No. 53/2020 of 23 April 2020, recital B. 7.6, https://www.const-court.be/public/n/2020/2020-053n.pdf. Accessed 20 August 2020.

59 The exclusion of volunteer firefighters from social security contributions can be partly explained by the idea that this is labour with a special social role.

60 See Constitutional Court, Judgement No. 53/2020 of 23 April 2020, recital B. 6.9, https://www.const-court.be/public/n/2020/2020-053n.pdf. Accessed 20 August 2020.

61 See Constitutional Court, Judgement No. 53/2020 of 23 April 2020, recital B. 7.6, https://www.const-court.be/public/n/2020/2020-053n.pdf. Accessed 20 August 2020.

62 See Constitutional Court, Judgement No. 53/2020 of 23 April 2020, recital B. 5.7, https://www.const-court.be/public/n/2020/2020-053n.pdf. Accessed 20 August 2020.

pact of this law could be so big for all parties concerned that the Constitutional Court did not proceed with the retroactive effect of the annulment of this law, which would have been as if the law had never existed. Precisely in order to avoid that persons carrying out side jobs could get into trouble and face all kinds of after-claims and fines, the annulment only applies as from the next tax year. This should also allow the sharing platforms to revise their entire business plan which was based on the sideline law.

III. Towards New Protection for Platform Workers?

In which direction should we now go regarding the protection of platform workers? No one can deny that the importance of the sharing economy is increasing. In fact, the Belgian Government set up the Recovery Act[63] to keep pace with developments. Moreover, the system of exemption from fiscal and parafiscal contributions indirectly subsidises the entire sharing economy.

The Government has already clarified the direct consequences of the annulment of this Act. It is only with the adoption of the Recovery Act of 2018 that an appeal was lodged with the Constitutional Court for the annulment of this Act. However, after the promulgation of any law, one has only 6 months to lodge an appeal for annulment before the Constitutional Court. No appeal had been lodged against the old separate status introduced in 2016. The Minister has already stated that from 2021, the old law granting a reduced tax rate will enter into force again. The question then arises as to whether this forthcoming Act could not be appealed against? The fact that the old law would be reinstated does not, in principle, oppose this. After all, the Council of Ministers had defended this argument in the case before the Constitutional Court. Thus, the Council of Ministers contested the admissibility of the pleas relating to the status of service provider through a recognised electronic platform, since that status was already introduced by the Programme Law of 1 July 2016, against which the applicants did not bring an action for annulment. An action brought against a difference in treatment which does not derive from the contested law but is already contained in a previous law is inadmissible. However, the Constitutional Court points out that when the legislator adopts an old provi-

63 Act on Economic Recovery and the Strengthening of Social Cohesion of 18 July 2018, https://www.ejustice.just.fgov.be/cgi_loi/change_lg.pl?language=nl&la=N&cn=2018071803&table_name=wet. Accessed 20 August 2020.

sion in a new legislation and thus appropriates its content, an appeal may be lodged against the provision within six months of its publication. Does this argument now backfire? The Constitutional Court already gives a certain indication: "Although the uncertainty about the correct classification may justify the need for a separate status, such a status was already created by the Programme Law of 1 July 2016. Moreover, the lack of clarity as to the classification does not justify the fact that the contested provisions attach to that status a total exemption from labour law, the social security system and tax obligations"[64].

In tax law, there is no longer a full exemption and the 10 percent net tax burden can be considered justified, but as far as the social aspect is concerned, it seems that this is not really justified. Furthermore, it is time to go down a different path, not only for the benefit of the platform worker but for the sake of our entire social security system.

Platform workers do not need a third separate status. In Belgium, social law is based on the traditional dichotomy between employees and self-employed persons, and creating a third group will certainly not help to avoid the traditional difficulties in distinguishing between the two categories. On the contrary, one may even expect that in this case, a heated discussion will emerge about who can be defined as a platform worker.[65] It is, in any case, very questionable to use a separate status for a special category of persons as a solution to the ever-increasing flexibility on the labour market. Are these persons really special? After all, do they not carry out the same activities as other people on the regular labour market?

IV. Conclusion

Platform workers do not need a third status, but they certainly do not need a non-status either. Is it also justified, on the basis of the marginal character and added value for society, to withdraw someone completely from social legislation, as is the case for platform workers? This is particular in times when social security also pays attention to work that can at least be considered socially useful. Thus, we see that the (Belgian) legislator pro-

64 See Constitutional Court, Judgement No. 53/2020 of 23 April 2020, recital B. 7.7, https://www.const-court.be/public/n/2020/2020-053n.pdf. Accessed 20 August 2020.

65 See also *Nerinckx, Stefan*, De "Uberisering" van de Arbeidsmarkt: Enkele Bedenkingen bij het Sociaal Statuut van de Actoren in de Platformeconomie, in: TSR 2018, p. 49.

vides for an increasing number of measures granting protection to those who do not perform "paid" work but still perform activities that are considered useful: people who take a career break to take care of a sick parent or sick child, or even just to pursue a dream, are – often even while receiving benefits – protected under the social security system. Even volunteering, the area par excellence where unpaid but useful work is provided, is economically encouraged by providing social protection. Work on the periphery or outside the traditional labour market is to a great extent recognised within social security.[66] So why exclude platform workers from social security? This creates a dilemma: the greater the number of people doing such work and the more important it is for these people, the more incomprehensible it is that these people would be deprived of any social protection and at the same time, however, the more difficult it is to carry out work that does not support the financial capacity of the social security system. The fundamental starting point of the Belgian social security system is that regular or productive labour constitutes the basis for the development of our welfare system. The looser the link with professional employment becomes, the more questions arise about the financing of social security, certainly in a professional system.

However, today's flexible workforce consists of people who not only switch between employers, but who also alternate between periods of professional activity and voluntary work. Individuals may no longer only carry out one secondary activity alongside a main activity, but rather different (secondary) activities, whereby the distinction between main and secondary activities fades. In addition, many platform workers also perform work that may not be considered professional work today, but which is of great use. It is not because this work is not carried out on the labour market that these activities should be considered as inferior, as chores, as a second-class activity.[67] It is not up to our social security system to exclude people who perform useful work and work in the platform sector. On the contrary, we should embrace them. This is not done by giving them a non-status, but by including them in the current system of social protection. It is not a question of robbing the platform worker of any social protection. In fact, he needs adequate protection precisely because of his precarious work situation.

---

66 *Van Steenberge, Josse*, Arbeid en Sociale Bescherming: Een LAT-relatie?, in: Ministerie van Sociale Voorzorg, 50 Jaar Sociale Zekerheid…en Daarna?, Brussels: Bruylant 1995, p. 97.

67 *Van Steenberge, Josse/Delanote, Liliane*, Maak er Werk van, Bruges: die Keure 1998, p. 37.

However, as long as our social security system only focuses on regular employment, the sharing economy will pose a threat to our welfare state.[68] Perhaps it is time to put forward a new concept of labour. Labour is more than earning an income; it is also the right to usefulness: to be given, acquire and earn a useful place in society.[69] Social security should therefore also be opened up for activities that do not or not always follow the normal scope of employment. The big advantage would be that precisely those activities floating between the commercial and non-commercial labour market, often in a grey zone, are made visible again. Labour then becomes not so much the basis of social security, but rather its purpose.[70] May platform work act as a trigger for this development!

---

68 See also *De Vos, Marc*, De Toekomst van Arbeidsrecht, in: De Corte, Rogier/De Vos, Marc/Humblet, Patrick/Kefer, Fabienne/Van Hoorde, Eva (eds.), De Taal is gans het Recht: Liber Amicorum Willy van Eeckhoutte, Mechelen: Wolters Kluwer 2018, p. 31.

69 *Van Steenberge, Josse/Delanote, Liliane*, Maak er Werk van (fn. 67), p. 37.

70 *Van Steenberge, Josse*, Arbeid en Sociale Bescherming: een LAT-relatie? (fn. 66), p. 89.

Chapter 4
Is the Classification of Work Relationships Still a Relevant Issue for Social Security? An Italian Point of View in the Era of Platform Work

Edoardo Ales

I. Introduction

This chapter aims at analysing the connection between the classifications of work activities in labour law and the protective statute they enjoy in social security. After a period during which a "tailor-made" approach has prevailed, linking a specific protective statute to a certain typology (subordination and autonomy), as classified by the labour law legislator, the deconstruction of those typologies as well as of the undertaking organisation has, more recently, pushed the legislator to effect change. The new approach of the Italian legislator consists of an arbitrary application of a social protection statute (as a "package") according to a political assessment of the weaknesses of specific groups of workers ("social types"), taking into account the new forms of integration into the organisation of increasingly "deconstructed" undertakings. Paramount examples would be the issue of "hetero-organised" collaborations and that of riders.

II. The Classification of Work Relationships: The Beginning

From a historical perspective, Italian legislation was confronted with the challenge of classifying work for the first time when mandatory social insurance against work accidents (*Infortuni sul lavoro*) was introduced by Act No. 80 of 17 March 1898. This Act defined who should be covered as a "worker" (*operaio*) for social law purposes: This is anyone who "is employed" outside his or her premises, permanently or temporarily, with fixed or piecework remuneration or anyone in the same situation who supervises the work of others, even without participating in it, if his or her salary does not exceed a certain amount and the pay periods remain within the month. The definition is completed by a list of activities regarded as particularly dangerous, such as working in mines and on construction sites, or other construction activities where more than five workers are employed. In general, the understanding of the term "operaio" referred to manual workers. However, the legislator did not provide any definition of employment, probably counting on the fact that the very notion of worker (*operaio*) was undisputed. It is worth noting that such a notion, at least for the purpose of Act No. 80, included *supervisors* and *apprentices*, paid or unpaid, who from a labour law perspective may not necessarily be regarded as workers (*operai*). By consequence, one has to stress that social security legislation uses a different, autonomous classification of workers covered by mandatory insurance for accidents at work, deviating from the one used for labour relations.

A second important turning point in the evolution of notions and classifications is represented by the introduction of the Mandatory Old Age and Invalidity Insurance[1] established immediately after WWI. It applied to male and female persons aged between 15 and 65 who work "in the employ" of a third party, as workers (*operai*), busboys (*garzoni*), apprentices, janitors (*inservienti*), assistants, shop assistants, supervisors and clerks (*impiegati*), in the private as well as in the public sector, home workers included. Interestingly, social insurance definitions did not replicate those provided for in the legislation on employment contracts in the private sector enacted two months earlier.[2] The latter had defined the *contract of employment in the private sector* as a contract under which a legal or physical person who runs a business, hires "at the service" of that business, usually on an open-ended basis, the professional activity of the other party for the purpose of "cooperation" as a staff member, with the exclusion of any manual work. The legislator refrained from providing any explanation of what was meant either by "in the employ" ("*alle dipendenze*") or by "at the service" ("*al servizio*"). Both expressions exclude, however, persons under contract working *independently*, although allowing *for some shades of dependency*. Furthermore, manual workers (*operai*) were covered by the mandatory old age and invalidity social insurance whereas they did not fall under the notion of contract of employment in the private sector. As a consequence, access to and protection by early social security legislation in Italy was provided in an autonomous way, not linked to labour law and its classifications.[3]

---

1 Royal Lieutenant Decree-Law No. 603 of 21 April 1919.

2 Royal Lieutenant Decree-Law No. 112 of 9 February 1919.

3 Indeed, the labour law legislation of that time did ignore, on purpose, the conditions of the worker (operaio) in order to exclude any recognition of rights during a period in which the worker movement was still struggling to overturn the existing

The divide between social security law and labour law regarding the definition of the protected categories of workers in each field persisted over the Fascist period. In fact, Royal Decree-Law No. 1827 of 4 October 1935 (Article 37) recalled that mandatory old age and invalidity pension referred to people as "in the employ" ("*alle dipendenze*"), thus including *operai* as well as *impiegati*, excluding *impiegati* with income above a certain earnings level. At the same time, employment contract law still excluded manual workers.[4]

III. *Subordination and Autonomy: A Political and Legal Issue*

A third, decisive turning point in the evolution of notions and classifications is represented by the adoption, in the Civil Code of 1942, at the very sunset of the Fascist regime, of the notion of *subordination* that applies to all "collaborators" of the entrepreneur (Article 2094) at times seen as the head (*capo*) of the undertaking (Article 2086). Subordination eliminated any differences not only between workers (*operai*) and clerks (*impiegati*) but also in relation to managers (*dirigenti*), all gathered in Article 2095 as belonging to subordinated "collaborators", although of different categories (*categorie di prestatori di lavoro*) due to the hierarchical supremacy of the entrepreneur as employer. Even if subordination in the fascist Civil Code is more of a political than a legal notion,[5] the employer's managerial prerogatives are recognised explicitly by Article 2094 and 2104 (2) Civil Code. On the other hand, the subordination of managers who, at times, exercise those prerogatives on behalf of the entrepreneur as employer over the rest of "collaborators", seems to be justified in view of granting them some form of social security in terms of old age and inability pension in connection to having been "in the employ" of the undertaking. One can conclude that the notion of subordination has become the decisive classification

---

political order. On the contrary, in a clear Bismarckian approach, the social security legislator tried (in vain) to appease workers' protests by introducing old age and invalidity pensions on a mandatory basis. Cf. *Gaeta, Lorenzo*, Storia (illustrata) del Diritto del Lavoro Italiano, Turin: Giappichelli 2020, pp. 388 ff.; *Ales, Edoardo*, Die geistigen Grundlagen der Sozialgesetzgebung des Kanzlers Otto von Bismarck und das Entstehen des Sozialstaates in Italien, in: Eichenhofer, Eberhard (ed.), Bismarck, die Sozialversicherung und deren Zukunft, Berlin: Berlin Ver. A. Spitz 2000, pp. 55-74.

4 Royal Decree-Law No. 1825 of 13 November 1924.

5 *Gaeta, Lorenzo*, Storia (illustrata) del Diritto del Lavoro Italiano (fn. 3), p. 80 ff.

tool, both for labour law and social law purposes. Nevertheless, social law may pursue more comprehensive coverage strategies in an autonomous way, as has been the case for some liberal professions which already had their own categorical old-age protection schemes.[6]

At the beginning of the constitutional period (1948), the very notion of *hierarchical subordination* was questioned because of its negative political significance and progressively substituted with that of *technical subordination* – to be understood in terms of "hetero-direction" of the employer on his "collaborators". In the social security perspective, subordination as "hetero-direction", encompassing the entire workforce, easily matches the notion of "in the employ" of the entrepreneur, including any kind of work performed within the undertaking, to be understood as a physical structure organised and directed by the entrepreneur/employer. Integration through the subordination of "collaborators" in the undertaking as a hetero-organised structure excludes any form of autonomy inside it. From such a perspective, autonomy can be conceived only as a feature of any kind of work performed *without subordination to the entrepreneur* i.e. *without integration in the organisation of the undertaking* even if provided in favour of it. The provision of a service or of a workmanship (*opera*) is so defined by Article 2222 Civil Code and protected in a way that highlights the non-involvement of work in the organisation of the undertaking. The issue of protection of autonomous work (self-employment) is the product of a comprehensive approach to work as a *professional activity* (entrepreneurial included) typical of the corporatist view, as expressed in Article 2060 Civil Code, according to which "work is protected in all its *organisational and executive forms*, be it intellectual, technical or manual".

Although extrapolating the freedom to conduct a business (as recognised by Article 41), the same holistic approach to the protection of work has been adopted, at least theoretically,[7] by the 1948 Constitution in Article 35. Nevertheless, one could say that the labour law protection of "purely" autonomous work, i.e. work performed without any form of integration whatsoever in the undertaking, further to that already provided by the Civil Code (Articles 2223-2238), became an issue for the legislator only in 2017, when Act No. 81 was adopted (see below). One important point to be stressed is that, on the one hand, autonomous work may come in the

6 See below.

7 *Ales, Edoardo*, (The Right to) Work as Foundational Value: Italy and the Very Notion of a Constitutional Promise, in: Bellace, Janice/ter Haar, Beryl (eds.), Research Handbook on Labour, Business and Human Rights Law, Cheltenham: Edward Elgar 2019, pp. 34-49.

form of a registered intellectual profession (Articles 2229 ff. Civil Code), and is as such protected, as for social security, within the system of Professional Funds, while separated from the General Social Insurance System (*Assicurazione Generale Obbligatoria*). For instance, this was and still is the case for barristers and solicitors who, according to Act No. 406 of 13 April 1933, are mandatorily insured by *Cassa Forense*, originally a public law body that was, however, privatised in 1994 (Legislative Decree No. 509 of 30 June 1994), and has been run since then by a foundation under the control of the Ministry of Labour and Social Affairs. On the other hand, social protection had been extended to artisans and merchants, first under the limited scope of health insurance (respectively, Act No. 1533 of 29 December 1956, and Act No. 1397 of 27 November 1960), then under inability, old age and survivors insurance (respectively, Act No. 463 of 4 July 1959, and Act No. 613 of 22 July 1966).

The differences between the two groups are manifest, since persons in the second (artisans and merchants) are by definition (small) entrepreneurs, whereas in the first (barristers and solicitors), this is not necessarily the case. Nevertheless, both are required to contribute to their activity through personal work, which, in case of the latter, shall be prevalent (Article 2222 Civil Code). Mainly for this reason, more recently, the social security legislator has addressed artisans and merchants, too, as "autonomous workers" (Act No. 233 of 2 August 1990) with a view to distinguishing them from entrepreneurs falling outside the scope of social protection on the grounds that they "just" run a company. On the other hand, artisans and merchants are autonomous also in the sense that they organise their own activity and work, without being integrated into any alien organisation, at least as far as their personal work is concerned. Nowadays, the social security of artisans and merchant is managed by INPS through separate funds.

IV. Coordination: A New Star is Born

From the perspective of notions and classifications, specific consideration must be given to *sales agents or representatives* who operate under an *agency contract* as regulated by Article 1742 ff. Civil Code.[8] Although at least in view of the Civil Code, they do not belong to the "collaborators" of an entrepreneur (agency contracts do not fall within the scope of Book V of the

8 *Ghezzi, Giorgio*, Del contratto di agenzia, Bologna: Zanichelli 1970.

Civil Code dedicated to "Labour"), their activity has to be *coordinated* with that of the undertaking. For instance, the areas in which the sales agent is active are predefined within the contract and the proponent entrepreneur shall not assign another agent to them. Furthermore, the sales agents shall discharge their duties according to the instructions received and have to provide the proponent with all the information related to the market conditions of the assigned area as well as with any other information that may help in assessing the convenience of each business deal. The fact that sales agents and representatives find themselves *somewhere in the middle* between organisational integration and independence is confirmed by the circumstance that, since 1938, their activity has also been regulated by framework collective agreements (*accordi collettivi*), which, among other things, have introduced a first form of social security in relation to the guarantee of severance payments. In fact, the 1938 Agreement established a social security body (ENASARCO, which still exists as an integrative pension fund) which was transformed into a public body by Royal Decree No. 1305 of 6 June 1939, and which regained its private law status in 1997. As for their classification, Act No. 741 of 14 July 1959, which provided the just mentioned collective agreements with a temporary *erga omnes* effect, explicitly traced back the position of sales agents and representatives to a *coordinated and continuous collaboration* with the proponent undertaking.

Relationships of such kind caught on rapidly in the labour market also outside the realm of the agency contract. This is confirmed by the fact that, some years later, the legislator included in the scope of application of the new employment proceedings *coordinated and continuous collaboration other than that of the sales agents and representatives* (Act No. 533 of 11 August 1973 modifying Article 409 No. 3 Civil Procedure Code). Nevertheless, the legislator did not provide these groups immediately with any other form of protection, social security included. On top of that, it was specified that they did not fall under any subordination relationship (Article 409 No. 3 Civil Procedure Code) so that they could not be put on an equal footing with collaborators "in the employ" of the entrepreneur, being therefore excluded from the General Social Insurance System. On the other hand, as autonomous workers they could have been entitled to social security only if they fell within the scope of application of one of the specific schemes mentioned above, which was almost never the case. It is still highly disputed whether *coordinated and continuous collaboration* shall be regarded as an intermediate category between subordination and autonomy. For the time being, the conclusion is that workers in this category are self-employed persons of sorts (*collaborazioni autonome coordinate e continuative*).

The above situation did not help in tackling the already relevant problem of (mis)qualification of the work relationship, both from the employer's and the employee's side. For the former, it had and still has to do with an *escape from subordination* because of its heavy social security burden; for the latter, on the contrary, with a *run after subordination*, since outside it there was no (social) protection. The possibility to qualify a work relationship as "coordinated and continuous collaboration", *de facto* outside any social security scheme (and burden), accentuated the fraudulent contractual behaviour of a part of the employers, stimulating the doctrine and the case law to look for an intermediate classification of such collaborations as "para-subordinated"[9] – with the consequence that at least part of the labour law provisions could have applied to them.

From the social security perspective, with reference to pensions, the legislator in Act No. 335 of 8 August 1995[10] has adopted a decisive provision. In fact, Article 2(26) has extended the General Social Insurance System to any person who performs professionally, although not exclusively, an autonomous activity for which no registration by a professional board is required (as specified by Article 18(12), Decree-Law No. 98 of 6 July 2011). Truth be told, Article 2(26) also recalls the "coordinated and continuous collaborations". However, it does so with reference to a tax law provision that has been withdrawn in the meantime. Decisive is the idea that, as it happens with sales agents and representatives, autonomous work can be compatible with *a certain degree of coordination* if the modalities of the latter are co-determined by the parties in a kind of *co-organisation* of the activity. By specifying that, for the purpose of Article 409 No. 3 Civil Procedure Code, a collaboration is coordinated "when, in the respect of the modalities of coordination defined by consensus between the parties, the collaborator organises autonomously his or her activity", the legislator has confirmed, by Act No. 81 of 2017, the autonomous nature of those collaborations. By consequence, these collaborations fall within the scope of application of the so-called *Gestione Separata* of the General Social Insurance System, under specific conditions of entitlement to benefits that are financed from contributions, the rate of which now amounts to 34 percent of the annual income as defined for tax law purposes.

9 *Santoro Passarelli, Giuseppe*, Il lavoro "parasubordinato", Roma: Franco Angeli 1979.

10 Cinelli Maurizio/Persiani Mattia (eds.), Commentario della riforma previdenziale: dalle leggi "Amato" alla finanziaria 1995, Milano: Giuffré 1995.

V. The Beginning of Ambiguity

1. The Extension of Subordinated Social Protection to Autonomous Work

From the late nineties, the legislator extended to female self-employed workers insured only by the *Gestione Separata* the provisions on maternity, family allowances and hospitalisation grant, increasing proportionally the contribution rate. In particular, according to Article 64 of Legislative Decree No. 151 of 26 March 2001, maternity provisions have to be applied according to the same principles as for subordinate work, although without requiring the abstention of the worker from her activity during the maternity leave as a condition to receive the maternity allowance (adoption and foster cases included).[11] This is a sign that, on the one hand, the integration into the organisation of the undertaking is not quite the same as in case of subordinate work, but also, on the other hand, that the legislator considers the need for protection of the coordinated collaborator to be the same as that of the subordinated one.

Once again, from the perspective of notions and classifications, it is important to stress that in 2015 the legislator referred straightforward to "coordinated and continuous collaborators" insured by the *Gestione Separata*, but not entitled to a pension and without a VAT number, as beneficiaries of a specific unemployment grant (DIS-COLL). DIS-COLL was introduced by Article 15 of Legislative Decree No. 22 of 4 March 2015, and it is paid in case of involuntary unemployment for a maximum of six months. Its amount is calculated based on the beneficiary's yearly income and corresponds to 75 percent of the monthly income if this falls below a minimum threshold fixed by the law. On the contrary, subordinated workers are entitled to NASPI, an unemployment benefit that is calculated based on the last wage. Both are of a typical social insurance nature.[12]

A further and highly controversial turning point as far as notions and classifications are concerned is represented by Article 2 (1) Legislative Decree No. 81 of 15 June 2015, as recently modified by Article 1 Act No. 128 of 2 November 2019. In its original version, Article 2 (1) provided for the application of the protective statute of subordinate work (one could argue both from a labour law and social security perspective) to "collaborations

---

11 *Ales, Edoardo*, Maternità e congedi parentali, in: Enciclopedia del Diritto, Annali, Vol. IX, Milano: Giuffré 2015, pp. 531-556.

12 *Renga, Simonetta*, Post fata resurgo: la rivincita del principio assicurativo nella tutela della disoccupazione, in: Lavoro e Diritto, 29 (2015) 1, p. 77.

that consist of exclusively personal and continuous work the execution modalities which are organised by the client, with particular reference to the time and place of work". The difference regarding subordination has to be found in the use of "organisation" instead of "direction" in order to describe the way in which the client relates to the collaborator: as a result, one could not define the former as an employer. Contrary to coordinated and continuous collaborations, the execution modalities of the performance are unilaterally organised by the client, excluding any negotiation with the "collaborators", which is a decisive element of the notion contained in Article 409 of No. 3 Civil Procedure Code. Scholars have named this "hetero-organisation", with a view to distinguishing it from "hetero-direction". They have also debated whether such a notion can be classified under subordination or autonomy.[13] In our view, however, one has to refer to the way in which the performance "collocates" with the structure of the client undertaking, and to the notion of "organised by the client". This has also to do with the understanding of the very notion of subordination. What is clear is the clash between "hetero-direction" as a typical feature of "traditional" subordination, and "hetero-organisation" as main character of what we can call an "autonomised subordination",[14] in which *neither hetero-direction power nor full autonomy is at stake*. As for the very notion of "hetero-organisation", an important point was represented by the prerogative of the client to determine unilaterally the time and the place of the performance.[15] However, such specification has been withdrawn by Article 1 Act 2 No. 128 of November 2019, whereby "exclusively" was also changed into "mostly" as far as the personal character of the performance is concerned.

---

13 See, among others, *Nogler, Luca*, La subordinazione nel d.lgs. n. 81 del 2015: alla ricerca dell'"autorità del punto di vista giuridico", in: WP C.S.D.L.E. "Massimo D'Antona".IT, 267 (2015); *Perulli, Adalberto*, Il lavoro autonomo, le collaborazioni coordinate e le prestazioni organizzate dal committente, in: WP C.S.D.L.E. "Massimo D'Antona".IT, 272 (2015); *Santoro Passarelli, Giuseppe*, I rapporti di collaborazione organizzati dal committente e le collaborazioni continuative e coordinate *ex* art. 409 n. 3 c.p.c., in: WP C.S.D.L.E. "Massimo D'Antona".IT, 278 (2015); *Magnani, Mariella*, Autonomia, subordinazione, coordinazione nel d.lgs. n. 81/2015, in: WP C.S.D.L.E. "Massimo D'Antona".IT, 294 (2016).

14 *Ales, Edoardo*, Subordination at Risk (of "Autonomisation"): Evidences and Solutions from Three European Countries, in: Italian Labour Law e-Journal, 12 (2019) 1, p. 65.

15 *Magnani, Mariella*, I tempi e i luoghi del lavoro. L'uniformità non si addice al post-fordismo, in: WP C.S.D.L.E. "Massimo D'Antona".IT, 404 (2019).

2. *"Hetero-Organisation": A New Challenge for Subordination*

It is rather clear that, as far as notions and classifications are concerned, the very meaning of *hetero-organisation* has to be investigated.[16] This in order to understand whether there is a typological justification for the application of the protective statute of subordination to relationships that do not fall under the scope of "hetero-direction", being not integrated in the same way into the structure of the undertaking. In such a perspective, it has to be stressed that the Constitutional court has declared unlawful a legislative provision denying (for the purpose of both labour law and social security) the classification of subordinated to work relationships that actually showed the typical features thereof on the ground of its irrationality and self-contradictoriness.[17] In the same vein, one could argue that, even if made to the benefit of workers, the choice to apply the protective statue of subordination to "hetero-organised" relationships may be deemed unconstitutional as well. In fact, it imposes a *disproportionate burden* on the client who is not entitled to the managerial prerogatives he or she may enjoy as employer in terms of "hetero-direction".

A big chance to clarify the situation has been offered by the case of food delivery riders, contracted as coordinated and continuous collaborators, who have lodged claims before several Italian courts in order to be recognised as subordinated workers and to have access to the relevant protective statute. In parallel to the court proceedings, in a quite unfortunate timing, the legislator has classified riders as autonomous workers, by adopting a specific regulation (see below) that could have not been taken into account by the judges due to its nonretroactive effect. Deciding on the first claim brought to its knowledge, the *Cassazione*,[18] although aware of the stance taken by the legislator, upheld the judgement of the Court of Appeal of Turin, according to which the activity of riders must be classified as "hetero-organised" collaboration, thus falling within the scope of application of subordination according to Article 2 (1) Legislative Decree 81 of 2015. However, without a motivation worthy of the name, the *Cassazione*, confirming the conclusions of the Court of Appeal, did limit the application of the protective statute of subordinated work, excluding, among the others, the right to a wage and working time. Moreover, the *Cassazione* has

16 *Zoppoli, Antonello*, La collaborazione eterorganizzata: fattispecie e disciplina, in: WP C.S.D.L.E. "Massimo D'Antona".IT, 296 (2016).

17 Corte costituzionale, 23.03.1993, No. 121.

18 Cassazione, sez. lav., 24.01.2020, No. 1663.

deemed irrelevant any investigation of the very meaning of "hetero-organisation", on the assumption that, by recognizing the entitlement to the protective statute of subordination, Article 2 (1) constitutes a *remedial provision*. In the view of the *Cassazione*, the legislator does not intend to classify *a new typology of work relationship*, focusing, on the contrary, on the positive effects that the remedy will have on the worker. What remains obscure is how to figure out when a work relationship falls within the scope of Article 2 (1) without having any idea of the real meaning of "hetero-organisation". By abdicating its supreme interpretation role, the *Cassazione* puts that provision at risk of unconstitutionality for the reasons mentioned in the above.[19]

Finally, yet importantly, nothing is said about the social security aspects, neither by the legislator nor by the *Cassazione*. However, remaining consistent with the clear statement of the legislator, "hetero-organised" collaborators shall fall within the scope of application of the General Social Insurance System, in the *Fondo Pensioni Lavoratori Dipendenti* (FPLD). Against this background, one could conclude that "hetero-organisation" can be an option for entrepreneurs only if they have decided to bear anyhow the costs of subordination, renouncing, however, to the traditional understanding of the managerial prerogatives it entails and opting in favour of "autonomised subordination". From a classification point of view, "hetero-organised" collaborations are neither subordinated nor autonomous. However, the subordination protective status applies, social security included. The practical effects of such a solution are not yet perceivable.

VI. Platform Work and its Varieties

How does all this apply to platform work? Since 2017, the Italian legislator has intervened three times with reference to the possibility that work is performed through "technological instruments", platform included. This has happened once via the already mentioned Act No. 81 of 22 May 2017,[20] with reference to *smart working* (Article 18), and twice via Legis-

19 *Ales, Edoardo*, In favore dell'etero-organizzazione come "concetto" autonomo: timeo danos et remedia ferentes, in: Massimario di Giurisprudenza del Lavoro, 73 (2020) 2, p. 19.

20 *Perulli, Adalberto*, Il *Jobs Act* del lavoro autonomo e agile: come cambiano i concetti di subordinazione e autonomia nel diritto del lavoro, in: WP C.S.D.L.E. "Massimo D'Antona".IT, 341 (2017).

lative Decree No. 81 of 2015, as modified by Act No. 128 of 2019, in Article 2 (1) and Articles 47-*bis* ff., respectively, with reference to hetero-organised collaborations and autonomous work in the delivery sector.

1. *Smart Working (on Platform) as a Modality of Subordinate Work*

According to Article 18 of Act No. 81 of 2017, smart working (*lavoro agile*)[21] is a modality of execution of subordinate work, freely agreed between the parties, also organised by objectives, without predetermined working time and place, in which work is performed partly inside and partly outside the premises of the undertaking, in the absence of a stable work station. Nevertheless, work is understood to be smart also if performed regularly in a place chosen by the worker for his or her personal convenience within the limit of reasonableness (so-called hub). Maximum working hour limits as provided by the law or collective agreements shall be respected. The use of "technological instruments" is an option. Even if classified as subordinate work (Article 2094 ff. Civil Code), the legislator requires the parties specifying, within the written individual agreement:

- its nature, i.e. open-ended or fixed-term, and, as for the latter, its duration and termination notice period which, however, cannot be less than 30 days (90 in the case of workers with disabilities);
- how managerial prerogatives, with reference to control and disciplinary powers, are exercised when work is performed outside the premises of the undertaking;
- which instruments, if any, must be used by the worker;
- rest and disconnection periods, in cases where work is performed using "technological instruments".

Both open-ended and fixed-term agreements may be terminated for just cause. Equal treatment between smart workers and those working within the premises of the undertaking shall be guaranteed. The smart work agreement shall be communicated to the competent labour authorities. By introducing smart work, the legislator explicitly explains the goal, first, of improving the performance of subordinate workers through the establish-

21 *Spinelli, Carla*, Tecnologie digitali e lavoro agile, Bari: Cacucci 2018; *Tiraboschi, Michele*, Il lavoro agile tra legge e contrattazione collettiva: la tortuosa via italiana verso la modernizzazione del diritto del lavoro, in: WP C.S.D.L.E. "Massimo D'Antona".IT, 335 (2017); *Magnani, Mariella*, I tempi e i luoghi del lavoro. L'uniformità non si addice al post-fordismo (fn. 15).

ment of new forms of organisation, also by objectives, in the absence of direction and control, thus echoing "autonomised subordination". On the other hand, it aims at the improvement of the work-life balance, in particular by recognising a priority of smart work agreements signed with female workers within three years after the termination of maternity leaves, from a clear "adult worker model" view,[22] according to which care activity is a woman's job.

From a social security point of view, the fact that the legislator has classified smart work as a "modality of subordinate work" makes things very easy, above all if one smart work day has the same value as an ordinary working day as far as working time, wage and, therefore, contributions are concerned. However, due to the lack of control over performance, above all in cases where somebody is working off-line, the relationship shall be built on mutual trust that allows for an aggregation of the elements mentioned above. The adoption of an achievement-oriented approach to work organisation[23] may be of great help to support such a perspective.

2. *Platform Work as a Modality of Hetero-Organised Collaboration*

An explicit reference to platforms, not to be understood as the employer or the client, but only as the *technical tool* through which the modalities of work are defined (see below), is provided by Article 2 (1) Legislative Decree No. 81 of 2015, as modified by Act No. 124 of 2019. As already illustrated above, one could think about "hetero-organisation", to which the protective statute of subordination applies, in terms of "autonomised subordination", within the framework of an achievement-oriented approach to work organisation. In such a framework, it is not at all problematic to reconcile platform work with subordination that has abandoned the dog-

22 *Ales, Edoardo*, Geschlechterspezifische Rollenmodelle und ihre Überwindung: das Adult-Worker-Modell in der italienischen Gesetzgebung, in: Eigenverantwortung, private und öffentliche Solidarität – Rollenleitbilder im Familien- und Sozialrecht im europäischen Vergleich, Bundesministerium für Familie, Senioren, Frauen und Jugend, Forschungsreihe Band 3, Baden-Baden: Nomos 2008, pp. 195-211.

23 *Ales, Edoardo*, Is Performance Appraisal Compatible with the Employment Relationship? A Conclusive Plea in Favour of an Achievement-Oriented Approach to Work Organisation, in: Addabbo, Tindara/Curzi, Ylenia/Fabbri, Tommaso/Rymkevich, Olga/Senatori, Iacopo (eds.), Performance Appraisal in Modern Employment Relations. An Interdisciplinary Approach, London – New York – Shanghai: Palgrave Macmillan 2020, pp. 255-263.

ma of "hetero-direction", above all if the very notion of work organisation is an immaterial one.[24] Indeed, a problematic point is the transnational nature of "digital work", above all if the principle of territoriality continues to apply to labour law and social security, as is the case with the Court of Justice.[25] According to the Court, "in the absence of harmonisation or coordination measures at Union level in the field concerned, the Member States remain, in principle, free to set the criteria for defining the scope of application of their legislation, to the extent that those criteria are objective and non-discriminatory".[26] Quite surprisingly, the Court offers no reflection on the notion of the "objective and non-discriminatory nature", thus apodictically supporting the territoriality principle of labour law.[27] In fact, in the view of the Court, "EU law does not (…) prevent a Member State from providing that the legislation it has adopted be applicable only to workers employed by establishments located in its national territory." In the same way, "it is open to another Member State to rely on a different *linking factor* for the purposes of the application of its own national legislation."[28] It is evident that according to such an interpretation it will be difficult, even in case the "owner" of the platform is located in an EU Member State, to advocate for the application of the more favourable social security system. The consequence is to jeopardise the possibility for delocalised ("digital") workers to invoke the law of the country of origin of their "real" employer and to favour the flourishing of fictitious employers (platforms) in their country of establishment and vice versa.[29]

3. *Platform Work as a Modality of ("False") Autonomous Work*

As already highlighted, Act No. 128 of 2019 adds a Chapter V-*bis* to Legislative Decree No. 81 of 2015, with the very promising heading "Protection

24 *Ales, Edoardo*, Subordination at Risk (of "Autonomisation"): Evidences and Solutions from Three European Countries (fn. 14), p. 65.

25 CJEU of 18 July 2017, C-566/15, Erzberger, ECLI:EU:C:2017:562. See *Ales, Edoardo*, Adapting Labour Law to "Digital" Work Between Scholarly Interpretation, Case Law and Legislative Intervention", forthcoming essy in a book edited by Perulli, Adalberto and Treu, Tiziano.

26 CJEU of 18 July 2017, C-566/15, Erzberger, para. 36.

27 Ibid., para. 38.

28 Ibid., para. 37.

29 *Ales, Edoardo*, Adapting Labour Law to "Digital" Work (fn. 25).

of Work through Digital Platforms" (Articles 47-*bis* to 47-*octies*).[30] Quite surprisingly, however, Chapter V-*bis* does not apply to all forms of platform work, but only to "autonomous workers who carry out activities of goods delivery on behalf of others, in urban areas by bicycle or motor vehicles", the so-called riders (Article 47-*bis*). Of high interest, on the contrary, is how the legislator defines digital platforms as "the software used by the client (undertaking) for the delivery service, in order to fix the remuneration due to the rider and to determine the way in which the service is performed". Therefore, in the legislator's view, the platform is only an instrument that can be used in order to organise work, and is not regarded as the employer as such. This is a very important assumption, since it means that the physical or legal person owning the platform can be held responsible for the violation of any labour law and social security provision as a "normal" employer or client. Moreover, that person takes the risk that the self-learning algorithm will act unlawfully, outside any possible human control. With the algorithm being no legal person, it cannot be sanctioned as would happen to the real employer.

The contracts of the riders shall be in written form *ad probationem*, meaning the absence of the written form does not effect the nullity of the contract. In the absence of a written form, one may advocate the existence of a subordinate contract, as it is useful to prove the actual conditions applied to the relationship and, if applicable, the infringement of workers' rights. Riders shall receive adequate information on their rights and on health and safety regulations. Failure to comply with this information duty results in a violation of Legislative Decree No. 152 of 1997, implementing the Written Statement Directive.[31] Effective sanctions are provided in such a case[32] (Article 47-*ter*).

Riders shall receive remuneration (*compenso*) that, notwithstanding their classification as autonomous workers, can be determined by national

30 *Ales, Edoardo*, Oggetto, modalità di esecuzione e tutele del "nuovo" lavoro autonomo. Un primo commento, in: Massimario di Giurisprudenza del Lavoro, 72 (2019) 3, p. 719.

31 Directive 91/533/EEC. After 1 August 2022 Directive 2019/1152/EU of 20 June 2019, relating to Transparent and Predictable Working Conditions in the European Union.

32 According to Article 4 Legislative Decree No. 152 of 1997, the worker can contact the Provincial Labour Office so that the latter obliges the employer to provide the information required by the decree within fifteen days. If the employer does not comply with the order, the worker is entitled to an indemnity that cannot exceed the remuneration received in the last year and which must be determined based on the seriousness and duration of the violations and the behaviour of the parties.

collective agreements, signed by the comparatively more representative trade unions at national level. This is a very controversial point since it implies that in order to have their pay defined by collective bargaining riders shall be represented by already existing unions, usually focused on subordinate workers. The same reference to *contratti collettivi*, typical of subordinate work, instead of *accordi collettivi*, typical of autonomous work, confirms the ambiguity of the legislative intervention. Yet, by defining pay, collective agreements shall take into account the modalities of the provisions of service and the organisation of the client (undertaking). In the absence of collective agreements, workers cannot be paid by the piece (delivery) and shall have a minimum hourly wage taking into account that already set by collective agreements of similar sectors. Such a provision seems to be aimed at stimulating the conclusion of collective agreements that could introduce piecework payment in the light of the modalities of the provision of service and of the organisation of the undertaking.

In any case, workers shall be entitled to a supplementary indemnity, not less than 10 percent of the minimum hourly wage, for work performed at night or on holidays or in adverse weather conditions. The amount of the indemnity is fixed by collective agreements or, in their absence, by Decree of the Ministry of Labour (Art. 47-*quarter*). Wage setting through collective agreements risks to clash with the case law of the Court of Justice. In fact, as decided in *FNV*,[33] a collective labour agreement, containing minimum rates for self-employed persons who carry out for an employer the same activity as his employees, falls outside the scope of Article 101 TFEU (and therefore does not conflict with competition law) only where such workers are "false" self-employed persons, i.e. workers who are in the same situation as employees. Since the legislator has explicitly classified riders as "real" self-employed persons, the regulation or even the definition of criteria determining their remuneration by collective agreements is difficult to reconcile with what the Court has stated. One had to assume that the just mentioned ambiguous approach has been adopted on purpose in order to cast doubt on the "real" autonomous nature of riders and to avoid the clash with competition law. However, the classification of riders as autonomous workers seems to imply a non-rebuttable presumption such as to exclude that they could be also hired as subordinate (hetero-organised)

33 CJEU of 4 December 2014, C-413/13, FNV, ECLI:EU:C:2014:2411, para. 42. *Biasi, Marco*, Ripensando il rapporto tra il diritto della concorrenza e la contrattazione collettiva relativa al lavoro autonomo all'indomani della l. n. 81 del 2017, in: WP C.S.D.L.E. "Massimo D'Antona".IT, 358 (2018).

workers, thus eliminating the comparator needed in order to make the *FNV* doctrine applicable. Provisions regarding the remuneration of riders will apply from November 2020.

Antidiscrimination law and the guarantee for the worker's freedom and dignity, as provided by the subordinate protective statute shall apply to riders. This is a further sign of the ambiguity mentioned above, taking into account that, at least as far as antidiscrimination law is concerned, autonomous work has its own rules. The refusal to accept a delivery does not justify the exclusion of riders from the platform, nor does a reduction of delivery opportunities, which is, on the contrary, a clear signal of the autonomous nature of riders, since no subordinate worker can lawfully refuse a task that has been required by the employer (Article 47-*quinquies*).[34]

Riders shall be insured against work accidents and occupational diseases, which is not anymore a typical feature of subordinate work only. Contributions are fixed according to the risk rate of the performed activity with reference to the general minimum daily remuneration for Social Security and Assistance contribution (EUR 48.98 – INPS circular letter No. 9 of 29 January 2020), related to the days of actual activity. The physical or legal person using the platform is responsible for the issue of work accidents and occupational diseases legislation, as provided by Decree of the President of the Republic No. 1124 of 30 June 1965, as well as of the health and safety regulation, as provided by Legislative Decree No. 81 of 9 April 2008, (Article 47-*septies*). As far as social security is concerned, being classified as autonomous workers, riders perform "an autonomous activity for which no registration by a professional board is required", thus falling within the scope of application of the *Gestione Separata* (Article 2 (1) Act No. 335 of 1995). Nevertheless, one may wonder whether as "false" self-employed persons to whom a wage is paid as set by collective agreements, they should not fall within the scope of application of the General Social Insurance System, in the *Fondo Pensioni Lavoratori Dipendenti* (FPLD).

Although in a different way, compared to "hetero-organisation" protected as subordination, also in the case of riders, a further inconsistency is at stake between their formal classification and the protective statute that the legislator applies to them. In fact, that statute is closer to subordination than to autonomy. Indeed, formally classified as autonomous workers, riders seem to have been provided by the same legislator with all that is need-

34 In the same vein see CJEU of 22 April 2020, C-692/19, Yodel, ECLI:EU:C:2020:288, point 40.

ed to be reclassified by the Court of justice as "false" self-employed workers.

VII. Conclusion

"Hetero-organised" collaborators and riders are paramount examples of a clear trend towards the abandonment of a "tailor-made protective statute" based on (old-fashioned) labour law classifications of activities, such as subordinated or autonomous work. The current approach of the Italian legislator consists of an "arbitrary" application of labour law and social security protective statute (as a "package"), according to a political assessment of the weaknesses of specific groups of workers ("social types"), without taking into account the way in which they are integrated into the organisation of increasingly "deconstructed" undertakings. From such a "package" perspective, the financing of pensions remains linked to contributions either from wage or from annual income (for those classified as self-employed), within the framework of a (virtually) contribution-based system of calculation of benefits, still run on a pay-as-you-go basis because of its unspeakable financial imbalance. State pay-offs will be needed for many years to come in order to support pensions that might be reduced substantially in their amount, due to the abandonment of the retribution-based system of benefits calculation. However, considering the high contribution rate,[35] the possibility of success for complementary pension funds remains relatively low – unless the legislator decides to transform from option to duty the use of the *Trattamento di Fine Rapporto* (Employment Termination Grant) in order to finance occupation pension schemes.[36]

The conclusion can be that the labour law classification of the work relationship is still a relevant issue for social security although increasingly in a way that does not necessarily coincide with the way of assessing the needs of a certain category of workers in order to understand if new forms of protection should be introduced that are specifically designed for them in accordance with their degree of integration within the organisation of an undertaking. The "package" perspective, according to which the subordination protective status can be "attached" by the legislator to workers

35 Harmonised at 34 percent of wage/income both for subordinate and autonomous work insured by the Gestione Separata, of which two thirds are paid by the employer/client.

36 *Ales, Edoardo*, Il sistema pensionistico a 25 anni dalla riforma, in: Rivista Giuridica del Lavoro e della Previdenza Sociale, 70 (2020) 3, forthcoming.

whose performance does not necessarily recall the features of "hetero-direction" ("hetero-organisation", for instance), is a sweeping one that entails a contingent choice on the part of the legislator, who decides to protect one "politically sensitive" group (riders, for instance), whatever the configuration of their social needs. In this view, further to the absence of "hetero-direction", one major point of reflection can be the lack of an exclusive link to one unique employer that puts the worker in a "false-employee" or "employee-unlike" position, in contrast to the position of the "false self-employed" or the "employee-like" worker. Whether this can cause the emergence of an intermediate category of work between subordination and autonomy, in terms of coordination, is still a matter of debate. In any case, such a solution would require the "design" of specific social security schemes and the abandoning of the "package" approach.

Chapter 5
Relationship between Employment Status and Scope of Social Security Protection: The United Kingdom Example

Philip Larkin

I. Introduction

In common with many other advanced western economies, in both common law and civil law jurisdictions, the United Kingdom labour market has experienced the proliferation of non-standard forms of employment, in particular over the last decade and beyond. These developments have generated much academic and political comment. These forms of non-standard employment include part-time work, agency work, "zero-hours" contracts,[1] and "gig" work, in which workers are paid per piece of work supplied through digital platforms.[2] A further distinguishing feature of many workers in the "gig" economy is that they are regarded as self-employed for both revenue and social security purposes, rather than as employees, or even as "workers".[3] The intermediate category of "worker" has a long pedigree in UK legislation, going back to the Employers and Workmen Act 1875, designed to allow county courts an enlarged and flexible jurisdiction in disputes between an employer and a "workman".[4] As a discrete category within the labour market, "workers" are entitled to the national minimum

1 These are work contracts in which the worker is not guaranteed a set number of working hours weekly, and their weekly hours of work are liable to fluctuate considerably, along with their weekly wage or salary.

2 The Rise of the Sharing Economy, The Economist, 9 March 2013, www.economist.com/news/leaders/21573104-internet-everything-hire-rise-sharing-economy. Accessed 15 April 2020.

3 On certain occasions the UK courts have ruled that certain categories of "gig" workers are, in reality, "workers" rather than self-employed persons. This will be examined below.

4 See Pimlico Plumbers Ltd and Another (Appellants) v. Smith (Respondent) UKSC 29, at para. 8. Section 10 of the Employers and Workmen Act 1875 defines a "workman" as a manual labourer working for an employer under "a contract of service or a contract personally to execute any work or labour."

wage, and paid holidays, but are taxed at the same level as self-employed persons, and are unable to bring claims in unfair dismissal.[5]

One problem which has frequently beset those in non-standard forms of employment has been that many of them are prone to fall into the "poverty trap" (whereby it remains more profitable for citizens, especially those with dependent children, to sustain themselves through welfare benefit receipt rather than engage in gainful employment[6]), due to the irregular weekly hours which they work, and subsequent varying wage rates. It is fortuitous that the UK Coalition Government of 2010 - 2015 initiated both a policy initiative and legislation to deal with the "poverty trap" while the non-regular sector of the labour market was expanding. In the absence of any form of judicially enforceable, entrenched, bill of rights in the UK guaranteeing a minimum income and access to the basic means of life, it remains for legislators to continue to address the problem of the poverty trap.[7] Parliament has made various legislative attempts to incentivise paid work and subsequent employment skills acquisition, the most significant being the introduction of Universal Credit (hereinafter: UC) in the Welfare Reform Act 2012, a process which is still ongoing.[8] In conjunction with the introduction of the National Living Wage in 2016,[9] it was anticipated in Government circles that UC, with its considerably lower clawback rates when recipients' number of working hours and wages rise, would lead both to an alleviation of poverty among low-paid families and

5 It should be mentioned, however, that workers who are not included in the "Pay As You Earn" (PAYE) tax scheme for employers are not entitled to the financial protection of the "Job Retention Scheme" initiated during the recent Covid-19 lockdown, as employees are. The Court of Appeal recently held in Adiatu v. Her Majesty's Treasury, CO/1636/2020, that this policy decision is compatible with the relevant provisions in the ECHR.

6 The problem of poverty caused by wages of just subsistence level or even below was first identified among agricultural workers in Southern English counties during the 1790s, which obliged magistrates to instigate the "Speenhamland System", providing labourers a payment out of local rates based on the price of bread and the number of people in their families. Essentially the same principle forms the foundations of Family Income Supplement, Family Credit, Working Tax Credits, Tax Credits, and, indeed, Universal Credit.

7 Indeed, the incorporation of the European Convention of Human Rights into UK law has made minimal impact on the increasing conditionality which has been a feature of welfare legislation for more than three decades.

8 Universal Credit is gradually becoming operational in various regions throughout the UK.

9 The National Living Wage replaced the National Minimum Wage in 2016 for citizens over the age of 25.

individuals, and an increase in the number of UK citizens accepting lower-paid positions in the labour market.[10] Such developments were expected to have concomitant social benefits, with the civic virtues of industry and thrift being inculcated in citizens, permitting the lower-paid to achieve the economic independence which Hayek believed necessary for a "market order" to flourish.[11] By 2022 an estimated 7.2 million families will receive Universal Credit, 3.9 million of whom will be in work.[12]

The aim of this chapter is to examine the relationship between employment status and the entitlement to social security, in particular UC, but including other benefits, analysing the factors which could prevent their successful operation. The chapter will also examine the question of whether, and how, the Welfare Reform Act (WRA) 2012 can be made effective through legislative and technological reform.

II. Evaluation of Non-Standard Forms of Employment

While it is difficult to arrive at exact figures for those in non-standard forms of work, it has been estimated that by the end of 2019 there were some 974,000 people in the labour market on zero-hours contracts,[13] while some 4.7 million people were estimated to be self-employed as part of the gig economy,[14] a number which had effectively doubled since 2016, and

---

10 This must certainly have been a consideration for MPs at the time of the passage of the Welfare Reform Bill, with the possible prospect of the UK leaving the European Union and a restriction in the number of migrant workers to fill up the low-paid positions in the labour market.

11 See *Hayek, Friedrich*, Law, Legislation and Liberty, Volume Three: The Political Order of a Free People, Chicago: University of Chicago Press 1979, p. 12. See also *Larkin, Philip*, Universal Credit, "Positive Citizenship", and the Working Poor: Squaring the Eternal Circle?, in: Modern Law Review, 81 (2018) 1, pp. 114 and 121.

12 Citizens Advice. Universal Credit Needs to Adapt to the Modern Labour Market, https://www.citizensadvice.org.uk/Global/CitizensAdvice/welfare%20publications/Summary%20briefing%20-%20UC%20and%20modern%20employment%20reports%20.pdf. Accessed 16 April 2020.

13 Office for National Statistics, People in Employment on Zero Hours Contracts, 18 February 2020, https://www.ons.gov.uk/employmentandlabourmarket/peopleinwork/employmentandemployeetypes/datasets/emp17peopleinemploymentonzerohourscontracts. Accessed 17 April 2020.

14 See Statistical Services and Consultancy Unit (SSCU) and University of Hertfordshire and Hertfordshire Business School (HBS), The TUC and University of Hertfordshire Joint Report Platform Work in the UK. 2016 - 2019, https://www.feps-e

now represents 9.6 per cent of the adult working population of the UK.[15] This steep increase demonstrates not only the omnipresence of the internet, but also the volume of demand for the products and services provided through digital platforms, which in turn creates the need for gig workers particularly in large centres of population.[16]

It is possible that this significant move towards the digital platform economy reflects not only the traditional Anglo-Saxon model flexibility of the UK economy, but the increasing "atomisation" of the labour force into a mass of self-employed individuals working off a digital platform also indicates that internet technology now undermines Coase's economic presumption formulated in the 1930s that the "firm" or company hiring employees under contract is the most efficient manner of production and directing the productive capacity of each individual employee, rather than continually contracting out for services.[17] Certainly the trend is symptomatic of the breakdown of the Fordist model in the UK, which involved large collective numbers of factory employees manufacturing all components of a particular product.[18] In socio-legal terms, the dilution of the traditional legal forms of employment in favour of the fluidity of the gig economy could represent what Delanty has labelled the "emerging crisis of solidarity"[19] not only in the UK but throughout Europe, hastened by recession, a development which manifests itself in the weakening of historical ties between employer and employee in the labour market, and, importantly, as Veitch states, changes to traditional assistance offered to citizens via the welfare state.[20]

---

urope.eu/attachments/publications/platform%20work%20in%20the%20uk%202016-2019%20v3-converted.pdf. Accessed 18 April 2020. See also *Partington, Richard*, Gig Economy in Britain Doubles, Accounting for 4.7 Million Workers, The Guardian, 28 June 2019.

15 See ibid.

16 For example, it was reported that London's gig economy has grown by 70 per cent since 2010. See *Osbourne, Hilary*, London's "Gig Economy" has Grown More than 70 Per Cent since 2010, The Guardian, 27 December 2016.

17 See *Coase, Ronald Harry*, The Nature of the Firm, in: Economica, 4 (1937) 16, pp. 386-405.

18 Davidov, Guy/Langille, Brian (eds.), The Idea of Labour Law, Oxford: Oxford University Press 2013, p. 45.

19 See *Delanty, Gerard*, Fear of Others: Social Exclusion and the European Crisis of Solidarity, in: Social Policy and Administration, 42 (2018) 6, pp. 676-690.

20 See *Veitch, Kenneth*, Social Solidarity and the Power of Contract, in: Journal of Law and Society, 38 (2011) 2, pp. 189-214.

In the UK context, this crisis of solidarity is perhaps aggravated by the welfare state regionalism effected by devolution, especially in Scotland and Northern Ireland.[21] In this theory the move away from the contributory Bismarckian welfare state based on social insurance contributions to a common fund is mirrored by developments such as the growth of the gig economy, changes which serve to erode the various contractual links between different social groups and institutions. Even the Conservative Party, most closely associated with neo-liberal policies over the past four decades in the UK, has been cognisant of these changes for over a decade now:

> Today the challenges facing Britain are immense. Our economy is overwhelmed by debt, our social fabric is frayed, and our political system has betrayed the people.[22]

1. *Advantages of Non-Standard Forms of Employment*

Whatever the negative effect on the traditional contractual labour market ties the gig economy and zero-hours contracts may have, the fact that these forms of work have proliferated to such an extent demonstrates how advantageous consumers find the services which they provide. The internet permits consumers instant connection with gig workers to promote efficiency, immediately linking individual demand to supply, reinforcing Veitch's notion of the new "cult of the consumer", and the concomitant notion that consumers should provide for their own care needs.[23] Neither are the benefits of non-standard forms of work confined to consumers: from the onset of the economic recession the gig economy in particular has helped create at least some income for a large sector of the working population, those who were unable to secure traditional type employment.

One feature of the last economic downturn in the UK was that rates of unemployment did not rise to the levels of the early 1980s, standing at 4.8 per cent in 2017.[24] Furthermore, platform work provides a level of flexibil-

---

21 See *Simpson, Mark*, Renegotiating Social Citizenship in the Age of Devolution, in: Journal of Law and Society, 44 (2017) 4, pp. 646-673.

22 Conservative Party, Invitation to Join the Government of Britain: Manifesto 2010, Conservative Research Department 2010.

23 See *Veitch, Kenneth*, Social Solidarity and the Power of Contract (fn. 20), p. 190.

24 This is practically equivalent to full employment. See Office for National Statistics, UK Labour Market: Estimates of Employment, Unemployment, Economic Inactivity and other Employment-Related Statistics for the UK, 15 March 2017,

ity to crowd workers to set their own hours of work around their family lives and other social commitments, a level of overall control which many employees do not normally possess.[25] For those citizens who already possess the status of full- or part-time employee, work in the gig economy offers them the opportunity to supplement their income, with research indicating that the pairing of employment and self-employment has grown over 20 per cent over the past decade.[26]

2. *Disadvantages of Non-Standard Forms of Employment*

It is nevertheless difficult to avoid a number of significant disadvantages which both the gig economy and zero-hours contracts contain for those who work under them. The first is the obvious point that, having the status of self-employed workers, they do not receive the statutory protection their employed counterparts enjoy, such as the rights to the national minimum wage,[27] statutory sick pay and the rights to bring claims for unfair dismissal and redundancy.[28] Furthermore, because they do not make the necessary national insurance contributions, they are not eligible for "new style" contributory jobseeker's allowance,[29] and, being self-employed, cannot receive Industrial Injuries Benefit for injuries sustained in the course of employment.[30] Neither do gig workers receive the protection of the tor-

---

https://www.ons.gov.uk/employmentandlabourmarket/peopleinwork/employmentandemployeetypes/bulletins/uklabourmarket/mar2017. Accessed 20 April 2020.

25 See *De Stefano, Valerio*, The Rise of the "Just-in-Time Workforce": On-Demand Work, Crowdwork, and Labour Protection in the "Gig" Economy, in: Conditions of Work and Employment Series, International Labour Office, Geneva, 71 (2016), p. 6, https://www.ilo.org/wcmsp5/groups/public/---ed_protect/---protrav/---travail/documents/publication/wcms_443267.pdf. Accessed 12 September 2020.

26 Office of Tax Simplification, The Gig Economy: An OTS Focus Paper, 2 December 2016, http://www.gov.uk/government/publications/the-gig-economy-an-ots-focus-paper. Accessed 20 April 2020. See also *De Stefano, Valerio*, The Rise of the "Just-in-Time Workforce": On-Demand Work, Crowdwork, and Labour Protection in the "Gig" Economy (fn. 25), p. 6.

27 Contained in the National Minimum Wage Act 1998. It should be noted, however, that zero-hours contract workers are entitled to certain rights such as the right to the national minimum wage and limits to working time.

28 These are contained in the Employment Rights Act 1996.

29 See below for a discussion of this.

30 Self-employed persons are eligible, however, for Council Tax reductions during periods of economic inactivity, and are also entitled to the hosing benefit element of UC. See below.

tious doctrine of vicarious liability if they carry out a tort in the course of their work, as do employees. However, for the purposes of this chapter the central problem of non-standard forms of work is their lack of stability and predictability of income for the worker. As De Stefano graphically asserts:

> "income stability remains a mirage for most of the workers in the gig economy [...]: as praised in the words of one of the businesses' managers quoted above, one of the chief sources of flexibility is exactly the possibility to hire people and "fire them after [...] ten minutes"[31].

Leaving aside the issue of the possibility of easy dismissal of gig and zero-hours workers, the reality is that the hours of work and the number of jobs ("gigs") they carry out may vary daily, weekly, or even seasonally, leading to an inevitable fluctuation in income, which in turn makes it difficult for individuals and families to plan and budget. Adams and Deakin have associated non-standard forms of work in the labour market with inequality and precariousness, mainly because there is little certainty in terms of regular income.[32] Indeed, zero-hours contracts and gig workers feature in much of non-academic literature on that sector of the workforce which has been labelled the "Precariat".[33] Irregularity of income has another negative consequence for such workers, namely, that it presents significant difficulties in the accurate calculation and delivery of social security benefits, in particular Universal Credit, a form of benefit specifically designed, amongst other purposes, to assist those on lower income. In order to understand the interrelation between non-standard contract workers and the social security system, some background must be given on UC and other relevant benefits.

---

31 See *De Stefano, Valerio*, The Rise of the "Just-in-Time Workforce": On-Demand Work, Crowdwork and Labour Protection in the "Gig" Economy (fn. 25), p. 6.

32 *Adams, Zoe/Deakin, Simon*, Institutional Solutions to Precariousness and Inequality in Labour Markets, Centre for Business Research, University of Cambridge Working Paper No. 463, September 2014, p. 1.

33 See, for example, *Bloodworth, James*, Hired: Six Months Undercover in Low-Wage Britain, London: Atlantic Books 2019, and *Standing, Guy*, The Precariat: The New Dangerous Class, London: Bloomsbury Press 2014.

III. Universal Credit and Other Related Social Security Benefits

1. Universal Credit, Unemployment and Work

Although structurally and technically innovative, there is little that is conceptually new in UC. Indeed, it builds upon the system of "tax relief payment", or "tax credits" introduced by the first New Labour Government of 1997 - 2001, a payment administered primarily through the revenue authorities, designed to support financially the family unit and provide parents with the incentive to find and retain paid employment.[34] The advantage of the tax credit system was that recipients could avoid the stigma of claiming a benefit, unlike Family Income Supplement and Family Credit which preceded it, and together with the introduction of the national minimum wage[35] it was hoped that paid employment would be sufficiently rewarding to encourage one or both parents to remain in employment.[36] Later New Labour governments developed the tax credits policy, with Working Families Tax Credit and Disabled Persons Tax Credit being replaced by "working tax credit", and forms of support for children through tax and social security with a "child tax credit" in the Tax Credits Act 2002.[37] Furthermore, by the time that the policy began in 1997, wage levels for the lowest decile of the workforce had fallen to historically low levels, as a result of deregulatory measures such as the abolition of Wages Councils and the legislative neutralisation of trade unions during the years of Conservative Government.[38] These factors not only occasioned a reduction in "job security", but also impacted negatively on employees' ability to negotiate reasonable wage increases.[39]

---

34 See *Larkin, Philip*, Universal Credit, "Positive Citizenship", and the Working Poor: Squaring the Eternal Circle? (fn. 11), pp. 114 and 117.

35 This was introduced in the National Minimum Wage Act 1998.

36 See *Larkin, Philip*, Universal Credit, "Positive Citizenship", and the Working Poor: Squaring the Eternal Circle? (fn. 11), pp. 114 and 117.

37 *Wikeley, Nick*, Tax Credits Act 2002: Annotated Legislation, London: Sweet and Maxwell 2002.

38 See *Puttick, Keith*, 21st Century Welfare and the Wage-Work-Welfare Bargain, in: Industrial Law Journal, 41 (2012) 1, p. 125. See also *Larkin, Philip*, Universal Credit, "Positive Citizenship", and the Working Poor: Squaring the Eternal Circle? (fn. 11), p. 117.

39 See *Gregg, Paul/Wadsworth, Jonathan*, Feeling Insecure? An Analysis of Job Tenure from 1975 to 1995, Employment Audit, London: Employment Policy Institute 1996. See also *Nickell, Stephen/Jones, Patricia/Quintini, Glenda*, A Picture of Job Insecurity Facing British Men, in: The Economic Journal, 112 (2002) 476.

Viewed in their entirety, tax credits appear to have been instrumental in improving the financial circumstances of a sizeable sector of the population out of poverty: Gordon Brown, as Chancellor, claimed that the means-tested Working Families Tax Credit, combined with child benefit, was responsible for raising 1.2 million children out of poverty.[40] The effectiveness of tax credits in reducing inequality and aiding social mobility in the UK is also evidenced by an OECD Report which demonstrates that while during the period between the late 1990s and the early years of the present decade the prospects of the poorest people in societies across the world worsened, in the UK they actually improved dramatically.[41] At the beginning of the period some six in ten people in the bottom income quintile were trapped in this position, but four years later this figure had fallen to four in ten.[42] This improvement in social mobility is important, because, as the Report emphasises, lack of social mobility can damage the foundations of growth in modern market economies, leading to the under-development of human talent and a dearth of spending power and a subsequent shortfall in investment in the economy.[43] The improvement itself is held to be a triumph of policy design, namely, the development of tax credits to ensure that paid work was sufficiently rewarding, and a minimum wage which steadily increased during the relevant period.[44] However, the tax credits system contained certain flaws, the main one being the high level of clawback which claimants experienced when their working hours, and subsequently salaries, increased, thus acting as a disincentive for both couples and individuals to engage further with the labour market, and ultimately become financially self-sufficient.[45]

The introduction of UC was brought about by two main policy aims. The first is to achieve maximum participation in the labour market by ensuring that paid employment will always be more lucrative than benefit re-

40 The measurement of poverty for these purposes is a household with less than 60 per cent of median national income. See Households Below Average Income Statistics Department for Work and Pensions (11 April 2002). See also *Lee, Natalie,* The New Tax Credits, in: Journal of Social Security Law, 10 (2003) 1, p. 10.

41 OECD, A Broken Social Elevator? How to Promote Social Mobility, OECD Publishing, Paris, 2018, http://dx.doi.org/10.1787/9789264301085-en. Accessed 30 July 2020.

42 Ibid., p. 23. See also *Strauss, Delphine*, Social Mobility Progress at Risk as EU Divorce Saps Economy, Financial Times, 13 July 2018.

43 Ibid., p. 23.

44 See *Larkin, Philip*, Universal Credit, "Positive Citizenship", and the Working Poor: Squaring the Eternal Circle? (fn. 11), p. 117.

45 See ibid.

ceipt. The second is to achieve greater administrative efficiency in terms of time and cost. UC, the outline structure of which is contained in the WRA 2012,[46] is essentially a form of income-based benefit, which incorporates six former means-tested benefits and tax credits,[47] and is administered and disbursed entirely by the Department for Work and Pensions.[48] These reforms were motivated by more than efficiency: it was also intended to simplify the system for claimants, since it proved difficult in practice to understand how the different tax credits and benefits they applied for related to each other.[49]

UC itself is an income-based benefit, although a remnant of social insurance-based is represented in the "new style" jobseekers allowance (JSA), which is payable to those claimants who have made sufficient national insurance contributions in the last two tax years before the claim.[50] In order to be eligible for UC, the claimant must be at least 18 years old, be in Great Britain, not receiving education, and has accepted a relevant

46 As with other welfare and tax credit legislation, the outline structure of UC is contained in the Welfare Reform Act (WRA) 2012, while much of the detail is set out in Regulations.

47 Income-based jobseeker's allowance, income support, income-related employment and support allowance, housing benefit, working tax credit, and child tax credit. This abolition is contained in WRA 2012, Section 33. See also *McKeever, Gráinne*, Social Citizenship and Social Security Fraud in the UK and Australia, in: Social Policy and Administration, 46 (2012) 4, pp. 465 ff., and *McKeever, Gráinne*, Balancing Rights and Responsibilities: The Case of Social Security Fraud, in: Journal of Social Security Law, 16 (2009) 3, p. 139.

48 This marks a change from the previous system of tax credits, which were administered entirely by the revenue authorities.

49 To exemplify the complexity of the previous system, a claimant with children in rented accommodation might have had to claim four different benefits from three different authorities. This was complicated by the fact that entitlement to tax benefits were calculated on the basis of an entire tax year, whereas four of the six benefits abolished by the WRA 2012 were calculated weekly and paid fortnightly. See *Mesher, John/Poynter, Richard/ Wikeley, Nick/Wood, Penny*, Universal Credit, Volume V: Social Security Legislation 2013/14, London: Sweet and Maxwell 2014, p. 4. See also *Larkin, Philip*, Universal Credit, "Positive Citizenship", and the Working Poor: Squaring the Eternal Circle? (fn. 11), p. 118.

50 New style JSA and UC may be claimed together, if the individual or household's finances do not reach sustenance level on JSA alone. Unlike UC, new style JSA may be claimed even if the claimant or their household have more than £16,000 in savings. See the Welfare Reform Act 2012 (Commencement No. 11 and Transitional and Transitory Provisions and Commencement No. 9 and Transitional and Transitory Provisions (Amendment)) Order 2013, SI 2013/1511. New style JSA claimants are subject to the more rigorous UC claimant commitment and the sanctions which accompany this.

claimant commitment.[51] Furthermore, claimants and households with financial resources over a certain threshold are not eligible for UC.[52] Section 1 of the WRA 2012 sets out the categories of claimant to whom UC may be awarded, namely, single persons, and couples jointly, both in and out of work.[53] This section of the WRA also outlines the structure of UC, affirming that it consists of a standard allowance, and separate amounts for children and young persons, for housing, and for other particular needs or circumstances.[54] The detailed rules on UC claims are contained in the Universal Credit, Personal Independence Payment, Jobseeker's Allowance and Employment and Support Allowance (Claims and Payments) Regulations 2013.[55] To create a notional link between receipt of UC and the labour market, it is paid fortnightly so as to reflect the reality that some 75 per cent of the working population now receive their earnings monthly and in arrears.[56]

Probably the most progressive reform made by the WRA 2012 is to change the manner of calculation of UC from that of tax credits, enhancing the incentive for families and individuals to enter and remain in the labour market. The "work allowance"[57] allows considerably higher earnings disregards than other income-based benefits such as income support or jobseeker's allowance. Claimants should thus be able to retain more of their earned income before their UC award is reduced, and if the figure calculated for earned income during the assessment period does not exceed the applicable work allowance then no deduction is made from the maximum amount.[58] Furthermore, once the reduction begins, claimants will only lose 65 per cent of the increase in their income rather than 100 per

---

51 Section 4 of the WRA 2012.

52 Section 5 of the WRA 2012. The threshold figure is £16,000.

53 Section 1 of the WRA 2012.

54 Section 1 (3) (a) – (d).

55 SI 2013/380. See also WRA 2012, Sections 3 and 4.

56 See *Puttick, Keith*, 21st Century Welfare and Universal Credit: Reconstructing the Wage-Work-Welfare Bargain Part 2, in: Industrial Law Journal, 41 (2012) 2, p. 239.

57 The structure of the "work allowance" and "higher work allowance" is set out in the WRA 2012, Section 8 (3) and UC Regulations 2013, Regulation 22. The higher and lower work allowances are each applied at six discrete rates which are specified in a table which forms part of Regulation 22.

58 See *Mesher, John/Poynter, Richard/Wikeley, Nick/Wood, Penny*, Universal Credit, Volume V: Social Security Legislation 2013/14 (fn. 49), p. 4. See also *Larkin, Philip*, Universal Credit, "Positive Citizenship", and the Working Poor: Squaring the Eternal Circle? (fn. 11), p. 125.

cent, a reform which accounts for the significant difference in outcome between working claimants on jobseeker's allowance and those on UC.[59] This reform in particular does make some headway in reducing the long-enduring disincentives for individual citizens and families of different types to engage with the labour market, particularly in the light of the post-2010 Coalition Government's commitment to ensure that 85 per cent of childcare costs for the least affluent UC recipients would be made by public funds.[60]

One might expect those citizens engaged in non-standard forms of work in particular to benefit from these reforms, occupying as they do many of the lower-paid positions in the labour market. The reforms also demonstrate a genuine desire on the part of legislators to remedy the shortcomings of the existing tax credits system.[61] It should also be noted that, like tax credits, UC may also be claimed by the self-employed, including the large number of gig workers, an important continuity since the self-employed proportion of the UK labour market began to rise since the early years of the century, and increased from 3.8 million in 2008 to 4.6 million in 2015, a trend hastened by the economic recession beginning in 2007.[62] Given that some 60 per cent of those families in poverty are actually working families,[63] one might expect UC to be instrumental in improving the living standards of such citizens. Seen through the prism of the WRA 2012, individual citizens are viewed very much as *producers* who should be economically active, rather than simply possessors of unearned rights, and in keeping with the view of Grover and Stewart that such reforms have been shaped by:

> […] ideas with a long standing tradition in England: that economically inactive people are lazy, and react rationally to the availability of social security by making themselves inactive, or prolonging their inactivity.[64]

---

59 See *Larkin*, ibid.

60 See *Wintour, Patrick/Mason, Rowena*, Prime Minister Pitches to Families with Childcare Cash, The Guardian, 18 March 2014.

61 See ibid.

62 See Office for National Statistics. Trends in Self-Employment in the UK: 2010 to 2015, https://www.ons.gov.uk/employmentandlabourmarket/peopleinwork/employmentandemployeetypes/articles/trendsinselfemploymentintheuk/2001to2015. Accessed 10 July 2020. These figures also include gig workers.

63 See ibid.

64 *Grover, Chris/Stewart, John*, Modernising Social Security? Labour and its Welfare-to-Work Strategy, in: Social Policy and Administration, 34 (2000) 3, p. 236.

2. *Universal Credit, New Style ESA, and Incapacity for Work*

Both zero-hours contract workers and gig workers may also be eligible to claim "new style" Employment and Support Allowance (ESA) if they are incapacitated or unable to work because of illness, and have made sufficient national insurance contributions over the past two tax years before the claim, and eligibility for this benefit also extends to the self-employed.[65] ESA was first introduced by the last Labour Government in the Welfare Reform Act 2007, replacing the former system of incapacity benefit and income support. Unlike UC, which was promoted primarily on the message of encouraging citizens to engage with the labour market, ESA was introduced for the more stringent purpose of ensuring what has been named "positive citizenship", or to almost coerce citizens back into the labour market and productivity as soon as possible.[66] The Welfare Reform Act 2007[67] is paradigmatic of the ideology which has underpinned much welfare reform legislation over the past four decades, reducing further the importance of national insurance benefits while rendering them more difficult to attain, with entitlement linked to increased conditionality.[68] As one UK former Secretary of State for Social Security asserted, "[...] people who earn a modest wage resent seeing neighbours, apparently as fit as themselves, living on invalidity benefit"[69]. This did not prevent the Labour Government from presenting the legislation as providing an opportunity for citizens to find fulfilment in the labour market, thus demonstrating the continuity in ideology at the foundation of welfare reform:

The reforms in the Bill set out a new direction of travel for our welfare system. They are underpinned by a belief in an active enabling welfare state that sees tackling poverty and social exclusion, with no-one left behind and no-one written off.[70]

---

65 The transition from ESA to "new style" ESA is set out in Regulation 23 of the Universal Credit (Transitional Provisions), Regulations 2013, SI 2013.

66 See *Larkin, Philip*, Incapacity, the Labour Market and Social Security: Coercion into "Positive" Citizenship, in: Modern Law Review, 74 (2011) 3, pp. 385 ff. It should be mentioned that receipt of UC is also hedged around with conditionality.

67 And the Welfare Reform Act 2012 which superseded it.

68 See *Larkin, Philip*, Incapacity, the Labour Market and Social Security: Coercion into "Positive" Citizenship (fn. 66).

69 HC Deb vol 236 cols 135 - 136 24 January 1994. This was the original core reason for replacing the former invalidity benefit with Incapacity benefit.

70 John Hutton MP, HC Debs vol. 449 col 616 24 July 2006.

As with UC, emphasis was placed on the idea of aspiration, and that citizens should strive to better their own social position through engagement in paid employment. For those non-standard workers who have made sufficient national insurance contributions, it is indeed possible to claim ESA, which has a contributory and non-contributory element, modelled closely on new style jobseeker's allowance.[71] Income-based ESA has been abolished by the WRA 2012,[72] but its essential structure was retained in the WRA and the Universal Credit Regulations 2013.[73] The basic entitlements are relatively uncontroversial, but in Section 37 of the WRA 2012 and Regulations 38 and 39 of the UC Regulations the key concepts of "limited capability for work" and "limited capability for work-related activity" the self-conscious aim is to place focus on what work the claimant can actually do, rather than their incapacity or illness.[74] In combination with these, the Work Capability Assessment, the framework for which is set out in the Regulations,[75] is designed to be a more stringent form of test than the personal capability assessment which preceded it. The majority of incapacitated UC claimants go through the first element of the procedure, which is the assessment of limited capability for work, usually decided on the basis of a face-to-face interview, and is judged on a series of activity descriptors, and scores are awarded for each activity.

The WCA was designed to modernise comprehensively the nature of those tasks prevalent in the contemporary labour market, and incapability to perform a task must arise from a specific bodily disease or disablement, or a mental equivalent. Establishing limited capability for work entitles the claimant only to the basic UC allowance, and the extra components they may receive will depend upon whether it is judged that they do or do not have limited capacity for work-related activity. This involves a claimant having to undergo more rigorous assessment and a person is deemed to have such a limited capability if, by reason of their physical or mental condition, at least one of the criteria contained in Schedule 9 to the UC Regulations applies to him or her. Those who fail to establish such limited capa-

71 See *Larkin, Philip*, Incapacity, the Labour Market and Social Security: Coercion into "Positive" Citizenship (fn. 66), p. 398. See also *Wikeley, Nick/Laurie, Emma*, Welfare Reform Act 2007, Annotated Legislation, London: Sweet and Maxwell 2007.

72 Section 33 of the Welfare Reform Act 2012.

73 SI 2013/376.

74 See *Larkin, Philip*, Incapacity, the Labour Market and Social Security: Coercion into "Positive" Citizenship (fn. 66), p. 398.

75 Schedules 6 to 9 to the UC Regulations 2013.

bility will receive the work-related activity component of UC, and are obliged to attend one or more work-focused interviews, the aim being to assess the claimant's chances of obtaining or remaining in work, and helping them back into the labour market.

New style ESA and UC for incapacitated claimants may have a special relevance for both zero-hours contract workers and those engaged in the gig economy: the introduction of the ESA coincided with some of the most arduous years of the economic recession, when positions in traditional forms of employment contract tended to be scarce. Even in the early years of the operation of income-based ESA statistics demonstrated that work capability assessments resulted in more than 66 per cent of ESA claimants being judged fit to work, with the decision of the Department for Work and Pensions being upheld in 62 per cent of appeals.[76] Given that the unemployment rate did not rise hugely during the recent recession, it is highly likely that many of those deemed fit for work or work-related activity may have been directed towards, or simply found, work in either the gig or zero-hours sector of the economy, work which frequently does not require a high level of skills or training. One of the central factors in the growth of digital platform and other such activity could have been the operation of the Welfare Reform Acts of 2007 and 2012, with claimants seeking to enter the labour market in any capacity not only to avoid legislative sanctions, but due to the opprobrium of an increasingly unsympathetic British public.[77] As Taylor-Gooby notes, it is this revival of lack of empathy for the less materially well-off that distinguishes the UK from continental Europe, and ensures that UK welfare legislation tends to be "sharper-edged and cruder" than that in continental nations.[78] It is unlikely that attitudes have changed greatly since the tailing-off of the last recession: they may even have been fortified by the knowledge that there appears to be a surfeit of positions in the non-regular economy.

---

76 Work Capability Assessment Statistical Release, para. 3, January 2010, https://www.gov.uk/government/statistics/employment-and-support-allowance-work-capability-assessment-july-2010. Accessed 10 July 2020.

77 A British Social Attitudes Survey, drawn up roughly at the early operation of the WRA 2012, indicated that the working population are less tolerant of the "plight" of their less affluent, unemployed counterparts in low-income social groups, especially if they perceive that benefit recipients are malingering.

78 This survey is cited in the Economist 26 January 2008.

3. *The Legislative Benefit Cap*

One central point which should be mentioned for the purposes of background information is that all welfare benefit recipients and their family units in the UK are subject to a legislative benefit cap, or limit, which was also contained in the Welfare Reform Act 2012,[79] representing another reform in the overall wide-ranging review of the social security system carried out by the Coalition Government, and as part of the austerity measures effected simultaneously. Introduced in April 2013, by 2014 some 36,471 households had experienced benefit reductions, with 17,102 being in London.[80] Originally set at £26,000 per household, the level of the cap was reduced to £20,000 for families from autumn 2016.[81] Like the WRA 2007, the benefit cap is credited with encouraging many citizens to enter or re-enter the labour market, with figures in 2014 indicating that some 8040 households had come off the benefit cap, and that 40 per cent of those who came off the cap had found gainful employment.[82] Lord Freud, Minister of Welfare Reform, also stated:

> Our reforms are creating an alternative to life on benefits and already we are seeing an increasing number of people changing their circumstances so they are no longer subject to the cap.[83]

It is entirely plausible that many people seeking to escape the financial strictures of the benefit cap, and to avoid the legislative sanctions contained in the Welfare Reform Act 2012 for those not deemed to be taking sufficient steps to find employment, have accepted zero-hours contracts or are online platform workers. The benefit cap has been subject to legal challenge on the grounds that it infringed provisions of international human

---

79 The framework for the benefit cap is contained in Sections 95 - 96 of the WRA 2012, and the Benefit Cap (Housing Benefit) Regulations 2012, SI 2012/2994, and the Benefit Cap (Housing Benefit and Universal Credit) (Amendment) Regulations 2016, SI 2016/909.

80 See Department for Work and Pensions, Benefit Cap: Number of Households Capped to December 2013, https://www.gov.uk/government/statistics/benefit-cap-number-of-households-capped-to-december-2013. Accessed 28 April 2020.

81 Apart from the London area, where the cap was reduced to £23,000, due to increased living costs.

82 See Department for Work and Pensions, Benefit Cap: Number of Households Capped to December 2013 (fn. 80).

83 Cited in BBC News. Thousands Hit by Government Benefit Cap Now in Work, 6 February 2014, https://www.bbc.co.uk/news/business-26065080. Accessed 10 July 2020.

rights law, but, in two majority decisions, the Supreme Court ruled that the relevant human rights law had not been breached.[84] As usual with issues relating to social policy and social security law, it was felt by some of the judges[85] that deliberations and action on such matters are best addressed in the political arena of the legislature.

IV. Non-Standard Forms of Work and the Social Security System

It would be inaccurate for the Coalition Government to claim that it had not been given advance warning of some of the main issues which could beset the operation of UC, which has caused perhaps most problems especially for those working non-standard contracts. While the operation of UC has revealed a variety of design defects in UC, it is this latter category of people that the sole focus will be upon. Referring to legislative measures towards simplicity and administrative efficiency, Baroness Hale stated that while such aims were self-evidently laudable, there was a good reason why the social security is so complicated in nature: the multipurpose welfare system must cope with a great number of life situations, which inevitably means that it must be, by nature, inherently complex.[86] A similar thesis is expounded by Harris, who argues that despite the longstanding ambition of both Labour and Conservative Governments to merge the tax and benefit systems in order to achieve administrative savings and a simplification of the frequently labyrinthine bureaucracy in both welfare and revenue systems, the life situations which both branches of law cover remain as complex as ever.[87] These views were also shared by Sainsbury,[88] Brewer,[89] and even the Policy Exchange on the Standing Committee for the Welfare

84 The cases are R (SG and Others) v Secretary of State for Work and Pensions [2015] UKSC 16, and R (DA & Ors) v Secretary of State for Work and Pensions and R (DS & Ors) v Secretary of State for Work and Pensions UKSC 21.

85 Lord Wilson, for example, in R (DA & Ors) v Secretary of State for Work and Pensions; R (DS & Ors) v Secretary of State for Work and Pensions [2019] UKSC 21.

86 See Hinchy v. Secretary of State for Work and Pensions [2005] UKHL 16 at para 48.

87 See *Harris, Neville*, Law in a Complex State: Complexity in the Law and Structure of Welfare, Oxford: Hart Publishing 2013, pp. 60-61.

88 Committee Debate – First Sitting: House of Commons 22 March 2011, col. 6.

89 Ibid.

Reform Bill.[90] In addition, the increased atomisation of the labour force, the factors which compel increasingly more citizens to accept non-standard forms of work, and the move towards what Bauman has called the "society of consumers",[91] has further compounded an already tangled socio-economic situation in the UK. Indeed, some commentators representing the more populist right of the political spectrum actively promoted the growth of the gig economy as a means of encouraging activism among unemployed citizens.[92] During the parliamentary debates relating to the passage of the Welfare Reform Bill 2012, John McDonnell MP[93] stated that in his own parliamentary constituency many of the jobs on offer tended to be casual and low-paid, with many of his constituents working on zero-hours contracts in which weekly rates of pay can fluctuate significantly.[94] He may also feasibly have mentioned the then growing number of gig workers in the economy, a development which had not yet really attracted a great degree of public attention.

The calculation of tax credits for those on non-standard contracts was already problematic under the previous system, and it appears that some of the same issues still beset the UC system. Before it came into operation, Seddon and O'Donovan criticised vociferously the information technology-dominated "industrial design" of UC, viewing it as fundamentally flawed, and they also predicted huge disruptions in its service flow, duplication of effort, and, as a result, rising costs.[95] These authors cite Adam Smith's notion of the division of labour to suggest that the administration of UC will actually be less efficient than that of tax credits, since in the case of the latter the burden of administrative tasks were shared by both the De-

---

90 This was Matthew Oakley, Head of Economics and Social Policy at Policy Exchange. See ibid. M. Oakley was acting as an expert witness in the Committee Debate.

91 *Bauman, Zygmunt*, Does Ethics have a Chance in a World of Consumers, Cambridge: Harvard University Press 2008, Chapter 3.

92 See *Kirkup, James*, Help Welfare Claimants to Join the Gig Economy, Daily Telegraph, 3 February 2016. See also *Bulman, May*, Amber Rudd Says People Should Take Zero-Hour Contracts to void Having Benefits cut, The Independent, 19 December 2018. Amber Rudd MP was then Secretary of State for Work and Pensions.

93 Member of Parliament for Hayes and Harlington and former Deputy Leader of the Labour Party.

94 HC Deb vol col 988 9 March 2011.

95 *Seddon, John/O'Donovan, Brendan*, The Achilles Heel of Scale Service design in Social Security Administration: The Case of the United Kingdom's Universal Credit, in: International Social Security Review, 66 (2013) 1, pp. 1 ff.

partment for Work and Pensions and the tax authorities.[96] To at least some extent these predictions have been borne out in the operation of the WRA 2012.

Non-standard work activities in the UK cover a wide variety of fields, and are not confined to courier work or other forms of manual or lower-skilled tasks. Research carried out in 2018 gave a broad definition of the gig economy, more comprehensive than that commonly understood.[97] The same research demonstrated that the age profile of those involved in the gig economy was skewed towards those aged 34 and under,[98] and more likely to be based in London.[99] While the provision of courier work was the most common type of gig activity, performing other types of job found through websites or apps was almost as common, and it was found that this could range from low-skilled work to professional work such as web development or work in the creative industries or media.[100] Very significantly, 25 per cent of survey respondents reported that they earned an hourly income of less than £7.50 per hour, which was then the national minimum wage, while the level of annual average earnings from the gig economy overall was relatively low, with 41 per cent stating that they normally earned less than £250 weekly through their services.[101] In addition, 87 per cent of everyone involved in the gig economy said that they had earned less than £10,000 in the past 12 months.[102] It is noteworthy, nevertheless that even with the issues which beset the gig economy, it was stated by Taylor that many self-employed persons experience greater financial

---

96 See ibid, pp. 3-5.

97 For example, the term was held to include not only individuals using platforms which play an active role in facilitating work and taking a proportion of the pay or charging providers' fees for using the platform (such as Deliveroo or TaskRabbit), but also the ad hoc provision of labour to either individuals and businesses, and, importantly, people providing services who are either freelancers or have set up a one-person business to offer their services, and people for whom the gig economy is the main source of income and those who use it to top up their income from other sources. See the Department for Business, Energy and Industrial Strategy. The Characteristics of those in the Gig Economy: Final Report, p. 12, https://assets.publishing.service.gov.uk/government/uploads/system/uploads/attachment_data/file/687553/The_characteristics_of_those_in_the_gig_economy.pdf. Accessed 30 April 2020.

98 Only some 10 per cent of the sample survey were aged 55 or over. See ibid, p. 14.

99 Some 24 per cent of the gig economy workers are based in London. See ibid., p. 17.

100 See ibid., p. 5.

101 See ibid., p. 6.

102 See ibid.

certainty than other labour market groups such as agency or zero-hours contract workers.[103] It might be expected that these would be exactly the people who would benefit from UC and the operation of the WRA 2012, and certainly many of these would come within its remit.

However, it is at this interface between the labour market and the social security system that real problems arise: for many, if not all, online platform workers and zero-hours contract workers, in whatever field they may be engaged, experience weekly and monthly fluctuations in earnings, and, unlike previous forms of benefit, UC is paid monthly in arrears. UC itself has been observed to operate most effectively for those engaged in traditional working arrangements of fixed hours and paid a fixed income each calendar month.[104] Yet in one survey on UC claimants, it was discovered that less than 50 per cent reported that they were being paid monthly, a finding backed up by analysis from the Resolution Foundation, which uncovered that 58 per cent of claimants moving on to UC were paid fortnightly or weekly in their current or previous job.[105] This held true for non-standard contract workers, whose income tends not to be received monthly (gig workers are remunerated per job), and, although the overall value of their annual benefit entitlement does not change, those trying to combine non-monthly wages with a monthly benefit.[106] For example, it is possible for a zero-hours contract worker, who may be paid weekly, and, due to the fact that each month does not contain the same number of weeks, their earnings in each calendar month will vary, since during some months they will receive four wage payments and in others five. This will undoubtedly lead to fluctuating UC payments, and subsequent problems in household budgeting. Furthermore, when two four-weekly wage pack-

---

103 *Taylor, Matthew/Marsh, Greg/Nicol, Diane/Broadbent, Paul*, Good Work: The Taylor Review of Modern Working Practices, Independent Report, July 2017. See https://assets.publishing.service.gov.uk/government/uploads/system/uploads/attachment_data/file/627671/good-work-taylor-review-modern-working-practices-rg.pdf. Accessed 30 April 2020.

104 See Citizens Advice. Universal Credit and Modern Employment: Non-Traditional Work, https://www.citizensadvice.org.uk/Global/CitizensAdvice/welfare%20publications/Universal%20Credit%20and%20non-traditional%20employment.pdf. Accessed 30 April 2020.

105 See *Brewer, Mike/Finch, David/Tomlinson, Daniel*, Universal Remedy: Ensuring Universal Credit is Fit for Purpose, The Resolution Foundation, October 2017, p. 6, https://www.resolutionfoundation.org/app/uploads/2017/10/Universal-Credit.pdf. Accessed 10 May 2020.

106 See Citizens Advice. Universal Credit and Modern Employment: Non-Traditional Work (fn. 104), p. 16.

ets are paid in the same month, this can push the overall earnings considerably over the threshold level, entitling the claimant to no UC for that month, causing difficulties for those used to a set amount of tax credit benefit.[107] For a benefit which was designed to inculcate regular habits of industry and thrift among recipients, one survey discovered that of over 800 working families receiving UC, 43 per cent stated that they were never able to put money aside as savings, while only 17 per cent were reported being able to do so regularly,[108] and this lack of flexibility in household budget prevents recipients from being able to plan for UC fluctuations. Zero-hours contract workers have the added problem of varying weekly income, causing them to have to make multiple claims in order to erode their surplus earnings.[109] Another problem which has beset many UC claimants has been the waiting time for the benefit, and it frequently takes some five to six weeks for the first payment to be made, a period during which those already in a precarious financial position can fall into poverty, requiring recourse to non-governmental sources of help such as charity food banks.[110]

The self-employed status of many gig workers, in combination with the irregularity of their earnings, brings to the fore a further factor compounding their frequent precarious financial position. In addition to not usually receiving a monthly wage or salary, gig workers and ordinary self-employed persons also face the inevitability of income fluctuation according to the vagaries of the market. Self-employed persons' access to UC is subject to them being deemed "gainfully self-employed",[111] a process which involves potential claimants undertaking a "Gateway Interview" carried out by Jobcentre Plus[112] Work Coaches who tend to lack specialist knowledge in assessing small business plans and activity for viability. It was not-

---

107 See ibid., at p. 17. Those familiar with tax credits are becoming fewer as the operation of UC progresses.

108 Citizens Advice. Universal Credit and Modern Employment: Non-Traditional Work (fn. 104), p. 18.

109 This problem was specifically mentioned by the Social Security Advisory Committee. See The Universal Credit, Miscellaneous Amendments, Savings and Transitional Provisions, SI 2018 No. 65. Report by the Social Security Advisory Committee, January 2018.

110 See *Purves, Libby*, The State has Earned Universal Discredit, The Times, 23 October 2017.

111 The definition of "gainful self-employment" is contained in Regulation 64 of the Universal Credit Regulations 2013, SI 2013/376.

112 The Jobcentre Plus serves not only as a form of labour exchange but also as a means of executive body which effects social security legislation and policy in the UK.

ed by the House of Commons Work and Pensions Committee that viability interviews of this nature require specialist knowledge and understanding of business development (knowledge usually beyond the remit of work coaches), since, in its view, it is vital that the DWP supports potentially successful businesses while not wasting resources on unsustainable ventures.[113] One key UK Government policy aim over the past decades, of both main political parties, has been to encourage entrepreneurship and individual self-reliance among citizens, and online platform and freelance workers could certainly be said to adhere to these criteria.

Like other self-employed UC claimants, online platform and other gig workers are subject to a "Minimum Income Floor" (MIF), which assumes that they are making a certain minimum amount of monthly income.[114] For the majority of claimants the MIF is the equivalent of a full-time worker's (which equals 35 hours weekly) wage on the national living wage. For the first year of business new self-employed persons are exempt from the MIF, a period known as the "Start-up Period", the rationale given by the DWP for this idea being that it is "to encourage individuals to increase their earnings through developing their self-employment" and to address "[…] flaws in legacy benefits which allowed self-employed claimants to receive state support while declaring low or zero earnings"[115]. The Resolution Foundation, a UK think tank, has voiced doubt about the effects of the MIF on self-employed UC claimants:

> Applying the MIF on a monthly basis could leave self-employed workers much worse off than employees, despite having identical incomes. This situation would arise as a result of a self-employed person's UC award being capped by the MIF when their income is low, without then being recovered in months when they earn more.[116]

---

113 See the House of Commons Work and Pensions Committee, Self-Employment and the Gig Economy: Thirteenth Report of Session 2016-17 HC 847, 1 May 2017.

114 This is set out in Regulation 62 of the Universal Credit Regulations 2013, SI 2013/376.

115 Reported in Citizens Advice. Universal Credit and Modern Employment: Non-Traditional Work (fn. 104), p. 16. It did constitute a valid concern among legislators that directors of small and medium-sized enterprises would deliberately pay themselves a very basic salary in order to be able to avail of UC.

116 *Finch, David*, Making the Most of UC: Resolution Foundation Report, June 2015, https://www.resolutionfoundation.org/app/uploads/2015/06/UC-FINAL-REPORT1.pdf.

The point was also underscored in the House of Commons Work and Pension Committee Report that the vagaries of self-employment, including seasonal variations in trade or payments made for ongoing work can easily confuse the true picture of annual income generation.[117] While this Report correctly suggests that this factor could deter people from self-employment,[118] for those who do not possess a high degree of skills, English language ability or education, there may be no alternative to persevering in online platform work, and perhaps taking on more than one set of online jobs in order to keep income at a reasonably steady level, while their financial situation continues to remain precarious. This is in addition to the pressures from the social security system set out above which propel citizens towards the gig economy. The uncertainty surrounding the intermediate category of "worker" was also noted, with many of such workers being on very flexible contracts and being similarly vulnerable to fluctuations, whether as employed or self-employed persons.[119]

V. *Judicial Action in the Sphere of Non-Standard Work*

On a number of significant occasions the UK courts have operated independently from legislation and used their common law powers to rule that some groups of people who engage in categories of labour market activity actually have the status of "worker" when previously they had been labelled and treated as self-employed gig workers by the on-line platform institutions for which they work. These developments could be declared as progressive insofar as they allow such people certain rights, such as the right to the national living wage. The most important of these cases is *Aslam and Others (Claimants) v. Uber BV and Others (Respondents)*,[120] in which two drivers for the online platform Uber, formerly classed as self-employed gig workers, claimed that they had the right to the national minimum wage and the right to be paid annual leave under the Working Time Regulations 1998,[121] rights enjoyed by both employees and workers.[122]

---

117 See Citizens Advice. Universal Credit and Modern Employment: Non-Traditional Work (fn. 104).

118 See ibid., p. 16.

119 See ibid., p. 17.

120 [2017] IRLR 4.

121 SI 1998/1833.

122 The definition of "worker" is contained in Section 230 (3) (b) of the Employment Rights Act 1996.

The Employment Tribunal held that the drivers fitted the relevant criteria under section 230 (3) (b) of the Employment Rights Act 1996. There were a number of reasons for this decision, the main one being that Uber in reality exerted a substantial amount of control over the drivers. Furthermore, Uber had engaged in conduct reminiscent of an employer, with the platform company deducting fares from the drivers' weekly pay without notice and enforcing the relationship between driver and passenger. The Tribunal also found persuasive the ruling of the North California District Court in *Uber Technologies Inc. v. Berwick,*[123] in which case it was decided that Uber was not simply selling a software package, but rather taxi rides. The Tribunal's decision was later upheld by a majority of the Court of Appeal. Initially there were significant reverberations from the ruling in *Aslam*, particularly when it brought to public attention the reality that the existing structure of the gig economy permitted it to operate with 20-30 per cent less in labour costs,[124] and that online platform providers had been able to evade paying their workers the national minimum wage.[125] Also, in the aftermath of the decision the Government announced a six month review of modern working practices with a special focus on self-employment and non-standard forms of work.[126] The precedent in *Aslam* had further legal impact, for example, in *Dewhurst v. CitySprint*[127] also involving a courier formerly labelled an online platform worker, and it was held that she was entitled to worker protection. Here, the tribunal focused upon whether the drivers were obliged to provide their services. It was discovered that the hiring procedure involved a two day induction, training on how to perform the job, and the supply of uniform and other equipment, so, in reality she could not be described as self-employed.[128]

However, the courts' approach to the gig economy has not been one of uniform extension of worker rights to all online platform workers. When Deliveroo workers brought the issue of their employment status before the

123 No. 15 – 546378.

124 *Kessler, Sarah*, The Gig Economy Won't Last Because It's Being Sued to Death, Fast Company. 17 February 2015, http://www.fastcompany.com/3042248/the-gig-economy-wont-last-because-its-being-sued-to-death. Accessed 4 May 2020.

125 *Croft, Jane*, Uber Challenged on UK Driver's Status, Financial Times, 20 July 2016.

126 *Taylor, Matthew/Marsh, Greg/Nicol, Diane/Broadbent, Paul*, Good Work: The Taylor Review of Modern Working Practices (fn. 103).

127 ET/220512/2016 of 5 January 2017.

128 Another case in which worker protection was extended to online platform courier workers was in Addison Lee Ltd v. Lange and Others UKEAT/0037/18/BA.

Central Arbitration Committee,[129] it was concluded that they were self-employed platform workers. Again, the central factor in the decision was the seemingly genuine ability of Deliveroo couriers to substitute other people to carry out their online platform duties.[130] Neither is the finding of employment law "worker" status by the courts necessarily entirely beneficial to the individual in question: while it was held in *Pimlico Plumbers Ltd and Another (Appellants) v. Smith (Respondent)*[131] that although the plumber who had previously been labelled self-employed was in reality a worker, he was not able to claim the substantial amount of back-dated holiday pay he believed that he was owed.[132] As former Supreme Court judge Lord Sumption has argued, courts are not the appropriate forum in which to formulate elements of social policy.[133] Furthermore, declaring that someone is a worker does not necessarily entail that their schedule of working hours and monthly pay remains at a constantly steady level in order to facilitate the regular payment of UC.

VI. Social Security Reforms for the 21st Century UK Labour Market

Given the consumer-led demands for the products and services which the gig economy provides, and its growing importance in the labour market, it is highly unlikely that Parliament can or will create legislation to transform all non-standard contracts into contracts of employment. Although it is possible to overstate the popularity of the flexibility of gig work, for at

---

129 This is an independent body which has the function of deciding whether any particular group of workers have the right to be part of a trade union or form a trade union of their own.

130 See *Butler, Sarah*, Deliveroo Riders Lose High Court Battle to Gain Union Recognition, The Guardian, 5 December 2018, https://www.theguardian.com/business/2018/dec/05/deliveroo-riders-lose-high-court-battle-gain-union-recognition. Accessed 10 July 2020.

131 [2018] UKSC 29.

132 See *Butler, Sarah*, Gig Economy: Worker Loses Pimlico Plumbers Holiday Pay Claim, The Guardian, 20 March 2019, https://www.theguardian.com/business/2019/mar/20/gig-economy-worker-loses-pimlico-plumbers-holiday-pay-claim. Accessed 10 July 2020.

133 Lord Sumption was inveighing against excessive judicial activism in the name of social justice, stating that Parliament was really the only place where these issues could be decided on collectively. See Lord Sumption, The Limits of Law, The 27th Sultan Azlan Shah Lecture, Kuala Lumpur, 20 November 2013, https://www.supremecourt.uk/docs/speech-131120.pdf. Accessed 10 July 2020.

least a significant section of self-employed platform workers it remains an important consideration, as does the status of self-employment. In the aftermath of the Deliveroo decision the company welcomed the decision by stating that it was "[…] a victory for riders who have consistently told us the flexibility to choose when and where they work, which comes with self-employment, is their number one reason for riding with Deliveroo"[134].

It is also the case that those in non-standard work contracts constitute one of the groups most in need of social protection, and the operation of UC still remains a flawed form of assistance. However, given the problems in UC outlined above, it should be remembered that what Adams and Deakin have called the "standard employment relationship" (SER), which may be defined as work which is carried out on an integrated physical site, on a continuous or indeterminate basis, by reference to a standard unit of working time such as a complete working day or week, continues to be a core legal and economic institution of market economies.[135] These authors assert that the rise in non-standard work is not entirely driven by social and technological factors external to the legal system, but rather it constitutes a response to developments within the law and the wider framework of legal developments, and that the stricter the degree of protection for core workers, the more likely it is that non-standard work will come to be acknowledged as discrete categories in their own right and regulated as such.[136] Although referring primarily to agency and part-time work, these authors' ideas on regulation could also be applied to gig and zero-hours contract workers. The recommendation for greater regulation of non-standard forms of work has also been made by the Resolution Foundation, which, recognising that the number of zero-hours contracts in the labour market had appeared to have reached a plateau, suggested that legislation should provide a legal right to guaranteed hours for anyone who has been working regular hours on a zero-hours contract for at least three months.[137] Given that research has demonstrated that over 25 per cent of

---

134 See *Butler, Sarah*, Gig Economy: Worker Loses Pimlico Plumbers Holiday Pay Claim (fn. 132).

135 See *Adams, Zoe/Deakin, Simon*, Institutional Solutions to Precariousness and Inequality in Labour Markets (fn. 32), p. 4.

136 See ibid., p. 18. See also *Schömann, Klaus/Rogowski, Ralf/Kruppe, Thomas*, Labour Market Efficiency in the European Union, Employment Protection and Fixed Term Contracts, London: Routledge 1998.

137 See *Tomlinson, Daniel*, The UK's Tight Labour Market and Zero Hours Contracts, 21 February 2018, https://www.resolutionfoundation.org/comment/the-uks-tight-labour-market-and-zero-hours-contracts/. Accessed 8 May 2020. See also

men working in low-paid part-time work wanted more working hours,[138] this would at least have the effect of ensuring security of income for those who wish regular hours of work, while allowing easier calculation of UC for the worker and their family unit. It would also bring more citizens into the SER category, with all the attendant rights which this status brings.

One alternative manner of providing social protection for non-standard workers may be to replace UC with some form of universal basic income (UBI), obviating the need for the complex calculations inherent in UC. This is a solution which has been suggested in several quarters, and essentially would mean that every UK citizen would be paid a certain sum of money, dependent on their personal circumstances, such as family size, disability, and employment status, which could take the form of a lump sum payment.[139] Some jurisdictions have already experimented with a universal basic income, including Finland and Luxembourg,[140] while in the UK the city of Hull applied in early 2020 to be the first region to pilot test such a scheme.[141] However, given the political and financial capital which has been expended on unrolling the UC system, it is unlikely that any government will seek to jettison the project in the near or medium future. Neither can it be proved definite that universal basic income would provide any more efficient protection, since, as with UC, the complexities of human life and life situations will remain, and it is possible that the generalised nature of the payment may not provide sufficient financial cover for certain disabilities or other contingencies:

> […] advocates of UBI either unconsciously or wilfully fail to acknowledge that the current system is designed to provide specific payments for people in specific circumstances (e.g. caring, disability, high housing costs, high childcare costs). If you sweep all of that away, you ei-

---

Kamm, Oliver, Zero-Hours Contracts are an Example of More Rules Needed, Not Fewer, The Times, 30 April 2018.

138 *Clarke, Clarke/Bangham, George*, Counting the Hours: Two Decades of Changes in Earnings and Hours Worked, London: Resolution Foundation 2018, https://www.resolutionfoundation.org/app/uploads/2018/01/Counting-the-hours.pdf. Accessed 8 May 2020.

139 See *Russell, Jenni*, Basic Income for All Could End the Benefits Trap, The Times, 10 December 2015.

140 See *Ametepe, Fofo*, The Effectiveness of Luxembourg's Minimum Income, in: International Social Security Review, 65 (2012) 1, pp. 99 ff.

141 See *Halliday, Josh*, Hull Asks to be First UK City to Trial Universal Basic Income, The Guardian, 19 January 2020, https://www.theguardian.com/uk-news/2020/jan/19/hull-universal-basic-income-trial. Accessed 8 May 2020.

> ther have to level up, giving a massive boost to people without those specific needs (at huge cost), or you create a fall in income for those with them. Neither is remotely acceptable in the real world.[142]

Given the somewhat confused situation in the labour market which non-standard contract workers inhabit, it is entirely conceivable that similar problems would affect them as have arisen under UC. The Luxembourg experience of UBI has not been one of uniform success, with a large percentage of the households eligible for the funds not taking them up, and an even larger percentage of EU migrants to the country do not take up UBI.[143] The abolition of UC would also preclude the possibility of reforms being made to the existing system, with its main flaw being that the administration of UC did not receive adequate funding, which had been cut quite drastically during the austerity programme of the Coalition Government.[144] Other changes to UC have been recommended to assist self-employed gig workers, such as specialist work coach advice, a legislative ban on declaring workers self-employed simply because their contracts offer none of the benefits of employment, and a temporary cessation of operation of the Minimum Income Floor until an independent review has been conducted of how UC can be reconciled to the realities of self-employment.[145]

VII. Conclusion

The notion of social protection for non-standard workers in the labour market places UK governments in a difficult position. On the one hand, they have the duty to provide social protection to all citizens, and especially those who fill lower-paid and often unskilled but very necessary positions in the economy, but on the other there exists the fear that over-regulation could cost jobs, especially among non-standard workers, and the de-

---

142 See *Goulden, Chris*, Universal Basic Income – Not the Answer to Poverty, The Joseph Rowntree Foundation, 25 April 2018, https://www.jrf.org.uk/blog/universal-basic-income-not-answer-poverty?gclid=EAIaIQobChMIhqWsua-k6QIVC7TtCh3KrgR3EAAYASAAEgLyl_D_BwE. Accessed 8 May 2020.

143 See *Ametepe, Fofo*, The Effectiveness of Luxembourg's Minimum Income (fn. 140), p. 107.

144 See *Nelson, Fraser*, If Universal Credit becomes Mrs May's Poll Tax, She Only has Herself to Blame, The Telegraph, 20 October 2017.

145 See Citizens Advice. Universal Credit and Modern Employment: Non-Traditional Work (fn. 104), pp. 19-20.

sire on the part of large employers to keep the market as flexible as possible.[146] Despite its flaws, the WRA 2012 and UC do go at least some way towards providing some social protection to this precarious sector of the labour market, and it does appear that governments are now cognisant that reforms must be made to UC, with £1.7 billion being invested during 2018-19 to increase the work allowance element of the benefit, a decision welcomed by anti-poverty campaigners.[147]

However, it is possible that the entire concept and structure of Universal Credit (UC) was outdated[148] and unfit for purpose even from the moments of its inception, and may not assist the very people in the labour market who were supposed to benefit most from it, the main reason being that UC (as with tax credits) was designed largely with a specific set of employment relationships in mind, mainly the traditional "master" and "servant" relationship.[149] With the proliferation of different forms of work contract in the UK labour market, one might assert that UC is, to some extent, already redundant in terms of both conception and structure. Furthermore, the growth of self-employment currently permits companies to evade making a proportionate contribution to the UK's social insurance system and revenue, and the reality that non-traditional forms of employment almost inevitably involve irregular patterns of weekly working hours, makes the calculation and administration of UC both difficult and expensive. It may be that there are limits to the efficacy of legislation in ensuring that non-standard contract workers and their families are able to sustain themselves and in encouraging citizens to remain in self-employment in the gig economy, which seems destined to continue and expand with the advance of technology. Perhaps the optimum solution to maintaining regular and stable payments of UC to gig workers in particular also lies in technology, with some form of integration of revenue authorities and digital platform software, so that gig workers have taxes automatically deducted from their earnings, relieving them of the burden of calculating this for themselves,

146 *Aldrick, Philip*, Reform of Gig Economy will Cost Jobs, Claim Business Groups, The Times, 12 July 2017.

147 *Anderson, Harriet*, An Important Step in Tackling In-Work Poverty – JRF Responds to the Budget, 29 October 2018, https://www.jrf.org.uk/press/important-step-tackling-work-poverty-jrf-responds-budget. Accessed 9 May 2020.

148 It will be argued below that Universal Credit in particular was designed primarily with those in full-time employment contracts in mind.

149 As set out in the landmark cases of Yewens v. Noakes 6 QBD 530, and Ready Mixed Concrete Ltd v Secretary of State for Pensions and National Insurance [1968] 2 QB 497.

and these calculations could be reported to the Department for Work and Pensions.[150] Certainly the WRA 2012 demonstrates the drawbacks inherent in creating legislation designed to provide social protection while focusing on a labour market which is changing at such a rapid pace.

150 Estonia already has integrated their tax system with the digital platforms of transport apps so that drivers pay tax as they earn. See *Silva, Rohan*, The Gig Economy is Here to Stay – Now Give the Workers Rights, London Evening Standard, 16 November 2017.

Chapter 6
Extending Social Insurance Schemes to "Non-Employees": The Dutch Example

Gijsbert Vonk

I. Introduction

The digital age is one of the drivers that results in a shift away from standard employment and towards various new forms of flexible employment, a process which represents a wider problem for the labour market and for society as a whole.[1] As for the Netherlands, this country is already a champion of flex work. It was one of the largest growers in the EU for both temporary work and solo self-employment with 4.7 percentage points of growth in the 10 years prior to 2018.[2] With a 30 percent flex share of workers, the Netherlands occupied third place in 2018 in the EU, with only Poland and Spain – which have a particularly high percentage of temporary workers – having a larger share of flexible work. Greece, where the share of self-employed persons in agriculture is particularly high, has almost as much flexible work as the Netherlands.[3] There are many factors that explain this trend, including typically Dutch institutional factors. These include: the liberal registration policy of self-employment by the Dutch Tax and Customs Administration prior to 2016, generous fiscal exemptions for

1 Digital Labour Platforms and the Future of Work: Towards Decent Work in the Online World, International Labour Office – Geneva, ILO, 2018, https://www.ilo.org/wcmsp5/groups/public/---dgreports/---dcomm/---publ/documents/publication/wcms_645337.pdf. Accessed 16 August 2020; *Pesole, Annarosa/Urzi Brancati, Cesira/Fernández-Macías Enrique/Biagi, Federico/González Vázquez Ignacio*, Platform Workers in Europe, EUR 29275 EN, Publications Office of the European Union, Luxembourg, 2018, doi:10.2760/742789, JRC112157, http://publications.jrc.ec.europa.eu/repository/handle/JRC112157. Accessed 17 April 2020.

2 Information from the Dutch Statistical Bureau CBS based on Eurostat data, https://www.cbs.nl/nl-nl/dossier/dossier-flexwerk/hoofdcategorieen/flexwerk-in-nederland-en-de-eu. Accessed on 17 April 2020.

3 Information from the Dutch Statistical Bureau CBS based on Eurostat data, https://www.cbs.nl/nl-nl/dossier/dossier-flexwerk/hoofdcategorieen/flexwerk-in-nederland-en-de-eu. Accessed on 17 April 2020.

the self-employed, and previous labour law reforms which regulated (and in doing so: facilitated) flexible employment relationships.[4]

The digital economy may result in an increase and diversification of flexible work forms due to platform activities[5] and changes in production methods in general. It may also expose groups of lower- and middle-income earners to labour-related risks, in particular unemployment; traditional factory workers are replaced by robots and administrative personnel are made redundant due to the introduction of the latest smart computer applications. Indeed, while technological change and the shift to flexible forms of employment have long been heralded as something positive for both the economy and society, there is now growing evidence that there are also negative effects to be taken into account. Thus, in a recent report written for the Netherlands Independent Commission on the Regulation of Work, the OECD noted that the solo self-employed are less productive than employees with equivalent characteristics. Moreover, it was pointed out that high shares of non-standard employment (combined with strict employment protection legislation on standard contracts) may lower the resilience of labour markets to economic shocks since such contracts are more cyclical in nature. Furthermore, it was pointed out in the OECD research that, because many non-standard workers are worse off in many aspects of job quality, such as earnings, job security or access to training, a rise in non-standard employment tends to contribute to higher inequality.[6]

These and other drawbacks that have come to the fore have resulted in a growing consensus in the Netherlands' policies that the trend towards flexible work has gone too far, or at least that something must be done to strengthen the position of those who do not work in standard full-time

4 Eindrapport Interdepartementaal Beleidsonderzoek Zelfstandigen zonder personeel, https://www.rijksoverheid.nl/documenten/rapporten/2015/10/02/eindrapport-ibo-zelfstandigen-zonder-personeel. Accessed on 25 September 2020.

5 Cf. inter alia *Schoukens, Paul/Barrio, Alberto/Montebovi, Saskia*, The EU Social Pillar: An Answer to the Challenge of the Social Protection of Platform Workers?, in: European Journal of Social Security, 20 (2018) 3, pp. 219-241, https://journals.sagepub.com/doi/full/10.1177/1388262718798393.

6 OECD Input to the Netherlands Independent Commission on the Regulation of Work, summarized in Annex 5 of Commissie Borstlap. In at voor land willen we werken. Naar een nieuw rapport voor de regulering van werk. Eindrapport van de Commissie voor de Regulering van Werk (Commissie Borstlap), 23 January 2020, https://www.rijksoverheid.nl/documenten/rapporten/2020/01/23/rapport-in-wat-voor-land-willen-wij-werken. Accessed 16 August 2020.

employment.[7] This growing consensus affects both labour law and social security law and the way these two areas are linked.

The purpose of this contribution is to offer a broad overview of the Netherlands' state of protection of non-standard workers (defined as everyone without a permanent contract of employment) under social security law. The objective is to map out what new approaches have been taken into consideration in order to fill protective gaps for these persons. It is divided into three parts:

(1) a description of the present state of social security law (Section III);
(2) an analysis of policy objectives, legislative change and proposals for change made by successive governments in the Netherlands and by official advisory agencies since 2010 (Section IV); and
(3) an overview of lessons that may (not) be learned from the Dutch experience (Section V).

These three parts are preceded by a short description of the Netherlands' system and the logical setup of this contribution connected to this system (Section II). The last Section V dealing with the lessons can also be read as a conclusion. This contribution focuses on public social security law. While regular excursions to (individual and collective) labour law and fiscal law are required, these fields of law are not the subject of separate analysis.

II. The System in the Netherlands and Logical Setup of this Contribution

The Dutch social security system bears the marks of different schools of thought, preferences and approaches in the history of European social security. Pre-war social security was in keeping with the continental, corporate approach, which was reflected in the first social insurance schemes that were based on the involvement of employer and employee organisations at sectoral level. After World War Two, social insurance was influenced more by the Beveridge approach to social security. This is visible in the emergence of *national insurance,* in Dutch: *volksverzekeringen.* This is a system of residence-based schemes that are based on the insurance principle and provide minimum income protection. National insurance schemes

7 *Brink, Barbara/Vonk, Gijsbert,* Naoorlogs universalisme in het huidige socialezekerheidsdebat, in: Beleid & Maatschappij, 47 (2020) 2, pp. 149-168, https://doi.org/10.5553/BenM/138900692020047002004. Accessed 16 August 2020.

in the Netherlands have been introduced for the risks of old age (AOW 1957), death (AWW 1959, currently Anw), children (AKW 1972), incapacity for work (AAW 1975) and special medical expenses (ABWZ 1976, currently Wlz). The present public/private insurance system for curative care (Zvw) can also be characterised as a national insurance scheme.

No national insurance schemes have been created to cover unemployment and sickness. Instead, there are employee insurance schemes (WW and ZW). The Sickness Benefit Scheme (ZW) is partly replaced by a civil law liability for the employee to continue to pay wages for an extended period of two years (Article 7: 629 Civil Code). The risk of incapacity for work currently also falls within the exclusive scope of an employee insurance scheme (the WIA Act, the Dutch Work and Income (Employment Capacity) Act). The former national insurance for incapacity for work (AAW) was abolished in 1998; it survived some time as a separate insurance scheme for the self-employed until that scheme was also abolished in 2004.

A system of social assistance and social care creates a general non-contributory safety net. The 21st century also marks the start of social allowances being paid through the taxation system. These social-fiscal allowances are paid by the Dutch Tax and Customs Administration and are gradually reduced as employees earn more. Allowances are paid as compensation for rent, healthcare contributions, childcare and children. These allowances fall under the regime of uniform concepts in the Awir (Dutch General Act on Income-Related Schemes). They are also fully residence-based.

The above description sets the scene for the further composition of this contribution. For it has to be borne in mind that, in principle, the whole problem of social security protection for non-standard workers does not exist in areas where national insurance schemes (and universal social fiscal allowances) have been established. The reason is that these are residence-based schemes and do not make any distinction between employees and the self-employed or, for that matter: between those who are economically active and those who are not. This observation also largely holds true for the financing of this part of the system. Contributions for the general social insurance schemes (with the exception of the curative care insurance Zvw) are integrated within the system of general income tax and are, as such, levied by the taxation authorities. All income from non-wage labour is subject to both national insurance contributions and general taxation liability. As there is a separate contribution liability for employee insurance schemes, there is a need to qualify the income as either generated from wage labour or non-wage labour. But within this wide band of non-wage labour all income from any economic activity is taken into account. There are no minimal income thresholds. The liability for taxation and national insurance contributions may be reduced by a number of tax credits. It is possible that for persons on low income the amount of tax credits which they are entitled to is higher than the amount of tax. In such cases, a person cannot fully offset their tax credits with the tax he or she has to pay. At least this is the case for single persons. When a person has a fiscal partner the situation may be different, when that partner earns an income which is high enough to incorporate the combined tax credits.

The foregoing implies that the problem of social security protection for non-standard workers in the Netherlands can be defined with reference to three major issues: 1) demarcation between those who are considered to be employees for the purposes of the employee insurance schemes and those who are not, i.e. the category of the self-employed at large (necessitated by the fact that there is a mixed system of employee and national insurance schemes and, parallel to that, between wage tax and general income tax); 2) protection against the risks for which only employee insurance schemes have been established (i.e. unemployment, sickness and incapacity for work); and 3) coverage for extra-minimal protection for old age and death through the occupational pension system (in view of the fact that the national insurance schemes for old age (AOW) and for death (Anw) only provide flat rate minimum subsistence benefits, which in the Netherlands system are supplemented by wage-related additions to be accrued on the occupational pension system).

The description of the present state of social security law for non-standard workers in the next section is set up according to this order. Thereby it has to be borne in mind that the analysis cannot always be limited to social security law, as there are important linking pins in the legal regime with both labour law and fiscal law.

III. The Present State of Social Security Law for Non-Standard Workers

1. Demarcation between Those Who are Considered to be Employees and Those Who are Not

In first instance, the distinction between employees and self-employment plays a specific role in the employee insurance schemes set up for the risks of illness (ZW), incapacity for work (Wet WIA) and unemployment (WW). Employees are insured under the employee insurance schemes. An employee is a natural person who has concluded an employment contract under private or public law and has not yet reached standard retirement age.[8]

a) Main Rules

An employment relationship under public law is based on an *appointment* by a public body. These employees are called *civil servants*. An employment relationship under private law is a relationship based on an employment contract as defined in the Dutch Civil Code. Whether or not the employment relationship has these features is dependent on the three classical criteria of personal work, wage and subordination. Employment practices operate on the basis of a variety of non-standard forms of employment. Only the agency contract is regulated in the Dutch Civil Code as separate from the general employment contract (Article 7:690 Civil Code). Other forms of non-standard employment, such as part-time work, on-call work, etc. are directly dealt with under the general employment contract rules set out in Article 7:610 Civil Code.

b) The Role of Case Law

Traditionally, it is pointed out that the Dutch Social Security Court (CRvB) uses a different basis than the Civil Court in establishing whether or not there is an employment relationship. Whereas the Civil Court attaches more importance to the parties' intentions when determining their employment relationship, the CRvB focuses on the factual relationship existing between the parties. In doing so, the CRvB aims to stop parties from acquiring a benefit or being granted a waiver of contributions on the basis of the contractual relationship. However, the significance of this difference in approach between the two courts should not be overemphasised. Recent years have seen a trend towards more convergence.[9]

But apart from this, jurisprudence is very much meandering and developing on a case-by-case basis. This can be illustrated by the case law on the status of post distributors, triggered by the FNV trade union. The largest postal company, *PostbedrijfNL* had traditionally resorted to employees

---

8 Article 3 (1) ZW, Article 3 (1) WW, Article 3 (1) WAO and Article 8 (1) Wet WIA.

9 Cf. *Klosse, Saskia/Vonk, Gijsbert*, Hoofdzaken socialezekerheidsrecht, The Hague: Boom Juridische Uitgevers 2019, pp. 67-70.

working for a wage but suddenly introduced a new business model in which the post deliverers were required to conclude contracts for services as solo self-employed workers with the company. Many courts ruled this to be a bogus construction but on appeal the Arnhem-Leeuwarden Court of Law[10] and the Amsterdam Court of Law[11] confirmed that the solo self-employed workers did indeed deliver post for *PostNL* as solo self-employed workers. According to the courts, the parties' intention as well as the actual performance of the work indicated that the parties' wanted to conclude a contract for services.

Another illustration of the ad hoc nature of the jurisprudence is the case law on Deliveroo personnel, also initiated by the FNV trade union. On 23 July 2018, the Amsterdam District Court was of the opinion that a Deliveroo worker does not have an employee status in view of the clear intention of the parties expressed in the agreement[12], but on 15 January 2019 the Court changed its mind and reached the decision that such a worker is deemed to be an employee, this time going beyond the mere formal expression of the intention of the parties and carefully looking at the material conditions of the case[13]. For example, in the latter case, the formal possibility of replacement by another person was disregarded because replacement did not occur in practice.

c) Extending and Limiting the Scope of Application of the Employee Insurance Schemes on the Basis of Legal Fiction

The definition of "employee" for the purpose of the employee insurance schemes is not limited to employees who are employed on the basis of a private or public employment contract. It also includes persons working in other employment relationships. These employment relationships are treated in the same way as employment relationships in which employee insurance is compulsory. The term "fictitious employment relationship" or "employment relationship by legal definition" is then used. Article 4 of the Dutch Sickness Benefits Act/Unemployment Act (ZW/WW), for example, stipulates that an employee is the person who performs work for which he or she has been contracted, unless he or she can be qualified as a self-em-

10 ECLI:NL:GHARL:2016:6621.
11 ECLI:NL:GHAMS:2016:2686.
12 ECLI:NL:RBAMS:2018:5183.
13 ECLI:NL:RBAMS:2019: 189 and 2010.

ployed entrepreneur in the fiscal sense. In specific circumstances intermediaries are also treated as employees. Article 5 ZW/WW extends the concept of employee further to musicians, professional sportsmen and women and homeworkers, at least inasmuch as they are not already classified as employees under private law.

These groups that are also brought within the scope of the employee insurance schemes are referred to in Dutch as "*rariteiten*", or rarities. A statutory instrument called the *Rariteitenbesluit* regulates the conditions under which the scope of the employee insurance schemes is extended to include special groups. Examples of these groups are: small contractors for work, intermediaries and their agencies (commercial agents, representatives etc.), share-fishermen, interns, conscripts, executives of cooperative societies, homeworkers and their agencies, musicians and artists, professional sportsmen and sportswomen and the remaining group of "people performing professional services". Sex workers are also included. Inasmuch as flexible workers qualify themselves as one of these groups and meet the set requirements, they are included in the insurance.

The most diverse group of people to whom the scope of the employee insurance schemes is extended, is a residual category of "people performing professional services". To qualify for compulsory insurance, several conditions have to be met. For instance, the scope of the work relationship is subject to certain minimums in terms of the number of working hours or duration of the work and earnings (at least 40 percent of the statutory minimum wage).

Finally, for the sake of completeness, it must be noted that the employee insurance acts do not only allow for an extension of insurance to persons without an employment contract. There are also general exclusions applying to persons who do have such a contract. Thus, persons working fewer than four days a week in a private person's household fall outside the scope of the employee insurance schemes (Article 6 (1c) ZW/WW): cleaners, gardeners and home carers, etc.

d) No (Formal) Definition of "Self-Employed Worker"

While there is a (not so) clear definition of "employee" for the purposes of both labour and social security law, a similar definition of a "self-employed person" is notably absent in the Netherlands. The self-employed work on the basis of different contracts is regulated in the Civil Code, i.e.: 1) *overeenkomst tot aanneming van werk*, i.e. producing work of a physical nature such as in construction (Civil Code Article 7:750) and 2) *overeenkomst van opdracht*, i.e. commissioned work (Civil Code Article 7:400). The second contract form is the dominant one for the self-employed. Despite the absence of a positive legal definition of self-employment, a number of positive indications have developed in the administrative practice of the tax authorities which play a major role in the practical assessment of the person's status as employed or self-employed. Below in the final part of this subsection I will pay further attention to this.

e) Practical Assessment of the Nature of the Employment Relationship by the Taxation Authorities

In practice, the distinction between being defined as an employee or as a self-employed person may not be an easy one. In order to offer more certainty, the taxation authorities play an important role in certifying the employment relationship. This system of certification, however, has run into rough political weather. The former system of registration of self-employed workers that was in force until 1 May 2016, i.e. the "VAR" (Declaration of Independent Contractor Status), imposed the risk of a wrongful registration on the employee. This made it attractive to employers to use (bogus) self-employed workers rather than employees working for a wage. In order to overcome this problem, the Wet DBA (Wet Deregulering Beoordeling Arbeidsrelaties – Act on the Deregulation of Judging Working Relationships) entered into force on 1 May 2016. This act introduces a system of prior mandatory certification of the employment relationship by the taxation administration. This new legislation shifted the risk for a wrongful assessment of the employment relationship from the employee to the employer. Amidst increasing legal uncertainty as to how employment relationships had to be qualified and due to a variety of implementation problems, the operation of the new act was soon suspended, pending the construction of yet another new assessment system. At the time of writing, this is still the case. In the meantime, employment relationships are not actively monitored by the tax authorities and enforcement measures are limited to manifestly fraudulent situations.

Generally speaking, the tax administration makes use of a variety of criteria for establishing employee insurance contribution liability and payroll tax liability. The criteria are set out in the *Handreiking beoordelingskader arbeidsrelaties* (guidelines for assessing employment relationships)[14]. These el-

---

14 www.belastingdienst.nl.

ements are derived from tax and social security law (which in their turn partly refer to labour law definitions). Examples are, *inter alia*: registration with the Chamber of Commerce, profit, the number of hours spent working for a company, the possibility of replacement, capital investment, entrepreneurial risk in the case of no payment, the number of customers, and how he or she actively presents him- or herself as a self-employed person to the public.

2. *Protection of the Self-Employed against the Risks for which only Employee Insurance Schemes have been Established (i.e. Unemployment, Sickness and Incapacity for Work)*

a) Sickness

Solo self-employed workers are not entitled to continued payment during illness, nor can they apply for a sickness benefit on the grounds of ZW. For a safety net in the event of sickness solo self-employed workers today have to rely on private insurance (referred to as AOV) or alternatively join a *broodfonds* (literally: bread fund). Below, both options will be described.

Self-employed workers seeking to take out private incapacity-for-work insurance (AOV) have to go through a technical and medical acceptance procedure. In the first case, the insurance company assesses what conditions it will attach to the insurance and whether it indeed wishes to offer insurance. The insurer offers AOV insurance based on the principle that the insurer is free to decide to do so or not, as long as this does not contravene mandatory legislation, for example on non-discrimination. During the medical acceptance procedure, the medical adviser's assessment plays a major role. This defines the risk. The insurer then establishes whether the self-employed worker seeking insurance is eligible for AOV and if so, under what conditions. The medical adviser must be in a position to act objectively and independently of the insurer and, on the basis of Article 7:435 of the Dutch Civil Code, the adviser should duly observe the professional medical standard. Generally speaking, the self-employed worker seeking insurance has no choice and will have to accept the examination. While the contribution rate and the amount and duration of the benefit formally depends on what is agreed between the parties, in practice there is no room for negotiation for the self-employed worker. Four out of every five solo self-employed workers have not taken out AOV, usually because they find this too expensive. Solo self-employed workers who are insured pay contributions of around 7 or 8 percent of their annual income.[15] Research conducted by the Social and Economic Council (SER) in the Netherlands shows that to receive a benefit of EUR 32,000 a year, contributions of about 15 percent have to be paid.

Due to the high cost of private insurance, *broodfondsen* are increasingly seen as the better alternative.[16] They are an intriguing phenomenon emerging from civil society initiatives. The funds are set up by a mutual agreement between small groups of solo self-employed workers in various occupational branches, designed to provide income protection during sickness of one or more of the members (for up to a maximum of two years). A group of self-employed workers deposit a specific amount each month on their own bank account. How much this is depends on the benefit they will need in the event of sickness. When a member falls ill, he or she can receive an annuity from the fund, the level of which depends on their deposits into the fund. When a member leaves the fund, their deposits in the fund are returned. An individual can only join such a fund after being introduced by a participant. The maximum size of a fund is 50 participants, in order to maintain the small-scale character which allows for mutual trust. The *broodfondsen* are new, but at the same time reminiscent of the types of mutual aid that came into being in the guilds and similar institutions a long time ago. This approach remains a relatively marginal, but continuously expanding phenomenon.[17]

b) Unemployment

There is no private insurance for the self-employed against unemployment. Indeed, according to the *Bond van Verzekeraars*, the umbrella organisation of private insurers, this risk does not lend itself to private insurance. There are merely some residual forms of protection for the self-employed in the public WW scheme. Thus, for example, unemployed persons who aim to

15 Pension Advice 2017/85.

16 *Hilhort, Pieter*, Sociale veerkracht als vangnet, in: s&d, 5 (2011) 6, p. 151.

17 In April 2020, there were about 562 *broodfondsen* for more than 20,000 persons. Between 2010 and 2018, the *broodfondsen* paid out in total almost EUR 3.1 million to 452 solo self-employed workers who had fallen ill. This is EUR 6,800 per person. The average duration of the incapacity for work was almost six months, cf. Broodfondsen: de stand van zaken, 1 April 2020, https://www.broodfonds.nl/nieuws/nieuws/broodfondsen_de_stand_van_zaken. Accessed 17 April 2020.

start their own company in self-employment, can take advantage of the Starters' Scheme (Article 77a WW).

c) Incapacity for Work

When the various national insurance schemes were established, self-employed workers were not included in the mandatory insurance schemes against long-term incapacity for work. However, in the 1970s this was increasingly seen as a shortcoming in view of the universal ambitions of the social security project. This culminated in the General Act on Incapacity for Work (AAW). While there were few thresholds for access to (partial) invalidity benefit, married women who were not the breadwinner of the family were excluded. When EU law opened the gates for this group to join the AAW, the system became untenable. In 1998, the act was replaced by two schemes, one of which was for self-employed workers: the Self-Employed Persons Act on Incapacity for Work (WAZ). This act was to be short-lived. It was considered to be too paternalistic and too expensive. In 2004, when neo-liberalism was still running high, the WAZ was abolished. From then onwards, the self-employed were supposed to look for solutions on the private insurance market. Private insurance alternatives turned out to be not as popular as expected. It now appears that more than two out of every three self-employed workers have not taken out private insurance against incapacity for work, with a strong overrepresentation amongst the low earners.[18] There is an increasing awareness that this figure, which includes large numbers of dependent self-employed workers, is not acceptable and that something needs to done to improve their protection (see below Section IV).

3. *Coverage for Extra-Minimal Protection for Old Age and Death through the Occupational Pension System*

Every resident of the Netherlands is entitled to an AOW benefit on reaching the standard retirement age, solo self-employed workers included. The

---

18 *Klosse, Saskia*, Flexibele arbeid, gebalanceerde bescherming, in: Kremer, Monique/ Went Robert/Knottnerus, André (eds.), Voor de zekerheid, de toekomst van flexibel werkenden en de moderne organisatie van arbeid, Den Haag: Wetenschappelijke Raad voor het Regeringsbeleid 2017, pp. 213-230.

AOW pension is a flat-rate minimum benefit. For supplementary pension entitlements people have to rely on the second and third pillar pensions arrangements.

a) Second Pillar

Solo self-employed workers are usually excluded from pension systems in the second pillar. Mandatory professional pension schemes for solo self-employed workers only exist for the medical professions and civil-law notaries. Both employees and self-employed workers participate in these professional pension funds. There are also branch pension funds for solo self-employed workers like plasterers and painters, but these operate on a voluntary basis. Employees who continue to work in self-employment have the option to continue to save for their pension voluntarily for up to ten years. However, the contributions for this are high; the self-employed person has to pay both the employee and employer contribution. It is probably because of this that interest in this option is so low. For solo self-employed workers who do not earn business profits this option is given only for the duration of three years. In recent years, several initiatives have arisen for pension funds for solo self-employed workers. But to date, there is little interest in these facilities.

b) Third Pillar

One quarter of all solo self-employed workers has made no arrangements for their old age in the third pillar. Better pension arrangements tend to be made as the business becomes more profitable. In most cases, people save or invest, and investing in their own home is also popular. Self-employed workers do have several tax benefits in relation to their provision for old age.[19] First of all, there is the annuity contribution deduction, a fiscally attractive way to save or invest for an old age benefit. In addition, advantage can be taken of the Fiscal Old Age Reserve (FOR). In 2019, up to 9.8 percent of the profit subject to a maximum of EUR 8,946 can be deducted

19 *Goudswaard, Kees and Caminada, Koen*, Pensioenen voor zelfstandigen, in: Kremer, Monique/Went Robert/Knottnerus, André (eds.), Voor de zekerheid, de toekomst van flexibel werkenden en de moderne organisatie van arbeid, Den Haag: Wetenschappelijke Raad voor het Regeringsbeleid 2017, pp. 231-256.

from the profit. This is a deferred tax debt; the Tax and Customs Administration will still have to be paid later when the pension materialises. Since 2016, there is a tax concession that ensures that self-employed workers are not required to have recourse to their pension savings when they apply for social assistance. As a result of this measure it is hoped that the self-employed will start to save more, knowing that their pension is safe when they are in danger of having to rely on social assistance.

IV. Policy Objectives, Legislative Change and Proposals for Change

1. Fighting Bogus Self-Employment and Enforcing Labour Law Protection

Long before 2010, the starting year of the first government led by the liberal conservative leader Mark Rutte, there were discussions about whether or not more protection and rights should be available to non-standard workers. The tone of the debate has changed over time. While during the turn of the century the flexible labour market was still often promoted as something positive for the economy and society, in subsequent years more attention was paid to the disadvantages of a flexible labour market strategy.

Due to the sharp increase in numbers, the solo self-employed are very much at the heart of the Dutch debate. The growth of solo self-employment is increasingly seen as problematic. Solo self-employment is seen as a problem for workers when the registration of the employment relationship is not correct or is bogus (*schijnzelfstandigheid*), or when the self-employed are highly dependent on a small number of commissioners (*afhankelijke zelfstandigheid*).[20] The problem of dependent self-employment is most manifest in lower-paid work, because the workers lack the negotiating position to keep up a decent income. Bogus self-employment is rejected in full because it does not only impact negatively upon the protection of the lower-paid workers but also because it corrupts the foundation of tax and contribution liability.

For a long time, the debate about solo self-employment failed to result in any conclusive results, both in labour law and in social security law. In the discourse, it is often pointed out that the group of self-employed persons is very differentiated in nature, so therefore difficult to catch in uni-

20 This distinction was made by IBO 2015.

form policy measures.[21] On the one hand, it is precisely freedom and opportunities that truly self-employed workers seek and benefit from. On the other hand, there are concerns about dependent and bogus self-employed workers who are more or less forced to become self-employed because they would otherwise be made redundant. It is for the latter reason that initially policy measures have focused strongly on reducing bogus self-employment and enforcing the rules of labour law. The currently stranded initiative for the Tax and Customs Administration to introduce a new assessment system (Employment Relationships (Deregulation) Act) described earlier in Section III.1.e), is one example of such efforts.

Another example is the Act Combating Bogus Self-Employment that entered into force on 1 January 2016. Bogus self-employment is defined as the situation in which a person officially performs work as a self-employed person while the facts and circumstances indicate the existence of an employment contract. In other words, it occurs when the factual situation is different from the situation as it is presented (on paper) with the aim of improperly competing on working conditions.[22] The bill for combating bogus constructions introduced *inter alia* an extended system to the hirers' liability.[23]

Also changes in the minimum wage legislation introduced in July 2017 were clearly inspired by the need to improve the possibilities for the enforcement of labour standards. While the changes extended the operation of the minimum wage legislation to more forms of marginal solo self-employment,[24] they simultaneously introduced different techniques for establishing the minimum wage in order to facilitate the work of the labour inspectorate. Thus, for example, the piece-wage scheme was adjusted in such

---

21 Centraal Bureau voor de Statistiek, Achtergrondkenmerken en ontwikkelingen van zzp'ers in Nederland, 1 December 2014, https://docplayer.nl/13379-Achtergrondkenmerken-en-ontwikkelingen-van-zzp-ers-in-nederland-1-12-2014-gepubliceerd-op-cbs-nl.html. Accessed 16 August 2020; Rijksoverheid. IBO-eindrapport Zelfstandigen zonder personeel, April 2015, https://www.rijksoverheid.nl/documenten/rapporten/2015/10/02/eindrapport-ibo-zelfstandigen-zonder-personeel. Accessed 16 August 2020.

22 Parliamentary papers II 2014/15, 32108, 2.

23 Set out in Article 7:616a-616f of the Dutch Civil Code which replaced Article 7:692 of the Dutch Civil Code.

24 For a more elaborate explanation, *Vonk, Gijsbert/Jansen, Annette*, Social Protection of Marginal Part-Time, Self-Employment and Secondary Jobs in the Netherlands, in: WSI Study No. 9, November 2017, pp. 34-35, https://www.wsi.de/de/faust-detail.htm?sync_id=7974. Accessed 16 August 2020.

a way that it is easier to establish whether the payments made fall below the minimum wage.

2. *Confronting the Great Divide*

Gradually the concerns about bogus and dependent self-employment are being overshadowed by a wider concern about a growing gap in the Netherlands between those who have relatively stable socio-economic positions and profit from welfare growth and those who lag behind. This gap is visible in the labour market where lower-qualified workers represent a much higher share in flexible and uncertain work relationships than higher-qualified workers (dual labour market). It is also visible in society as a whole, a phenomenon which in the Dutch discourse is often referred to as the *Kloof* (great divide). In particular the Social and Cultural Planning Bureau (SCP) has been active in exposing this divide. Thus, for example, in an influential report published in 2014 about the divide, called *Verschil in Nederland*, the SCP distinguished between six groups according to their economic, social, and cultural capital characteristics. Four groups representing 70 percent of the population do relatively well. These are the established elite (15 percent), young professionals (13 percent), the working middle class (27 percent) and comfortable pensioners (17 percent). However, on the other side of the spectrum we find two other groups who suffer economic insecurity and various forms of social exclusion, and these are the unsecure workers (14 percent) and the precariat (15 percent). In this manner a "soft divide" between the have and have-nots is clearly visible.

Over the last ten years, various public advisory agencies have called for action to confront the great divide, often stressing the advantages of universalism in social protection, without, however, making this very concrete.[25] In particular, the agencies refrained from explicitly addressing the "open wound" in Dutch social security for the self-employed, namely the absence of a public insurance scheme for incapacity for work, caused by the abolition of the AAW (1998) and WAZ (2004). Apparently, this was considered to be too politically sensitive or unrealistic.

A different attitude can be found amongst stakeholders and independent academics who have put forward various proposals to address the lack

25 *Brink, Barbara/Vonk, Gijsbert,* Naoorlogs universalisme in het huidige socialezekerheidsdebat (fn. 7), pp. 149-168.

of social protection for non-standard workers. These range from a differentiated system of social security protection for all workers (Klosse),[26] an extension of the fictitious labour relationship in the employee insurance schemes to more categories of solo self-employed and atypical workers (De Jong),[27] to the introduction of a completely new labour code which regulates various categories of labour in a coherent manner (Houweling).[28]

The first idea has been presented by the Maastricht professor of social law, Klosse, basing herself on previous work of interdepartmental think tanks. She envisages the rules of fiscal law, labour law and social security protection as a house to which all workers have access. Once inside the house there are four different chambers, access to which depends not only on the qualification of a worker as a self-employed or employed person, but also on the degree of economic dependence, as opposed to self-reliance. Thus, economically dependent employees will be entitled to the full package of labour law and social security protection, while self-reliant self-employed persons will merely enjoy certain fiscal stimuli. But this is not the end of it because economically dependent self-employed persons will equally enjoy large sections of traditional labour law and social security protection, while those employees who are self-reliant will have less protection under labour law and opt-outs in social security.

The second idea was advocated inter alia by De Jong for platform workers in her award-winning Master thesis at the University of Groningen. The default situation for all platform workers should be that they are statutorily subject to obligatory insurance for the employee insurance scheme. Only if the platform satisfies certain predetermined statutory requirements on governance and the treatment of their workers, the platform can apply for an exemption on behalf of their workers.

The third idea is advocated by the Rotterdam professor of labour law, Houweling. He suggests that the degree of labour law and social security protection should not be dependent on the formal contractual relationship

---

26 *Klosse, Saskia*, Flexibele arbeid, gebalanceerde bescherming (fn. 18), pp. 213-230.

27 *De Jong, Febe*, Platformwerk als fictieve dienstbetrekking. Scriptie Rijksuniversiteit Groningen, 2 November 2018, https://www.ser.nl/nl/actueel/Nieuws/nominaties-scripties-scriptieprijs-2020. Accessed 24 June 2020; *Van den Berg, Lucy*, Platformwerk, biedt het Rariteitenbesluit Soelaas?, in: Tijdschrift voor Recht en Arbeid, (2019) 15.

28 *Houweling, Ruben*, Modernisering van het arbeidsrecht, in: Tweede Kamer der Staten-Generaal (ed.), Ambtelijk rapport Onderzoek varianten kwalificatie arbeidsovereenkomst, pp. 91-100, https://www.tweedekamer.nl/kamerstukken/detail?id=2017D14208&did=2017D14208. Accessed 17 April 2020.

but on the quality of protection itself. Thus, for example, it is clear that all workers, regardless of their status and contract form should be protected against discrimination. On the other hand, severance should only be available to those who have a contractual relationship with an employer. Houweling proposes the introduction of a Code for all Work Relations which is to not only spell out the material rules of protection but which must also specify which categories of persons come under each of these rules.

None of these initiatives have been taken up by the government. Instead, reform has rather focused on incremental changes in labour law and social security legislation. In particular, reference must be made to the *Wet Werk en Zekerheid* (WWZ) of 2015 (Act on Work and Security) and the *Wet Arbeidsmarkt in Balans* (WAB) which entered into force on 1 January 2020 (Act on a Balanced Labour Market). The first act aimed, among other things, at making the systems of flexible labour law, dismissal law and labour law more activating and to reduce the growing divide between persons with a permanent and those with a flexible contract.[29] One of the reforms concerns the so-called Chain Regulation in Article 7:668a of the Dutch Civil Code, intended to prevent employers from being able to keep workers endlessly in a flexible employment relationship. The Chain Regulation limits the maximum number of temporary contracts that can be entered into consecutively and the maximum duration of these. The WWZ reduced the maximum contract duration from three to two years, thus limiting the possibilities for employers to keep workers on temporary contracts.

In many respects, the WAB – which followed four years later – can be seen as a technical amendment to the WWZ. This is visible in the recalibration of some rules on dismissal law and the Chain Regulation. A more substantive change involved the introduction of a new calculus for the contributions for unemployment benefits. These contributions no longer fluctuate according to the branches of industry and occupation, but according to the number of employees with a fixed-term employment contract as compared to flexible labour contracts. Employers with more flexible workers are liable to pay a higher contribution. The latter change is the first social security measure of a more radical nature with a direct financial consequence; it involves a form of pricing of flexible labour for the employers.

---

29 Parliamentary papers II 2014/15, 33818, 3.

In 2017, the latest government of Rutte III announced more substantive measures to confront the dual labour market by curbing the growth of solo self-employment.[30] The most eye-catching proposal included in the coalition programme included the following segmentation of workers according to their level of income: workers who earn less than 125 percent of the minimum wage defined in the statute or a collective labour agreement (less than between EUR 15 and EUR 18 per hour) will be deemed to have an employment contract. The duration of the employment should be longer than three months.

This proposal never made it because it was deemed to be contrary to EU law.[31] An alternative, but still substantive proposal was tabled to introduce minimum tariffs for the solo self-employed.[32] According to this proposal, which is deemed not to be contrary to EU law, self-employed workers will be entitled to a minimum tariff of EUR 16 an hour. This rate is higher than the minimum subsistence norm in the Netherlands; it is calculated so as to include a number of indirect costs, such as preparation, marketing, insurance against sickness, and incapacity for work. High-earning self-employed workers (earning more than EUR 75 an hour) will be given an opt-out for wage tax and the employee insurance schemes. The idea, which has been widely criticised for imposing far too much red tape on small, lower-qualified solo self-employed workers, has – at the time of writing – still not been sent to Parliament in the form of a concrete legislative proposal.

Lastly, for the sake of completeness, I will mention that preparations are underway to re-introduce the presently dormant system of prior certification of the employment relationship by the tax authorities. The failed system of model agreements is to be replaced by a web module which offers commissioners of work the possibility to obtain an assessment of the nature of the employment relationship based on the answers to a number of questions raised in this module. This system is to be operational in 2021.

3. *Borstlap Commission*

Another sign that the government is prepared to contemplate more fundamental change is the initiative to charge an independent commission with

30 Vertrouwen in de toekomst' Coalition Agreement 2017-2021; VVD, CDA, D66 en ChristenUnie, 10 October 2017.

31 Parliamentary Papers II, 2018/19, 31311, No. 212.

32 Proposal for internet consultation of 28 June 2019, https://www.internetconsultatie.nl/minimumbeloningzelfstandigen. Accessed 10 April 2020.

a wide-reaching mandate to investigate whether the entire regulatory system for work is still up to date. The Commission, which is often referred to as the Borstlap Commission (named after its chairman Hans Borstlap) gave its verdict in its final report in January 2020.[33] The shortest answer to the question raised by the government is that the regulatory framework is no longer up to date. According to the report, this threatens the economic potential of the Netherlands, ensures that groups of workers are structurally dependent on precarious and low-quality work and thus also threatens social cohesion. The Commission recommends that the Netherlands should quickly work on an integral redesign of the rules surrounding work in the areas of employment law, social security, taxation and personal development during the career. At the time of writing there is no official cabinet reaction to the report, but on the whole, it is well received in the public opinion.

Three recommendations of the Borstlap report need to be highlighted because of their direct relevance for the topic of this contribution. First of all, according to the Commission, flexible contracts should no longer be encouraged: temporary work should be truly temporary and the cost of the uncertainty should be reflected in the price of temporary work. This recommendation signals the end of decades of flexible employment strategies pursued by the respective Dutch governments. The fixed employment contract is rehabilitated as the default standard for employment relationships.

Indeed, secondly, the Commission is of the opinion that the variety of currently existing contract forms should be reduced to three forms only: dependent employment, self-employment and agency work. Cross-over forms of labour and hybrid contract forms are to be abolished. In order to avoid artificial incentives that pull labour away from its natural contract form into another, the fiscal and social security treatment of all three contract types must the equal. In other words, the price of labour may not fluctuate according to contract form.

Thirdly, the former also implies that for the risk of incapacity for work a new mandatory *public* insurance scheme at a minimum level for all workers must be introduced. The Commission refers to a *volksverzekering*, so it is better to speak of a compulsory social insurance for all residents who receive remuneration from work. Earnings-related supplements, either statutory or occupational, must complement this system. This proposal signals a change of heart in the political debate about public versus private social security which has been raging over decades. They imply a restoration and

33 Commissie Borstlap. In at voor land willen we werken (fn. 6).

an extension of the public universal insurance system. It is expected that concrete legislative proposals to this effect will be tabled in the second half of 2020. Finally, reference is made to the proposal to introduce a universal scheme for occupational training. According to its proposal, everybody will receive a personal development budget at birth, to which employers will subsequently contribute.

V. Conclusion: Lessons (not) to be Learned from the Dutch Experience

From this overview it follows that in the Netherlands non-wage earners are excluded from the protection of most of the corpus of labour law and of employee insurance schemes against sickness, unemployment and incapacity for work. Neither are they likely to be covered by collective second pillar pensions which supplement the universal state pension scheme. There are exceptions for special categories of self-employed workers who enjoy limited job and social security protection. These are diverse groups like artists, franchise holders, sales agents, homeworkers, etc.

As mentioned in the introduction, over the last decades the Netherlands has experienced a sharp increase in both solo self-employment and flexible employment. This can partly be explained by measures to encourage flexibility on the labour market, leading *inter alia* to the liberal registration policy of self-employment by the Dutch Tax and Customs Administration prior to 2016, generous fiscal exemptions for the self-employed, and previous labour law reforms which regulated (and in doing so: facilitated) flexible employment relationships. We have seen that growth in non-standard labour is increasingly seen as problematic. While attention focused initially mostly on the problem of bogus self-employment and lack of social protection for individuals who occupy a place in the lower echelons of the flexible labour market, the concerns have gradually shifted to the detrimental effects of a dual labour market on the economy and society as a whole. Reducing flexible work and bringing it back to its very essence is now seen as a way of confronting the great divide between stronger and weaker groups of citizens and as a way of investing in human capital.

This shift is reflected in the nature of the measures successive governments have taken or have contemplated. Initially, these measures were mostly practical, focusing for example on offering more legal certainty by introducing a certification of employment relationship by the tax authorities and combating bogus self-employment by simplifying legislation and strengthening enforcement measures. More recent measures are more robust in character, including a system of minimum tariffs for the self-employed and introducing forms of pricing of flexible labour. If it is up to the Borstlap Commission, the reforms should spill over to structural changes in the regulation of labour, but if and how these ambitions will materialise in the post COVID 19-era remains to be seen. At the time of writing, i.e. at the height of the coronavirus crisis, the government priority has been to respond to the economic effects of this crisis by introducing a temporary income support regime for the self-employed who are faced with a reduction or cessation of business activity. For our subject of social security, the most exciting prospect will be the re-emergence of a universal scheme for basic protection against incapacity for work, which had existed until 1998 (and further in its revised form until 2004). The abolition of the universal scheme for incapacity for work around the turn of the century has proven to be a historical anomaly. If this is to be translated into a lesson, it is: Do not temper with broad solidarity institutions, because once abolished they are very hard to reintroduce.

Another lesson is that it is worthwhile to continue to invest in a properly functioning registration system of work relationships. Despite all its mishaps and teething problems, the binding registration may qualify as an interesting practice from a comparative point of view. This is because the registration system does not only provide legal certainty, but can also operate as a steering instrument to regulate employment relationships in a proactive manner according to policy objectives pursued. Thus, for example, when the feeling is that solo self-employment should be tested more vigorously in relation to the traditional criteria of the employment contract, this can be done by changing how authorities judge the labour relationship as part of the registration system. While the previously existing system of the *VAR-verklaring* failed to realise this ambition because it was too liberal and shifted the burden of wrongful registration too much to the worker, the new system of so-called model agreements (which seeks to address these wrongs) failed because of implementation problems. But this does not mean to say that the system cannot work. Arguably, the new approach should be given time and space to be tried out. The latest government of Rutte III is taking its time. It announced the development of a new web module in 2017 which should give clarity to employers/commissions of work of the status of the worker as employee or self-employed worker. But at the time of writing, the module is still not fully in operation. However, there are first signs of hope. The web module has completed its test phase and is now entering its first pilot phase. In a letter to Parliament of 15 June 2020, the Minister of Social Affairs reported to Parliament that the test phase shows that the web module provides clarity in a large number of cases.[34] Only in 25 percent of the cases the commissioners of work received a declaration of self-employment. In 27 percent of the cases the web module could not create sufficient clarity, but in 48 percent of the assignments, the web module indicated employment, which means that an employment contract is probably required. This last relatively large percentage could be seen as an indication that the web module steers employment relationships in the direction of the employment contract, or at least that it does not bias in favour of solo self-employment in the way that the previous system of VAR declarations did. Indeed, the Minister warned that companies who wanted to establish working relationships with self-employed workers should structure such relationships differently in the future. Perhaps the web module can also work as a stepping stone towards the creation of more legal certainty for platform workers, in the sense that platforms who engage such workers and who use the web module will realise in time that the workers do not necessarily have the status of solo self-employed workers merely due to the fact that they work for platforms.

34 Cf. Voortgangsbrief werken als zelfstandige, Minister van Sociale Zaken en Werkgelegenheid, 15 June 2020, https://www.rijksoverheid.nl/actueel/nieuws/2020/06/15/webmodule-zzp-start-als-pilot. Accessed 25 September 2020.

Chapter 7
Collective Agreements and Social Security Protection for Non-Standard Workers and Particularly for Platform Workers: The Danish Experience

Natalie Videbæk Munkholm

I. Introduction

In Denmark, the flexibility of employers to align their labour with the ebb and flow of a fluctuating market goes hand in hand with a strong social security system, providing income benefits as well as fully funded retraining opportunities for persons whilst unemployed or otherwise not receiving salaries. A solid and broad social security system is an essential element of the Danish flexicurity system.

The Danish Constitution in Section 75 (2) provides, that "any person unable to support himself or his family shall, when no other person is responsible for his or their maintenance, be entitled to receive public assistance, provided that he shall comply with the obligations imposed by statute in such respect". The provision gives the right to any person residing lawfully in Denmark; citizenship is not a prerequisite. The specific state assistance is established in the social legislation. In 1933, as part of the "Kanslergade compromise", the social security system underwent a major reform, ensuring that social security measures were provided to everyone in a rights-based system on objective criteria, and without a loss of other types of fundamental citizens' rights.[1]

The social security system consists of a range of public social security benefits awarded in case of sickness (sick leave benefits), childbirth and parental leave (maternity/parental leave benefits), unemployment for those not insured (basic living benefits), and retirement (early retirement pensions and old-age retirement pensions). Some social security measures are co-financed by compulsory employer insurance, such as coverage for acci-

1 Petersen, Jørn Henrik/Petersen, Klaus/Christiansen, Niels Finn (eds.), Dansk Velfærdshistorie, Vol. 1 and 2, Odense: University of Southern Denmark Publishing 2011.

dents at work and occupational diseases. Unemployment benefits are co-financed by personal private membership (unemployment insurance benefits). Occupational pensions for early retirement and old-age retirement are also contribution-based. In addition, a number of benefits in kind are offered to everyone regardless of their connection to the labour market, such as residence-based universal health care regardless of employment status, universal family benefits, public childcare from age 0 which is heavily subsidised, and free secondary and tertiary educations.

In addition to the social security measures in legislative acts, collective agreements improve the content as well as the scope for persons eligible for social security measures. In Denmark, 84 percent of all workers are covered by a collective agreement, i.e. 100 percent in the public sector and 67 percent in the private sector. The unionisation rate is also very high at an average of 74 percent for all workers in Denmark. The social partners are highly valued by the legislators and participate in the rule-making. Participation takes place in standing expert committees advising the Government on topics relating to the labour market, as well as in ad hoc expert committees when reforms are considered. In addition, the social partners on their own account negotiate and bring joint proposals to the Government for new steps in regulation aiming at addressing aspects that are particularly current challenges to the market. One recent example is the joint proposal by the main social partners to provide minimum salaries for workers in the goods transportation sector in order to counteract abuse of the rules on cabotage transportation. More recently, the social partners worked closely with the Danish Government to negotiate a number of efficient help packages to avoid and reduce lay-offs during the Covid-19 pandemic in 2020. In addition, the social partners contribute in all consultation procedures on legislation aiming at the labour market and interaction with social security measures.

With regard to social security measures, the public social security system is supplemented by the social partners by additional social benefits, such as occupational pensions, paid sick leave and paid maternity/parental leave. Likewise, the public system is supplemented by the social partners extending certain labour protections to persons in non-standard work such as platform workers.

The close involvement of the social partners in committees and councils recently resulted in a reform of the unemployment insurance system, with a view specifically to erasing systemic barriers for persons in non-standard employment, such as platform workers. As part of the former Government's overall focus on changes to the labour market and the drive to include everyone in the system, an interdisciplinary Disruption Council was established for two years (2017-2019), with a view to discussing risks and opportunities and to producing policy and regulatory recommendations.[2] One risk identified was the poor match between the way work is now performed – in a combination of different types of employment and self-employment, including platform work – and the system for being eligible for unemployment insurance benefits, based on the more traditional full employment or full self-employment.[3] A tripartite work group presented recommendations for a reform allowing for all income to count in the Unemployment Insurance Benefit System.[4] The proposal was adopted, and the new regulation for Unemployment Insurance came into force on 1 January 2018.[5] In other social security areas, similar developments have not yet taken place.[6]

In Denmark, a person can provide work either as an employee/worker[7] or as a self-employed person. This binary divide regulates rights under labour law, as well as in most other areas of law, including social security law.[8] There is no general definition of who is an employee in Danish labour or social security law, and the assessment of belonging to one or the other category can vary across legal bases. The categorisation in labour law and social security law is made on the basis of the factual circumstances in a case-by-case approach. In labour law, it is possible to have a status as employee under one act, and a status as self-employed under another act. The respective status as either employee or self-employed in the social security system, however, often decides on the method for being eligible for benefits, and on which types of income to use for calculation of the amount of benefits. This will be further explained below.

---

2 About the Disruption Council, an initiative of the former Government see https://www.regeringen.dk/partnerskab/. Accessed 21 July 2020.

3 Output from the Disruption Council includes No. 3: A modern and flexible labour market, https://bm.dk/media/9598/output-fra-disruptionraadet.pdf. Accessed 21 July 2020.

4 For recommendations of the work group see https://bm.dk/arbejdsomraader/kommissioner-ekspertudvalg/arbejdsgruppe-selvstaendige-i-dagpengesystemet/oversigt-over-hovedforslag/. Accessed 21 July 2020.

5 Amendment Act No. 1670 of 26 December 2017 to the Act on Unemployment Insurance, https://www.retsinformation.dk/eli/lta/2017/1670. Accessed 21 July 2020.

6 September 2020.

7 In Denmark, both terms are used interchangeably; there is only one category of worker/employee.

8 Only in tax law has a third category recently been introduced for the income year 2018 and forward. The contents do not challenge the existing binary divide in labour law or social security law.

This chapter presents *the overall social security measures* in Denmark and the implications of the *uncertain employment status of non-standard workers, in casu platform workers*. Furthermore, the role of the social partners in developing the *regulatory* measures in tripartite negotiations, and in negotiating *supplementing or specialised social security measures* in collective agreements for persons in non-standard forms of employment and particularly for platform workers. The role of the social partners is then discussed, with a view to *highlighting the strengths and weaknesses of the Danish experiences of providing platform workers* with access to the social security systems so far.

II. Social Security Measures – The Legislative Framework and Recent Reforms

Statutory acts provide the primary framework for most of the social security elements. This includes sick leave (*sygedagpenge*) and maternity/parental leave benefits (*barsels/forældreorlovsdagpenge*), basic living benefits (*kontanthjælp*), early retirement pensions in case of inability to work (*førtidspension*), and a small public old age pension (*folkepension*). Statutory acts also provide the framework for unemployment insurance (*arbejdsløshedsdagpenge*), but this is available only to members of unemployment insurance associations, independent of the trade unions.

1. Sick Leave Benefits

The right to sick leave benefits is provided in the Act on Sick Leave Benefits.[9] This differs for employed and self-employed persons. It is a requirement that the person applying for sick leave benefits has a current connection to the labour market. This is established in the basis of a number of working hours within a certain reference period.

Persons applying for sick leave benefits must choose whether to apply as employed or as self-employed, as the hours cannot be accumulated across different types of employment categories. The system uses *the labour market standard* for assessing whether a person is in employment or not. Hours can thus be counted towards being eligible *either* as employed *or* as self-employed. The system for being eligible for sick leave benefits differs for employees and self-employed persons. Non-standard employees and self-employed persons are covered by the right to sick leave benefits, but may have

9 Statutory Act on Sick Leave Benefits No. 68 of 25 January 2019.

trouble achieving the required number of working hours, either as employed or as self-employed persons. Non-standard or self-employed persons are often caught between systems, and can end up without sick leave benefits. The local municipality assesses the status as employed/self-employed. There is a free public complaints procedure, but so far, no complaints have been heard about a right to sick leave benefits from the platform company as employer or from the local municipality.

The payment of sick leave benefits is shared between the employer/self-employed and the local municipality. The employer pays for the first two weeks of benefits for their employees on sick leave, after which the local municipality takes over. Employees can be entitled to receive *salaries* rather than sick leave benefits during sick leave, whereas such a right requires explicit legal basis.[10] This section focuses only on the right to public sick leave benefits.

An employee in current employment is entitled to receive sick leave benefits. The first 30 days of sick leave benefits are paid by the employer, if the employee has been employed with the employer in the last 8 weeks prior to his/her sickness and has worked a minimum of 74 hours with the employer during those 8 weeks.[11] After the first 30 days of sick leave, the local municipality pays the sick leave benefits. If the work relationship with the employer does not entitle to employer-paid sick leave benefits, but the work history entitles to municipality-paid sick leave benefits, the employee will receive sick leave benefits from the local municipality from day 1.

Non-standard workers, such as casual workers and platform workers who are not genuinely self-employed, who have worked the required hours, are eligible to receive sick leave benefits from the employer during the first 30 days of sick leave. For workers in casual employment, where the work is provided on an ad-hoc basis at the initiative of the employer, from day to day and without a set number of working hours or days per week, the biggest challenge is that sick leave benefits compensate for the loss of income during sick leave, and is therefore conditional on the employee being employed and having missed working hours/expected income due to the sickness. This is not an issue in ongoing employments, with planned or expected working hours during the sick leave. For workers performing work on a casual basis, such as 0-hour contracts, on-call employees or platform workers, this criteria is difficult to fulfil, as eligibility presupposes being "em-

10 A right to salaries during sick leave can be provided either by special statutory law, e.g. Section 5 of the Salaried Employees Act or by collective agreement.

11 Section 30 of the Sick Leave Benefits Act.

ployed" the day before the sick leave as well as having missed working hours during the days when off on sick leave. An administrative ruling has assessed how to handle casual workers in this respect.[12] The ruling stated that casual workers are only viewed as "in employment" in periods where the worker is actually currently working for the employer. If the casual work, on the other hand, has ended on a day earlier than the day before the leave, the criterion of being "in employment" is not met. Elements such as having agreed to an average working time, a notice of termination, how and for how far ahead the work is planned, whether the employer is obliged to offer assignments, and whether the worker is obliged to accept offers of assignments can indicate a current employment relationship. If the employment is assessed as current, it is of less influence that the worker is not performing work specifically on the day before the leave. If the worker, on the other hand, is not viewed as in current employment and is not working on the day before the leave, he or she is not eligible for sick leave benefits. In this case, there is no need to go on to assess whether the requirement of working hours has been met.

Platform workers would face the same challenge as casual workers. Platform workers who have worked regularly over a longer period of time, and have worked a considerable amount of hours each week, and where there are e.g. a number of assignments lined up for the future days, could perhaps be considered in "current" employment with planned working hours, and thus fulfil this requirement for sick leave benefits from the platform company and the local municipality. The typical contract of work for platform workers may not have elements indicating that the work is current. Most platform workers would most likely be assessed as not in current employment, if they did not perform assignments the day before the leave.

Genuinely self-employed persons are entitled to sick leave benefits from the local municipality after two weeks of self-financed sick leave.[13] Sick leave benefits require that the self-employed person has been conducting business to a substantial degree (more than 50 percent of part-time, i.e. 18.5 hours per week) during at least 6 out of the last 12 months. The information provided by the self-employed platform worker is used as a starting point. If the number of months with the required level of activities is less, hours in employment *prior* to being genuinely self-employed can be in-

12 Section 2.1.2.10 and Ruling 100-15 in Guideline 9510 of 26 June 2018; cf. Appeal Committee Ruling 100-15 on the right to sick leave benefits, https://www.retsinformation.dk/Forms/R0710.aspx?id=176826. Accessed 21 July 2020.

13 Cf. Section 42 of the Sick Leave Benefits Act.

cluded. Self-employed persons can take out a voluntary private insurance granting a right to sick leave benefits from the municipality from day one or day three respectively, instead of financing the first two weeks of sick leave themselves. This applies to genuinely self-employed persons also in non-standard work relationships, such as platform workers. This means that platform workers who have worked less intensively with their business, i.e. for less than 18.5 hours per week, or who have worked for less than 6 months, are ineligible for sick leave benefits from the municipality.

The system for sick leave benefits is difficult for persons in non-standard employment, in particular for those who are not in a stable work relationship with foreseeable work tasks. This applies also to platform workers. If assessed as employees, the biggest hindrance is being considered in "current" employment, as there are often no mandatory assignments or working hours for platform workers. If assessed as genuinely self-employed, they would have to finance the first two weeks of sick leave out of their own pocket, unless having taken out the voluntary sick leave insurance. In reality, periods of being indisposed for providing work in causal employment, 0-hour-contracts or via platform work would, to a large extent, be at risk of having to be self-financed by the worker, regardless of employment status.

2. *Maternity Leave Benefits*

The right to take parental leave and to receive benefits during parental leave is governed by the Act on Entitlement to Leave and Benefits.[14] Also concerning access to maternity/parental leave benefits, non-standard employees and self-employed persons are covered, but may have trouble achieving the required number of working hours in order to be eligible, either as employed or as self-employed persons. The purpose of the Act is to ensure all parents a right to take leave in case of pregnancy, childbirth and adoption, and that parents connected to the labour market are entitled to receive benefits during these periods of leave.[15] The Act applies to all parents and both employees and self-employed persons have a right under

14 Statutory Act No. 67 of 25 January on Entitlement to Leave and Benefits in the Event of Childbirth (The Maternity Leave Act).

15 Section 1 of the Act on Entitlement to Leave and Benefits.

the Act to receive benefits.[16] Maternity/parental leave benefits are paid to employees as well as to self-employed persons by the local municipality.

Employees and genuinely self-employed persons are in most aspects treated equally under the Act. One difference is that the Act grants employees a right to take parental leave, which can be enforced vis-à-vis the employer. Self-employed persons must plan their own work schedules and their own periods of leave. The assessment of whether one is considered to be an employee or self-employed is based on the labour law assessment.[17]

Employees are eligible for maternity/parental leave benefits on terms similar to being eligible for sick leave benefits. Employees are eligible only if employed on the day before the leave, and having worked a minimum of 160 hours within the last four months.[18] Being employed on the day before the leave is taken literally.[19] For persons in non-standard employment with atypical employment patterns, such as part-time work, fixed-term work, casual work or temporary agency work, assessment of the end date will be determined *inter alia* from a work schedule.[20] The 160 working hours for being eligible are counted on the basis of income and working hours registered with the tax authorities.[21] If the hours are not registered (unknown working hours), the number of working hours are calculated on the basis of registered income divided by an hourly income rate,[22] which in 2020 is set at DKK 202 per hour.[23]

Persons in non-standard employment, including platform workers who are assessed as employees must be "in employment" on the last day before the

16 Sections 2 and 2 (2) of the Act on Entitlement to Leave and Benefits.

17 Section 4 (1) in Executive Order No. 953 of 17 September 2019 on the Calculation of Maternity Leave Benefits.

18 Section 27 (1) (1) of the Maternity Leave Act. Additional requirements apply.

19 Section 2.1 in Guideline No. 9510 of 26 June 2018 on Employment Requirements for the Right to Maternity or Parental Leave Benefits, *Vejledning om beskæftigelseskravet for ret til barselsdagpenge*.

20 Section 2.1.1 of Guideline No. 9510 of 26 June 2018.

21 Section 27 (2) of the Maternity Leave Act.

22 Section 2 (2) of Executive Order No. 953 of 17 September 2019 on the Calculation of the Employment Requirement and Calculation of the Rate of Benefits for Maternity and Parental Leave, *Bekendtgørelse om opgørelse af beskæftigelseskrav og beregning af barselsdagpenge mv*, set each year in January by the tax authorities.

23 Section 2 (2) of Executive Order No. 953 of 17 September 2019, Section 2 (8) of the Executive Order on Supplemental Occupational Pension, *Bekendtgørelse om Arbejdsmarkedets Tillægspension*, No. 1385 of 25 November 2015. The level in Section 2 (8) is amended each year, and in 2020 is set at DKK 211.93 for men and DKK 191.39 for women, https://indberet.virk.dk/sites/default/files/ukendt_arbejdstid_timeloenssatser.pdf. Accessed 21 July 2020.

leave. The rules regarding maternity leave benefits reflect the rules for sick leave benefits on this issue, see above. The assessment of being in "current" employment is uncertain for persons in casual work, on 0-hour contracts and engaged in platform work under the current legislation. Particularly as regards platform workers and the requirement of having worked 160 hours, the income for platform workers will most likely not be registered with the tax authorities as a number of working hours, but instead as a total income. In this case, the number of working hours must be calculated at the rate of DKK 202 per hour. Most hourly rates for platform workers in Denmark are considerably lower than DKK 202 per hour. The hours calculated for platform workers, and any other worker in non-standard employment with an hourly rate of less than DKK 202, would then not reflect the actual hours worked.

A genuinely self-employed person is entitled to parental benefits if the person for 6 months out of the last 12 months has had activities amounting at least to half of the normal weekly working hours.[24] All hours with activities as a self-employed person can be included, as the calculation is not limited to hours with assignments.[25] The authorities take as a starting point the information provided by the self-employed person for the number of hours in activities as a self-employed person.[26] If specific circumstances give rise to doubt, the authority can ask for further information. This applies also to genuinely self-employed workers in non-standard work relations, such as genuinely self-employed platform workers. It is doubtful whether "logging on" and being available for assignments counts as "hours with activities as a self-employed person" in relation to being eligible for Maternity Leave Benefits.

The rate of benefits received depends on the income before taking leave.[27] The amount is capped, in 2019 at DKK 4,355 (approx. EUR 581) per week,[28] and the cap is the same for the employed and the self-em-

24 Section 28 (1) of the Act on Maternity Leave.

25 Section 5 of Executive Order No. 953 of 17 September 2019.

26 Section 3.1 of Guideline No. 9510 of 26 June 2018.

27 Section 32 of the Act on Maternity Leave. The manner of calculation is provided in chapters 8 and 9 of the Act, in Sections 6-21 of the Executive Order 953 of 17 September 2019, and further explained in the Guideline on Calculating Rates of Benefits for Maternity and Parental Leave, No. 9829 of 27 September 2019, *Vejledning om beregning af barselsdagpenge*. Only registered and otherwise documented income counts.

28 Maximum benefits per week for employees and self-employed persons are the same, cf. Sections 35 (1) and 37 of the Act on Maternity Leave. The maximum level in 2019 is set at DKK 4355 (approx. EUR 581) per week.

ployed. The income level is calculated either on the basis of income in employment or on the basis of income as a self-employed person.[29] The income sources are *not* cumulated.

For employees, the benefits are paid for a number of hours per week at a certain rate per hour, reflecting the levels before commencing the leave. Benefits are paid on the basis of the average hourly income and the average weekly hours before the leave.[30] For employees with *varying* weekly working hours, such as many workers in non-standard employment, the number of hours is calculated from the average working hours per week during the last 4 weeks before the commencement of leave.[31] For employees with *unforeseeable* working hours, the number of hours is calculated using the total income and dividing it by the hourly rate of DKK 202 in 2020.[32] These calculations then arrive at a number of average weekly working hours, and an average payment per working hour for the employee.

For workers in non-standard employment, where the number of working hours is not registered by the employer, such as platform workers performing work via a platform company, the working hours are considered "unknown". The number of hours will be calculated on the basis of the overall income divided by the set hourly rate of DKK 202. This means that platform workers, and other workers in non-standard work relationships where the employer does not register the working hours but rather the income, are likely to be eligible for fewer hours of maternity/parental benefits per week. This results in reduced benefits per week, compared to employments where the weekly or monthly working hours are registered by an employer.

For the self-employed, the benefit rate is based on the annual income as a self-employed person the year before the commencement of leave, regardless of the hours worked.[33] The annual tax return, *Årsopgørelsen*, is used as the basis.[34] This applies to all self-employed persons, including platform

29 Section 4 of Executive Order No. 953 of 17 September 2019. The tax authorities' assessment is the starting point for categorising the income, unless this would be in breach of a labour law assessment, cf. Section 4 of Executive Order No. 953 of 17 September 2019.

30 During the 3 months just prior to the commencement of the leave, cf. Section 33 (1) of the Act on Maternity Leave.

31 Section 11 of Executive Order No. 953 of 17 September 2019.

32 Set in the Executive Order on ATP, mentioned above, in 2020 on average amounting to DKK 202 per hour.

33 Section 6 (1) of Executive Order No. 953.

34 Section 6 (2) and 7 (1) of Executive Order No. 953.

workers who are genuinely self-employed. The benefits will match the income, regardless of working hours, but cannot exceed the cap.

In particular non-standard workers in casual employment will have difficulties obtaining a right to benefits during maternity and parental leave, similar to the difficulties of obtaining a right to sick leave benefits. The problem lies in the "current" employment status, where the employment must not have ceased prior to commencing the leave. If eligible, workers in non-standard employment, where the employer does not register the working hours, in particular platform workers, can encounter problems with the calculation of the hourly benefits. As the working hours are unknown, the calculation results in reduced weekly maternity benefits. Genuinely self-employed persons who have worked a significant amount of hours over at least 6 months have better access to maternity and parental leave benefits from the local municipality. Their rate of benefits will match the annual income in the tax returns, the year before commencing the leave.

These major problems with sick leave benefits and maternity leave benefits for persons with more fragmented work relationships that do not resemble the standard unlimited full-time employment with one employer, or for genuinely full time self-employed persons are evident. These issues surfacing in particular due to the non-standard character of the work patterns in fragmented work was to a certain degree solved by the reform of the unemployment insurance system in 2018 focusing on *global income* rather than *hours* worked.

3. *Unemployment Insurance*

Income during periods of unemployment can be divided into two separate sources: Unemployment Benefits, *Arbejdsløshedsdagpenge*, which is an insurance-based source relying on membership of unemployment benefit associations;[35] and Basic Social Assistance, *Kontanthjælp*, provided by the local municipality, for those who are not members hence not insured. More than 70 percent of employees are members of an unemployment insurance fund.[36] Unemployment insurance is almost fully state-financed, with a

35 Now independent of trade unions and available across industries.

36 *Mailand, Mikkel/Larsen, Trine P.*, Study: Hybrid Work – Social Protection of Atypical Employment in Denmark, WSI Institute of Economic and Social Research, Hans-Böckler-Stiftung, March 2018, p. 5, https://www.boeckler.de/pdf/p_wsi_studies_11_2018.pdf. Accessed 21 July 2020.

small fee-based contribution. Membership fees are tax-deductible, i.e. supplementing state-financing. The rules on Unemployment Insurance Benefits (UIB) are provided in the Act on Unemployment Insurance.[37]

In 2018, the unemployment insurance system underwent a substantial reform with a view to adapting the system to the changed labour market reality.[38] The system now focuses on the *activities* of a person, rather than on the *employment status* of a person. The amendment was a response to recommendations by the Disruption Council, which pointed to the rigidity of the existing categorisation of persons as either employees or as self-employed in two separate pillars in the system, which was not reflecting the modern pattern of fragmented or atypical employments.[39] The reform entailed that all income earned can be cumulated towards being eligible for unemployment benefits. This adapts the current system of unemployment insurance benefits to the work reality of persons in atypical employments, including self-employment.

All forms of work count, i.e. either self-employed work, A-employment (primary employment), B-employment (supplementary employment), or honorarium-based employment. The assessment of income generated from either self-employed or employed work in the Act on Unemployment Insurance is aligned with the definition in tax law.[40] Any activity with the purpose of generating income on the basis of personal work activities can be viewed as self-employment if one of five criteria is met. One of these criteria is registration with the Central Business Registry, unless the tax authorities tax the income as salaries in employment.[41] Registration with the Central Business Registry is a prerequisite for contracting as a self-employed person in Denmark. Registration is carried out online via a simple registration of information without a test, it is immediate and completely free of charge. Having registered a business with the Central Business Registry is not in itself decisive for the status as genuinely self-employed in relation to unemployment benefits, but an individual assessment of the status should be carried out. The tax authority's assessment is a primacy-of-

37 Statutory Act No. 199 of 11 March 2020 on Unemployment Insurance.

38 Statutory Amendment Act No. 1670 of 20 December 2017 to the Act on Unemployment Insurance.

39 See Proposal for Amendment to the Act on Unemployment Insurance, L88, 2017-18, https://www.ft.dk/samling/20171/lovforslag/l88/index.htm. Accessed 21 July 2020.

40 Section 57a of the Act on Unemployment Insurance.

41 Section 57a (1) of the Act on Unemployment Insurance.

facts test, to a large extent resembling the labour law assessment of employment status.[42]

Membership of an Unemployment Insurance Association for one year is a prerequisite for unemployment benefits.[43] Everyone, regardless of employment status can be a member of an unemployment insurance fund, also self-employed persons. A person seeking unemployment insurance benefits must first of all be unemployed. For self-employed persons, whose work under self-employed status is the primary or sole source of income, this requires the person to close and liquidate all self-employed activities.[44] If the self-employed work is a secondary or supplementing source of income, the relevant activities must be reduced. In order to be eligible for benefits, the person must document a connection to the labour market. This must be documented in the form of an accumulated income over the last three years, a total of DKK 233,376 in 2019 (EUR 31,117). All income earned as an employee as well as income earned as a self-employed person are accumulated towards meeting the income level. Supplementing work also counts.[45] In order to count income from "employment", the work must be performed in a traditional employment relationship, i.e. on terms similar to pay and working conditions in collective agreements for the type of work performed.[46] Hours worked in non-standard work relationships, where the salaries are not similar to those in collective agreements, such as is the case for most platform workers, would in this regard not count as hours in "employment".

The rate of benefits is calculated as hourly rates on the basis of all income within a set reference period.[47] All types of registered income are accumulated to form the basis for calculating the rate of benefits.[48] Unemployment benefits can be granted as *supplementing unemployment benefits* for persons temporarily in part-time employment.[49] Supplementing unem-

42 Tax Legal Guidelines 2020-21, C.C.1.2.1 Self-Employed Work, Delimitation towards Employees, https://skat.dk/skat.aspx?oID=2048530&chk=216701. Accessed 21 July 2020.

43 Statutory Act No. 1213 of 11 October 2018 on Unemployment Insurance.

44 Sections 13 and 20 of Executive Order No. 1182 of 26 September 2018 on Self-Employment in the Social Security System.

45 Section 53 (3) and (15) of the Act on Unemployment Insurance.

46 Section 53 (6) of the Act on Unemployment Insurance.

47 Section 46 (1) and Section 49 (2) of the Act on Unemployment Insurance.

48 Section 53 (15) of the Act on Unemployment Insurance, and preparatory works to the Amendment Act No. 88 of 17 November 2017, p. 13.

49 Section 59 of the Act on Unemployment Insurance.

ployment benefits are available for a period of up to 30 weeks.[50] Only persons performing work in part-time employment or in self-employment as a secondary or supplementing source of income can be eligible for supplementing unemployment benefits. Genuinely self-employed persons whose main or sole income is under self-employed status, such as is the case for some platform workers, cannot receive supplementing unemployment benefits.

Access to Unemployment Insurance Benefits for workers in non-standard work, such as platform workers and workers providing work in a number of work-relations, is in principle more flexible now, as eligibility and calculation of benefits can be based on an accumulated income from any type of work, employed as well as self-employed. However, income from employment can only be included, if it is earned on terms similar to those in collective agreements, which primarily refers to a certain level of remuneration. This is an obstacle, as e.g. much non-standard work, including most forms of platform work, is not remunerated at the level of collective agreements. Income received by workers under self-employed status can count fully towards being eligible for unemployment benefits and towards calculating the rate of unemployment benefits that can be received. A genuinely self-employed person who has a business as his or her primary source of income must however cease activities in the business before being eligible for such benefits. If persons in non-standard work are eligible for unemployment insurance, supplementing unemployment benefits can be awarded for up to 30 weeks if these persons temporarily work part-time. If work under self-employed status generates the primary income, supplementing unemployment benefits cannot be awarded.

4. Cash Benefits

Basic Cash Benefits, *Kontanthjælp,* are provided by the local municipality, for those who do not receive unemployment insurance. The Cash Benefit rate is significantly lower than unemployment insurance rates. The rules on Cash Benefits are provided in the Act on an Active Social Policy.[51] The Act on an Active Social Policy was not amended as part of the unemployment insurance reform. The Act on an Active Social Policy continues to categorise persons as either employees or as a self-employed.

50 Section 60 of the Act on Unemployment Insurance.
51 Act on Active Social Policy No. 981 of 23 September 2019.

Cash Benefits are available to persons who are unable to provide for themselves, including by way of savings, who are not provided for by a family member, and who do not receive other benefits.[52] Eligibility is based on assessment of the current financial situation of the household, i.e. it is means-tested. In order to be eligible, the person must have had ordinary full-time employment for 2.5 years within the last 10 years.[53] Furthermore, the person must be available for job offers, and must actively pursue employment.[54] Actively pursuing employment for persons that are married or who have received Cash Benefits for one year requires a demonstration of a minimum of 225 working hours within the preceding year.[55] These working hours can be accrued via employment on terms similar to those in collective agreements[56] via self-employment as a supplementing source of income[57] or via substantive self-employment with activities of a minimum of 18.5 hours per week.[58] For the self-employed, the hours are calculated on the basis of annual income from the business in the preceding calendar year.[59] Access to Cash Benefits furthermore requires that the applicant is unemployed and available for work. For self-employed persons, this means that the company has to be shut down.

For workers in non-standard employment, such as platform workers, access to Cash Benefits requires that the applicant has held ordinary employment for 2 years and 6 months within the last 10 years. Furthermore, when the worker has received Cash Benefits for one year, or if the worker is married, the worker must in addition document 225 working hours within the preceding year. The 225 working hours can be performed in employment, but only hours performed on terms similar to those in collective agreements count, i.e. not hours provided by performing work via a digital platform. Alternatively, the 225 working hours can be performed to generate secondary income as a self-employed person, or in terms of substantial self-employment if the work is carried out during at least 18.5 hours per week. Platform work that is substantial genuine self-employed platform work

---

52 Section 11 (2) of the Act on Active Social Policy.

53 Section 11 (8) of the Act on Active Social Policy. Certain groups, such as young persons who have not had the opportunity to work 2.5 years, are subject to different criteria.

54 Section 13 (1) and 13a of the Act on Active Social Policy.

55 Section 13f (6) and (7) of the Act on Active Social Policy. If this requirement is not met, the rates are reduced, cf. Section 13f (2).

56 Section 13f (14) of the Act on Active Social Policy.

57 Section 13f (15) of the Act on Active Social Policy.

58 Section 13f (16) of the Act on Active Social Policy.

59 Section 11 (9) of the Act on Active Social Policy.

would in this case count towards the 225 working hours. Ministerial guidelines provide, as a starting point, that work performed via digital platforms counts as self-employed working time.[60] The company of the platform worker would, accordingly, have to be shut down in order for the respective worker to be eligible for Cash Benefits.

There have been no accounts of the situation of platform workers that had their profile with a platform company deactivated temporarily or permanently by unilateral decision on the part of the platform company. This presents a new situation, where the assessment of the status of the platform worker would most likely depend on the circumstances of the deactivation decision. A permanent deactivation made unilaterally by the platform company resembles a termination in employment. Deactivations of self-employed platform workers would influence only the provision of work via that particular platform, and as assessment of being genuinely self-employed is not dependent on the business relationship with one customer only, this would not in itself be sufficient to document that a genuinely self-employed platform worker has ceased business. The platform worker could already be – or could choose to be – registered with another platform company providing the same kind of services. As mentioned, this has not yet been assessed by administrative or judicial review.

5. Retirement Pensions

Pensions in Denmark consist of public and private pension programs, in a three-pillar system: state-funded public old-age pension, employer/employee funded private occupational pensions, and employee-funded private pensions. About 90 percent of all workers have supplementary private pensions, either in the form of occupational pension plans or individual pension plans.

The public old-age pension scheme is a universal, residence-based, non-contributory, statutory old-age pension scheme, regulated in the Act on Social Pensions.[61] The public old age pension scheme is designed to secure a decent minimum standard of living for all citizens of pension age. The pension is paid out to everyone who resides in Denmark and who has lived

60 Ministry of Employment. Statement in Collaborative Economy and the Basic Social Assistance System. Statement No. 9433 of 14 June 2018, https://www.ft.dk/samling/20171/almdel/BEU/bilag/378/1911151.pdf. Accessed 28 July 2020.

61 Act on Social Pensions No. 983 of 23 September 2019.

in Denmark for a significant part of their working life, currently amounting to 30 years between the age of 15 and retirement age.[62] The public old age pension scheme consists of a flat-rate benefit. In 2020, the age for being eligible for public pension is 66 years (planned to increase over the next decades). The public pension is the same for retired employees and retired self-employed persons, irrespective of any earlier income sources and levels. The number of years of permanent residency influences the rate.[63] Depending on marital status, household income and/or income earned, the flat-rate can be supplemented or reduced.[64] This includes reduction for income earned via platform work performed as an employed or self-employed person.

Occupational pension schemes are provided in collective agreements, often as industry-specific plans with an appointed pension provider.[65] Occupational pension schemes are applicable only to employees who work in a company that is covered by a collective agreement. If provided, the employer is obliged to make pension contributions to the agreed private pension fund of the employee. Payment to the employees directly, as part of their salaries, would be a breach of the collective agreement. Employer contributions are typically set at a percentage in addition to the salaries, e.g. 5-15 percent in private employment and 10-17 percent in public employment. The employee also contributes, typically with half of the employer's percentage, which is withdrawn from the salaries and deposited in the pension fund alongside the employer's contribution. Employee deposits are tax-deductible. The collective agreement determines which groups of employees are covered. This could include traditional employees as well as freelancers working on terms similar to employees. Genuinely self-employed persons do not have access to the occupational pension schemes provided in collective agreements. Genuinely self-employed platform workers must make their own private pension agreement, and pay the pension contributions out of their own earnings.

---

62 Section 2 and 3 of the Act on Social Pensions. The number of required years of residence for being eligible fluctuates over time with the political climate.

63 Section 5 of the Act on Social Pensions.

64 Section 15 and 27 of the Act on Social Pensions.

65 Except for Civil Servants, *Tjenestemænd*, who are a special group of public employees (approx. 6.50 percent of public employees, approx. 1.95 percent of the entire workforce). Source: Statistics Denmark, Work, Income and Assets Tables 2018 with a special public retirement scheme. In 2018, the number of *Tjenestemænd* was 54,640, out of 832,557, being 6.56 percent of all public employees, i.e. is approx. 30 percent of the entire work force in 2018.

Platform workers who are employees or "false self-employed" persons could technically be covered by a collective agreement. Collective agreements can obligate the platform company to make contributions to occupational pension schemes of the platform workers' choice, including mandatory contributions from the platform worker. In reality, by far most platform workers are not covered by an occupational pension scheme, obligating the employer to make pension contributions in addition to their salary. Platform workers who are not covered by a collective agreement do not receive pension contributions paid by the employer. They are left to make their own savings from their remuneration.

Private pension schemes can be established by self-employed persons and employees alike. The terms are set by the private pension provider. Deposits into pension plans with life-long payments are tax-deductible. Deposits into pension saving accounts with lump sum payments (or a set number of payments) are tax-deductible up to a certain amount each year. Due to the character of non-standard work with fluctuating income, such as platform work with irregular earnings, it can be difficult to engage in a private pension plan with set contributions each month.

The overall question for platform workers with regard to retirement pensions is whether they do engage in private pension schemes supplementing the public old-age retirement pension, as does 90 percent of the workforce in Denmark. Very few platform workers are covered by a collective agreement with provisions on mandatory employer contributions. In reality, it is the platform workers themselves who must take the initiative to establish a private pension plan with a pension provider of their choice. As a private pension scheme is established at the initiative of the worker rather than set in a collective agreement at the commencement of employment also in younger years, it is likely that this takes place only at a later stage in their career. It is a simple fact that very few young people choose to start their own pension plan at the beginning of their career. A second issue is the question of earning interests on the pension deposits, as there could be a difference between the industry-wide occupational pension schemes with appointed pension providers, and the privately established pension schemes with any form of pension provider. Workers who generate their main income through platform work over a large portion of their lives are likely left with considerably less in pension income compared to the average workers in Denmark.

6. Occupational Injury Insurance

Statutory acts mandate employers to contribute to the public occupational injury insurance system as well as take out private occupational accident insurance. Any size employer must insure their employees. This duty rests also with self-employed persons who are their own employer.

Liability for industrial injuries is regulated by the Workers' Compensation Act.[66] The Workers' Compensation Act covers persons engaged to perform work for an employer in Denmark.[67] The work can be paid or unpaid and may be permanent, temporary, or casual. The employer is under a duty to take out occupational accident insurance and contribute to the public occupational injury insurance for all employees.[68] The Workers' Compensation Act grants employees a number of compensatory benefits in case of injuries incurred when performing work, *inter alia* compensation for loss of ability to work and compensation for permanent injuries. If an employer has not taken out insurance as prescribed, and one of the employees becomes injured at work, the public Labour Market Insurance will provide the benefits to the employee irrespective of the violation by the employer.[69] The funds are then retrieved by the Labour Market Insurance from the employer.

The Workers' Compensation Act applies to employers. An employer is defined as the entity with an economic interest in the work as well as having the right to instruct and control the work. If this is not clear, an entity can be the responsible employer under the Act according to an overall assessment of the social and occupational status of the parties.[70] In this, the formal setup of the self-employed company is assessed as well as the relationship between the self-employed and the alleged employee. The assessment takes into consideration the social purposes of the Act in the interest of general society. Genuinely self-employed persons are not covered by the definition of employee in the Act, and are not insured by an employer. Instead, genuinely self-employed persons have the option of voluntarily tak-

---

66 Act on Workers' Compensation No. 977 of 9 September 2019.

67 Section 2 (1) of the Act on Workers' Compensation.

68 Sections 48 and 50 of the Act on Workers' Compensation.

69 Section 52 of the Act on Workers' Compensation.

70 This was established in early case law under the Act e.g. Supreme Court ruling U.1920.529 H, cf. detailed analysis in *Magnus Nørgaard, Sørensen*, Platformsøkonomien og arbejdsskadesikringsloven, 2018, https://law.au.dk/fileadmin/Jura/dokumenter/forskning/rettid/Afh_2018/afh27-2018.pdf. Accessed 28 July 2020.

ing out an insurance for themselves.[71] If the genuinely self-employed person has not taken out insurance against occupational injury, the costs must be borne by themselves in case of injury, unless a third party is liable for the injury according to personal injury law.

For platform workers this entails, that the platform company can be viewed as the employer, due to a traditional assessment of the relationship between the platform worker and the platform company, including an assessment of the degree of instruction and control of the platform company. If this is not clear, the formal company setup of the platform worker will be considered as part of an overall assessment. In addition, the overall protective purpose of the regulation will be considered as part of the overall assessment. For this reason, the platform company is, in relation to industrial injury insurance, more likely to be assessed as an employer under the Workers' Compensation Act due to the protective purpose of the regulation. Platform companies could be obliged under the Workers' Compensation Act to provide coverage for platform workers who provide services as self-employed persons but without a formal business setup outside of the relation to the platform company. If a platform company has an injury in connection with work and the platform company has not taken out industrial injury insurance, the Labour Market Insurance will cover the payments incurred to the platform worker, and have the payments reimbursed by the platform company. Genuinely self-employed platform workers are not covered by the definition of employee in the Act, and are not automatically insured by an employer. Instead, genuinely self-employed persons can take out voluntary occupational injury insurance for themselves. Genuinely self-employed platform workers must take out cover against the financial risk of occupational injuries themselves.

No complaints have been assessed on occupational injuries of platform workers and the question of liability of the platform company in its role as employer. Many platform companies offer a special occupational injury insurance that can be taken out by platform workers with self-employed status. The insurance scheme is provided especially for platform work by a private insurer.

71 Section 48 (2) of the Act on Workers' Compensation.

III. The Role of Social Partners in Improving Social Security for Platform Workers

Social partners participate in improving social security measures in several ways. Occupational retirement pensions with mandatory employer contributions are found only in collective agreements. Sick leave benefits are regulated by statutory acts, but some collective agreements improve the rights of the employees to receive salaries during sick leave and/or during maternity/parental leave. Furthermore, some agreements include additional work-life-balance elements, such as days off in the case of children's illness, additional days off for seniors, etc. These elements could be extended as terms of work also to platform workers, if the negotiations for collective agreements for platform workers are continued. The Danish social partners have used a number of ways to improve the social security rights of platform workers.

First of all, the social partners have a long history of being closely consulted or directly involved in tripartite negotiations with the Government and in expert committees on reforms affecting social security and the labour market. The role of the social partners representing both employers and employees is essential to the legislators when preparing regulations aimed at the labour market and is well-established in Denmark – by tacit understanding, as there is no legislation obliging the legislators to include the social partners. This is understood as making rules of a better quality and, as such, with better effects on the market, as well as with the support of employers as well as employees for reforms. This respected role in society is a preunderstanding of the social partners, and part of the goodwill in society – with rule-makers, workers and employers alike. For platform workers, this was very clear in the negotiations for the 2017 reform of the unemployment insurance system, which aimed at moving away from categorising platform work and at setting up a universal income model.

Second, the social partners extend negotiated rights in collective agreements to non-standard groups of workers. Negotiating agreements specifically for persons in non-standard work had taken place several times before the emergence of platform work, such as for e.g. *freelance* journalists and photographers. Negotiating agreements that cover platform workers has likewise taken place. Three models have been used for this: A tailor-made collective agreement for the Danish platform company *Hilfr* offering cleaning services to private users, an accession agreement with the Danish platform company *Voocali* offering translation services to private and public entities, and temporary agency work models used by the platform companies *meploy* offering logistics services, and *Chabber* offering restaurant staff temps.

The most innovative development was the negotiation of a tailor-made collective agreement for the platform company *Hilfr* as a pilot-project in 2018. The platform company *Hilfr* was set up in 2017 by three young Danes, who started the platform making use of digital technology to match small cleaning jobs with a wider audience of cleaners. The platform is the second largest platform offering cleaning services in Denmark, with 216 cleaners and 1.700 customers.[72] The entrepreneurs initiated contact with the trade unions, as a way to develop their business and give their platform a competitive edge in the market.[73] The platform company owners negotiated with 3F, the largest trade union in Denmark for unskilled workers. In 2018, the parties agreed to the *Hilfr*-agreement.

The agreement entails[74] that cleaners at the *Hilfr* platform are either *FreelanceHilfr* or *SuperHilfr*. *SuperHilfr* are covered by the agreement, *FreelanceHilfrs* are not. The agreement ensures that a *SuperHilfr* is employed by *Hilfr.dk*, and works at an hourly minimum rate of DKK 141.21 has a right to paid holidays, and to sick leave benefits. The agreement settled the issue of scope with an innovative provision stating that freelancers automatically obtain employee status as *SuperHilfrs* after 100 hours of work via the platform. However, freelancers who wish to transfer their status from freelancer to employee before having worked 100 hours can notify *Hilfr* of this, and in this case the agreement covers new work assignments accepted after the notification. Likewise, freelancers who wish to remain freelancers after 100 hours of work facilitated by the platform must inform *Hilfr* of this decision, and in this case they will not obtain employee status and will not be covered by the collective agreement. In reality, the agreement was based on a fully individual opt-in-opt-out mechanism for the individual cleaner.[75] The agreement instituted a pension plan for cleaners above the age of 20, with employer contributions at 4.15 percent and employee con-

72 https://hilfr.dk. Accessed 28 July 2020.

73 *Anna, Ilsøe*, The Hilfr Agreement, Negotiating the Platform Economy in Denmark, FAOS Research Paper No. 176, March 2018, https://faos.ku.dk/publikationer/forskningsnotater/rapporter-2019/Rapport_176_-_The_Hilfr_agreement.pdf, p. 6. Accessed 28 July 2020.

74 Collective Agreement between Hilfr ApS. CBR.no.: 37297267 and 3F Private Service, Hotel and Restaurant, 2018, https://www2.3f.dk/~/media/files/mainsite/forside/fagforening/privat%20service/overenskomster/hilfr%20collective%20agreement%202018.pdf. Accessed 28 July 2020.

75 This element was heavily criticised.

tributions at 4 percent. In addition, all employees were covered by a health care plan, also paid by employer contributions. The right to pension contributions is earned after a minimum of 320 hours of paid employment with *Hilfr* within a 3-year-period. The agreement protects against dismissal by stating that deletion or depersonalisation of the employee's profile on the platform can only take place after a 2 weeks' notice in writing, and a discretionary decision of dismissal must be based on substantial reasons relating to the company or the employee.

The *Hilfr* agreement was in force from 1 August 2018 to 31 July 2019. The parties are currently renegotiating the terms, and the provisions have been extended to cover *SuperHilfrs* in the negotiations. The agreement has shown that it is possible to create a collective agreement for platform workers that is fully adjustable to the special working situation of platform workers. However, as is clear, having a *special* agreement for platform work comes at a cost. In the *Hilfr* agreement, the cost was to sacrifice an essential principle of industrial relations, namely that the individual worker and employer cannot derogate the protections of the collective agreement to the detriment of the worker by individual opt-in-opt-out provisions. However, as mentioned, no cases have arisen since the agreement came into force in August 2018.

The pilot project has also shown that it is possible to *clarify* the status of persons providing work via digital platform by way of collective agreement. This is a supplementary aspect of concluding collective agreements that could have a normative effect also on clarifying the rights and duties between the parties in matters regulated by statutory acts, such as mandatory occupational injury insurance. The fact that the agreement determines who is an employee under the agreement could have some bearing on the public social security systems regarding eligibility – in that working hours in employment are counted towards eligibility for sick leave benefits, maternity/parental leave benefits, and towards the requirement of 225 hours of annual work for continuing to receive basic living benefits from the local municipality. The assessments under these regulations are based on the assessments of employment status carried out in labour law. The project has shown that it is possible to engage in negotiations with platform owners, with a view to establishing the working conditions for service providers along the existing Danish standards for work, specifically with regards to *social security contributions* similar to those of more standard employment relationships. The platform is to pay sick leave benefits for the first 30 days of sick leave, and to make contributions to occupational pension schemes.

A specific learning point to take home from the *Hilfr* agreements during their first year of existence was the response of the users. When booking assistance, the user can choose between a *FreelanceHilfr,* at individual hourly rates, and a *SuperHilfr* covered by the collective agreement starting at 141.21 DKK per hour. 1 out of 7 cleaners in *Hilfr*, approx. 14 percent, are *SuperHilfrs,* covered by the collective agreement.[76] Approximately 35 percent of all assignments are however carried out by a *SuperHilfr.* This large proportion indicates a preference to use *SuperHilfrs*, despite the services being performed at a higher rate. There are no empirical studies on why the end users prefer *SuperHilfrs*. Explanations could be that the users prefer to engage persons that provide work on approved terms, or to avoid circumvention of the Danish model. More details can be found in a new report on *Hilfr* agreements and lessons learned.[77]

The pilot project did not give guidance on future negotiations with more uncooperative platforms. *Hilfr.dk* initiated the negotiations by contacting the trade unions. However, the largest platform company providing cleaning services to private homes, *HappyHelper*, has refused to enter into negotiations at all. A further unclear topic is that there is yet to be a specific judicial review of the right of trade unions to engage in industrial action against digital platforms as a follow-up to potential unsuccessful negotiations with uncooperative platform companies. Earlier caselaw on non-standard workers and causal self-employed persons may suggest that industrial action is indeed possible, but caselaw has not yet confirmed this in relation specifically to non-standard workers on platforms.

Another agreement negotiated in 2018 was the *Voocali* agreement.[78] The *Voocali* agreement was an accession agreement. *Voocali.com* is an interpretation platform company which offers interpretation services to public and private entities. The agreement entails that interpreters, who are employees, are provided with all the rights of the Collective Agreement for White

---

76 32 out of 212 in all, cf. Denmarks Radio. Kun hver syvende rengøringsmedarbejder er på banebrydende overenskomst, 27 November 2019, https://www.dr.dk/nyheder/penge/kun-hver-syvende-rengoeringsmedarbejder-er-paa-banebrydende-overenskomst. Accessed 28 July 2020.

77 *Anna, Ilsøe*, The Hilfr agreement (fn. 73).

78 HK Danmark, HK indgår overenskomst med platformsvirksomhed, 1 October 2018, https://www.hk.dk/aktuelt/nyheder/2018/10/01/hk-indgaar-overenskomst-med-platformsvirksomhed. Accessed 28 July 2020. The accession agreement is available in Danish at https://www.hk.dk/-/media/dokumenter/raad-og-stoette-v2/freelancer/erklringvoocalihkprivatendelig.pdf?la=da&hash=F220F50F58285F3F4681F9AE6A81E2E716EF953C. Accessed 28 July 2020.

Collar Workers in Trade, Knowledge and Service,[79] as negotiated between *HK Privat*, the largest union for salaried employees, and *Dansk Erhverv*, the Danish Chamber of Commerce. The parties agreed to conclude a *special* collective agreement for freelance interpreters at *Voocali*.[80] This agreement entails[81] that freelance interpreters receive a guaranteed fee agreed to in the collective agreement with HK Privat, transportation supplements, a no-show fee in event of cancellation, a requirement of objective reasons for being excluded from the platform, registration of taxes for freelancers without a Business Registration Number, no restrictions with regards to carrying out assignments outside of *Voocali.com*, and data portability to take their user ratings with them. The freelance agreement did not include occupational pensions, retraining programmes, additional tax registrations, a complaints mechanism for ratings, as these elements were part of the future negotiations envisaged in mid-2018. The rates were negotiated on the basis of the salary statistics, which includes salary, holiday pay, hardship allowances, sickness pay, supplements, employee fringe benefits, pension contributions on the part of the employer, special holidays, education costs and insurance. These elements were not separated in the agreement, and the rates for the freelancers included these elements indicating that the freelancers themselves should put aside money from the salaries to cover these additional costs, also those relating to pension payments and sickness pay. The freelance agreement was in force for one year in a trial basis. The agreement was renegotiated in 2019, and now also covers police interpreters[82] providing services via *Voocali.com*.

Finally, a few platform companies have chosen to provide services under terms similar to those of the Act on Temporary Agency Workers. This is the case for the platform companies *Chabber*,[83] offering catering personnel such as bartenders, chefs, waiters and receptionists, and *meploy*, offering temporary work agents to retail, production, warehouses. *Chabber* is an

79 https://www.danskerhverv.dk/siteassets/mediafolder/dokumenter/03-overenskomster/overenskomster-2017-2020/funktionaroverenskomsten-2017-2020.

80 Standard contracts and terms for freelancers available at https://www.hk.dk/-/media/dokumenter/raad-og-stoette-v2/freelancer/appendix41.pdf?la=da&hash=62EC78D86F778B2EAC6042E523299052. Accessed 28 July 2020.

81 Appendix 7.4 to the Agreement between Voocali and HK Privat, https://www.hk.dk/-/media/dokumenter/raad-og-stoette-v2/freelancer/appendix74.pdf?la=da&hash=4F6B32877A1D5F6A50AD08129D961D6A. Accessed 28 July 2020.

82 HK Danmark, Ny aftale for polititolke skal sikre fair vilkår i nyt udbud, 29 July 2019, https://www.hk.dk/aktuelt/nyheder/2019/07/29/ny-aftale-for-polititolke-skal-sikre-fair-vilkaar-i-nyt-udbud. Accessed 28 July 2020.

83 Chabber Homepage, https://www.chabber.com/. Accessed 28 July 2020.

online freelance platform, tailor-made to the hotel and restaurant industry. Freelancers are employed by *Chabber*, and the latter platform takes care of salary payments and tax registration. Rather than direct payments between the customers and the freelancers, the company ProLøn[84] has tailored a solution so salaries are paid out by *Chabber* to the freelancers. In *Chabber's* Terms and Conditions the user entity is defined as the employer, obliging the user entity to pay the *Chabber* employee all benefits under the collective agreement applicable at the user entity, with *Chabber* administrating the payments and registrations. *meploy* is a Danish platform company matching the needs of temporary workers in the retail, warehouse and production sectors. *meploy* is set up like a temporary work agency. The temporary work agencies provide services based on an equality principle, meaning that temporary agency workers will receive salaries and benefits similar to those of the other workers in the user entity. If the user entity is covered by a collective agreement, *Chabber* and *meploy* will receive these rates. If the user entity is not covered by a collective agreement, *Chabber* and *meploy* will receive the rates of the other workers in the user entity. *Chabber* and *meploy* do not have their own collective agreements for the temporary agency workers, and as such any right to pension contributions, sickness pay, and other benefits depends entirely on the user entity. *meploy* is a member of Dansk Industri, the Confederation of Danish Industry, a private business and employers' organisation representing approximately 11,000 companies in Denmark.[85]

However, the biggest amendment to the social security status of non-standard workers and the self-employed was not the platform agreements but the statutory amendment in 2017 for unemployment insurance. In this regard, the important and essential role of the social partners in tripartite negotiation and consultation with the Government in any matters relating to the labour market and social security system was evident and also a prerequisite for aiming to make the interaction between the labour market and the social security system a smooth and dynamic match. The unemployment insurance reform was a good example, and the reform could be seen as a consequence of unemployment insurance traditionally being an issue provided by the trade union membership and insurance-based. The sick leave benefit and maternity/parental leave benefit scheme, however, have not yet been reformed to match the new labour market. This lack of

84 https://proloen.dk/kundecases/chabber/. Accessed 28 July 2020.
85 DI Digital, meploy, 1 April 2019, https://www.danskindustri.dk/brancher/di-digital/nyhedsarkiv/manedens-medlem/meploy/. Accessed 28 July 2020.

reform could be explained by the fact that these types of benefits are seen as traditionally part of a fully public social benefit system, rather than related to trade union membership or insurance.

For social security rights, in order to counteract abuses, only hours earned in employment that resembles the terms provided by collective agreements used to be counted towards being eligible. This element is of less significance in the reformed unemployment insurance system, as the focus switched to *income*, which can be accumulated from any type of work, rather than *status*. The element is still significant with regard to all other social security measures. However, as illustrated, being covered by a collective agreement improves the retirement pensions of employees compared to pension rights following from statutory legislation only. Mandatory employer contributions to the occupational pension schemes of their employees follow only from collective agreements. These schemes in collective agreements are normative also for employment relationships that are not covered by collective agreements. Employers not covered by a collective agreement sometimes opt to offer company-level pension schemes as an avenue to attract and keep qualified employees, either as a company policy or negotiated in the individual employment contracts. For platform workers, however, there are no indications that they are offered occupational pension plans or similar in their contracts. Occupational pensions are still left to the private initiative of the platform worker.

Likewise, many collective agreements improve the rights during sick leave by providing a right to sickness pay. Salaries during sick leave and partial salaries during maternity/parental leave are provided for white collar workers in the White Collar Workers' Act. Collective agreements can extend these rights to other groups of workers not covered by the White Collar Workers' Act. Salaries during maternity/parental leave likewise have a normative effect for relationships not covered by a collective agreement, as an employee benefit provided by the company.

Additionally, collective agreements often improve the work-life balance of employees, e.g. by providing periods with paid leave during maternity/parental leave, or days off in case of children's sickness. These provisions are mandatory only for employers covered by a collective agreement stipulating these rights. However, the provisions are normative also for employment/self-employment not covered by a collective agreement. This can be either in the form of general company level policies to this end, or of negotiated provisions in individual employment contracts. There is, however, no indication that such work-life balancing provisions have as yet been part of the regulations of platform companies.

The categorisation of the platform workers is still unclear and heavily debated by practitioners, tax authorities, social security authorities, and labour lawyers. Recently, the competition law authorities have established a task force monitoring digital platforms as potentially in breach of competition law. In August 2020, the Competition Authority task force issued their first ruling on the platforms *HappyHelper* and *Hilfr*.[86] Both platforms were found in breach of competition law by posting minimum prices for the services on their websites, concerning the platform workers who are genuine self-employed. For *Hilfr*, the Competition Authority did not find that the current collective agreement established "an employment situation" as understood in competition law. The *Hilfr* platform agreed to ensure that the persons covered by the collective agreement are more clearly "employed". The implications of this ruling and development are not yet certain.

At the same time, the social partners and the platform companies themselves have made significant progress in Denmark with regards to ensuring decent working conditions for platform workers, as well as some progress in including social security measures alongside. The drivers of this development have primarily been the platforms themselves, wanting to use digital technology to meet the demands of the market and at the same time ensure decent working conditions for the platform workers. The public discourse on the status of platform workers and the role of collective agreements has likewise intensified over the last years. There is an ongoing dialogue between the trade unions and the platforms, with a view to informing the platforms about certain problems for the service providers. Negotiations for new collective agreements are currently taking place with the delivery platform *JustEat*.[87]

IV. Conclusion

The Danish experience with improving the social security of platform workers yields a number of learning points. First of all, the drivers in the first wave of platform companies and collective agreements were the platform companies themselves, looking to align their company with the Danish model as well as to create a competitive edge to their platform with the

86 https://www.kfst.dk/pressemeddelelser/kfst/2020/20200826-rengoringsplatforme-fjerner-minimumspriser/. Accessed 28 July 2020.

87 *Anna, Ilsøe*, The Hilfr Agreement (fn. 73), p. 18.

customers. The first wave of collective agreements used different strategies for providing the platform workers with basic working conditions, i.e. the tailor-made collective agreement of *Hilfr.dk*, the accession agreement of *Voocali* with a tailormade freelance agreement as a supplement, and the temporary agency strategies of *Chabber* and *meploy*. Across these attempts, the focus was on essential working terms rather than social security measures. In particular, the lack of mandatory employer pension contributions is clear, as is sickness pay and pay during maternity/parental leave. To this end, the *Hilfr.dk* and *Voocali.com* agreements are still pending, whereas *Chabber* and *meploy* delegate these matters to the user entity in principle providing the platform workers with a better coverage and additional benefits – at par with the standard workers with the user entity.

Second, the lack of focus on social security matters could be seen in continuance of the reform of the unemployment insurance system in 2017, changing a system of accruing working *hours* in either employment or self-employment in order to be eligible for unemployment benefits, to a system of accrual of rights based on universal income. The reform received a lot of public attention, as it was the first tangible result of the work in the highly promoted Disruption Council of the former Government. However, as has been described above, the reform is still experiencing systemic setbacks for platform workers.

Collective agreements for platform workers *can* improve social security in areas where the public system is less strong, such as in areas with a low public system for platform workers, most notably retirement pensions. Also in areas where the public system is not yet aligned smoothly with new ways of providing work, such as sick leave and maternity/parental leave benefits, and occupational injury insurance, collective agreements could clarify the status of platform workers and in this way assist their accrual of rights in the public benefits system. Most influential to the social security of platform workers was, however, the amendment to the statutory act on unemployment insurance changing the accrual method to universal income from all types of work, rather than single-employment-based accrual either in employment or self-employment.

The outcomes from the first attempts are varied. The uncertain status of platform workers has spurred attention also from the competition authorities. For the sake of the companies and of the platform workers as well as the users and broader society, it would be recommended that the stakeholders engage in dialogue on how to assess and distinguish between freelancers working on terms more similar to employees and freelancers working on terms more similar to genuine self-employment via the platforms. This clarification and understanding could also pave the way for more collective agreements for platform workers as the preferred avenue of improving not only the basic working conditions of platform workers, but also their overall social security coverage in their active work life, when injured at work, when on sick-leave and maternity/parental leave, and during their retirement.

The involvement of social partners in the rulemaking of the legislators, the invitation to be part of the consulting and negotiation of new initiatives is probably the most influential element. The social partners are always close to new developments and influence the systemic choices of the legislators. This cooperation is not based on any legally binding instruments, but is at the free choice of the legislators at any time. This influenced the 2017 reform of the unemployment benefit insurance system, and recently resulted in a historic proposal by the social partners to the legislators for statutory regulation of minimum pay in the transportation industry for foreign transporters with a view to counteracting abuse and circumvention of the collective agreements in this specific sector.[88] Such dual and tripartite negotiations could perhaps over time also open up further dialogue at the political level to provide solutions for platform workers. There are still questions outstanding with regard to collective agreements and platform workers, such as the lawfulness of collective action against platform companies and, in this respect, the status of the platform workers, how categorisations of the platform workers in collective agreements can influence assessments in the public social security system. There have been no complaints reviewed under the *Hilfr* agreement or the *Voocali* agreement.

The platform companies in Denmark provide services within all areas. The work performed is not new, but the form of organising the work is new and based on digital technology which has a number of administrative benefits. The work is performed on non-standard contracts; however, this is not necessarily precarious work. Some platform companies offer services by highly skilled workers, some offer services in highly regulated areas, and some in less regulated and more at-risk areas. Platform companies are different and vary in their social and commercial outlook, much like other types of companies. In this, the platform companies represent a new form of company model rather than new forms of work. The need for social security of persons performing work has likewise not changed – persons are still in need for social security. The fragmentation of work pat-

---

88 Aftale om vejtransport, January 2020, https://www.bm.dk/media/12316/aftale-om-vejtransport.pdf. Accessed 28 July 2020.

terns, as well as the uncertain and fragmented categorisation of the status of platform workers under the variety of social security regulation and collective agreements, contribute to the social security status of platform workers being indeed very uncertain. The steps forward taken by the Danish Government and the social partners in providing the 2017 reform of unemployment insurance, as well as by the social partners in testing collective agreements tailormade for platform workers have definitely improved the status. However, the agreements were made with friendly platform owners, and so far no industrial action has been taken against more uncooperative platform companies in Denmark. Also, the preliminary results focused on parts of the social security system and parts of social security provisions in the collective agreement. The learning points and good results from these processes could form a better starting point for the next wave of focus on the rights of platform workers – their overall standing in the social security system in Denmark, allowing them to be part of the Danish flexicurity system also when utilising the new digital forms of flexible work made possible by platform work.

Chapter 8
Looking for the (Fictitious) Employer – Umbrella Companies: The Swedish Example

Annamaria Westregård

I. Introduction

A new business model – a version of the umbrella company, or *egenanställningsföretag* as they are called in Swedish – has been adopted in Sweden.[1] It is not a new phenomenon – it was first seen in Sweden during the 1990s[2] – but it was not until the collaborative economy developed that the industry grew, as the business model suits the digitalised world well.[3] In the collaborative economy some platforms assign umbrella companies as middlemen to handle the transactions between the umbrella company worker and the client (service consumer).[4] The parties rarely meet in real life: all contacts

1 Eurofound, New Forms of Employment, Publications Office of the European Union, Luxembourg, 2015, pp. 118 ff., https://www.eurofound.europa.eu/sites/default/files/ef_publication/field_ef_document/ef1461en.pdf. Accessed 12 September 2020, those companies are called umbrella companies. See also Government White Paper SOU 2017:24, Ett arbetsliv i förändring – hur påverkas ansvaret för arbetsmiljön?, pp. 159 ff.

2 For more on the historical development of umbrella companies in Sweden see Government White Paper SOU 2017:24 (fn. 1), pp. 159 ff.

3 It is difficult to determine how widespread the business model is and how many umbrella company workers there currently are. According to the branch organisation, the number of umbrella company employees grew from 4,000 in 2011 to 44,000 in 2017 (see homepage of the Egenanställningsföretagens Branschorganisation, http://www.egenanstallning.org/index/news. Accessed 19 June 2019), and according to the Government White Paper SOU 2017:24 (fn. 1), p. 167, 18,650 persons worked at 7 (big) umbrella companies in 2015. There were approximately 29,500 active umbrella company workers in 2018 and 32,300 during 2019, according to the Swedish Statistic Service (SCB), https://www.scb.se/AM0103. Accessed 19 June 2020. In this book chapter the focus is not on the number of workers but on the fact that it is a phenomenon that exists and is here to stay.

4 The term *service consumer* is used in the same way as in the European Commission, Communication from the Commission to the European Parliament, the Council, the European Economic and Social Committee and the Committee of the Regions. A European Agenda for the Collaborative Economy, COM (2016) 356 final, of 2

between them are conducted electronically. The Swedish umbrella companies' business model is that the umbrella company worker (to be) finds an assignment. He either bids for work on a digitalised platform or finds it in some other way. If successful, the umbrella company worker (to be) negotiates both the working conditions and the remuneration with the client. The umbrella company worker (to be) then makes sure the client has signed a contract with the umbrella company. The umbrella company worker is employed by the umbrella company on a short fixed-term employment contract for the duration of the assignment. When the work is done the client is invoiced by the umbrella company. Once the client has paid the umbrella company, the platform worker is credited his remuneration, after deductions for tax, social security contributions, and the umbrella company's commission.[5]

Umbrella companies are promoted as an easy way for people who do not want the administrative burden of having a company of their own, to work and concentrate on their work performance instead of on administration. Umbrella companies attract many different types of performing parties, both in the digitalised economy and in the "old" economy in traditional freelance sectors like journalism, acting etc. In Sweden, it is the employer and not the employee who pays taxes and social security contributions to the Swedish Tax Agency. Self-employed persons with a Business Tax Certificate pay themselves and the administrative burden of being self-employed is significant compared to that of being an employee. There are, from a social security perspective, no particular reasons for using umbrella companies since e.g. the social security fees are the same for employees and self-employed persons.

Swedish umbrella companies have a trade organisation where membership is conditioned on companies taking responsibility for the performing parties during the time they are working.[6] The organisation's point of view is that the performing parties are employed by the umbrella companies for the duration of their assignments and that the umbrella companies take full responsibility for their umbrella company workers. Umbrella com-

---

June 2016, p. 3, https://ec.europa.eu/transparency/regdoc/rep/1/2016/EN/1-2016-356-EN-F1-1.PDF. Accessed 20 August 2020.

5 See Government White Paper SOU 2017:24 (fn. 1), p. 161 ff, p. 198; the Swedish Tax Agency, https://www.skatteverket.se/privat/skatter/arbeteochinkomst/inkomster/egenanstallning. Accessed 15 June 2020; Eurofound, New Forms of Employment (fn. 1), p. 120.

6 See homepage of the Egenanställningsföretagens Branschorganisation, http://www.egenanstallning.org. Accessed 30 March 2020.

panies of a similar construction can be found in France and Austria.[7] In France and Austria the employment in itself does, however, not seem to be as important for the umbrella companies' identity as it is in Sweden. In France, *portage salarial* is described as a construction in between employment and self-employment.[8] In contrast to the Swedish system, *portage salarial* in France is regulated in the statutory legislation.[9] In Sweden, there is no particular regulation about umbrella companies, so it is the already existing legislation that applies to umbrella companies. In Austria, some of the umbrella companies are described as not-for-profit organisations.[10] That is not a suitable description of umbrella companies in Sweden, which make up a special business model in a particular niche of the labour market. Their reason for handling administration is that they are commercial companies that make their profit by charging a percentage of the worker's income.[11] Platform and other companies that do not want to employ employees need a middleman who can take on the responsibilities of the employer during assignments. This explains the demand for umbrella company services in the collaborative economy.

In Section II, I will analyse the legal prerequisites in Swedish labour legislation for the umbrella companies' business model and the concept of employment in labour law. I will then analyse the concept of employment in social security legislation, and the particular gaps and problems in the social security system and in unemployment insurance for umbrella company workers in Section III. In Section IV, the importance of supplemental social security benefits in industry-wide collective agreements are presented. In Section V, I will present conclusions. I will, for instance, analyse the umbrella companies' role as employers and in whose interest they operate. I will also analyse the business model's significance for the social security protection of umbrella company workers with the intention of determining whether or not umbrella companies are a possible way of extending

7 Eurofound, New Forms of Employment (fn. 1), pp. 118 ff.

8 *Kessler, Francis*, Chapter 10: New Forms of Employment in France, in: Blanpain, Roger/Hendrickx, Frank/Wass, Bernd (eds.), New Forms of Employment in Europe. Bulletin of Comparative Labour Relations Series Volume 9, Alphen aan den Rijn: Wolters Kluwer 2016, pp. 203 f.

9 Article 8 of the Law of 2008; see *Kessler, Francis*, Chapter 10: New Forms of Employment in France (fn. 8), p. 203 f.

10 Eurofound, New Forms of Employment (fn. 1), pp. 118 ff.

11 Frilands Finans e.g. charges 6 per cent, see homepage of Frilands Finans, https://www.frilansfinans.se/fragor-och-svar/. Accessed 18 July 2020.

the social security protection to include this group of vulnerable employees and self-employed persons.

II. Legal Prerequisites in Swedish Labour Legislation for the Umbrella Company Business Model

1. Basics

The Swedish variety of umbrella companies does not exist in the other Nordic countries, in spite of the fact that these countries have seen similar developments in the collaborative economy.[12] There might be several reasons for this. In this section, I will analyse the prerequisites in Swedish labour legislation that have created a demand for this particular business model and the statutory regulations that have aided its emergence.

The Swedish legislation is built on a binary system where the performing party is either employed or self-employed. The concept of employment in the 1982 Employment Protection Act is wide and covers both the concept of "workers" and that of "employees" as referred to in other countries.[13] The Swedish Labour Court has not yet[14] decided on any cases where they have had to determine whether umbrella company workers and platform workers are employees according to the concept of the employee in the 1982 Employment Protection Act, or whether they are self-employed. It may very well be the case that the Labour Court will regard the relationship between the umbrella company and the umbrella company worker as one of employment with a short fixed-term contract. If the statutory act only allowed permanent full-time employment, there would be no legal prerequisites for the business model. In this respect, the 1982

12 Eurofound, New Forms of Employment (fn. 1), pp. 118 ff. and *Hotvedt, Marianne Jenum/Munkholm, Natalie Videbæk*, Labour Law in the Future of Work, Fafo-paper 2019:06, https://www.fafo.no/pillar-vi. Accessed 20 August 2020.

13 The legislation in the United Kingdom, unlike in Sweden, separates employees from workers (cf. Section 230 (1)-(3) of the Employment Rights Act 1996) and the concept of the worker is broader and different from the concept of the employee, see *Kenner, Jeff*, Inverting the Flexicurity Paradigm: The United Kingdom and Zero Hours Contracts, in: Ales, Edoardo/Deinert, Olaf/Kenner, Jeff (eds.) Core and Contingent Work in the European Union: A Comparative Analysis, Oxford: Hart Publishing 2017, pp. 153-183.

14 There have been cases where the Court has had to decide whether umbrella company workers are employees in terms of the Unemployment Insurance Act, with differing results, see below.

Employment Protection Act is flexible and allows very short employment contracts and offers generous possibilities for fixed-term employment.

2. *A Wide Concept of Employment in Labour Law*[15]

The employee is identified in an overall assessment of relevant criteria.[16] The concept of employment is based on a core criterion: *a contract by which a performing party must personally perform work on behalf of another party.*[17] The core criterion is so important that it must always be present. In addition to the core criterion there are other circumstances of importance to the Labour Court when they make their overall assessment of all relevant criteria. The list varies depending on the author.[18] Examples of circumstances taken into account are:

---

15 See further *Westregård, Annamaria*, The Notion of "Employee" in Swedish and European Union Law: An Exercise in Harmony or Disharmony?, in: Carlson, Laura/Edström, Örjan/Nyström, Birgitta (eds.), Globalisation, Fragmentation, Labour and Employment Law: A Swedish Perspective, Uppsala: Iustus Förlag 2016, pp. 185-204; *Westregård, Annamaria,* Collaborative Economy: A New Challenge for the Social Partners, in: Ahlberg, Kerstin/ Herzfeld Olsson, Petra /Malmberg, Jonas (eds.), Niklas Bruun I Sverige. En vänbok, Uppsala: Iustus Förlag 2017, pp. 427-438; *Westregård, Annamaria,* Digital Collaborative Platforms: A Challenge for Social Partners in the Nordic Model, in: Nordic Journal of Commercial Law, 1 (2018), pp. 92 ff., https://doi.org/10.5278/ojs.njcl.v0i1.2486. Accessed 18 July 2020; *Westregård, Annamaria,* Key Concepts and Changing Labour Relations in Sweden, Nordic Future of Work Project 2017-2020: Working Paper 8. Pillar VI, 2019, https://www.fafo.no/pillar-vi. Accessed 20 August 2020.

16 For more about the overall assessment, see *Westregård, Annamaria*, The Notion of "Employee" in Swedish and European Union Law: An Exercise in Harmony or Disharmony? (fn. 15), pp. 185-204; *Westregård, Annamaria,* Collaborative Economy: A New Challenge for the Social Partners (fn. 15), pp. 427-438; *Westregård, Annamaria,* Digital Collaborative Platforms: A Challenge for Social Partners in the Nordic Model (fn. 15), pp. 92 ff.; *Westregård, Annamaria,* Key Concepts and Changing Labour Relations in Sweden (fn. 15).

17 Originally *Adlercreutz, Axel*, Arbetstagarbegreppet, Stockholm: Norstedts 1964, p. 186, 276 ff. and later *Malmberg, Jonas/Bruun, Niklas*, Ds. 2002:56 Hållfast arbetsrätt för ett föränderligt arbetsliv, Stockholm: Fritzes 2002, p. 111 n. 63 identified the set of relevant circumstances or criteria, all of them fundamental prerequisites (*grundrekvisit*).

18 *Adlercreutz, Axel*, Arbetstagarbegreppet (fn. 17), p. 186 and pp. 276 ff.; *Malmberg, Jonas/Bruun, Niklas*, Ds. 2002:56 Hållfast arbetsrätt för ett föränderligt arbetsliv (fn. 17), p. 111 n. 63; *Källström, Kent/Malmberg, Jonas,* Anställningsförhållandet: inledning till den individuella arbetsrätten, Uppsala: Iustus 2016, p. 26; *Sigemen, Tore/Sjödin, Erik*, Arbetsätten: En översikt, Alphen aan den Rijn: Wolter Kluwer

Is the work performed under the principal's leadership and control (salaried employment) or not (self-employment)? Is the workload measured by duration (employment) rather than by specific duties (self-employment)? Does the performing party have only one principal (salaried employment) or several (self-employment)? Who owns machinery and equipment (employees use the employer's equipment and the self-employed provide their own equipment)? What are the parties' intentions? This is a criterion of special interest when it comes to umbrella companies, as the parties have signed a fixed-term employment contract for the duration of the assignment. Does someone become an employer just because the parties have concluded an employment contract as umbrella companies and umbrella company workers do?[19]

The intention of the umbrella company and the umbrella company worker is for the umbrella company worker to have a fixed-term employment contract for the duration of the assignment. If the Labour Court has to decide whether a relation is to be considered an employment according to the 1982 Employment Protection Act, the Court balances the different interests between the contracting parties. In labour law it is the real circumstances between the parties rather than the intention of the parties or the written contract that matters most for the overall assessment. In cases of "false self-employment" the Labour Court ignores the contract. In such cases the employment contract may instead create "false employees". An umbrella company is definitely not an ordinary employer. A self-employed person could probably perform the same assignment without the umbrella company. On the other hand, it would not be problematic for the Labour Court to follow the intention of the parties, were it beneficial for the weaker party – here the umbrella company worker. In a recent Government White Paper, umbrella company workers were recognised as employees, see Section III 3 below.[20] The Swedish Labour Court has not yet had a case where they have had to decide whether umbrella company workers should be regarded as employed by the umbrella company.

2017, p. 31; *Inghammar, Andreas*, The Concept of "Employee": The Position in Sweden, Restatement of Labour Law, in: Waas, Bernd/van Voss, Guus Heerma (eds.), The Concept of Employee, Oxford: Hart Publishing 2017, p. 686; *Lunning, Lars/Toijer, Gudmund*, Anställningsskydd: En lagkommentar, 11th Edition, Alphen aan den Rijn: Wolters Kluwer 2016, p. 27.

19 *Westregård, Annamaria*, Key Concepts and Changing Labour Relations in Sweden (fn. 15), p. 9 ff.

20 Government White Paper SOU 2020:26, En sjukförsäkring anpassad efter individen, p. 62 ff.

One circumstance that speaks for a wide employment concept is that it was the legislator's intention according to the *travaux préparatoires* that the concept of employment should, in dubious cases, be interpreted as if there was an employment in hand.[21] This statement in the Bill to Parliament[22] was about the concept of employment in the 1976 Co-Determination Act (1976:580), but it has been repeated by the Supreme Court according to the 1992 Pay Guarantee Act in the case of bankruptcy.[23] Whether the interpretation principle is still valid for the Labour Court has been put into question and the principle has been found to probably not be valid when the concept is interpreted in social security legislation.[24] As we will see in Section III below, the concept of employment is interpreted differently in social security legislation than in labour law. This can prove fatal for the umbrella company worker, who can be employed by the umbrella company for the duration of the assignment but after the assignment be regarded as self-employed according to the 1997 Unemployment Insurance Act and therefore not be entitled to unemployment benefits in the same way as other short fixed-term employees.

The employer is "the party on whose behalf the employee performs work".[25] In the private sector, where the umbrella companies operate, the concept of the employer in the labour legislation is based on the *principle of the legal subject*. This means that the employer is the legal or physical person who concludes the employment contract. In this business model it is the umbrella company that signs the employment contract with the performing party and therefore is the employer according to this principle.

---

21 In Sweden, the legislation is interpreted according to the sources of the statutory acts. If the interpretation of the statutory act is unclear, the *travaux préparatoires* are important sources, particularly Government White Papers (SOU) and Bills to Parliament (*proposition*). The content of statutory acts is clarified by caselaw, and here the Labour Court's rulings are of special interest. The doctrine in the legal literature has an impact, especially the arguments about how to interpret the other sources. See *Fahlbeck, Reinhold/Sigeman, Tore,* European Employment and Industrial Relations Glossary: Sweden, London: Sweet & Maxwell 2001, p. 286 ff.

22 Bill to Parliament (prop. med förslag till arbetsrättsreform) 1975/76:105 bil. 1 pp. 309 and 324 and *Lunning, Lars/Toijer, Gudmund,* Anställningsskydd: En lagkommentar (fn. 18), p. 26.

23 Supreme Court ruling NJA 1996, p. 311.

24 *Lunning, Lars/Toijer, Gudmund,* Anställningsskydd: En lagkommentar (fn. 18), p. 26.

25 Section 1 (2) of the 1976 Co-Determination Act (1976:580).

3. No Requirement for Duration of Time

Another prerequisite in the concept of employment that is crucial for the umbrella company business model is that the labour law concept of employment in the statutory regulation (the 1982 Employment Protection Act) does not demand any *duration of time*. An employment can be very short and last only a few hours or even minutes. There are restrictions in some collective agreements that prohibit very short fixed-term employment, but as there are no collective agreements at industry or local level at the moment, there are no such restrictions for umbrella companies.[26]

4. Generous Possibilities for Fixed-Term Employment

The generous possibilities in statutory regulations for fixed-term employment in Sweden are essential for the umbrella companies' business model. The business model is that umbrella company workers have short fixed-term contracts for the duration of an assignment. This is possible due to Section 5 and 5(a) of the 1982 Employment Protection Act. The legislation

---

26 In the recent White-Collar Employee Agreement between the white-collar trade union Unionen and Almega (the employers' organisation for the Swedish service sector), there is a special form of fixed-term employment which must exceed a minimum employment period – missing in the law – of seven days, unless the employer and the employee specifically agree on a shorter period. If this rule is abused there are restrictions. The regulations concerning automatic conversion to permanent employment are extended to a total period of three years – a year more than the law requires – in a five-year period. This regulation is particularly important as it covers the service sector where a lot of the "new" precarious forms of employment exist (Section 2.2. and 2.3. of Collective agreement between Unionen and Almega concerning tech and media companies for the period 1 May 2017 to 30 April 2020. The new regulations are in Section 2.2. and valid from 1 November 2017. See also Labour Court ruling 2015 No. 50, reinterpretation of the previous rules. The regulation is the same in all Almega's 22 collective agreements for white-collar workers).
Another example is the Restaurant Collective Agreement, which regulates employment for single days (*anställning för enstaka dagar*). The employee is entitled to refuse the work offered if the minimum chargeable time is three hours a day. Here, the parties have struck a balance between the employer's interest in only having staff in place when there is work to be done, and the employee's interest in having to endure no more short fixed-term employment than is necessary and in rules for minimum hours (4 § 1.2. *Anställning för enstaka dagar* in the collective agreement between Visita and Hotel and Restaurant, HRF for the period 1 April 2017 to 31 March 2020).

allows a general fixed-term employment for a maximum of two years (within a frame of five years) and after that the employment is converted into a permanent employment. General fixed-term employment, in contrast to other forms of work, entails that employers can hire on a temporary basis without having to give particular reasons for why the positions are temporary.[27] The statutory regulation on fixed-term employment is what distinguishes Sweden from the other Nordic countries, where legislation does not to the same extent allow fixed-term employment. This is probably a crucial element of the expansion of umbrella companies in Sweden as opposed to the other Nordic countries, as the concept of employment is similar in all Nordic countries and platform work has developed at about the same level (except, so far, in Iceland).[28]

Short fixed-term employment is regarded as a problem for the employees. In a Government White Paper (SOU 2019:5 *Tid för trygghet*) the investigating committee presented a legislative proposal with the intention of improving the conditions for employees with short fixed-term employment contracts. If an employee has more than two short fixed-term employment contracts within 30 days, the time between the employment should also be regarded as employment in accordance with the 1982 Employment Protection Act and its statutory regulations about re-employment (after twelve months if the employer rehires someone within nine months)[29] and conversion to permanent employment (after two years within a frame of five years). It is currently uncertain if the proposal will be turned into legislation. Nothing in particular is said about umbrella company workers. There will be application difficulties in respect to both re-employment and conversion to permanent employment owing to the umbrella companies' special business model.

5. *Umbrella Companies and Temporary Work Agencies*

Umbrella companies operate in much the same way as temporary work agencies, with one difference being that it is the employer who decides when a temporary employee works, while an umbrella company worker

---

27 Bill to Parliament (prop. 2006/07:111 Bättre möjligheter till tidsbegränsad anställning, m.m.), p. 32; *Lunning, Lars/Toijer, Gudmund*, Anställningsskydd: En lagkommentar (fn. 18), p. 251.

28 *Hotvedt, Marianne Jenum/Munkholm, Natalie Videbæk*, Labour Law in the Future of Work (fn. 12).

29 Section 25 in the 1982 Employment Protection Act.

decides for himself when to work and then "hires" an employer. From a labour perspective, temporary agency workers in Sweden are also employed between assignments and receive a salary. The employer provides them with work. Umbrella company workers are not employed between assignments and find their own assignments. From a social security perspective umbrella company workers will have problems entering social security between their assignments as their legal status is unclear, see Section III 3 and 4 below, while temporary agency workers, who are employees, do not encounter the same problems.

If an umbrella company is judged to be a temporary work agency, the consequence is that its employees are entitled to the basic working and employment conditions set down in the end user's collective agreements and other binding general provisions.[30] The question of whether umbrella companies are covered by the 2012 Agency Work Act (2012:854) depends on the interpretation of the definition of temporary work agencies in Section 5 (1). When the statutory act was passed, umbrella companies were not mentioned in the preparatory work for the Bill to Parliament.[31] At the time, the digital economy was still in its infancy and the umbrella companies were few. According to the statutory act, temporary agency work is when a company employs temporary agency workers in order to assign them work for users, under the company's supervision and direction. If a company instead places its employees to perform a particular job under its direction for another company, then that is considered contract work, which is not covered by the 2012 Agency Work Act.[32] The decision whether a company should be considered a temporary work agency or not, must also correspond to the interpretation under the Temporary Agency Work Directive.[33] There have not yet been any cases in the Labour Court determining whether umbrella companies should be regarded as temporary work agencies in accordance with the 2012 Agency Work Act.

---

30 Sections 5 (3) and 6 in the 2012 Agency Work Act (2012:854).

31 Government White Paper SOU 2011:5, Bemanningsdirektivets genomförande i Sverige; Government Bill Prop. 2011/12:178 Lag om uthyrning av arbetstagare.

32 Government White Paper SOU 2011:5 (fn. 31), p. 55; see also Labour Court ruling 2006 No. 24 on contract versus agency work.

33 Directive 2008/104/EC of the European Parliament and the Council of 19 November 2008 on Temporary Agency Work.

III. Umbrella Companies and the Concept of Employment according to Social Security Legislation and Unemployment Insurances

1. The Concept of Employment in Social Security Legislation

The concepts of employee and employer are not defined in the same way in social security legislation as they are in labour law. There is a close connection between the concepts in social security legislation and tax law, but the concepts in labour law are different. In the social security regulations, an employee is defined as someone who has an income from employment. Income from employment or income from business is identified according to tax law.[34]

There is no general definition of the employer in tax and social security legislation, as it mirrors the concept of the employee. When needed, the concept of the employer is defined in statutory regulation. An example is statutory rule in the Social Security Act, which stipulates that remuneration of less than 1,000 SEK a year (1 EUR is around 10.50 SEK) is always regarded as income from employment and that the person (whether legal or natural) who pays the remuneration is regarded as an *employer*.[35] The main reason for identifying *the employer* in tax and social security legislation is that according to the 2000 Social Insurance Contribution Act (2000:980) *employers* pay tax and social fees for their employees. The employer's responsibility for paying tax and social fees in some cases goes beyond even the concept of employment. These responsibilities also include principals that hire independent self-employed persons without a registered firm.[36] Self-employed persons deemed to be owners of a business pay taxes and social fees themselves. In Sweden, there is little difference in social security expenses between hiring a self-employed person or having an employee do the work.[37] The umbrella companies pay both taxes and so-

34 See e.g. Supreme Court ruling NJA 1982, p. 784. Chapter 6 Section 2 and Chapter 25 Section 10 of the 2010 Social Insurance Code (2010:110) that refers to persons who according to Chapter 13 Section 1 in the 1999 Income Tax Law are approved for a Business Tax Certificate.

35 Chapter 25 Section 7 of the 2010 Social Insurance Code.

36 Chapter 2 of the 2000 Social Insurance Contribution Act (2000:980); see also *Källström, Kent,* Employment and Contract Work, in: Comparative Labour Law & Policy Journal, 21 (1999) 1, p. 162.

37 For 2020, the total mandatory employer contribution (social security fee) is 31.42 per cent of paid gross salary. It is the same for employees and for the self-employed. The employer's contribution is based on the whole income. The benefits to the individual are limited to 8 price base amounts (380,000 SEK), https://www.

cial fees for the umbrella company workers so in this sense they are employers. This does not mean that the umbrella company worker will be regarded as an employee, since the concept of the employee does not mirror the concept of the employer (see Section III 3 and 4 below about social security and unemployment benefits for umbrella company workers).

The main reason for identifying the umbrella company workers as either *employees or self-employed* in social security legislation is to decide in the binary legal system which statutory regulation about access to and the calculation of benefits will apply, as there are different regulations for employees and self-employed persons. One of the most significant and important aspects of the Swedish social security system is that the self-employed are covered in a way that does not give them the exact same protection, but similar protection to that of employees. Despite the regulations creating far from exact parity, they still offer much more protection than the social security system, from which the self-employed are excluded. As we will see in the analysis in Section III 4 and 5 below, there are still gaps and problems in both the accessing and calculation of benefits.[38]

There are also parts of the social security system that are similar for self-employed persons and employees. One example is occupational injury annuity and injury insurance. Anyone who works in Sweden is insured against occupational injury (illness and accidents at the workplace, while travelling to and from work, or at home if you have to stay at home because of an epidemic like the Covid-19 crisis).[39] The insurance is mandatory and covers both employees and self-employed persons, which means that both are entitled to occupational injury annuity if approved by the Social Insurance Agency. The insurance against occupational injury covers the self-employed, here defined as those operating a company as a simple partnership (*enskild firma*), trading partnership (*handelsbolag*) or limited

---

skatteverket.se/foretagochorganisationer/arbetsgivare/arbetsgivaravgifterochskatteavdrag/arbetsgivaravgifter.4.233f91f71260075abe8800020817.html. Accessed 7 June 2020.

38 For a more general description of the Swedish social security system for employees, self-employed and precarious workers (like platform workers and others with untraditional employment contracts), see *Westregård, Annamaria*, Protection of Platform Workers in Sweden, Nordic Future of Work Project 2017-2020: Working Paper 12. Pillar VI. 2020, https://www.fafo.no/pillar-vi. Accessed 20 August 2020.
See also *Johansson, Caroline*, Autonomous Workers and Social Security – A Swedish Example, in: Revista del Ministerio de Trabajo Migraciones y Seguridad Social, 144 (2019), pp. 89-102.

39 Chapters 39-42 in the 2010 Social Insurance Code.

partnership (*kommanditbolag*), but also assignment workers (*tillfälliga uppdragstagare*). If the classification of some employees is unclear this can pose a problem, since they may not fit into either of the insured categories (employees and self-employed persons). The aim of the Swedish legislator is to create parity in the social security system between employees and genuinely self-employed persons, but also between different business models and company structures. This can be seen in the reforms of the last decade. In 2010, social security and tax regulations were reformed with the express ambition of encouraging all types of work, including work performed in non-traditional forms.[40] Complementary reforms were initiated or carried out in 2018 and 2019.[41] The legislator also investigated the possibilities of improving the protection in the social security system with a focus on the collaborative economy and platform workers. The investigation has not resulted in any concrete suggestions of improvements since more analyses and research will be needed.[42]

2. *The "Intention of the Parties" Criterion*

Within tax law, changes were made ten years ago to facilitate the start-up of small businesses, and these changes will also affect the concept of employment in social security, since this relies on the concept in tax law. An amendment called the Reinfeldt amendment was added to Chapter 13 Section 1 of the 1999 Income Tax Act. The aim was to facilitate the issuing of

40 Legislative Bill (prop. 2009/10:120).

41 A legal change in SFS 2018:670 and Legislative Bill (prop. 2017/18:168 Stärkt försäkringsskydd för studerande och företagare); proposal for legal changes in Government White Paper SOU 2018:49, F-skattesystemet – några särskilt utvalda frågor; inquiry for new legislation in Kommittédirektiv Dir. 2017:56 Trygghet och utveckling i anställning vad gäller arbetstid och ledighet; Kommittédirektiv Dir. 2018:8 En ny arbetslöshetsförsäkring för fler, grundad på inkomst; Dir 2018:26 En trygg sjukförsäkring med människan i centrum; Government White Paper SOU 2019:2, Ingen regel utan undantag – en trygg sjukförsäkring med människan i centrum. In the inquiry for legislation, Government White Paper SOU 2019:41, Företagare i de social trygghetssystemen is the intention to create more explicit regulations for calculating SGI for the genuinely self-employed operating with a company as a simple partnership (enskild firma), the qualification days in sickness insurance to create parity between different company forms, an analysis of the regulations on part-time sickness benefits and, generally, a focus on the collaborative economy and platform workers.

42 Government White Paper SOU 2019:41, Företagare i de sociala trygghetssystemen, pp. 106 ff. and 122.

Business Tax Certificates (godkänd för F-skatt) and to thereby make it easier to start businesses with one or few principals.

The amendments to the legislation seem to be more or less a codification of existing caselaw.[43] Just as before, an overall assessment is made to determine the level of independence. The difference is that now, particular criteria are emphasised and the *travaux préparatoires* therefore have greater importance. *The intention of the parties* is one example of a criterion given special weight, while the number of clients is accorded less importance.[44] Other criteria mentioned in the text include the degree to which the contractor is dependent on the principal and how much he is involved in the principal's operations. The fact that the principal determines how, when and where the work is to be carried out, or that it is to be carried out on his premises and with his equipment does not, according to the preparatory works, automatically mean that the contractor is under the principal's supervision and that there is an employment at hand.

The present rules for Business Tax Certificate approval have resulted in more people being hired as sole traders, even though they are actually employed ("false" self-employed). The Ministry of Finance appointed an inquiry to look at possible alterations to the legislation.[45] In the Government White Paper (SOU 2018:49) the commissioner was particularly critical of the fact that the former employer can be the new company's only client and that the importance of the intention of the parties is given. The final Government White Paper (SOU 2019:31) however decided not to change the concept of employment but to improve and facilitate the Swedish Tax Agency's ability to follow up and ensure that those approved for a Business Tax Certificate fulfil the business criteria to avoid classification as false self-employed in tax law (and social security legislation).[46]

In labour law, it is the real circumstances between the parties rather than the intention of the parties or the written contract that matter most for the overall assessment, particularly if it is a question of classifying "false self-employment". In tax law, on the other hand, the *intention of the parties* is a very important criterion for the overall assessment when deciding whether the performing party is self-employed or not. The intention of the parties does not seem to be of the same importance when deciding if um-

---

43 See Supreme Administrative Court, 2001 ref. 25 (RÅ 2001 ref. 25) and Council of Legislation's comments and Legislative Bill 2008/09:62 F-skatt åt fler, p. 25.

44 Legislative Bill 2008/09:62, pp. 25-26.

45 Dir. 2017:108 Översyn av F-skattesystemet.

46 Government White Paper SOU 2019:31, F-skattesystemet – en översyn, pp. 31 and 200.

brella company workers will receive social security benefits. This is despite the fact that the employment concept in social security legislation is normally connected to the concept in tax law. Here again, the real circumstances seem most important, probably owing to the interest in avoiding that "false employees" receive benefits from a third party (Swedish Social Insurance Agency or unemployment insurance funds), see Section III 3 and 4 below. The result of the different approaches in different areas of legislation is that someone might well be regarded as an employee in the labour legislation but at the same time as self-employed in the social security legislation and this is exactly what can happen to umbrella company workers.

3. *Social Security for Umbrella Company Workers*[47]

How does the Swedish social security system function in respect to umbrella company workers? There are problems at different levels. The first problem pertains to whether the umbrella company worker is employed or self-employed according to the legislation in question. This depends on whether the umbrella company workers are regarded as employed by the umbrella company or if the relation is regarded as something else, which in the binary system means self-employed. If umbrella company workers are regarded as self-employed, they are entitled to social security benefits for the self-employed, which can be less favourable than benefits for employees.[48] The second problem is that *if* umbrella company workers are regarded as employees according to the parties' intentions, they share the same problem in sickness insurances as other employees with irregular intermittent on-demand employment. If a person engaging in on-demand work becomes ill and does not have work scheduled, the Swedish Social Insurance Agency investigates if there is any job at all on the labour market that he or she can perform, just as they would with an unemployed person who becomes sick. This makes it more difficult for on-demand workers than for ordinary employees to receive sickness benefits. The on-demand worker also receives sickness benefits at unemployment benefits

47 Sickness and injury benefits and parental allowance benefits are regulated in the 2010 Social Insurance Code (2010:110). For further details see *Westregård, Annamaria*, Protection of Platform Workers in Sweden (fn. 38), pp. 25 ff.

48 Both access to and calculation of benefits for employees and self-employed are regulated in the 2010 Social Insurance Code (2010:110) see Chapters 6, 25, 27 and 28.

level, which is lower than ordinary sickness benefits. When umbrella company workers work with an assignment and have signed a fixed-term employment contract, they are entitled to sickness benefits if they were to become ill during this period.

The legislator in Sweden has recently suggested a solution for persons with on-demand work which entails that they will receive sickness benefits for 90 days on the same conditions as other employees.[49] Umbrella companies and solo self-employed persons are particularly exempted from the proposed legislation. The Government White Paper (SOU 2020:26) states that although umbrella company workers are indeed employed by the umbrella company on a general fixed-term employment,[50] their fixed-term employment is limited by their assignments for other clients. If their assignments were ended by the employer they would have been included in the directive for investigation in the legislative committee (kommittédirektiv Dir. 2018:26), but they are not. It is the umbrella companies' special business model that has resulted in the exclusion of umbrella company workers from the suggested changes in the statutory regulations. The solo self-employed are excluded since they are not employed at all by the principal.[51] The developments in the legislative process described above are an example of how the social security insurances are generally not adapted to the particular working conditions of umbrella company workers, who work with short assignments on an irregular basis.

4. *Unemployment Benefits for Umbrella Company Workers*

The Administrative Court of Appeal has in a few cases decided on whether umbrella company workers are entitled to unemployment benefits according to the 1997 Unemployment Insurance Act (1997:238). There are 25 unemployment insurance funds in Sweden that administrate unemployment benefits. They are regulated in the 1997 Unemployment Funds Act (1997:239). Most of them are administrated by different unions but there are also funds for the self-employed (Småa).[52] A decision by the unemployment insurance fund about access to an insurance and calculation of benefits for a certain individual can be appealed to the administrative courts. It

49 Government White Paper SOU 2020:26, En sjukförsäkring anpassad efter individen, p. 62 ff.

50 According to Section 5 in the 1982 Employment Protection Act.

51 Government White Paper SOU 2020:26 (fn. 49), p. 71, reference 9.

52 See https://www.sverigesakassor.se/om-oss/in-english/. Accessed 19 June 2020.

is of crucial importance for umbrella company workers whether they are regarded as employees or self-employed. An employee is unemployed between assignments and thus entitled to unemployment benefits. An independent contractor or a self-employed person is entitled to unemployment benefits according to the statutory regulation for the self-employed but access to unemployment benefits for the self-employed is far more complicated. If umbrella company workers are regarded as self-employed they will in most cases probably be denied unemployment benefits between assignments.[53] As for unemployment insurance, the main difference between employees and the self-employed is that the self-employed have to take a hiatus in their business operations (which they can do once every fifth year) or close down the company in order to be eligible for benefits. In practice, this means that short-fixed term employees are entitled to unemployment benefits between assignments while self-employed persons are not.

Whether the umbrella company worker is regarded as an employee or self-employed depends on how the concept of employment is assessed according to the Income Tax Act (1999:1229) as the 1997 Unemployment Insurance Act (1997:238) refers to that concept of employment.[54] The statutory regulation on unemployment benefits unfortunately causes problems for umbrella company workers, as they are sometimes regarded as independent contractors (even if they do not have a company of their own) and therefore as not being entitled to unemployment benefits between assignments. It is difficult to foresee whether a person will be entitled to unemployment benefits or not.

There are two legal questions here. The first concerns the role of the umbrella company as an employer and what impact that role has for the judgement, and the second concerns the question as to how the degree of independence of the umbrella company workers is to be judged. The Administrative Court of Appeal has in a few cases discussed the umbrella

53 When a self-employed individual shifts from working in his or her own company to the unemployment insurance he or she either has to close down all business activity completely or make a temporary hiatus in operations. The temporary hiatus can be made so that the company owner does not need to close down the company in order to receive unemployment insurance. If a hiatus has been made and the business activity has started again, a period of five years has to pass before the company owner can receive unemployment benefits again under a new hiatus. This regulation is therefore of no use between assignments (Section 35 in the 1997 Unemployment Insurance Act).

54 Section 34 in the 1997 Unemployment Insurance Act (1997:238) refers to Chapter 13 Section 1 in the Income Tax Act (1999:1229).

company's role as an employer and what impact it will have for decisions on whether the umbrella company worker is an employee or not according to the 1997 Unemployment Insurance Act.[55] The Court states that even if the umbrella company formally is the employer, it is implied that the employer's responsibilities will not come into force. According to the Court this, together with other operative facts, such as management, setting of wages etc., means that the umbrella companies do not have the role of an employer in the ordinary sense, and cannot from the perspective of the 1997 Unemployment Insurance Act be regarded as employers in the same way as other employers. The fact that the umbrella company acts as an administrator and contract party "between" the umbrella company worker and the client does not on its own make the umbrella company worker an employee. If other circumstances indicate that the umbrella company worker without the presence of the umbrella company would instead have been regarded as an independent contractor, then the Court can ignore that there is an employment contract between the umbrella company and the umbrella company worker. In other words, if the umbrella company worker could just as well have handled the client and the administration through a company of his own, without the umbrella company, then the umbrella company worker will be regarded as an independent contractor. He or she will then not be entitled to any unemployment benefits between assignments.

Settled caselaw from the Administrative Court of Appeal varies and the most essential criterion has been the *degree of independence*.[56] The Administrative Court of Appeal balances different operative facts in each specific case. In one case[57] the Administrative Court of Appeal stated that the operative facts that pointed in the direction of the umbrella company worker being an employee according to the 1997 Unemployment Insurance Act,

---

55 See e.g. Judgement of the Administrative Court of Appeal in Gothenburg of 11 May 2010 (Case No. 3059-09).

56 Judgement of the Administrative Court of Appeal in Gothenburg of 11 May 2010 (Case No. 3059-09); Judgement of the Administrative Court of Appeal in Gothenburg of 17 February 2015 (Case No. 911-15); see also the Swedish Unemployment Insurance Board (IAF) appeal to the Supreme Administrative Court in the Judgement of the Administrative Court of Appeal in Gothenburg of 11 May 2010 (Case No. 3059-09), review not granted (Case No. 4218-10). See also report from the Unemployment Insurance Board (IAF) Uppdragstagare i arbetslöshetsförsäkringen, 2016:3, pp. 15-16, about the particular difficulties relating to the solo self-employed.

57 Judgement of the Administrative Court of Appeal in Gothenburg of 17 February 2015 (Case No. 911-15).

were that the worker was employed by the umbrella company, payed employee taxes (A-tax) and did not have a Business Tax Certificate for self-employment (F-skatt), that the umbrella company took all employers' responsibilities for him, that the client decided when and where the assignment was to be carried out and that the worker did not market his services independently but simply made his labour available. There were also operative facts that pointed in the direction of the worker being an independent contractor. The client's first contact was with the umbrella company worker and not the umbrella company and the worker used his own computer and camera. In this case the Administrative Court of Appeal decided that the umbrella company worker was not an independent contractor and was therefore entitled to unemployment benefits.

A new Unemployment Insurance Act has recently been put forward in a Government White Paper.[58] Regrettably, it does not propose any solution to the problem of how to assess the degree of independence, so the problems will remain according to umbrella companies.[59] One thing that might, on the other hand, ease access to unemployment benefits for umbrella company workers is that in the present legislation there is a qualifying condition requiring a person to work a specific number of hours.[60] For umbrella company workers, and a lot of other non-traditional workers, it can be difficult to prove the number of hours worked. This is one possible explanation for why the unemployment benefits' degree of coverage has decreased in recent years. Out of all unemployed persons, only 40 per cent receive unemployment benefits out of a loss-of-income insurance scheme.[61] It has been suggested that the minimum working hour condition be replaced with a minimum wage condition – relating to both a total income and a minimum monthly income during four months.[62]

The varying judgements in settled caselaw have made it difficult to foresee whether an individual umbrella company worker will be entitled to

58 The Government White Paper SOU 2020:37, Ett nytt regelverk för arbetslöshetsförsäkringen.

59 The Government White Paper SOU 2020:37 (fn. 58), p. 209 f.

60 The basic work requirements are that the person has worked at least 80 hours a month for 6 months during the last year or 480 hours in total, and at least 50 hours a month for 6 consecutive months during the last year, Section 12 in the Unemployment Insurance Act.

61 See the Homepage of Arbetslöshetsrapporten, https://arbetsloshetsrapporten.se/ersattning-akassa/. Accessed 20 August 2020.

62 The Government White Paper SOU 2020:37 (fn. 58), p. 260 ff.

unemployment benefits or not.[63] It seems important for the legislator and the courts to find "false employees", and that will have an impact on how the interests are balanced between the Swedish Social Insurance Agency or the unemployment insurance fund and the umbrella company workers.

IV. The Importance of Collective Agreements – Supplemental Benefits

1. The Social Parties and New Phenomena in the Labour Market

The Nordic model relies on the regulation of the most important working conditions being arranged through collective agreements, and not via the statutory regulations. There are thus no statutory regulations on minimum wages, overtime pay, guaranteed minimum working hours, and so on.

In Sweden, there are currently no collective agreements for umbrella companies nor any industry-wide collective agreements specific to platform work. This is probably due to the fact that Swedish platform companies do not yet take on a more organised form as employers since they imply that platform workers are self-employed.[64] It seems likely that those closest to collective bargaining and to concluding a collective agreement are the umbrella companies – this is despite the lack of clarity about their position as parties. The umbrella companies already have a trade organisation and claim that they are meeting their responsibilities as employers. A stumbling block in collective bargaining is the business model with short fixed-term employment. That all employees have permanent employment is one of the most important issues for the unions.

The Swedish social partners are very good at handling new situations. An example is the collective agreements for temporary work agencies – a brand new service industry in Sweden born in the early 1990s.[65] Almega and LO, the blue-collar trade union, and again Almega and the white-collar trade unions, arrived at a collective agreement for staff working for

63 See report from Unemployment Insurance Board (IAF), Uppdragstagare i arbetslöshetsförsäkringen. 2016:3. p. 15 f., https://www.iaf.se/globalassets/dokument/rapporter/2015-2016/2016-3-uppdragstagare-i-arbetsloshetsforsakringen.pdf. Accessed 20 August 2020.

64 *Westregård, Annamaria,* Digital Collaborative Platforms: A Challenge for Social Partners in the Nordic Model, in: Nordic Journal of Commercial Law, 1 (2018), pp. 104 ff., https://doi.org/10.5278/ojs.njcl.v0i1.2486. Accessed 20 August 2020.

65 *Eklund, Ronnie,* Temporary Employment Agencies in the Nordic Countries, in: Scandinavian Studies in Law, 43 (2002), pp. 311-333.

temporary work agencies in 2000.[66] What is interesting about these two collective agreements is that they cover the entire private sector. This means that a temporary work employee can work in any of the sectors covered by the collective agreement and enjoy the same collective agreement and conditions. The exact details of the agreements differ, but the principles are the same: both cover all temporary work employees, regardless of the industry they are hired out to. Temporary work agencies and their employees are now considered to be a service industry in their own right.[67] An industry-wide collective agreement for umbrella companies might have a different construction than that of the temporary work agencies, but in Sweden an industry-wide collective agreement is important in that it establishes an industry as a recognised industry. An umbrella company can conclude a collective agreement at company level.

---

66 The collective agreement on general employment conditions for temporary work blue-collar workers, between Temporary Work Agencies Almega (Bemanningsföretagen Almega) and the blue-collar unions Fastighetsanställdas Förbund, GS-Facket för skogs, trä och grafisk bransch, Handelsanställdas förbund, Hotell och Restaurang Facket, IF Metall, SEKO-Service- och kommunikationsfacket, Svenska Byggnadsarbetareförbundet, Svenska Elektrikerförbundet, Svenska Kommunalarbetareförbundet, Svenska Livsmedelsarbetareförbundet, Svenska Musikerförbundet, Svenska Målareförbundet, Svenska Pappersindustriarbetareförbundet and Svenska Transportarbetareförbundet, for 1 May 2017 to 30 April 2020.
The collective agreement on general employment conditions for temporary work white-collar workers and professionals between Temporary Work Agencies Almega and the white-collar workers and professional unions Unionen and the Academic Alliance. The Swedish Association of Graduate Engineers is the representative for the Academic Alliance. The Academic Alliance includes a variety of professions, including university lecturers, physiotherapists, scientists, and engineers, such as Akademikerförbundet SSR, Civilekonomerna, DIK, Sveriges Arbetsterapeuter, Fysioterapeuterna, Jusek, Naturvetarna, Sveriges Farmaceuter, Sveriges Ingenjörer, Sveriges Psykologförbund, Sveriges Skolledarförbund, Sveriges Universitetslärarförbund, Sveriges Veterinärförbund, for 1 May 2017 to 30 April 2020. The collective agreement for white-collar workers and professionals has one set of conditions used throughout the temporary work industry. The blue-collar agreement has the same regulations for salary (§ 4-5) and working hours (§ 7-9) in the industry where the person currently works. Other conditions such as holiday pay and insurance (§ 10–22) are the same for temporary work employees, regardless of the industry.

67 See especially the blue-collar workers' collective agreement (3) and the social partners' common declaration of intent; see also the agreement's importance for temporary work in the Government White Paper SOU 2011:5, Chapter 6.5-6.

2. *Supplemental Collective Agreements*

The collective agreements between Sweden's major federations contain important supplemental compensation to the state social security insurance and pensions.[68] All employers with a collective agreement, 92 per cent in the private sector, are obliged in the collective agreement at industry level to also keep their employees insured in accordance with the federal collective agreements. Those federal collective agreements contain sickness insurance, occupational injury insurance, supplementary industrial injury insurance, occupational life insurance, ITP-pension schemes for white-collar workers and occupational pension schemes for blue-collar workers, occupational group health insurance etc. There are also more supplemental benefits in the industry-wide collective agreements.

If a collective agreement does not cover the workplace, the employees do not get any of the benefits in the federal collective agreements. They only have the state social security insurance levels on sickness and injury benefits, parental allowance and retirement and old age benefits.[69] An employer who is a not a member of any employers' association with an industry-wide collective agreement can, of course, sign up with a private insurance.[70] They are normally more expensive than the federal collective agreement insurances. The collectively agreed federal social security schemes, including pensions, normally offer better and cheaper terms than other private social security schemes that are available for individual companies, due to the large number of insured persons. This is one of the reasons why, aside from regulation wages and working conditions, it is important for the umbrella company industry to conclude industry-wide collective agreements.

---

68 The federal level comprises the private-sector employers – the Confederation of Swedish Enterprise and Industry (Svenskt Näringsliv – SN). The union representatives are the Swedish Federation of Professional Associations (Sveriges akademikers centralorganisation – SACO) for academically qualified personnel, the Federation of White-Collar Workers (Tjänstemännens centralorganisation – TCO) for white-collar workers, and the Swedish Trade Union Confederation (Landsorganisationen – LO) for blue-collar workers.

69 *Westregård, Annamaria*, Protection of Platform Workers in Sweden (fn. 38), pp. 27 f.

70 For more on industrial relations in Sweden, see *Westregård, Annamaria,* Sweden, in: Liukkunen, Ulla (eds.) Collective Bargaining in Labour Law Regimes: A Global Perspective, Springer 2019.

V. Conclusion

Are umbrella companies employers and umbrella company workers employees? The intention of the parties in the employment contract is that there should be a short fixed-term employment for the duration of the assignment. The legal problem is that umbrella companies do not take on the role of an employer in the usual sense. It is the umbrella company worker and the client that have control of the assignments and over when and how the work will be carried out. The umbrella company's role is to administrate taxes, social security fees, invoice the client and pay remuneration. The umbrella company worker could however, with some administrative effort, just as well handle the situation as a self-employed worker and does not actually need the umbrella company as a middleman.

Umbrella companies have found their own niche in the labour market and are commercial enterprises that aim to make a profit. One reason why umbrella companies are anxious to take on full employer's responsibilities from a labour law perspective, is that this will further their goal of creating an industry of their own. If umbrella company workers are not employed by the umbrella companies, there will in practice be very little that separates them from ordinary accounting firms that administrate taxes and pay out salaries etc. for small solo self-employed clients with a registered firm of their own. Umbrella companies' employer responsibilities are limited to the duration of the assignment, so their burden is not particularly heavy.

In *labour law* the employment concept is wide, particularly in the relation between the contracting parties according to the 1982 Employment Protection Act. Nothing speaks against the fact that the Labour Court can decide on the relation between the umbrella company and the umbrella company worker as being an employment according to the intention of the parties in the employment contract. The labour legislation generally tries to prevent classification of persons as "false self-employed" workers and to reclassify them. The caselaw of the Labour Court shows that the Labour Court is more cautious about classifying anyone as self-employed. According to the principle of the legal subject, the umbrella company – not the client – is the employer.

From an *employment protectio*n perspective, one problem for umbrella company workers is thus short fixed-term employment and the precariousness this creates in times of crisis, such as the Covid-19 crisis. Another problem is that the working conditions for umbrella company workers, with regard to e.g. minimum wage, overtime pay but also benefits supplemental to the Swedish social security insurances etc., have so far not been regulated in an industry-wide collective agreement. Such agreements constitute the normal way of regulating working conditions in Sweden, since working conditions are for the most part not regulated at all in statutory law, and if they are regulated, most of the labour legislation is semi-discretionary.[71] At the moment it is the umbrella company workers themselves that negotiate the terms and conditions with the clients. Naturally, umbrella companies, whose commissions are normally a percentage of the workers' commissions, will not allow remuneration to be too low. Hopefully, the social parties will in a traditional Swedish way find solutions for the working conditions through an industry-wide collective agreement.

In *tax law* it has been a political goal to facilitate the setting up of companies for sole traders. The concept of self-employment is therefore wider there than in labour law. This will also reflect on how the concept is interpreted in *social security legislation*, as the concepts are linked by statutory regulations. The employer's responsibility to pay tax and social security fees covers both employees and dependent contractors. Umbrella companies therefore have to pay taxes and social security fees, regardless of whether the umbrella company workers are employees or dependent contractors (umbrella company workers do not have their own companies and do not pay tax and social security fees themselves, according to the business model). There is no legal contradiction in that an umbrella company, from a social security legislation perspective, pays taxes and social security fees for its fixed-term employees who are employees according to labour legislation, while at the same time the umbrella company workers, when it comes to social security regulations and unemployment insurance, will be regarded as self-employed persons without current assignments instead of as unemployed employees.

The concept of employment in *social security legislation* and with regard to *unemployment benefits* is more limited than in labour law. The intention of the parties in the employment contract has little impact when it comes to classification in social security legislation. If the object is to identify employees, it is more important to determine whether the income comes from an employment or from business activity, as this will determine which statutory regulations are applicable: the ones for employees or the ones for the self-employed. The aim in social security legislation seems rather to be to identify "false employees" in order to avoid that e.g. umbrella company workers are deemed entitled to benefits for employees if they are in fact independent.

71 *Westregård, Annamaria,* Sweden (fn. 70).

From a *social security perspective*, the main problem is that umbrella company workers so easily fall between the regulations for employees and the self-employed, due to their significant level of independence. The uncertain situation for umbrella company workers – at what level their social security and unemployment benefits should be calculated or indeed if they should receive any at all – is naturally a huge disadvantage. This will also in times of crisis make them more vulnerable than other employees. The introduction of a "new" business model, like that of umbrella companies, might rather – from a social security perspective – complicate than ease the situation of the employees at the moment, since the uncertainty with regard to how those new workers should be classified has increased. It might not make a huge difference to the final decisions whether umbrella company workers are entitled to e.g. unemployment benefits. Without the umbrella companies, a large part of the umbrella company workers would probably automatically have been regarded as self-employed persons instead of as employees; at least some of them are regarded as the latter now.

The problem of access to and calculation of benefits at basic level in the social security insurance for a new business model in Sweden remains for the legislator to solve. So far, the legislator has not shown much interest in including umbrella company workers in the inquiries for new legislation to improve the statutory regulations for this vulnerable group.

Part III:
Financing of Social Security: Experiences and New Approaches

Chapter 9
The Influence of the Platform Economy on the Financing of Social Security: the Spanish Case

Borja Suárez Corujo

I. Introduction

So far, the debate on the future sustainability of social security has mainly focused on the impact that ageing populations will have on public expenditure. Due to the demographic change – growing numbers of pensioners whose life expectancy is longer – the upward trend of pension expenditure has placed social security and public pension systems, in particular, at the centre of the debate on the long-term budgetary and economic policies since the end of the 20th century. However, it should not be overlooked that, along with the process of ageing, the sustainability of social security systems will also be challenged by the rise of the platform economy. With robotisation embedded as a component part of the "digitalisation of the economy" phenomenon, the platform economy is transforming employment and labour markets[1] in a way that threatens to undermine the foundations of welfare state institutions. Along these lines, labour law is facing the question of how to preserve the traditional guarantees which have historically balanced the relationship between labour and capital. But likewise, this deep transformation threatens the current design of those social security systems where benefits are primarily based on previous contributions made by employers and employees.[2] It is therefore not an exaggeration to say that the framework of the debate on the long-term sustainability of social security systems has changed. Leaving aside the still unknown

1 *Degryse, Christophe*, Shaping the World of Work in the Digital Economy, 1 January 2017, ETUI, Brussels, p. 2, https://www.etui.org/sites/default/files/Foresight%20brief_01_EN_web.pdf. Accessed 7 August 2020.

2 See Economic Policy Committee/Social Protection Committee, Joint Paper on Pensions 2019, 22 January 2020, Brussels, p. 44, https://europa.eu/epc/system/files/2020-01/Joint-Paper-on-Pensions-2019.pdf. Accessed 07 August 2020. In this Joint Paper an appropriate, though insufficient, reference to this technology-driven transformation and its consequences on the sustainability of pension systems is made.

impact of Covid-19, from now on policymakers will have to tackle two major structural transformations: population ageing and the emergence of the platform economy. This paper will draw attention to the latter, focusing on the issues regarding its financial side and taking Spain as a study case.

More in particular, the aim of this article is to reflect on how this major technological shift could modify the financing structure of Bismarckian social security systems. Given the fact that in this model social security is principally financed through social contributions, my argument is that dependence on such a model could seriously harm the financial balance of the system once the platform economy gains greater weight. Therefore, potential weak points in the system need to be tackled through a progressive redesign of social security financial resources or a reconfiguration of benefits. After some considerations on the legal classification of platform workers, my attention is drawn to two of the main factors that pose financial risks. One is that some platform-like service provisions could be excluded from the obligation to pay social contributions because of, for example, their sporadic character. The other is that the growth of "just-in-time" work will normally entail lower social contributions even if the activity is based on an employment relationship.

Further, I will carefully consider the advantages and disadvantages of the three possible paths that Bismarckian systems (taking Spain as a case study) could follow in the coming scenario.

The first option would imply preserving the same financial structure, basically based upon contributions. Such a solution would surely lead to benefit cuts since the system would not have the capacity to overcome the financial burdens caused by ageing. A reflection on the negative consequences that this situation would create for platform workers, among the more vulnerable workforce, seems appropriate. The second and third options would be initially channelled through the increase of State funds and deployed in two different manners. This broader involvement of the Government in financing social security could prompt a reduction of funds coming from contributions in order to maintain public expenditure. This could represent a first step towards a more Beveridgean system which focuses on reducing poverty through assistance benefits and encourages the development of occupational (or even individual) private plans. Again, a specific analysis of the capacity of platform workers to engage in these complementary schemes should be thoroughly analysed. The alternative is that this increase in tax-based financing would not call into question the current financial structure where contributions determine both the funding of the system and the granting of benefits. Two main questions are to be examined. One deals with the tax options to implement said increase.

The proposal of a "robot tax" merits an in-depth study, as well as the pros and cons of direct and indirect (earmarked or non-earmarked) taxes. Likewise, attention should be paid to how the career paths of platform workers will necessitate a potentially large-scale change to the design of social benefits.

II. The Legal Classification of Platform Workers

Up to now, analysis concerning the influence of economic activities based on the use of online platforms has mainly concentrated on how (labour) law treats these new forms of work and the ability of the applied regulation to secure decent working conditions. According to Spanish law, what is the appropriate legal classification of this type of contractual relationship? Theoretically, we find three possible classifications with regard to the respective workers.

Two of these types of platform "collaborators" (using a neutral term) fall outside the scope of labour law. First, they can be classified as *independent contractors* or, to be more precise, self-employed workers who are in business on their own account and, therefore, do not enjoy specific guarantees with respect to the digital platform. And second, still beyond the employment relationship, the Spanish *Self-Employed Workers' Statute* also foresees an intermediate category: the so-called "economically dependent self-employed workers" (in Spanish *trabajadores autónomos económicamente dependientes*), who render services mainly (at least 75 percent of their income) for one client. This type of "dependent contractor" reflects the combination of features that makes it difficult to give a clear-cut response according to traditional patterns; and it could certainly be an attractive solution for both parties as it offers a minimum level of professional guarantees to the service provider while it gives the platform flexibility and reduced "labour" costs – basically, social security contributions. But, as a matter of fact, it is not a real option in practice: the number of the economically dependent self-employed workers has always been very low since creation of this category in 2007, and has not been affected in any way by the emergence of the platform economy despite the interest of platforms.

As an alternative, platform collaborators can also be classified as employees falling within the scope of the Workers' Statute enjoying all labour guarantees with the corresponding employer obligations. But in Spain, this is certainly not the case in practice since virtually all digital platforms treat their "collaborators" – i.e. service providers – as independent contractors. As in other European countries, it is not surprising that this arguably inadequate classification of a self-employed person has given rise to a controversial debate on the employment status of platform workers – in most cases, riders. And a good illustration of such a heated discussion is the high number of court decisions that have been taken so far in Spain.[3] In a previous research,[4] I analysed the main evidence supporting both legal classifications – as employee or as self-employed person – based on Spanish case law and the extent to which subordination plays a key role in determining the characteristics of the relationship between the digital platform and its collaborators.

From one perspective leaning towards the self-employed status, evidence of independence – from subordination – stems from the following contractual conditions. First, the most relevant one arguably is that working time is determined at the collaborator's discretion, which means that there is no fixed timetable and, even more importantly, that the very "collaborator" decides when to be active in the platform. Second, and along the same lines, it is common that (s)he enjoys the freedom to refuse tasks commanded through the platform. Third, it seems to show autonomy that the performance of the activity is basically self-directed, notwithstanding the existence of common instructions directed at all "collaborators". Fourth, the non-exclusivity of the contractual engagement, which is to say, the possibility of "collaborating" with several platforms is generally considered a sign of independence (ancillary income). And, fifth, the fact that activity-related spending is not compensated for by the platform could also indicate that the service is provided on the worker's own account.

Conversely, and thus leaning towards the employee status, evidence of dependence of the "collaborator" on the platform is also frequently found in practice, some of it being typical of the traditional idea of subordination and some other showing new forms of such dependence. Firstly, in cases of

---

3 It should be noted that, despite the estimates that show very high numbers of platform workers in Spain (see *Urzi Brancati, Maria Cesira/Pesole, Annarosa/Fernandez Macias, Enrique*, New Evidence on Platform Workers in Europe, EUR 29958 EN, Luxembourg: Publications Office of the European Union 2020, doi:10.2760/459278 (online), p. 16), real figures seem to point at a more limited proportion. Just as an example, a study published by a prominent Spanish Trade Union, Unión General de Trabajadores (UGT), quantifies the number of riders working for delivery platforms as little more than 14,000, which represents a mere 0.07 percent of the active workforce (UGT 2019, 15).

4 *Corujo, Borja Suárez*, The "Gig" Economy and its Impact on Social Security: The Spanish Example, in: European Journal of Social Security, 19 (2017) 4, p. 297, doi: 10.1177/1388262717745751.

work on-demand via apps, where the performance is physically carried out, it is common to have "collaborators" fulfil certain conditions before they are "activated". Secondly, another sign of subordination lies in the personal dimension of the performance in the sense that it is not transferable. Thirdly, according to the experiences analysed in Spain, the supremacy of platforms is obvious in very different aspects: strict (no matter if indirect) supervision and control; detailed indications of how to perform the tasks; price fixing of services performed; sham incentives on "activation" that hide a minimum level of availability. Fourthly, the fact that the platform is allowed to "deactivate" "collaborators" in a wide range of circumstances shows a sort of disciplinary power, one of the most typical characteristic of employers. And fifthly, without being exhaustive, it is also a sign of subordination of "collaborators" that the relationship established with the client (payment included) is always channeled through the platform.

What is the Spanish courts' view on this issue? The number of claims related to the legal classification of platform workers – always concerning delivery platforms, in most cases Deliveroo and Glovo – is growing[5] and, as we shall see, it appears to be favourable to the recognition of an employee status. The first court rulings date back to 2018. At that point, first instance courts did not have a clear-cut position: two court decisions held that the services rendered through the platform by formally self-employed persons really described a subordinate relationship and, therefore, recognised their employee status[6] whereas another ruling classified the claimant "rider" as a self-employed person[7]. Throughout 2019 we found court decisions – up to July coming from first-instance social courts – defending both positions favourable or contrary to the employee status, with a slight tendency to-

5 Highly recommended is professor Beltrán de Heredia's blog where he compiles judicial decisions on the employment status of platform workers in Spain and also in a wide range of countries: *Beltrán de Heredia Ruiz, Ignasi,* Employment Status of Platform Workers (national courts decisions overview – Argentina, Australia, Belgium, Brazil, Canada, Chile, France, Germany, Italy, The Netherlands, Panama, Switzerland, United Kingdom, United States and Uruguay), 9 December 2018, https://ignasibeltran.com/2018/12/09/employment-status-of-platform-workers-national-courts-decisions-overview-australia-brazil-chile-france-italy-united-kingdom-united-states-spain/#spa2. Accessed 7 August 2020.

6 Judgement of Social Court No. 11 of Barcelona of 29 May 2018 and Judgement of Social Court No. 6 of Valencia of 1 June 2018.

7 Judgement of Social Court No. 39 of Madrid of 3 September 2018.

wards the former.[8] This tie still existed when the "regional" – Autonomous Communities – courts of Asturias and Madrid ruled the first appeals.[9] But from that point onwards, the state of play seemed to have changed (definitely?) leaning towards the employment status. The same High Court of Justice of Madrid (Social Chamber) modified its view through a "plenary" decision taken by its twenty-one members – the former decision had been taken by a section of the court – who held that the claimant (Glovo rider) had an employment relationship with the platform.[10]

8 Nine decisions classified riders as employees: Judgement of Social Court No. 33 of Madrid of 11 February 2019, Judgement of Social Court No. 1 of Gijón – Asturias – of 20 February 2019, Judgements of Social Court No. 1 of Madrid of 3 and 4 – two rulings – April 2019, Judgement of Social Court No. 6 of Valencia of 10 June 2019, Judgement of Social Court No. 31 of Barcelona of 11 June 2019, Judgement of Social Court No. 19 of Madrid of 22 July 2019, and Judgement of Social Court No. 3 of Barcelona of 18 November 2019. On the contrary, six rulings hold that there is not a subordinate relationship, but an activity that is carried out on its own by self-employed persons (Judgements of Social Court No. 24 of Barcelona of 21 and 29 May 2019), in certain cases – to be more precise – by economically dependent self-employed persons (see Judgement of Social Court No. 39 of Madrid of 11 January 2019, Judgement of Social Court No. 4 of Oviedo – Asturias – of 25 February 2019, Judgement of Social Court No. 1 of Salamanca – Castilla y León – of 1 June 2019 and Judgement of Social Court No. 2 of Vigo – Galicia – of 12 November 2019). See again *Beltrán de Heredia Ruiz, Ignasi,* Employment Status of Platform Workers (national courts decisions overview – Argentina, Australia, Belgium, Brazil, Canada, Chile, France, Germany, Italy, The Netherlands, Panama, Switzerland, United Kingdom, United States and Uruguay), (fn. 5).

9 The Judgement of the High Court of Justice of Asturias (Social Chamber) of 25 July 2019 recognised the labour status, whereas the Judgement of the High Court of Justice of Madrid (Social Chamber) of 19 September 2019 held that the rider was an independent contractor.

10 See Judgement of the High Court of Justice of Madrid (Social Chamber) of 27 November of 2019. As Beltrán de Heredia highlights, the Court based its decision on the following main arguments (see *Beltrán de Heredia Ruiz, Ignasi*, Employment Status of Platform Workers (fn. 5). First, a "primacy of fact principle" rules and, therefore, it is facts and not labels which determine the attribution of employee status or non-status; along these lines, written documentation did not reflect the legal nature of the relationship and without any substantial change in the fact situation the rider, who was initially classified as an independent contractor, turned into an economically dependent self-employed person. Second, in this case there was subordination to the authority of the platform since it was said platform that unilaterally established rates, and the rider's activity was fully integrated into the digital platform's business. And thirdly, in order to carry out the activity (delivery) what was relevant in economic terms was the app and not the means provided by the rider.

In some way, we could speak of a true turning point, given the fact that all court decisions taken by high courts of justice (Social Chamber) or by first-instance social courts since that ruling have stuck to that view defending the employee status of riders.[11] And it is particularly relevant that in some cases it was the result of an action taken by the Labour and Social Security Inspectorate – and thus affecting more than 500 riders.[12] Although we still have to wait for the "final" decision of the Supreme Court[13], it seems that the judiciary clearly leans towards the employment relationship. As a matter of fact, it is probable that this heated controversy will have an end before that ruling sees the light of day on account of the fact that the Spanish Government has finally taken a first step to regulate this issue announcing its intention to present a bill that will reinforce the employee classification of platform workers.[14]

III. The Platform Economy and its Impact on Social Security[15]

Much less attention has been paid to the implications of on-demand work via apps on social security. It is true that there seems to be growing interest in this issue, but in general terms these new research studies and political

---

11 See Judgements of the High Court of Justice of Madrid (Social Chamber) of 18 December 2019, 17 January 2020 and 2 February 2020; Judgement of the High Court of Justice of Castilla-León (Social Chamber) of 17 February 2020; and Judgement of the High Court of Justice of Catalonia (Social Chamber) of 21 February 2020. Likewise, Judgement of Social Court No. 2 of Zaragoza of 27 April 2020 and Judgement of Social Court No. 21 of Madrid of 11 June 2020.

12 Judgements of the High Court of Justice of Madrid (Social Chamber) of 17 January 2020. Also Judgement of Social Court No. 2 of Zaragoza of 27 April 2020.

13 On 23 September 2020, the Supreme Court announced a judgement to be published in the coming days whereby the employee status of riders is confirmed.

14 See the public enquiry previous to the draft of a bill on platform work that has recently been opened by the Spanish Ministry of Labour and Social Economy (Consulta pública previa a la elaboración de un proyecto normativo consistente en la modificación del Real Decreto Legislativo 2/2015, de 23 de octubre, por el que se aprueba el texto refundido de la Ley del Estatuto de los Trabajadores y de la Ley 20/2007, de 11 de julio, del Estatuto del trabajo autónomo, sobre determinados aspectos de la prestación de trabajo por cuenta propia y ajena del trabajo a través de plataformas), http://www.mites.gob.es/ficheros/participacion/historico/consulta-publica/2020/Proyecto_07_20200606_consulta_publica_gabinete_empleo.pdf.

15 A short draft of Sections III, IV and V was first presented at the ISLSSL World Congress 2018.

initiatives have focused on platform workers and their conditions of access to social security benefits as well as the serious risk of benefit inadequacy they are exposed to.[16] In this sense, ILO (2016) considers their work (in their different profiles) as types of non-standard employment that demand specific measures in order to improve access to benefits and to ensure portability of entitlements. Likewise, the European Union has taken steps to address the challenges of access to social protection for people in all forms of employment – platform workers included – through the achievement of three objectives: ensuring effective coverage (access to social benefits), transferability of social protection rights, and transparency (access to user-friendly information on rights and obligations).[17] Given that these difficulties in guaranteeing benefit adequacy are so crucial, it tends to be ignored that there is also a very serious financial risk that threatens social protection in the platform economy: the reduction or insufficiency of social contributions endangering the long-term financing of social security and thus the adequacy of individual social benefits.[18]

Before focusing on the social security field, we should make some considerations from a more general perspective on the impact that the process of digitalisation of the economy could have on fair taxation and the sustainability of State budgets. The question would be whether digitalisation

16 Very illustrative: *Forde, Chris/Stuart, Mark/Joyce, Simon/Oliver, Liz/Valizade, Danat/Alberti, Gabriella/Hardy, Kate/Trappmann, Vera/Umney, Charles/Carson, Calum*, The Social Protection of Workers in the Platform Economy, Study for the EMPL Committee, 2017, European Union, Brussels, 2017, https://www.europarl.europa.eu/RegData/etudes/STUD/2017/614184/IPOL_STU%282017%29614184_EN.pdf. Accessed 7 August 2020. In particular regarding pensions in European Commission, Pension Adequacy Report 2018, https://op.europa.eu/en/publication-detail/-/publication/62f83ed2-7821-11e8-ac6a-01aa75ed71a1/language-en. Accessed 07 August 2020. An attempt of analysis of the different aspects of social security in *Suárez Corujo, Borja*, The "Gig" Economy and its Impact on Social Security: The Spanish Example (fn. 4).

17 Council Recommendation of 8 November 2019 on Access to Social Protection for Workers and the Self-Employed 2019/C 387/01, https://eur-lex.europa.eu/legal-content/EN/TXT/?uri=CELEX%3A32019H1115%2801%29. Accessed 7 August 2020.

18 Implicit in: Federal Ministry of Labour and Social Affairs. White Book 4.0, 1 March 2018, p. 179, https://www.bmas.de/EN/Services/Publications/a883-white-paper.html;jsessionid=0A171136D7FF1D358063F3960C2C18E5. Accessed 7 August 2020; *Spasova, Slavina/Bouget, Denis/Ghailani, Dalila/Vanhercke, Bart*, Access to Social Protection for People Working on Non-Standard Contracts and as Self-Employed in Europe. A Study of National Policies, European Social Policy Network (ESPN), Brussels: European Commission, 2017, p. 8, https://ec.europa.eu/social/main.jsp?catId=1135&intPageId=3588. Accessed 7 August 2020.

– and, in particular, the platform economy – affects the sustainability of public finances. As the European Commission has acknowledged, "[…] the growing challenge of ensuring that the digital economy is fairly taxed has still not been adequately addressed",[19] leading to tax avoidance and/or to the loss of tax revenues. In brief, in a globalised and digitally connected world the redesign of tax systems appears to be a key issue in order to preserve welfare state institutions and social fairness.[20]

In this regard, the legitimacy of the claim in favour of the reinforcement of taxation of digital (in particular, platform) activities is based, at least, on two aspects. The first one is that long-term economic projections are moderately positive; as an illustration, the average annual potential GDP growth in the EU for 2016-2070 is projected at 1.4 percent largely thanks to a 1.5 percent average annual growth in labour productivity per hour worked over the entire period.[21] Therefore, there is no question that European member states will be significantly richer in thirty years' time, despite the much more modest trend of total EU population and, in particular, the decrease of labour supply. If output is less dependent on labour, it is reasonable to redesign taxation so as to keep its efficacy on collecting funds.

But, secondly, the necessity to adapt the tax system to a changing economic environment adds another factor that has to be taken into account: numerous examples show that the quick development of platform business and the way this business is being driven is partly related to an "ill" (business-biased) motivation that seeks to reduce labour cost through eluding or limiting the obligation to pay taxes (or social contributions). We need

---

19 European Commission, Second Phase Consultation of Social Partners under Article 154 TFEU on a Possible Action addressing the Challenges of Access to Social Protection for People in all Forms of Employment in the Framework of the European Pillar of Social Rights. Consultation Document C (2017) 7773 final, 20 November 2017, http://ec.europa.eu/social/BlobServlet?docId=18619&langId=en. Accessed 17 August 2020. Note that these projections were made previous to the Covid-19 crisis.

20 European Commission, Staff Working Document, Impact Assessment Accompanying the document Proposal for a Council Directive laying down Rules relating to the Corporate Taxation of a Significant Digital Presence and Proposal for a Council Directive on the Common System of a Digital Services Tax on Revenues resulting from the Provision of Certain Digital Services, SWD (2018) 81 final/2, 21 March 2018, p. 5, https://ec.europa.eu/transparency/regdoc/rep/10102/2018/EN/SWD-2018-81-F1-EN-MAIN-PART-1.PDF. Accessed 17 August 2020.

21 European Commission, The 2018 Ageing Report, Underlying Assumptions & Projection Methodologies, Institutional Paper 065, Brussels, November 2017, pp. 71-72, https://ec.europa.eu/info/sites/info/files/economy-finance/ip065_en.pdf. Accessed 17 August 2020.

to be conscious that this economic model – now questioned by the social and economic consequences of the Covid-19 crisis? – destabilises the level playing field for businesses putting at risk EU competitiveness and, moreover, reduces financial contributions to social protection schemes.[22]

The threat of erosion of the social budgets associated with this major technological shift affects all social security models. But my attention focuses on Bismarckian systems (social insurance schemes) given the special vulnerability of social contributions – in this context the principal source of financing – in the new economic environment. My argument is that this dependence on employer and employee contributions could seriously harm the financial balance of the system once the platform economy gains greater weight. What is the best way to tackle this threat? And is it possible to turn this risk into an opportunity to redesign an established institutional solution?[23] Again Spain will be a reference case.

The mainly professional basis of this type of social security system makes the contractual relationship between platform and service provider particularly relevant. Legal classification (employment relationship or not), but also the specific working conditions are key aspects in determining the level of contributions and therefore could end up generating a financial risk to social security in three ways.

First of all, some platform-like service provisions can be excluded from the obligation to pay social contributions if they are not registered with any scheme of social security due to the terms in which the activity is carried out. This could be the case, for example, if said activity has a sporadic character or, more broadly, if the service provider's income remains below legal thresholds.[24] Certainly, these sorts of situations are not new; the

22 *Forde, Chris/Stuart, Mark/Joyce, Simon/Oliver, Liz/Valizade, Danat/Alberti, Gabriella/ Hardy, Kate/Trappmann, Vera/Umney, Charles/Carson, Calum*, The Social Protection of Workers in the Platform Economy (fn. 16), p. 40.

23 *Eichhorst, Werner/Rinne, Ulf*, Digital Challenges for the Welfare State, in: IZA Policy Paper No. 134, 2017, p. 10.

24 Gupta, Sanjeev/Keen, Michael/Shah, Alpa/Verdier, Genevieve (eds.), Digital Revolution in Public Finance, Washington D.C.: International Monetary Fund 2017, p. 73. In Spain, the obligation to register with the Special Scheme of Social Security for the Self-Employed is subject to the requirement that the activity must be performed regularly (in Spanish, "*de forma habitual*"). Case law gives an answer not using a time criterion, but pointing at a minimum level of (net) income, equivalent to the national minimum wage. Considering the characteristics of platform work, it is clear that a new rule is necessary in order to give an adequate response to the new type of activities associated with the emergence of the platform economy.

difference now is that they are becoming more frequent as "gig" activities increase and income distribution polarises.[25] Furthermore, there is an additional risk (a major one in countries like Spain) of informality[26] or under-declaration of income to avoid such duties.

A second risk has to do with legal classification. There are well-known implications in terms of the applicable contractual regulations. As we have already seen, whether the service provider is to be considered an employee of the platform or an independent contractor (or even a third, intermediate, category) is crucial in ascertaining whether said relation is subject to labour law or not. But sometimes it seems that it is not sufficiently highlighted that it also has important consequences for social security, given the fact that it will determine the correspondent scheme for registration. And this is not a minor thing.[27] On the one hand, there are still differences in terms of social coverage[28] and the risk of benefit inadequacy[29]. But, on the other, since the amount of contributions diverges depending on the scheme my interest here is the impact that such classification might have on social security funding. From the perspective of the financial condition of the system, and taking once again Spain as an example, the status of either employee (registration with the General Scheme of Social Security) or that of independent contractor (registration with the Special Scheme for

25 On the new social cleavage that has emerged between those working in highly paid sectors, and those working in low-paid services, see *Palier, Bruno*, The Politics of Social Risks and Social Protection in Digitalised Economies, Policy Network, 17 May 2018, https://policynetwork.org/opinions/essays/politics-social-risks-social-protection-digitalised-economies. Accessed 17 August 2020.

26 OECD, Pensions at a Glance 2019: OECD and G20 Indicators, OECD Publishing, Paris, 2019, p. 94, https://doi.org/10.1787/b6d3dcfc-en. Accessed 17 August 2020.

27 Note that the relevance of this issue is today more evident in the context of the Covid-19 crisis. See an illustration in *Rasche, Matthias*, Coronavirus Highlights Sick Pay Void for Platform Workers, Eurofound, 19 March 2020, https://www.eurofound.europa.eu/publications/article/2020/coronavirus-highlights-sick-pay-void-for-platform-workers. Accessed 17 August 2020.

28 The Covid-19 pandemic has openly – very often dramatically – shown the acute vulnerability of platform workers, who in some countries have been forced to face the economic, social and health consequences derived from the crisis without access to adequate social benefits. That is the case, for example, for sickness protection in countries like Belgium, cf. *Rasche, Matthias*, Coronavirus Highlights Sick Pay Void for Platform Workers (fn. 27).

29 It is certainly true that Spain has made significant progress in extending the (social protection) coverage of self-employed persons: full coverage against accidents at work and occupational disease, and "unemployment" (cessation of activity) became compulsory since 2019 (Royal Decree-Law 28/2018 of 28 December). Nevertheless, an important gap still remains in terms of adequacy as we will see below.

the Self-Employed) makes a real difference in terms of average contribution: on average, self-employed persons pay only 60 percent of what employees pay in contributions. The legal design of this issue explains this worrying outcome:[30] employees contribute according to their real income (salary), whereas self-employed persons are entitled to freely decide, within certain limits, their contribution base. Not surprisingly – interested in underestimation – the vast majority of them, circa 85 percent, opt for the legal minimum base[31] harming their future benefit rights, but also social security revenues at present. So we might conclude that, even if there is no fraudulent purpose, not considering the service provider as an employee of the digital platform will have a negative impact on the financing of social security.[32]

And finally, the third and probably most relevant factor that exposes the system to a risk of underfunding has to do with the new world of work that will result from the process of major change (digitalisation) that the economy is undergoing. To be more precise, what matters at this point is that the growth of *"just-in-time"* work will normally entail lower social contributions as a projection of the income linked to short-time activities. Note that this trend is compatible with a – foreseeable – scenario where the economy keeps on an upward path, showing the already mentioned job polarisation.[33] And note as well that this problem of low income and

30 Note that this unbalanced result is not caused by a divergence on the percentage of the contribution base (relatively similar in both cases), but by the legal provisions regarding such bases.

31 The current minimum contribution base stands at EUR 944 per month, in contrast with the corresponding General Scheme's minimum base: EUR 1,050 per month. After the significant increase of the minimum wage, such a difference makes it more "attractive" in terms of labour costs to register with the Special Scheme for the Self-Employed.

32 *Spasova, Slavina/Bouget, Denis/Ghailani, Dalila/Vanhercke, Bart*, Access to Social Protection for People Working on Non-Standard Contracts and as Self-Employed in Europe (fn. 18). As a matter of fact, the impact on the revenue side depends on how the payment of contributions by self-employed persons is regulated: in Spain, that difference exists but it is not that big once the self-employed are obliged to contribute once all social risks are fully covered after the 2018 reform. But the interest of digital platforms in the self-employment status is clear: the socialist trade union UGT (*Unión General de Trabajadores*) estimates that delivery platforms (Glovo, Deliveroo, Ubereats y Stuart) could be saving EUR 76 million per year (UGT 2019, 31).

33 *Autor, David/Mindell, David/Reynolds, Elisabeth*, The Work of the Future: Shaping Technology and Institutions, MIT Work of the Future, Fall 2019 Report, p. 22, https://workofthefuture.mit.edu/report/work-future. Accessed 17 August 2020.

subsequent low social security contributions does not only affect self-employed persons (especially in countries like Spain, if they choose their contribution base), but also those activities based on an employment relationship. In this regard, the response to the problem that we are facing is not just a question of "ensuring neutral social protection against unemployment, sickness and other life circumstances independent of employment status",[34] but a deeper, structural change that reflects the growing importance of capital with respect to labour.

As a matter of fact, this vulnerable position of platform workers is not new and, above all, not exclusive of this type of service provision; on the contrary, this characteristic is common to all forms of non-standard employment[35] in a context where employers try to preserve the competitiveness of their enterprises mainly by seeking to reduce labour costs. However, rather than mitigating the problem, it appears to aggravate it, because the extraordinary potential growth of the digital platform economy threatens to turn what today is atypical into typical work.[36]

All in all, we might conclude that the role of social contributions as the main source of financing of Bismarckian-type social security systems is, partly at least, in question. In countries like Spain, it is itself a major structural change – the dimension varies depending on the specific characteristics of the system – but its dimension becomes even more dramatic as this transformation takes place at the same time as population ageing, the retirement of the baby boom generation and a significant increase of pension expenditure. So at a moment when the social security system experiences a significant increase in financial needs, its central financing pillar is weakening, threatening long-term sustainability. Is there a margin to react

34 European Commission, Final Report of the High-Level Expert Group on the Impact of the Digital Transformation on EU Labour Markets, April 2019, Luxembourg: Publications Office of the European Union 2019, p. 42, https://ec.europa.eu/digital-single-market/en/news/final-report-high-level-expert-group-impact-digital-transformation-eu-labour-markets. Accessed 17 August 2020.

35 *Matsaganis, Manos/Özdemir, Erhan/Ward, Terry/Zavakou, Alkistis,* Non-Standard Employment and Access to Social Security Benefits, Research Note 8/2015, European Commission, Brussels, 2016, https://www.eurofound.europa.eu/data/platform-economy/records/non-standard-employment-and-access-to-social-security-benefits. Accessed 07 August 2020; OECD, The Future of Social Protection: What Works for Non-Standard Workers?, OECD Publishing, Paris, 2018, https://doi.org/10.1787/9789264306943-en. Accessed 17 August 2020.

36 *Schoukens, Paul/Barrio, Alberto,* The Changing Concept of Work: When does Typical Work Become Atypical?, in: European Labour Law Journal, 8 (2017) 4, doi:10.1177/2031952517743871.

and cope with this challenge so the main characteristics of said social insurance systems can be preserved? Or are we on the verge of a radical shift?

IV. Coping with the Financial Risks Associated with the Platform Economy? Small Steps, So Far

Certain actions can be useful to partly correct the three problems that have just been examined as causes of financial risks to social security. These "flanking policies" could involve taking steps against those activities that are developed outside the scope of the system and consequently without the obligation to pay social contributions. In a benchmarking analysis we come across legal reforms conceived to include sporadic or irregular activities within the scope of obligatory contributions. In some cases (France), regulation has sought to give coverage to a wide range of activities – not necessarily connected to platform economy – that, fraudulent or not, were not taxed in the past.[37] In others (Belgium),[38] there has been a specific legal response for platform workers limited so far to taxation, but that could certainly favour future registration with the correspondent social security scheme. Both orientations are not incompatible and could inspire legal reforms in countries such as Spain where there is a high proportion of irregular economy and where self-employed persons are only obliged to register with social security (Special Scheme for the Self-Employed) in cases where the activity is performed on a regular basis.[39]

Alongside the regularisation of activities that fall outside the scope of social security, we might find other actions aimed at increasing today's low contributions. Having noted the different positions occupied by employees and self-employed persons (also) in the field of social security and its projection on the financing system, a first achievement would be to correct the frequent cases of misclassification – platforms seeking to circumvent

37 See the French case (*chèque emploi-service universel*, Article L1271 Code du Travail).

38 Belgian law foresees an exemption from the payment of social security contributions for those working for digital platforms with earnings below 5,000 EUR, cf. *Schoukens, Paul/Barrio, Alberto,* The Changing Concept of Work: When does Typical Work Become Atypical? (fn. 36), p. 318.

39 In fact, case law tries to give an answer not using a time criterion, but pointing at a minimum level of (net) income, equivalent to the national minimum wage. Given the low salary level characteristic of the Spanish economy the contribution leak is easily imaginable: a new design of the social contribution system according to real income seems to be an adequate response.

applicable quality standards and rules governing the protection of workers and, particularly, social security contributions.[40] Adequate recognition of professional status would reinforce the scope of the social security scheme for employees (the so-called General Scheme in Spain) and favour an improvement of working conditions, including wages and, therefore, social contributions. But there are two aspects that we have to take into account.

First, the Spanish ongoing experience shows very limited results in terms of additional financial resources so far. Most of the judgements regarding legal classification of platform workers that have been mentioned above derived from actions of dismissal brought before the courts by individual workers claiming their status as employees. Only in isolated cases, legal action has been taken by the Inspectorate of Labour and Social Security on the grounds of misclassification of the so-called "collaborators"[41]. Said legal actions were based on previous administrative actions by the same Labour Inspectorate related to underpayment of social contributions. To be more precise, the relevant aspect is not so much the amount of unpaid social contribution[42], but the identification of the individual entity obliged to pay these: the digital platform, as the employer in the General Scheme of Social Security; therefore, not platform workers as self-employed persons in their own Special Scheme.

And second, it is important to be conscious that the labour framework itself is not enough as the increase of non-standard employment proves. Furthermore, the positive impact stemming from the employee status has probably a more individual than collective dimension. What is meant is that enriching labour and social guarantees could possibly drive the reinforcement of benefit adequacy (in individual terms). But from the perspective of financing, the extension of "just-in-time" service provision will inevitably limit the amount of contributions paid by employers and employees even if the productivity growth benefits wages.

As an alternative – beyond the employment scope, the improvement of the professional status of self-employed persons might also be a way of

40 Federal Ministry of Labour and Social Affairs. White Book 4.0 (fn. 18), p. 61.

41 See Judgements of Social Court No. 6 of Valencia of 1 June 2018 and 10 June 2019; Judgement of the High Court of Justice of Madrid (Social Chamber) of 17 January 2020; Judgement of Social Court No. 2 of Zaragoza of 27 April 2020 and Judgement of Social Court No. 21 of Madrid of 11 June 2020.

42 The administrative actions claiming for social security contributions are not that numerous so far. They have enabled the Labour Inspectorate to claw back a total of app. EUR 20 million in social security contributions, an amount that is insignificant in terms of social security funding.

counterbalancing the financial risk to social security associated with platform activities. Always focusing on Bismarckian systems, we observe a growing attention paid to the unsatisfactory, in general terms, social protection "enjoyed" by this group.[43] Again, it could be stated that there is a margin for real progress in terms of adequacy (access to the system and extent of coverage).[44] This is particularly the case for social schemes – like the Spanish one – that exclude from registration the self-employed whose income does not reach the legal threshold, and that enables said independent contractors to choose their contribution bases without taking into account real earnings. However, we should be conscious of the burden that paying contributions represents for the self-employed, given the fact that in this type of relationship those who are in business on their own account are the only ones responsible for such duty. Once more, this step forward does not seem to go very far.

To recap, we have shown the potential negative impact that the platform economy could have on the financing of social security systems mainly based on contributions. On the one hand, we have pointed out dysfunctional aspects concerning service provision through digital platforms (undefined labour status and social security framework) that could lead to a serious drop of social contributions. While, on the other, we have also suggested the adoption of certain measures that would improve the social conditions of platform workers and reinforce contribution collection. Nevertheless, the digital transformation that enhances the platform economy is so profound that it is to be acknowledged that those changes will not be enough to guarantee the long-term sustainability of Bismarckian social security systems, especially if/when they have to face the retirement wave of the huge baby boom generation. Further actions regarding sources of financing are urgently needed.

V. Preserving or Transforming the Financial Structure of Social Security Systems in a Context of Ageing?

Another relevant aim of this article is to carefully consider the advantages and disadvantages of the three possible paths that a Bismarckian system

43 OECD, Policy Responses to New Forms of Work, OECD Publishing, Paris, 2019, p. 52, https://doi.org/10.1787/0763f1b7-en. Accessed 17 August 2020.

44 *Forde, Chris/Stuart, Mark/Joyce, Simon/Oliver, Liz/Valizade, Danat/Alberti, Gabriella/Hardy, Kate/Trappmann, Vera/Umney, Charles/Carson, Calum*, The Social Protection of Workers in the Platform Economy (fn. 16), p. 51.

like the Spanish one could follow in terms of financial structure reform in the coming economic scenario associated with the platform economy. It is certainly a major issue since this decision will be determinant of the design of social security and its economic and social sustainability.

The first option would imply preserving the same financial structure of social security, at this moment largely based upon contributions.[45] We have already examined legal reforms that could (partly?) offset the potential financial risk. In fact, it is reasonable to think that these amendments will probably see the light of day sooner or later in all European countries to guarantee minimum working conditions to platform workers. Focusing on Spain, some important decisions in terms of revenue have been taken by the Spanish Government in recent years. Particularly relevant was the significant increase of the minimum wage (plus 22.3 percent in 2019 and plus 5.5 percent in 2020), a controversial decision that did not hinder job creation and that enabled, along with some other measures adopted by the *Royal Decree-Law 28/2018 of 28 December, on the revaluation of public pensions and other urgent social, labour and employment measures,*[46] an impressive increase of revenue (social contributions). Likewise, the steps taken by the Labour Inspectorate and, foreseeably, by the Government to reinforce the employment status of platform workers could also have some positive (though very limited) impact.

Notwithstanding this actual – or hypothetical – achievement that certainly favours average contributions, it would be irresponsible not to acknowledge that social security will not have the capacity to overcome the financial strain caused by the structural weaknesses linked to labour precariousness and, above all, ageing. This demographic change stemming from the retirement of the baby boom generation and, to a minor extent, the upward trend of life expectancy will significantly push up pension ex-

45 In 2019, social contributions (124 billion EUR) accounted for circa 90 percent of total public revenues of the Spanish social security system. That figure does not include financial resources: a loan allocated by the State to the social security system (13.8 billion EUR) and the withdrawal of assets from the Reserve Fund (3.6 billion EUR).

46 Said Royal Decree-Law 28/2018 foresaw full coverage against accidents at work and occupational diseases (besides "unemployment", i.e. cessation of activity) for self-employed persons. Although the increase of contribution rate associated with the new regulation is small (and gradual), the amount of social contributions collected is growing: 174 million (accidents at work and occupational disease) and 144 million (cessation of activity). Whereas, conversely, expenditure on benefits increases very moderately (Source: Secretary of State of Social Security and Pensions).

penditure – the main component of social security – requiring additional resources throughout a time period of around twenty years.

That said, preserving the current financial structure would surely lead to growing imbalances of the social security budget since the revenues coming from employer and employee contributions will not amount to the resources needed to pay benefits (mainly retirement pensions), even if further legal adjustments are adopted and even in a context of solid economic growth. In this respect, the evolution of social security in recent years has shown how constrained employer's and employee's contributions are when it comes to facing the maturation of social security and the process of ageing of society. As we have just seen, in 2019 some decisions on the revenue side of social security were taken by the Spanish Government with a very significant growth of social contributions (an increase of 7.9 percentage points, EUR 9 billion in absolute terms). And yet, the social security deficit still stood at a worrisome level (16.9 billion EUR, 1.5 percent of GDP), despite having reduced in size with respect to 2018. Leaving aside the uncertain consequences of the Covid-19 crisis, this type of situation – budgetary deficit – could be bearable in the short term through public debt, especially if the economic juncture is not favourable. But beyond that, a "structural" (long-term) imbalance is not sustainable and would certainly end up giving way to reforms seeking a retrenchment of the spending by means of benefit cuts (eligibility-restricting or generosity-reducing reforms). The result would be particularly negative for precarious workers, platform ones included, assuming that a close connection between professional trajectory and benefits is basically preserved. What we would probably see is an exacerbated polarisation of the workforce that could leave all those working in precarious conditions (low income) in a more vulnerable social position: insufficiently protected by social security (no eligibilty for benefits or less generous benefit enjoyment); and, due to their weak level of income, with no capacity – or a very limited one – to obtain in the private sector additional (retirement) savings to make up for the public shortage. In view of this outcome, I would conclude that a different path should be taken in order to preserve the sustainability of the social security system.

The second and third options would be initially channeled through the increase of general government revenue from taxation (tax-financed benefits),[47] but deployed in two very different manners; in fact, one would push the (originally) Bismarckian social security system towards a more

47 OECD, Policy Responses to New Forms of Work (fn. 43), p. 57.

Beveridgean one, whereas the other would avoid this shift maintaining its typical (mainly) contributive, earnings-related, design.

On reflection, it seems foreseeable that the stagnation of revenues coming from social contributions caused by an increasingly digitalised economy will give way to a broader involvement of the Government in financing social security. But we must be conscious that, if the outcome is an equivalent level of total funds, this movement could have very serious implications in terms of adequacy due to the growing (pension) spending associated with the ageing process. In other words, such a reconfiguration of the financial structure could just mean a change in the financing sources of social security without an alteration of the level of public expenditure.[48] But this would entail a major shift in the system since the number of beneficiaries (most of them pensioners) will peak in coming years: the level of social insurance benefits is then to be reduced assuming that private instruments will make up for such downsizing. In this regard, said shift ("path switching"[49]) could represent a first step towards a more *Beveridgean* system which in the specific field of pensions would correspond to what is known as a "multi-pillar model of first generation"[50]. Here the role of social security – the public social protection system – is characterised by mainly focusing on poverty prevention through the provision of assistance-rooted flat-rate or means-tested entitlements;[51] while, as a key supplement, policy-makers encourage the development of occupational (normally also individual) private plans. Again, the position of platform workers in this scheme looks troubling, maybe not in terms of severe poverty, but certainly in terms of risk of lack of protection and inequality.

Obviously, the problem does not lie in the (assistance) public pillar as it could be an effective instrument to fight against (working) poverty. The difficulties for non-standard workers (platform ones included) come from

48 To illustrate this remark, attention is drawn to the fact that the current level of public pension expenditure stands at 12 percent of GDP in Spain. In coming decades, the numbers of pensioners will sharply peak putting a strain on the pension system.

49 *Ebbinghaus, Bernhard*, Can Path Dependence Explain Institutional Change? Two Approaches Applied to Welfare State Reform, MPIfG Discussion Paper 05/2, 2005, p. 17, http://hdl.handle.net/10419/19916. Accessed 17 August 2020.

50 *Natali, David*, Pensions After the Financial and Economic Crisis, ETUI, Working Paper 2011.07, Brussels, 2011, p. 7, https://www.etui.org/sites/default/files/11%20WP%202011%2007%20WEB.pdf. Accessed 17 August 2020.

51 See *Behrendt, Christina/Quynh Anh Nguyen*, Ensuring Universal Social Protection for the Future of Work, in: Transfer, 25 (2019) 2, p. 30, doi:10.1177/1024258919857031. Accessed 17 August 2020.

their precarious status in the labour market and their subsequent doubtful capacity to engage in satisfactory terms in the complementary schemes (occupational or individual private plans).[52] Two, at least, potential risks for individuals within typical Bismarckian systems would then arise. First, from a general point of view, the restrained role played by social security and its redistributive mechanisms implies a greater dependence of individuals' social benefits on their professional trajectory. This would be particularly harmful for workers in countries with highly precarious labour markets. In this sense, it is easy to anticipate that the same precariousness that is suffered by atypical workers at the present time in Spain will also harm – in fact, already is incipiently harming – the professional status of platform workers. Second, even in countries where the quality of employment is better, this reinforced close relationship between benefits and previous wages brings along a serious risk of inequality. The "just-in-time" nature of platform activities seems to bring downward total working time, leading (inevitably?) to flat earnings. In such conditions, the saving capacity of workers – badly needed to complement their public basic pension – is more than doubtful.[53] The alternative is that this increase in tax-based financing would not call into question the current financial structure of Bismarckian inspiration where social contributions paid by employers and employees largely determine both the funding of the system and the granting of benefits. As a correction, the reform of the financial structure would consist of a deeper involvement of the State in funding social security – progressively seeking less dependence on said contributions.

Drawing our attention once again to Spain, in the short term this deeper involvement of the State in the financing of social security would be useful to correct a structural flaw by which certain expenditure items (i.e. operating expenses of social security, measures for the promotion of employment and temporary reduction of contributions, or subsidies to special

52 Private pension schemes play a limited role in Spain: assets in pension funds held 133 billion dollars in 2018, 9.5 percent of GDP – in contrast to 60 percent of GDP on OECD average. But it is particularly small when it comes to occupational schemes. The proportion of workers participating in this type of plans is low: 1.9 million participants, approximately 10 percent of the total working population in 2019. With two additional problems: first, the number of workers covered is frozen, has even been shrinking in recent years; and second, coverage is skewed to permanent – often well-paid – workers, see www.inverco.es/en/38/0/104/2020/3. Accessed 17 August 2020.

53 Economic Policy Committee/Social Protection Committee, Joint Paper on Pensions 2019 (fn. 2), p. 61.

schemes) are currently supported by contributions.[54] In the medium term, this more balanced design would provide for additional resources, the ones needed to cope with the impact of the retirement of the baby boom generation and to compensate the (relative) loss of relevance of contributions. And once this demographic phenomenon is exhausted, the system would be in a better position to adapt its financial structure to the economic environment.

In essence, this amendment would focus on reinforcing the redistributive component of social security, making it compatible with the preservation of the contributory (earnings-related) principle that defines social insurance schemes. It would mean smoothing the proportionality base of benefits through redistributive measures that are tax-financed. And this would be key to guaranteeing the adequacy (social sustainability) of benefits. The reason is that said solidarity component goes beyond ensuring a basic level of coverage, since it becomes useful to combat inequality in two ways. On the one hand, the combination of contributory and non-contributory elements is important to reduce the dependence of workers on private social protection mechanisms with a double effect of retaining high-income workers within social security and thus strengthening the legitimacy of the system. And on the other, even more significant, the redistribution element turns to be the instrument through which social security offers adequate access and coverage to platform workers – all non-standard workers in general.

How to implement this deeper involvement of the State in the financing of social security? It could be said that the platform economy is one of the factors that contributes to forging a deep trend whereby the distribution of income is shifting towards capital and against labour: capital is gaining importance relative to labour in the functional distribution of income; which is to say that the position of the owners of capital has been reinforced to the detriment of workers, very especially those in more precarious jobs. And the problem is that this shift comes with a continued decline of the share of tax revenues from capital in overall taxation in a context of economic globalisation. As a whole, both trends threaten to make it increasingly difficult to count on contributions as a main source of financing social security. In this scenario, the already mentioned dependence of

54 As the Independent Authority for Fiscal Responsibility (AIREF 2019, 56) has pointed out, the transfer of expenditure responsibilities from the social security system to the State would be one key measure to close the existing deficit in social security (1.5 percent of GDP in 2019).

social security financing on contributions calls for a response to preserve the labour-capital trade-off. The answer could come from collective bargaining if it could guarantee the transfer of productivity gains to wages, but recent reforms in this field in the EU countries have been oriented to weaken these instruments. Some experts also suggest favouring the access of workers to the ownership of capital.[55] In any case, neither of these solutions would be satisfactory enough. At present, and looking ahead, the emphasis must be put on taxing.

We find different options to diversify the financing mix of social protection. Some of them are related to capital. In this purview, new taxes are being created in Spain such as the tax on financial transactions, consisting of taxing all share purchase transactions carried out by financial operators, and the tax on digital services, ensuring that revenues generated by large companies that engage in certain digital activities not covered by the current fiscal framework are taxed.[56]

But the most relevant proposal so far is the *robot tax*, understood as the levy of a tax on the work performed by a robot. In fact, this new way of taxation has specifically to do with the impact of machinery (robots) replacing work currently performed by workers. It is not unthinkable that a rapid process of robotisation could demand an urgent and firm response of the State aiming at both slowing down the speed of automatisation and giving support to the redundant workers affected. There would be born the idea of a robot tax to face a potentially major social problem.[57] There are alternative means to compensate for the loss of relevance of labour in the financing mix in an emerging digital economy. Along these lines, environmental taxes could play a role, especially in those countries, such as Spain, where this type of taxing is still low. Note that both environment and social security (pensions) are very closely linked to the concept of sustainability and their intergenerational dimension. Likewise, consumption

55 *Freeman, B. Richard*, Who Owns the Robots Rules the World, IZA World of Labor 2015:5, doi: 10.15185/izawol.5.

56 Both bills are currently in Parliament. Though still modest in terms of revenue (their impact amounts to 1.2 billion and 850 million EUR, respectively), they trace a path that could provide for an increase of financial resources.

57 The Committee on Legal Affairs presented a motion for a European Parliament resolution on Civil Law Rules on Robotics that included a specific reference to a robot tax. However this remark was deleted from the text finally passed [European Parliament resolution of 16 February 2017 with recommendations to the Commission on Civil Law Rules on Robotics (2015/2103(INL))].

taxes (value added tax, VAT) play a role as an increasingly relevant source of financing.[58]

That said, an additional issue that should be seriously discussed is whether these potential new sources of financing social security should be earmarked. A well-known example is the French *contribution sociale généralisée* (CSG), which is levied as a separate tax on different types of income; but it can also be designed as part of general taxes on property or consumers.[59] In this way, earmarking could be an interesting solution to partly replace (offset) contributions as a stable source of social security financing. This motion for debate is still pending in Spain: the challenges to the sustainability of its social security system urge to open it.

VI. Conclusion

Throughout this chapter, attention has been drawn to the impact of the rise of platform economy on the financing of Spanish social security, a typical Bismarckian system. To recap, the following concluding remarks should be highlighted.

1. The rise of the platform economy and, in a broader sense, the process of digitalisation will affect the sustainability of public finances. Although long-term economic projections are moderately positive, we already observe that output is less dependent on labour. The consequence of this shift of income distribution is that tax systems will have to be (partly) redesigned to preserve welfare states. And in particular, in this new economic environment the dependence of typical earnings-related (social insurance) social security systems on social contributions threatens to seriously harm the financial balance of the system once the platform economy gains greater weight. The question lies in assessing the best way to tackle this threat.
2. Focusing on Spain, the emergence of the platform economy potentially generates financial risks to the social security system which stem from

58 *Spasova, Slavina/Ward, Terry*, Social Protection Expenditure and its Financing in Europe. A Study of National Policies, European Social Policy Network (ESPN), Brussels: European Commission 2019, p. 122, doi: 10.2767/145960.

59 See, for example, the Belgian case where part of VAT revenue is earmarked for social security. See *Hindriks, Jean/Baurin, Arno*, Financement des pensions: rétrospectives et perspectives, in: Reflets et perspectives de la vie économique, 58 (2019) 1, doi: 10.3917/rpve.581.0097.

three circumstances. One, the exclusion from the obligation to pay contributions of self-employed persons who are only obliged to register with social security if the activity is performed on a regular basis in the sense that a minimum level of income is reached. Two, legal misclassification, given the fact that the inadequate – though frequently sought – status of self-employment entails in practice a lower amount of contributions. And three, lower social contributions as a projection of the income linked to short-time activities, a new form of "atypical" employment progressively becoming typical.

3. Some steps could be taken in order to adapt the system to the new economic environment and to cope with these financial risks. Namely, regularise activities that fall outside the scope of the Special Scheme for the Self-Employed; implement a new system of social contribution for self-employed persons; and, above all, correct legal misclassification of platform workers through an adequate recognition of their professional status (employees) by reinforcing the scope of the General Scheme of Social Security.
4. Nevertheless, these measures will not be enough to tackle the major challenges faced by a typical Bismarckian social security system. On the one hand, the role of social contributions as the main source of financing of an earnings-related system of social security is partly in question due to the already mentioned shift of income distribution towards capital – against labour. And, on the other, the population is ageing as a consequence of a longer life expectancy and the retirement of baby boomers, bringing along a substantial increase of pension expenditure.
5. In order to preserve its long-term sustainability, the financial structure of the Spanish social security system should be adapted. It is important to note that not doing so in a context of population ageing would imply growing imbalances due to the financial strain caused by said process of ageing that would probably lead to reforms seeking a retrenchment of expenditure and causing an exacerbated polarisation of the labour force.
6. A first (and, in my view, unsatisfactory) response would be the increase of State funds to offset the foreseeable stagnation of social contributions. In this case, we would see a change in the financing sources of social security without altering the level of public expenditure. In an ageing society, it would entail that social security focuses on poverty relief moving towards a Beveridgean system where precarious (platform) workers face great difficulties to ensure an adequate social protection given their limited ability to enrol second pillar schemes.

7. The alternative takes a different path: increasing State funds to offset the stagnation of social contributions while preserving the current earnings-related system and its financial structure. This deeper involvement of the State in funding social security would enable the Spanish system to cope with the impact of ageing and, at the same time, reinforce its solidarity component to guarantee the adequacy of benefits. Its implementation in Spain demands a major tax reform to increase tax-revenue-to-GDP.

Chapter 10
Social Security in the Platform Economy: The French Example – New Actors, New Regulations, Old Problems?

Francis Kessler

I. Introduction

Digital technologies have led to new business models bearing various (mostly positive) names, e.g. "platform economy" or "collaborative economy". The only common factor of all these models is, however, that digital technology is used and that in most cases a physical workplace is not necessarily required for these activities. The organisation model of digital platforms is based on a triangular relationship.[1] A platform can play the role of an intermediary between a professional service provider and a "(platform) user-consumer", or of an intermediary between a "non-professional user-provider" and a "user-consumer". Work could be paid in each situation, but the provided work could also be without any payment. There is a great variety of business models active in multiple sectors, each of which has its own market characteristics.[2]

Both the overall organisation of the French social security scheme and the status of the worker influence the financing of social security. The compartmentalisation of social protection systems between employees and self-employed persons, and between the different categories of self-employed persons is one of the core characteristics of the French basic social security organisation (*sécurité sociale*). Apart from family benefits and health care, French Social Security includes several schemes, each covering one or more specific socio-professional categories:

– The general scheme covers employed persons and any person entitled to residence rights for family benefits and health care benefits. Unem-

1 *Dirringer, Josépha*, L'Avenir du droit de la protection sociale dans un monde ubérisé, in: Revue française des affaires sociales (RFAS), (2018) 2, p. 34.

2 *Petropoulos, Georgios*, An Economic Review on the Collaborative Economy, Policy Department A: Economic and Scientific Policy. Study for the IMCO Committee, May 2016, pp. 6, 12 f., https://www.europarl.europa.eu/thinktank/en/document.html?reference=IPOL_IDA(2016)595358. Accessed 19 June 2020.

ployment insurance is not part of the administrative organisation of *sécurité sociale* for historical reasons; it is instituted as a special fund.

- The specific schemes are geared for self-employed persons; most of the latter are managed by the general scheme,[3] while some of them – especially the so-called "liberal professions" (attorneys, medical doctors, etc.) – have kept their own old age and invalidity pension systems.[4] French self-employed workers are not insured against unemployment, accidents at work or occupational diseases.
- The agricultural regime (*Mutualité sociale agricole*) covers employed and self-employed workers in agriculture.
- "Special schemes" cover employees who are not in the general scheme (e.g. public servants, employees of SNCF and of the French utility companies providing gas and electricity).

3 Social security for self-employed workers (*"Régime social des indépendants*" – RSI) has been integrated in the general scheme as of 1 January 2020.

4 The construction of social protection in France is historically linked to the development and structuring of the employed salaried workforce. However, although it originally only covered employees, according to its founding order of 4 October 1945, the social security system was intended to cover all workers and their families. However, the non-agricultural self-employed occupations strongly resisted this generalisation for economic and sociological reasons, with the exception of compensation for family benefits. A compromise was finally reached with the public authorities, with the agreement that social security would be extended to self-employed persons, however through their own schemes to take into account the specific characteristics of their activities and aspirations. Established in stages, first in the form of autonomous pension insurance schemes starting in 1948, then health insurance schemes from the 1960s, the social security system for self-employed persons is characterised by a juxtaposition of different basic social security schemes which are themselves subject to a range of managing organisations. Membership with these schemes is mandatory.
The pension scheme for traders and the pension scheme for craftspeople are both managed by the *Régime social des indépendants* (RSI), which is under its way to be integrated into the general scheme under the name of *Sécurité sociale des indépendants* (SSI).
The pension scheme for the self-employed and the pension scheme for lawyers, are respectively managed by different funds under an overall umbrella of the fund for the self-employed (*Caisse Nationale d'Assurance Vieillesse Profession Libéral*, CNAV-PL) and the national fund for the French bar (*Caisse Nationale des Barreaux Français*, CNBF).
The health insurance scheme for traders, craftspeople and the liberal professions, managed formerly by the *Regime social des indépendants* is now administratively integrated into the general schema via the SSI.
The health insurance scheme, pension scheme and occupational accident scheme for farmers is managed by the agricultural social mutual scheme (MSA).

While one can observe a (slow but steady) move towards a harmonisation of the social protection schemes, there is a persistent gap between the costs of contributions and the coverage of social risks. Compulsory complementary pay-as-you-go old age pensions schemes, compulsory private collective health care insurance schemes, as well as complementary schemes on incapacity and invalidity based on collective agreements provide for a substantial part of social protection for employees. Self-employed persons who choose to do so can take out optional complementary insurance with a health plan or insurance company to top up their pension, health or unemployment insurance. Since the so-called "Madelin" Act of 1994,[5] they have been able to benefit from tax advantages, whereby they can deduct the amount of the contribution or insurance premium from their professional income. In 2013, within the framework of a National Inter-Professional Agreement (NIA), the French government required all employers (irrespective of the size of their businesses) to offer private complementary health insurance to their employees, and this agreement was taken over by the legislator to become law. This "generalisation" of complementary group health insurance to all employees is accompanied by tax incentives which target both the nature of contracts (collective), the content of collective health insurance contracts, and the fact that the individual premium has to be independent of the individual state of health of the insured ("responsible contracts"). In 2013, the "responsible contract" was still defined as a contract that encourages compliance with the gatekeeping pathway and does not reimburse non-refundable franchises but has to offer higher packages for dental and optical care.[6] The self-employed are not affected by these compulsory private health insurances but they can fall under the means-test criteria of the so-called "C2S" system.[7]

5 Law No. 94-126 of 11 February 1994 (Loi Madelin), in: Journal officiel de la République française (JORF), No. 37, 13 February 1994, p. 2493 ff.

6 The "Subsidized Individual Supplementary Health Insurance Program" ("*Complémentaire Santé Solidaire*", CSS) enrols insured individuals who are entitled to health care coverage on the basis of their employment or legal ongoing residence in France and whose income is below an amount that is determined by their household makeup. Income taken into account is that of the 12 months prior to their application. CSS members' health insurance expenses are covered by their health insurance funds and by the delegated supplementary insurer ("*organisme gestionnaire*") which they have chosen. These insurers will benefit from a tax relief.

7 Individual complementary health contracts, whether publicly aided (C2S) or not, will concern self-employed individuals, civil servants, students, precarious workers, the long-term unemployed, some inactive persons and a majority of retired persons. This population is composed of "good" risks and of "bad risks" such that it is

Platform workers are not a particularly homogeneous group in terms of legal status.[8] In France, in relation to services provided to the user-consumer of a particular platform, involved "platform workers" have the status of either an employee – for example for the storage of goods by Amazon – or that of a single-person limited company (*entreprise unipersonnelle à responsabilité limitée,* EURL) combined with the status of micro-entrepreneur, which is a subtype of self-employed status (see below). Others – especially the high-skilled work force – tend to opt for the single-person corporation (SASU[9]): a president of such a simplified company is considered an employee of the company and so pays normal social security contributions to the general system (except for unemployment insurance).[10] "Platform work" is, in this case, the expression of individuals of a preference for self-employed work or, of persons who may dread being submitted to a hierarchy and prefer to work on their own, the wish to deliver a higher performance under the conditions of self-employed work. The contractor can conclude a contract with the platform for the provision of services (*louage d'ouvrage*, as defined in Article 1710 of the Civil Code). The advantage for the platform lies in the set of conditions applicable to the

---

difficult to state how the risk structure of the individual collective health insurance market will evolve and whether this will result in an increase in premiums rates.

8 For alternative classifications: European Commission, "Don't Gig Up!" State of the Art Report. Working Paper 2/2019, April 2019, p. 5, http://www.ires.fr/index.php/etudes-recherches-ouvrages/documents-de-travail-de-l-ires/item/5935-n-02-2019-don-t-gig-up-state-of-the-art-report. Accessed 15 June 2020; *Allaire, Nolwenn/Colin, Nicolas/Palier, Bruno/Tran, Laurène*, Covering Risks for Platform Workers in the Digital Age. Working Paper. Sciences Po, Chaire numérique, gouvernance et innovations institutionnelles, 1 May 2019, p. 10, https://www.sciencespo.fr/public/chaire-numerique/wp-content/uploads/2019/05/covering-risks-plateform-workers-digital-age.pdf. Accessed 15 June 2020.

9 A SASU (société par action unipersonnelle) is a one-man company and a simplified version of an SAS (société par action simplifiée), which can be set up by a single person. The minimum capital is EUR 37,000 or EUR 25,000 if you want your stock to be publicly traded. *Abdelnour, Sarah/Méda, Dominique*, Les nouveaux travailleurs des applis, Paris: PUF, 2019.

10 As an example, many UBER Drivers opt for single-owner limited liability companies (EURL), simplified shareholder company (SAS), or simplified single-shareholder company (SASU). According to preliminary results, more than 30 percent of UBER independent drivers have a SAS-SASU status, 15 percent are auto-entrepreneurs (AE), 15 percent have a EURL/SARL/EI/EIRL status, whereas others are employees or cumulate different statuses. *Abdelnour, Sarah/Bernard, Sophie*, Vers un Capitalisme de Plateforme? Mobiliser le travail, Contourner les régulations, in: La nouvelle revue du travail, 13 (2018) 2, doi: 10.4000/nrt.3797.

manpower: fee-for-service arrangement, possibility to terminate the contractual relationship at any time, and possibility to circumvent labour law and social contributions and unemployment contributions as an employee.

In this context, several parallel discussions have taken place. A "classical" debate has been on the labour law status of the worker sometimes leading to the requalification of service contracts to employment contracts, which has implications for the social security status of the platform workers. Classification as an employee will result in the payment of social contributions related to that status. The *Court de Cassation*, the French highest court in private litigations, has held on 28 November 2018[11] that delivery riders working for online delivery platforms are to be treated as employees rather than self-employed workers. French Uber drivers also claimed to be in a subordination relationship with Uber. The French Court of Cassation has decided to reclassify the contractual relationship between Uber and a driver as an employment contract. Indeed, when connecting to the Uber digital platform, a subordination relationship has been established between the driver and the company. Hence, the driver does not provide services as a self-employed person, but as an employee.[12] Consequently, the French Social Security Recovery Agency, i.e. the institution in charge of collecting social security contributions (*Union de recouvrement des cotisations de Sécurité Sociale et d'Allocations Familiales*, URSSAF) has publicly claimed that the regularisation of the reclassification of platform workers as employees is Uber's responsibility, who is required to declare and pay social security contributions for its drivers. The French Social Security authority also stated that they "may subsequently initiate actions on their own initiative to check whether the expected regularisation has indeed been carried out".[13]

This chapter will deal with the financing of social security *stricto sensu*. We will examine the major outputs of a discussion mostly driven by a taxi

11 Cour de cassation, Social Chamber of 28 November 2018, Case No. 137 (17-20.079), ECLI:FR:CCASS:2018:SO01737, https://www.courdecassation.fr/jurisprudence_2/chamber_sociale_576/1737_28_40778.html. Accessed 16 July 2020.

12 Cour de cassation, Social Chamber of 4 March 2020, Case No. 374 (Uber), https://www.courdecassation.fr/IMG/20200304_arret_uber_english.pdf. Accessed 16 July 2020.

13 *Taquet, François*, Les démêlés d'Uber avec l'Urssaf... : Uber 1/Urssaf, JSL, 2017, No. 433, p. 27 ; Dernièrement, Cour de cassation, Chambre civile 2, 28 novembre 2019, 18-15.333, F-P+B+I (No. Lexbase: A3474Z4G); *Meiffret-Delsanto, Karine,* Recours à un auto-entrepreneur et contrôle URSSAF: attention au redressement!, Lexbase Social, 2020, No. 809 (No. Lexbase: N1858BYH).

drivers' riot against VTC drivers,[14] by the creation of a professional association of self-employed VTC drivers (called "union") and by the requalification of self-employed persons as employees and the application of the corresponding social security contributions. In Section III, we will examine the major output of this debate, namely specific legislative measures trying to protect VTC drivers beyond the social security system. In Section IV, we will examine the other path that has been chosen by the French legislator on the income of short-term furnished rentals.[15] With the so-called "*Airbnb rule*" the French legislator has tried to combine two goals: collect social security contributions on income generated by such rental activity via a platform, but also promote these individual activities by (partial) exemptions of some of that same income. In Section V, the new anti-fraud measures will be reviewed. Indeed, France has introduced, via Law No. 2018-898 of 23 October 2018, the obligation for all electronic platforms to transfer to tax authorities the complete data on transactions, bank accounts used, and all identification details, including those of the service provider. Under the Amending Finance Act for 2016 and, in particular, the Anti-Fraud Act of October 2018, platforms are now required to submit the data on income received by each person renting out this kind of accommodation to the tax authorities, which in turn share this information with the social security collecting institutions. So as to understand these – most often very sophisticated – sectorial rules, Section II will deal with the overall financial organisation of the French social security system(s).

---

14 In January 2016, French taxi unions had staged a nationwide strike, shutting down roadways across Paris in a protest against ride-hailing companies like Uber. Thousands of taxi drivers participated in demonstrations across Paris today, disrupting traffic to and from the French capital's two major airports. Protesters burned tires at a major thoroughfare on the western edge of Paris, where police used tear gas to disperse some, and two taxi drivers were injured after a shuttle bus drove through a blockade at Orly airport.

15 In the area of short-term furnished rental, in particular relating to Airbnb, France has adopted a complete regulation. The rules focus on owners who offer short-term rental of dwellings they do not occupy, i.e. secondary residences. It is then necessary, before any announcement online, to make an administrative pre-rental declaration, and to address it to the mayor of the municipality where the housing is located. The platforms are also responsible for and have an obligation to inform the owners about their obligations, and must ask them for a declaration on the honour attesting the respect of the rules. The municipal declaration number must appear in the ad on the site. The platform must also ensure that an owner who rents his own accommodation does not exceed 120 nights per year, beyond which the dwelling can no longer be considered as his main residence.

II. Financing Social Security: Main Principles

The French Social Security is mainly financed through contributions based on income. All income earned from professional activities is subject to social contributions. Social security contributions are a major part of taxation in France, as they represent 37.1 percent of total tax revenues, and with 17 percent of GDP, French social security contributions are the highest among OECD countries. The share nominally ascribed to employers is also more important in France than in other countries, representing 11.3 percent of GDP, more than twice the OECD average of 5.2 percent.[16] As a general trend, the overall percentage of contributions is slowly decreasing; the part of taxes or assimilated taxes is growing especially for employees. The general scheme for employees and the "special schemes" for certain categories of employees and civil servants are mainly financed through contributions from both employees and employers. The rates applicable differ according to the nature of the risk. These rates, set by decree, are uniform and are intended to apply to all employers and employees. Only the rates for accidents at work are determined according to the activity and the value of the risk specific to the company (i.e. the cost of accidents at work or occupational illnesses arising for employees).

Although self-employed workers are now administratively integrated into the general scheme, the level of their contributions is still slightly different from that of employees and depends on the legal and tax status of the company. Since 2009, a simple business status has been available to anyone who wishes to establish a small business in France. The term micro-entrepreneur (formerly known as auto-entrepreneur) is the usual term for the "*régime micro-social*" tax system. It is not a legal form (the legal status is still that of one form of single company), but a simplified reporting system and payment of contributions and social charges is effected by proportion of turnover, according to the principle of "no turnover, no dues". The micro-entrepreneur is not registered for VAT and limits are imposed on annual turnover: EUR 170,000 for commercial businesses and EUR 70,000 for service professionals and artisans. Those adopting this status run the business as a *micro-entreprise*, which leads to a rather complex and often changing contribution system, i.e. the self-employed social security scheme, which

16 *Bozio, Antoine/Breda, Thomas/Grenet, Julien*, Incidence of Social Security Contributions: Evidence from France, March 2017, https://www.tresor.economie.gouv.fr/Articles/231ab136-d997-4563-9ece-f885dac3c8a5/files/1c6489fa-099b-4ed6-ab6a-0554305997d3. Accessed 15 June 2020.

could be summed up in (i) a liability to social security contributions based on cash receipts, not on profit or loss, and (ii) relief for new micro-enterprises available at the rate of 50 percent for the first year of activity.

Earmarked taxes (*impôts et taxes affectés*, ITAF) are mandatory withholdings that are explicitly earmarked for social security financing. These include the General Social Contribution (*Cotisation Sociale Généralisée*, CSG), which alone amounts to more than half of all ITAF and various other taxes especially on the pharmaceutical sector. This CSG, but also the Social Debt Repayment Contribution (*Contribution pour le Remboursement de la Dette Sociale*, CRDS) are paid on employment income, replacement income, property income, investment income and gambling income. All persons treated as French residents for income tax purposes and subject to a French compulsory health insurance scheme are liable to CSG at the following rates:

- 9.2 percent on employment income,
- 6.2 percent on "replacement incomes" (e.g. daily sickness benefits, unemployment benefits, retirement pensions etc.).

Individuals drawing a French pension are either exempted from or liable to CSG, CRDS and/or CASA (*Contribution Additionnelle de Solidarité pour l'Autonomie*, Additional Solidarity Contribution for Autonomy[17]) as determined by their reference taxable income.

A steadily growing part of the *value added tax* is dedicated to the financing of social security. The main idea of what is sometimes called "Social VAT" in the French debate is reducing the tax burden on labour via an exemption from social security contributions by offsetting the loss of revenue to the public finances caused by an increase in VAT. As an example, VAT earmarked to finance social security reached EUR 10.1 billion in 2018; it had been no less than EUR 46 billion in 2019 according to the projections of the High Council for the Financing of Social Protection. This is mainly due to the 6-point reduction in the health insurance contribution rate, estimated at almost EUR 23 billion.[18]

---

17 See: Comment s'applique la contribution de Solidarité pour l'Autonomie (Casa)?, March 2020, https://www.service-public.fr/particuliers/vosdroits/F31408. Accessed 16 July 2020.

18 Haut conseil du financement de la protection sociale, Etat des lieux du financement de la protection sociale, May 2019, https://www.strategie.gouv.fr/sites/strategie.gouv.fr/files/atoms/files/hcfips-2019-05-10_etat_des_lieux_actualise.pdf. Accessed 16 July 2020.

III. First Legislative Initiatives to Take Account of the Platform Economy

The French Labour Code contains express provisions seeking to assimilate particular typologies of workers, such as journalists, models, performing artists, etc., to the legal regime applicable to standard employees and, as an important consequence thereof, the application of the rules of the general social security system to these categories. Also, Article L.311-3 of the Social Security Code lists the professional categories that are integrated in the general scheme, such as managers of limited liability companies and private limited liability companies with minority or egalitarian remuneration, chairmen and chief executive officers of public limited companies and private limited companies, and chairmen of the cooperative banking companies. However, the French legislator has, up to now, chosen another path for "gig workers".

1. The Premises: The Mettling Report and the France Stratégie Report

The issue of digital labour and the awareness of digital transformation with its consequences on the labour market has re-launched the debate. Two reports were published in 2015 within a short period of time: the Mettling report "*Transformation numérique et vie au travail*" (digital transformation and life at work)[19] and the France Stratégie[20] report "*Le Compte personnel d'activité (CPA): de l'utopie au concret*" (the personal activity account: from utopia to concrete practices).

For its part, the Mettling report lays out recommendations in order to "reintegrate the new forms of work into our social protection scheme". The report underlines that digital technology is increasing the number of freelancers and the porosity between salaried activity and other forms of

19 It follows various reports on the topic since 2013, but it is the first study on the implications of the digital transformation for the workplace. This work was complemented by studies entrusted to several major consulting firms and a survey carried out among 4,500 young company managers. It is based on interviews with a number of leading figures in the trade union sector, but also with consultants, and has resulted in thirty-six recommendations.

20 Stratégie, administratively called "Commissariat général à la Stratégie et à la Prospective" (CGSP), is an institution attached to the Prime Minister. Its objective is to contribute to the determination of the broad guidelines for the nation's future and the medium- and long-term objectives of its economic, social, cultural and environmental development, as well as to the preparation of reforms.

work. It demonstrates the need for a set of rights attached to the person and transferable from one company to another, from one status to another. The new forms of work must also contribute to the financing of social protection. Recommendation No. 17 of 36 proposes to update the jurisprudence concerning the classification as a salaried worker, by introducing a wider range of criteria, such as the level of autonomy at work, the exclusivity of services, the decision-making of remuneration, etc.

The France Stratégie's report states that "no one knows exactly what its consequences will be for work and employment, but it is clear that its emergence calls into question the belief in a generalized trend towards a monoactivity wage model. It is therefore important, as a matter of urgency, to rethink the mechanisms for the protection and support of individuals for a world where there will be a plurality of activities and statutes". In 2016, France Stratégie published another report called "*Nouvelles formes de travail et de la protection des actifs*" (New forms of work and protection of the workforce). It stresses the new risks to consider (fluctuation in revenues for independent workers, accidents and disease for freelancers and nomadic workers) and exposes (not so surprisingly) the different options for a new social protection scheme, namely (i) to maintain the distinction between employment and independent work, while broadening the scope of salaried work and improving transition security, or (ii) to create a third status for economically dependent self-employed workers, or (iii) to go beyond the distinction between employment and independent work, while establishing a unique worker's status.

The CESE (*Conseil économique, social et environnemental*) has also recommended[21] to develop the social dialogue between public authorities, social partners and representative bodies of the self-employed; to promote the responsibility of third parties (social responsibility of platforms and BEC, extension of the status of "*entrepreneur-salarié*", etc.); to secure the social rights of the new independent workers, especially by allowing workers on digital platforms to benefit from unemployment insurance in case of total

21 *Thiéry, Sophie*, Les nouvelles formes du travail indépendant, in: Les Avis du CESE, Journal officiel de la République Française, November 2017, https://www.lecese.fr/sites/default/files/pdf/Avis/2017/2017_25_travail_independant.pdf. Accessed 16 July 2020;
Conseil économique social et environnemental - The Economic, Social and Environmental Council (ESEC) is a constitutional consultative assembly. It represents key economic, social and environmental fields, promoting cooperation between different socio-professional interest groups and ensuring they are part of the process of shaping and reviewing public policy.

revenue loss. An IGAS report has discussed various scenarios regarding the extension of the unemployment scheme to the self-employed.[22]

2. *Legislative Attempts*

The legislative attempts are exclusively aimed at "Uber drivers" or "VTC drivers".[23] No overall rule for platform workers has been adopted yet.

a) First Attempt: Law on Work, Modernising the Social Dialogue of 2016

VTC platforms owe their success to a reduction in transaction costs (lack of taximeters and dispatchers, integrated payment system), better allocation of resources (increased vehicle utilisation rate, reduced waiting time) and, in principle, more efficient price information than taxis. Tensions between French taxi drivers and VTC (Uber) drivers in 2015, with Uber drivers and taxi drivers taking aim – literally – at each other's cars have prompted the French legislator to become active. The so-called "Labour Law" of August 2016[24] has established a legal framework under which the relations between some digital platforms and workers are regulated and, above all, has established a definition of collaborative platforms. The legislator has defined the scope of its intervention. An "electronic platform" (this is the terminology in the French Labour Code) is understood as a "company that irrespective of its place of establishment puts into electronic contact a client and a worker, with the purpose of selling or exchanging a good or service". This definition echoes the definition of Article L.111-7 of the French Consumer Code, which considers as an online platform provider "any natural or legal person offering, on a professional basis, including for free, an online communication service to the public that is

22 Inspection Générale des Affaires Sociales (IGAS), Rapport: Ouverture de l'Assurance chômage aux travailleurs indépendants, No. 2017-096R, October 2017, http://www.igas.gouv.fr/IMG/pdf/Rapport-Assurance_chomage_independants.pdf. Accessed 16 July 2020. The IGAS is the French Government audit, evaluation and inspection office for health, social security, social cohesion, employment and labour policies and organisations.

23 French law distinguishes "taxis", heirs of cabs and then of so-called square cars, and "transport vehicles with drivers", heirs of so-called discount cars.

24 Law No. 2016-1088 of 8 August 2016 (regarding work and modernising the social dialogue), in: JORF, No. 0184, 9 August 2016.

based on: 1) ranking or referencing contents, goods or services offered or uploaded by third parties by using computerised algorithms; 2) allowing several parties to get in contact with one another for the sale of goods, the provision of services or the exchange or sharing of content, goods or services".

It also created a social responsibility for platforms by inserting Articles L.7341-1 to L.7341-6 into the Labour Code. According to Article L.7342-1 of the Labour Code, "when the platform determines the characteristics of the service provided or the good sold and fixes its price, it has, with regard to the workers concerned, a social responsibility that is exercised under the conditions provided for in this chapter". Article 60 of the so-called "*loi travail*" conferred two specific rights concerning social protection on platform workers. The regulation supports platform workers in receiving professional training and introduces coverage against accidents at work to these platform workers. This provision does not apply to all platforms, but only to those that determine the characteristics of the service provided or of the goods sold, and that fix the price of the service.[25]

The first part of this social responsibility requires the platform to cover insurance costs related to the risk of occupational accidents.[26] Platforms must either reimburse the contributions paid by self-employed workers in respect of their subscription to an insurance covering the risk of accident at work or their subscription to voluntary insurance against accident at work,[27] or otherwise offer self-employed workers a collective insurance contract covering the risk of accidents at work.[28] When the self-employed worker has taken out insurance covering the risk of accidents at work or joins the voluntary insurance scheme for accidents at work, the costs are covered by the platform if the self-employed worker has achieved a turnover greater than or equal to 13 percent of the annual social security ceiling.[29] For 2020, the annual social security ceiling is EUR 40,524. The worker's turnover must therefore be equal to or above EUR 5,268.12 (EUR 40,524 x 13 percent). Where the self-employed person works for several collaborative platforms, the costs shall be reimbursed by each of them in proportion to the turnover which the self-employed person has achieved

25 Article L.7342-1 of the Labour Code.

26 *Desbarrats, Isabelle*, Quel statut social pour les travailleurs des plateformes numériques? La RSE en renfort de la loi, in: Droit social, (2017) 11, p. 971.

27 Article L.7242-2 para. 1 of the Labour Code.

28 Article L.7242-2 para. 2 of the Labour Code.

29 Article D.7342-1 of the Labour Code.

through it, in relation to the total turnover which he has achieved through the platforms.[30]

The contribution due by the platform is equal to the contribution due for voluntary insurance against accidents at work and occupational diseases, assessed by means of an annual salary lower than a minimum determined on 1 April of each year calculated on the basis of the change in the annual average of consumer prices, excluding tobacco, published by the National Institute of Statistics and Economic Studies on the penultimate month preceding the date of revaluation of the benefits concerned.[31] The rate of the voluntary insurance contribution is equal to 80 percent of the rate of the contribution for accidents at work and occupational diseases fixed for the same type of activity.[32] The maximum amount of contribution paid by the platform will therefore be calculated as follows[33]: accident rate × 80 percent × reference minimum wage.

The overall financing of social security is concerned: each self-employed person can deduct the cost of this insurance from his revenue. The decree specifies that the worker who wishes to be reimbursed for these costs must apply to the platform, justifying the costs and indicating the turnover achieved. This request can be made online and free of charge. The platform must inform its workers of the existence of such repayment terms.[34] If the aforementioned conditions are met, the platform reimburses contributions up to a ceiling equal to the contribution due under the voluntary insurance for accidents at work and occupational diseases, calculated on the basis of the minimum wage.[35]

The platform is exempt from this obligation if the worker adheres to the collective insurance contract the platform puts in place for its workers, provided that the platform contract offers guarantees at least equivalent to those provided for by the individual insurance.[36] In the absence of any indication to the contrary, it does not seem that the worker must subscribe to the collective insurance contract put in place by the platform. Therefore, it would seem that the worker who prefers to take out voluntary or individual insurance rather than subscribe to the collective insurance con-

30 Article D.7342-4 of the Labour Code.

31 The Decree of 4 May 2017 and the Interministerial Circular published on 8 July 2017.

32 Article D.24-6-11 of the Social Security Code.

33 Circular DGT-RT1-DGEFP-SDPFC-DSS-2C 2017-256 of 8 June 2017.

34 Article D.7342-5 of the Labour Code.

35 Article D.7342-2 of the Labour Code.

36 Article L.7342-2 of the Labour Code.

tract will be able to obtain the reimbursement of contributions paid. When the worker subscribes to a collective contract that includes guarantees at least equivalent to those provided for in the voluntary insurance for accidents at work, the contribution to this contract is entirely paid by the platform.[37]

Many platforms have partnered with insurance companies to offer insurance policies for accident and liability protection. Uber announced a partnership with AXA in July 2017, and in May 2018 it declared that it was expanding the partnership on a European scale. Deliveroo also entered into a partnership with AXA in March 2017. On their part, Brigad – a platform connecting companies from all sectors with qualified freelancers and specialists in the hotel and restaurant business – offers its self-employed partners (known as "Brigaders") access to complementary health care at a negotiated rate, with progressive reimbursement by the platform according to the worker's level of activity. There is no actual discussion on this topic but a recent report of the French Senate states that these attempts to build up private social protection beyond the social security system might be unsuccessful given that "while they may be beneficial to workers, these initiatives fall short of genuine social protection in the face of major risks, in particular that of accidents at work".[38]

b) Second Attempt: Law to Choose One's Professional Future of 2018

In a second attempt the so-called "Law to Choose One's Professional Future"[39] the legislator tried to include additional provisions that would have given platforms the possibility to set up a "social charter" in favour of these workers. The purpose of this charter was to afford workers a higher level of protection while setting aside any risk of reclassification of the contractual relationship as an employer-employee relationship. Thus, the Constitutional Council has declared that the article related to Article 66 of the Law was

---

37 Article L.7342-2 al. 2 of the Labour Code.

38 *De Forssier, Michel/Fournier, Catherine/Puissat, Frédérique*, Travailleurs des plateformes: au-delà de la question du statut, quelles protections? Rapport d'Information No. 452 (2019-2020). Fait au nom de la commission des affaires sociales, 20 Mai 2020.

39 Law No. 2018-771 of 5 September 2018.

adopted according to a procedure contrary to the Constitution and therefore void.[40]

c) Law on Mobilities of 2019

Following this unsuccessful attempt, the measure reappeared in the draft of a "Law on Mobilities" (*Loi d'orientation des mobilités*), presented by the Council of the Ministers on 26 November 2018 and adopted by the National Assembly on 19 November 2019, and is still under discussion at the Parliament; it offers platforms to voluntarily enter into a charter additional social rights for the self-employed in return for the non-reclassification of a legal relationship of subordination between the platforms and the workers. Article 20 of the Law foresees that, through a charter, platforms offer additional social rights to self-employed workers. Among the various provisions relating to VTC platforms the Law encourages the latter to set up social responsibility charters (forthcoming Articles L.7342-8 and L.7342-9 of the Labour Code). This Article states that "the platform may establish a charter determining the terms and conditions for the exercise of its social responsibility, defining its rights and obligations as well as those of the workers with whom it is in contact". Concerning social protection, the Article adds that the charter specifies in particular "under its point 8° the supplementary social protection guarantees negotiated by the platform and from which workers may benefit, in particular for the coverage of the risk of death, risks affecting the physical integrity of the person or linked to maternity, risks of incapacity for work or disability, as well as the provision of benefits in the form of retirement pensions, allowances or bonuses for retirement". This charter must first be validated by the administration responsible for measuring its relevance.

On 27 November 2019, the Constitutional Council was called on by more than 60 Members of the National Assembly in an ex ante review pro-

---

40 Constitutional Council Decision No. 2018-769 DC of 4 September 2018 "The last sentence of the first paragraph of Article 45, last sentence, of the Constitution states: "Without prejudice to the application of Articles 40 and 41, any amendment shall be admissible at first reading if it is related, even indirectly, to the text tabled or transmitted". Introduced at first reading, Article 66 does not have any link, even indirectly, with the provisions contained in the bill tabled on the National Assembly's desk. It was therefore adopted according to a procedure contrary to the Constitution".

cedure[41] especially on Article 20. The Members of the National Assembly, who referred the matter to the Constitutional Council, questioned the various aspects of this reform. The authors of the referral deplored the purely "optional" nature of the social responsibility charter. In addition, the uncertainties surrounding the legal value and normative scope of this charter raised questions about its opposability. They also emphasised the presumption of a non-salaried status for platform workers. According to them, the option would seek to circumvent the judicial judge's case law on the subordination relationship, whereas in a judgment of 28 November 2018, the Social Chamber of the Court of Cassation opened the way for a possible reclassification in relation to employee benefits.[42] The legislator would thus have favoured as far as possible the legal security of the economic model of platforms to the detriment of the effective protection of the "self-employed" in their relationship with these platforms. The initiators of the referral also complained that the legislator had confined himself to listing eight mandatory topics to be included in the charter without specifying the minimum social guarantees that should apply to platform workers. Finally, the wording of the provisions concerned would establish, for several reasons, a difference in treatment between self-employed persons in relation to a platform and that of other self-employed persons. According to the law providing for the scope of the charter to be reserved for workers on VTC, not all self-employed workers would be covered, nor even all workers independent of electronic contact platforms. On the other hand, there would also be a breach of equality between self-employed workers in relation to a platform having established a charter and those in relation with a platform that has not engaged in this approach.

41 The Constitutional Council is seized on a mandatory basis with organic laws and the regulations of the Houses of Parliament prior to promulgation of the former and prior to the entry into force of the latter.

42 Cour de cassation, Social Chamber, 28 November 2018, No. 1720079 FPPBRI. In this case, a rider filed a claim before the Court to obtain the reclassification of the relationship with Take Eat Easy into an employment contract. The Labour Chamber of the Court of Cassation admitted the status of employee, on the grounds that the platform included a geo-tracking system to monitor the rider's position in real time and record the number of kilometers ridden. In addition, the company held disciplinary power over the delivery rider (in particular based on the bonus/malus system applied by the platform), and would give the rider instructions. The Court of Cassation granted the status of employee to the self-employed delivery driver.

The Constitutional Council has given its decision on 20 December 2019[43] regarding the conformity of the "Law on Mobilities" with the French Constitution. Most of the provisions referred to the Constitutional Council were validated, but the latter nevertheless censors the provision which provided that compliance with the commitments established in the charter cannot characterise a relationship of subordination between the platform and the worker. For this matter, the Constitutional Council recalls that "while, in principle, workers in relation to a platform that has established a charter exercise their activity independently, it is up to the judge, in accordance with the Labour Code, to reclassify their relationship as an employment contract when it is characterized by the existence of a legal relationship of subordination". Yet, the contested provisions were intended to prevent such reclassification by the judge, which leads to a change in the calculation of social security contributions and to sanctions against the platform then considered as an employer.

IV. *New Sources of Financing in a Gig Economy: The Example of Rental of Furnished Accommodation for Short Periods*

France has adopted on 24 July 2019 a Digital Tax Bill.[44] The tax consists of a 3 percent levy applied to revenue derived from specific digital activities by companies with a qualifying revenue of more than EUR 750 million worldwide and EUR 25 million in France. The tax is applied retroactively as of January 2019 with the first payments due in November 2019.[45] As re-

---

43 Constitutional Council Decision No. 2019-794 DC of 20 December 2019.

44 Largely inspired by the EU Directive, for which no consensus was found.

45 The following services are subject to the DST:
"The supply, by electronic means, of a digital interface that allows users to contact and interact with other users, including for the delivery of goods or services directly between those users";
"Services provided to advertisers or their agents enabling them to purchase advertising space located on a digital interface accessible by electronic means in order to display targeted advertisements to users located in France, based on data provided by such users.
These services include, among others, the buying, stocking and diffusion of advertising messages and the management and communication of users' data.
The Law excludes from the scope the following services:
Direct sale of goods or services online;
Making a digital interface available as a primary means to provide users with digital content, communication services and payment services".

gards social contributions and, moreover, the financing of the basic social security schemes, in principle all income derived from professional activities is subject to social contributions and results in affiliation to a social security regime (see above Section II). But the picture is a little more complicated than that as shows the example of rental by private persons of furnished accommodation. The rise of digital platforms in the economy of seasonal rentals and their easy use have led to a tenfold increase in short-term rentals: the social security contribution rules on the revenue generated by this type of activity largely via a digital platform (*Airbnb, HomeAway, HouseTrip, 9Flats, Wimdu, Abritel, SeLoger Vacances*) shows the contradictory intentions of the legislator – which on the one hand tries to encourage private initiative and new forms of earnings through digital platforms and, on the other hand, wants these kind of earnings to contribute to the financing of the social security system. The result is an extraordinarily complex legislation especially because the legislator has chosen to keep the traditional categories and is only trying to adapt them to the "new economy".

1. *Definition(s)*

The situation of people renting furnished accommodation for short periods has always been complex because there are two legal categories that tenants now operating with digital platforms had to fit in: "bed and breakfast" or "guest rooms" (*chambre d'hôtes*) and "furnished tourist accommodation" (*meublé de tourisme*). The rental of bed and breakfast and furnished accommodation is governed by the legislation concerning seasonal rentals, i.e. the Tourism Code. As such, the stay may not exceed 90 consecutive days whatever the form of short-term rental.

a) Bed and Breakfast

"Bed and breakfasts" are furnished rooms located in the home of a host that are rented out for a fee, for one or more nights, accompanied by services[46] and in line with the rules of hygiene and sanitation[47]. The services are a minimum: overnight stay, breakfast and the supply of household

46 Article L.324-3 of the Tourism Code.
47 Article D.324-14 of the Tourism Code.

linen[48]. Tourists must be received by the host.[49] The number of rooms rented in the same dwelling may not exceed 5 and the number of persons accommodated at the same time may not exceed 15.[50]

b) Furnished Tourist Accommodation

Furnished tourist accommodation means furnished villas, apartments or studios, for the exclusive use of the tenant, offered for rent to a visiting clientele who do not choose to live there and who are staying there for a stay characterised by daily, weekly or monthly rentals (cf. Article L.324-1-1 of the Tourism Code).

2. *Affiliation and Contributions*

a) Bed and Breakfast

The will to promote the development of "non-professional" bed and breakfast activities via a digital platform has led the legislator to introduce a capped exemption of income from bed and breakfast rentals. When the annual revenue (turnover excluding taxes) is less than 13 percent of the annual social security ceiling (EUR 5,348) the lessor is exempt from social security contributions because the rental activity is not of a professional nature.[51] The lessor is therefore not obliged to join the general scheme for neither employees nor for the self-employed. However, when annual revenues are below the above-mentioned threshold, they are subject to social contributions on income from assets – namely, the CSG, the CRDS and the solidarity levy[52] – at the overall rate of 17.2 percent of taxable income.[53] If the income exceeds the cap, the bed and breakfast landlord affiliated to the general regime is subject to the rules of social security for self-employed persons.[54] A bed and breakfast landlord who has set up a Sole

48 Articles D.324-13 and D. 324-14 of the Tourism Code.

49 Article D.324-13 of the Tourism Code.

50 Article D.324-13 of the Tourism Code.

51 Article D.611-1, II of the Social Security Code.

52 Ministry of social security DSS/SD5B/2013-100 of 14 March 2013, § 1-5.

53 Article L.136-8 of the Social Security Code; Ordinance No. 96-50 of 24 January 1996; Article 235 ter of the General Taxation Code.

54 Article L.611-1, 5 of the Social Security Code.

Proprietorship (SP) or a Sole Proprietorship with Limited Liability (SPL) for his rental activity and who benefits from the micro tax regime in calendar year N is automatically subject to the micro entrepreneur social scheme that same year.[55] Turnover must not exceed EUR 176,200 in calendar year N - 1 or N – 2.[56]

b) Furnished Tourist Accommodation

When the natural person's gross annual income is less than or equal to EUR 23,000, the lessor of furnished accommodation does not carry out a rental activity on a professional basis and is not obliged to join the general regime.[57] Since 1 January 2017, it has been stipulated that rental activity is regarded to be carried out on a professional basis, giving rise to contributions, when the natural person's gross annual income exceeds EUR 23,000. The lessor is obliged to join the general scheme as soon as this threshold is reached.[58] As soon as the annual income exceeds EUR 23,000 but does not exceed EUR 70,000, the income from this self-employed activity is then deemed to be of a professional nature and the person concerned can opt:

- to join the general social security scheme for employees;
- to join the self-employed scheme (*Sécurité sociale des indépendants* SSI);
- to join the micro-entrepreneur system within the SSI.

When the income exceeds EUR 70,000 in annual income, the income from such self-employed activity is then of a professional nature and the person concerned has the choice to join the general social security scheme; if the annual income does not exceed EUR 85,800 the person has to join the self-employed scheme SSI.[59]

55 Official tax administration bulletin (BOFiP)-BIC-DECLA-10-40-10-§ 100-01/06/2018.
56 Article 50-01.2 of the General Tax Code; Article L.613-7, I of the Social Security Code.
57 Article L.611-1, 6 of the Social Security Code.
58 Article 155, IV 2 of the General Tax Code, Article L.611-1 6° of the Social Security Code.
59 Article 293 B, I, 1 of the General Tax Code.

	Rental of Short-term Furnished Accommodation[60]		
Exemption of social security contributions up to	EUR 23,000		
Social Security System	General System micro-entrepreneur	General System (employee)	General System (self-employed)
Maximum	EUR 70,000	EUR 85,800	EUR 85,800
Basis for contributions	Income	Profit	(Income- 60 percent)

V. *Anti-Fraud Measures: New Forms of Control*

France has also reformed its laws and aims to facilitate the operations of the platform economy. As work on a platform is done or organised via the Internet and could easily escape the traditional regulatory framework, reporting often depends on the individual's awareness and conscientiousness. Sometimes workers do not consider platform work as "work" and are therefore unaware of their obligations.[61] Article 10 of Law No. 2018-898 of 23 October 2018 relating to the fight against fraud modifies Article 242 bis of the General Tax Code on the reporting obligations on platforms with regard to users and the administration. This law simplifies the drafting of the texts, by merging all the obligations of the platforms into a single Article 242 bis of the General Tax Code. The main objective of the Anti-Fraud Act is to require online platform operators to have a robust mechanism (i) to inform their users about their tax and social obligations and (ii) to transmit information to the tax authorities.

The Decree of 27 December 2018[62] issued for the application of Article 242 bis of the General Tax Code is thus a reminder of the fact that the platforms are still required to inform the users, at the time of each transaction, of "information relating to the tax regimes and social regulations applica-

60 *Bocquet, Michel/Bouvard, Michel/Canevet, Maurice/Carcenac, Thierry/Chiron, Jean/Dallier, Pierre/Delahaye, Véronique/Gattolin, Arnaud/Guené, Claude/Lalande Bruno/De Montgolfier Arnaud*, Report made in the name of the finance committee (1) on taxation and the collaborative economy: The Need for a Fair, Simple and Unified System, No. 481, French Senate Ordinary Session 2016-2017, pp. 37-38.

61 European Social Insurance Platform (ESIP), Are Social Security Systems Adapted to New Forms of Work Created by Digital Platforms?, 30 January 2019, https://esip.eu/images/pdf_docs/ESIP_Study_Platform_Work.pdf. Accessed 16 July 2020.

62 Arrêté of 27 December 2018 issued for the application of Article 242 bis of the General Tax Code (NOR: CPAE1825922A).

ble to these sums, the resulting reporting and payment obligations to the tax authorities and social contribution collection agencies, as well as the penalties incurred in the event of failure to meet these obligations".[63] The decree also clarifies the thresholds above which these new platform reporting obligations are applicable. Pursuant to Article 242 bis of the General Tax Code, platforms have to provide, in particular, the status of the individual (*statut de particulier*) or professional indicated by the platform user and the number and total gross amount of transactions carried out by the user during the previous calendar year. The platforms must:

- provide for each transaction loyal, clear and transparent information on the tax and social obligations of declaration and payment of the lessor who carries out commercial transactions through the platform;[64]
- provide an electronic link to the websites of the administrations allowing for compliance, where appropriate, with these obligations;
- send each year to the lessor an electronic document summarising the sums received during the year through the platform;[65]
- send each year to the tax authorities a document summarising all the information provided to the lessor.[66]

The assets concerned by the absence of a declaration are:

- furniture, household appliances and motor vehicles, with the exception of works of art, antiques or collectibles for which the option provided for in Article 150 VL of the General Tax Code has been exercised;
- furniture, other than precious metals, for which the sale price is less than or equal to EUR 5,000.

However, this reporting exemption is limited to users whose cumulative transactions over the year meet the following thresholds:

- the user has received income of less than EUR 3,000 over the entire year;
- the number of transactions of the same user over the year is limited to 20.

Platforms have to send all this information electronically to the tax authorities by 31 January at the latest for users who have received more than

63 Article 23 L sexies of the General Tax Code.

64 Annex IV Articles 23 L sexies of the General Tax Code.

65 Article 242 bis, 2 of the General Tax Code, Annex IV Articles 23 L septies to 23 L decies of the General Tax Code.

66 Article 242 bis, 3 of the General Tax Code.

EUR 3,000 or made more than 20 transactions during the previous year. This is the result of the implementation of the recommendation made by a recent Commission expert report on Digital Transformation[67] to set up a "Single Digital Window in Europe" for the payment of taxes and contributions of platform workers that would allow a better fight against social security tax evasion, while being a further step towards a simplification of procedures and a real single market for platform workers in Europe.[68] This annual reporting obligation by platforms has started to apply in January 2020 on the income received by users in 2019. In addition, it is now stipulated that it is up to the tax authorities to send this information to the social security bodies (Article L.114-19-1 of the Social Security Code).

VI. Conclusion

What can we learn from the French legislation on social security contributions facing the development of the "gig economy"? First of all, digital platforms have, through their networking activities, not only changed consumption habits but also the supply of certain services, creating new markets and, at times, distortions of competition. These upheavals have generated a legislation of social protection to the sometimes protective ambitions of the beneficiaries, sometimes only as an incentive for the development of the activity in question, or its restructuring. But the traditional categories still remain, and the legislator did not wish or was not able to create *sui generis* rules. The legislator has preferred to marginally modify the already existing rules and create particular sub-categories of self-employment, to partially call into question already existing rules. The question of financing social protection in a "new economy" has only been tackled on the margins, under pressure from different groups with sometimes conflicting interests, which is reflected in a multitude of detailed rules that do not respond to any overall logic but to situations that are sometimes urgent but always high-profile. As a result, the Labour Code, for example, which is in principle dedicated to employees, now contains

---

67 European Commission, Final Report of the High-Level Expert Group on the Impact of the Digital Transformation on EU Labour Markets, April 2019, Luxembourg: Publications Office of the European Union 2019, p. 42, https://ec.europa.eu/digital-single-market/en/news/final-report-high-level-expert-group-impact-digital-transformation-eu-labour-markets. Accessed 16 July 2020.

68 *Viossat, Laurent-Charles,* Les enjeux clés de la protection sociale des travailleurs de plateforme, in: Regards, 55 (2019) 1, p. 85.

rules for the self-employed and organises *private* insurance contracts with reference to the rules on industrial injuries in the Social Security Code – mysterious and complex ways indeed.

It must be noticed that an unprecedented collaboration between the tax and social security authorities has been not only initiated but written down in the law. Only specific issues related to specific social crises (e.g. catastrophic social situation of self-employed service providers related to a platform and anarchic development of rentals by private individuals) were dealt with. It is to be feared that the foreseeable abysmal deficits in the social security health insurance for 2020, following the sanitary crisis linked to COVID-19, will relegate the difficult issue of work via digital platforms to the background from which it had only sporadically emerged.

Chapter 11
New Forms of Employment and Innovative Ways for the Collection of Social Security Contributions: The Example of Estonia

Gaabriel Tavits

I. Introduction

The spreading of new forms of work performance is not a new topic as the various ways of how people work have been changeable. Performance of short-time work-tasks (gigs)[1], working via platforms, renting (sharing) of dwelling space via platforms and obtaining income from it – they are all ways of performing work which ensure considerable income for a person. In some cases, it is ancillary activity which earns a person additional income. In other cases, it is a form of entrepreneurship that ensures the main income to a person. In the literature of labour law the new forms of work performance are discussed on a wide basis.[2]

New forms of work and changes in working conditions also challenge the social protection system, which must support employment, the economy and the well-being of society as a whole. As social protection requires resources, the important questions are how to finance social protection in

---

1 *Duszyński, Maciej*, Gig Economy: Definition, Statistics & Trends [2020 Update], https://zety.com/blog/gig-economy-statistics?gclid=CjwKCAjwte71BRBCEiwAU_V9h8jAgjCA9UmO2Eq8c51uiiT5f4pVQiosRk_uU1DSoJU1_2QeiHbArxoC0_wQAvD_BwE. Accessed 12 May 2020.

2 See e.g. *Perulli, Adalberto,* The Legal and Jurisprudential Evolution of the Notion of Employee, in: European Labour Law Journal, 11 (2020) 2, pp. 117-130, https://doi.org/10.1177/2031952520905145. Accessed 12 May 2020. *Risak, Martin/Dullinger, Thomas*, The Concept of "Worker" in EU Law: Status Quo and Potential for Change, ETUI, 2018, https://www.etui.org/Publications2/Reports/The-concept-of-worker-in-EU-law-status-quo-and-potential-for-change. Accessed 12 May 2020. For Estonia: *Erikson, Merle/Rosin, Annika*, Legal Position of Workers: An Employee or Independent Servant? (Tuleviku töötegija õiguslik staatus: Töötaja või iseseisev teenusepakkuja?), in Estonian, https://www.riigikogu.ee/wpcms/wp-content/uploads/2018/08/T%C3%B6%C3%B6tegija-%C3%B5iguslik-staatus.pdf. Accessed 12 May 2020.

changed situations and how to simplify the collection of the necessary means for financing social protection. Consequently, it is important that the social protection system is able to provide sufficient and adequate protection for all those who are engaged in some form of activity. This does not necessarily have to be a permanent activity. It is sufficient when work is ensured through a number of different short-term activities and short-term incomes.

Legislation in the area of social protection is widely based on the classical definition and principles regarding the employee (employment relationship) providing that both – the employer and the employee – must contribute to social protection. Under circumstances in which it is not clear whether the person performing work is an employee or not, there are considerable limits to ensuring social protection. When, as is common, the state collects the income tax based on the worker's income, these taxes and contributions required for social protection do not have to be related to income only, but to the person receiving the income (and the activity performed). Usually social protection is ensured to a person in a dependent employment relationship. In single cases it is possible to provide protection also to sole proprietors.

This chapter analyses the scope of regulation of the social protection legislation in Estonia and options of how new workers (platform workers) can make sure they are covered by the required social protection schemes (pension insurance, unemployment insurance, health insurance). New initiatives by the Estonian legislator in the field of financing social protection in order to protect platform workers are also discussed.

II. New Forms of Employment

New options of work performance have spread in the Estonian economy. There are numerous ways in which work can be performed via different platforms. At the same time, there are micro entrepreneurs in Estonia who earn income from entrepreneurship and have to pay only the income tax of the income obtained but no taxes/contributions related to social benefits.

New ways of work performance have not been regulated in the Estonian legislation. According to the changes in the Public Transport Act[3] the plan had been to regulate the ridesharing service; however, significant differences in comparison with the prototypical taxi service are not provided. The contractual relationship has remained unregulated on the legislative level, and due to that decisions on the respective type of relationship have to be made on an individual basis (whether employment relationship or any other relationship under the law of obligations).

According to different data, at least 8 percent of the Estonian working-age population is partially involved in new forms of work performance.[4] Therefore, the need for social protection covering new forms of work performance must not be underestimated. According to the Employment Contracts Act, wages must be presented in the employment contract as a gross amount.[5] This requirement is relevant so that the employee does not lose his salary if the state stipulates a reduction in certain payments. Withholding social security payments and taxes is the responsibility of the employer.

Apart from the common forms of platform work, e.g. car sharing services, courier services, house sharing through airbnb, sharing short-term jobs (gigs) is common in Estonia. The sharing of gigs takes place through a platform where companies can offer short-term employment and employees can enter into short-term contracts. With jobs offered through such a platform, employees can perform a variety of gigs without having to commit to a particular company for the long term. Such an opportunity opens up a chance to work under different fixed-term employment contracts[6]

---

3 Sections 65 and 66 of the Public Transport Act (Ühistranspordiseadus) - RT I, 23 March 2015, 2, English translation https://www.riigiteataja.ee/en/eli/518012019010/consolide. Accessed 12 May 2020.

4 See: https://www.riigikogu.ee/arenguseire-keskus/platvormitoo-saanud-eesti-inimeste-jaoks-oluliseks-lisasissetuleku-allikaks/. Accessed 12 May 2020. According to a survey carried out in Latvia, the spreading of new forms of work performance is significantly more modest being only 1 percent. *Piasna, Agnieszka/Drahokoupil, Jan*, Digital Labour in Central and Eastern Europe: Evidence from the ETUI Internet and Platform Work Survey, ETUI, 2020, https://www.etui.org/node/31491. Accessed 12 May 2020.

5 Section 29 of the Employment Contracts Act (Töölepingu seadus) - RT I 2009, 5, 35, English translation: https://www.riigiteataja.ee/en/eli/509052019005/consolide. Accessed 12 May 2020.

6 The possibility to apply fixed-term employment contracts is important in this case of employment. According to the Health Insurance Act, an important condition is

without the employee having to be associated with a specific company for a longer period of time.

Telework can no longer be regarded as a new form of work. Although teleworking means that the employee does not have to be physically present at an office all the time, teleworking is indicative of a clearly identifiable employment relationship as well as of a dependent employment relationship connected to social security coverage. Self-employment is not considered a new form of employment. In a situation where a person is self-employed[7], work is regulated separately at the legislative level. Self-employment can be considered as one form of entrepreneurship. Due to the current legal framework, in order to be self-employed, a person must register in the Commercial Register.

III. Scope of Regulation of the Social Protection Rights

1. The Constitutional Framework of Social Protection[8]

According to the Constitution of the Republic of Estonia, a person has the right of receiving support from the state in the following cases: old age, loss of provider, incapacity for work or need. Concurrently, every person is entitled to health protection as stipulated by the Constitution.[9] The scope of support and the terms and conditions for receiving benefits are estab-

---

that the employment contract lasts at least one month. If the duration of the employment contract is shorter than one month, the employee does not receive the health insurance protection prescribed by law. Section 5 of the Health Insurance Act (Ravikindlustuse seadus) - RT I 2002, 62, 377, English translation: https://www.riigiteataja.ee/en/eli/524042020006/consolide. Accessed 12 May 2020.

7 In Estonian: *füüsilisest isikust ettevõtja*, sometimes the official English translation is "sole proprietor".

8 Also: *Merusk, Kalle/Tavits, Gaabriel*, Der Schutz der sozialen Grundrechte in der Rechtsordnung Estlands, in: Iliopoulos-Strangas, Julia (ed.), Soziale Grundrechte in den "neuen" Mitgliedstaaten der Europäischen Union, Baden-Baden: Nomos, 2019, pp. 81-139; *Tavits, Gaabriel*, Estonia, in: The Right to Social Security in the Constitutions of the World: Broadening the Moral and Legal Space for Social Justice, ILO Global Study, Volume 1: Europe, International Labour Office – Geneva: ILO 2016, https://www.ilo.org/global/standards/subjects-covered-by-international-labour-standards/social-security/WCMS_518153/lang--en/index.htm. Accessed 12 May 2020.

9 § 28, The Constitution of the Republic of Estonia (Eesti Vabariigi põhiseadus) - RT 1992, 26, 349, English translation: https://www.riigiteataja.ee/en/eli/521052015001/consolide. Accessed 12 May 2020.

lished by the law. It is the legislator's task to ensure a minimum level of social protection.

Within the meaning of the constitutional context, the right to health protection does not automatically mean a right to health insurance for everyone.[10] The right to health insurance is established for a person when social tax is paid by or on behalf of the person, or in cases where the person is insured according to the law. In the latter case, health insurance is ensured according to the legislation irrespective of the payment of social tax. According to the Estonian Health Insurance Act, health insurance is provided to all people who work on the basis of an employment contract or in the civil service and for whom the employer pays the necessary taxes.[11] If a person has no income, or if no tax required for health insurance is paid by the person or on behalf of the latter, then no health insurance protection is guaranteed. The right to health protection in the Constitution denotes a person's right to emergency care.[12] The state pays for this kind of care irrespective of whether a person is covered by health insurance or not.

The constitutional right to get support from the state in case of need primarily denotes a situation in which a person has the right to get protection under the social welfare regulation. The person is entitled to receive support only when he has no personal resources and support provided by the state is the only option to improve the person's economic situation. The option to receive support due to age, loss of provider and incapacity for work primarily depends on the circumstances under which, irrespective of the person, the latter is not able to earn any income and due to which the state is obliged to support the person.[13]

---

10 *Nõmper, Ants/Annus, Taavi*, The Right to Health Protection in the Estonian Constitution, in: Juridica International, (2002) 7, https://www.juridicainternational.eu/public/pdf/ji_2002_1_117.pdf. Accessed 2 May 2020.

11 Section 5 (1) of the Health Insurance Act (Ravikindlustuse seadus) - RT I 2002, 62, 377, English translation: https://www.riigiteataja.ee/en/eli/524042020006/consolide. Accessed 12 May 2020.

12 Section 6 of the Health Services Organisation Act (Tervishoiuteenuste korraldamise seadus) - RT I 2001, 50, 284, English translation: https://www.riigiteataja.ee/en/eli/529042020006/consolide. Accessed 12 May 2020.

13 This provision by its essence is taken over from the Constitution empowered in 1938. See: *Siimets-Gross, Hesi*, Social and Economic Fundamental Rights in Estonian Constitutions between World Wars I and II: A Vanguard or Rearguard of Europe?, in: Juridica International, (2005) 10, https://www.juridicainternational.eu/public/pdf/ji_2005_1_135.pdf. Accessed 12 May 2020. The Constitution of the Republic of Estonia is rather modest in regard to guaranteeing social rights and only a minimal catalogue of social rights is provided. See also: *Alexy, Robert*, Põhiõigused Eesti põhiseaduses, in: Juridica, 2001, https://www.juridica.ee/article.

The wording of the Constitution, as well as the current interpretation, does not specify who should receive aid and under what conditions such aid should be provided. Since, according to the Constitution, the receipt of state aid is directly regulated through an ordinary law, the legislator has to decide in each case under what conditions and to whom the specific aid must be granted. According to the Constitution, all citizens of the Republic of Estonia and, in cases prescribed by law, also aliens have the right to state aid.[14] The Constitution does not stipulate any particular forms of employment or economic activities for persons to be entitled (whether they are self-employed, employed under an employment contract, employed on a short-term basis, etc.). Thus, according to the Constitution, social security protection is to be universal regardless of the economic activity in which a particular person is engaged. Pursuant to § 29 of the Constitution, everyone has the right to freely choose his or her field of activity and profession. Consequently, if such freedom is guaranteed pursuant to § 29 of the Constitution, then in order to ensure the necessary social protection, the freedom provided for in the Constitution in choosing a profession and field of activity must be taken into account. Thus, if a person is free to choose an activity, this must be accompanied by the state-guaranteed social protection. A person must be able to receive state aid against the social risks provided for in § 28 of the Constitution, regardless of the form of economic activity or field which the person has freely chosen on the basis of the Constitution.[15]

As mentioned above, the social security system in Estonia today is mainly based on the fact that social benefits are provided to people who pay social tax or other social security contributions themselves or for whom such tax or contributions are paid. When dealing with circumstances under which a person receives some income from his activity, it does not automatically mean that he is guaranteed social security benefits. All people who exercise new forms of employment run the risk of not being covered by health insurance or unemployment insurance and they might have no opportunity to contribute to the pension insurance. Although § 28 of the

---

php?uri=2001_eriv_ljaanne_p_hi_igused_eesti_p_hiseaduses. Accessed 12 May 2020.

14 § 28, Comment 23, The Constitution of the Republic of Estonia. Comments (Eesti Vabariigi põhiseadus. Kommenteeritud väljaanne), Tallinn: Juura, 2017, https://www.pohiseadus.ee/. Accessed 12 May 2020.

15 § 28, Comments 19, 20, 23, The Constitution of the Republic of Estonia. Comments (Eesti Vabariigi põhiseadus. Kommenteeritud väljaanne), Tallinn: Juura, 2017, https://www.pohiseadus.ee/. Accessed 12 May 2020.

Constitution gives everyone the right to turn to the state for aid in the event of the risks specified in the Constitution, this right can be significantly adjusted (restricted) on the grounds of law. Consequently, the Constitution of the Republic of Estonia does not guarantee universal access to the social protection system.

Pursuant to the Constitution, the General Part of the Social Code Act specifies the purpose of social protection. According to Section 2 (2) of the General Part of the Social Code Act,[16] the objective of social protection is to support and increase a person's independent living and social inclusion, create equal opportunities, achieve a high level of employment, prevent unemployment, and support reconciliation of work and private life. The goal of the Social Code has been determined in Section 1 (1). The Social Code will contribute to ensuring social rights protected by the Constitution of the Republic of Estonia, European Union law, and international agreements binding on the Republic of Estonia. As one can see, the General Part of the Social Code Act will also form part of the general principles determined in § 28 of the Constitution.

2. *Benefits Included in the Social Protection System and Personal Scope*

Estonian social benefits can be divided into two categories depending on the way in which the benefits are financed: 1) benefits which can be provided to persons working in an employment relationship where contributions are paid; 2) benefits paid from the state budget – in this case it is not important for the receipt of the benefit whether separate taxes/contributions are paid, and it is also not important which kind of economic activity the entitled person is engaged in.

Social protection benefits for the receipt of which different special-purpose payments are required are:

(1) state pension insurance,
(2) health insurance,
(3) unemployment insurance,
(4) mandatory funded pension.

16 General Part of the Social Code Act (Sotsiaalseadustiku üldosa seadus) - RT I, 13 March 2019, 157, English translation: https://www.riigiteataja.ee/en/eli/521032019012/consolide. Accessed 12 May 2020.

Different legal acts concerning social protection define the scope of application in a different way, and the circle of insured people is also different. However, the common feature is the fact that the insurees have a permanent income primarily based on an employment contract or work in the civil service. Without the legal basis mentioned above, no corresponding insurance payments have to be paid and no insurance protection is provided. Therefore, social protection is, in the first place, guaranteed to people who work in dependent employment relationships. If work is performed based on the contract under the Law of Obligations Act[17] and without the existence of a dependent employment relationship, the obligation to pay social protection contributions exists, but the minimum level for contributions can be determined.[18]

According to the State Pension Insurance Act, the following are considered to be persons covered by pension insurance:[19]

(1) persons who, pursuant to the Social Tax Act, pay the pension insurance part of social tax or for whom it must be paid;
(2) persons for whom the right to receive a state pension is derived from other bases pursuant to this Act.

Due to the regulation mentioned, the important criterion is not work itself or the nature of work; the important aspect is to make sure social tax is paid. Whether the payment of social tax is guaranteed by the employer or another person is irrelevant to the provision of social protection. What really matters is that social tax obligations are fulfilled and that social tax in both pension insurance and health insurance budgets is collected.

17 Law of Obligations Act (Võlaõigusseadus) - RT I 2001, 81, 487, English translation: https://www.riigiteataja.ee/en/eli/515012020004/consolide. Accessed 12 May 2020.

18 Section 5(2) 4) 5) of the Health Insurance Act (Ravikindlustuse seadus) - RT I 2002, 62, 377, English translation: https://www.riigiteataja.ee/en/eli/524042020006/consolide. Accessed 12 May 2020. In such a situation it is not necessary to be registered as self-employed. In situations were the services are granted based on a civil law contract, the person who receives services has to pay also social security taxes and contributions, see Section 9 (1) 2 of the Social Tax Act (Sotsiaalmaksuseadus) - RT I 2000, 102, 675, English translation: https://www.riigiteataja.ee/en/eli/527042020012/consolide. Accessed 12 May 2020.

19 Section 3 of the State Pension Insurance Act (Riikliku pensionikindlustuse seadus) - RT I 2001, 100, 648, English translation: https://www.riigiteataja.ee/en/eli/530042020003/consolide. Accessed 12 May 2020.

According to the Health Insurance Act[20], the circle of persons covered by health insurance is divided into three different categories:

(1) persons for whom the corresponding insurance tax must be paid. The health insurance part of the social tax is usually paid by the employer, in some cases also by the state (e.g. if the person is in the military service of the Defence Forces). In the case of persons registered as unemployed, the social tax necessary for obtaining health insurance is paid, for example, by the Unemployment Insurance Fund;
(2) self-employed persons who have to pay social tax themselves in order to receive health insurance cover; as mentioned above, there is an obligation for self-employed persons to register in the Commercial Register;
(3) persons treated as insurees. There is no obligation for these persons to pay social tax (this group includes, for example, pregnant women, children up to the age of 19, persons receiving a state pension[21]).

The Unemployment Insurance Act defines protected persons differently than the State Pension Insurance Act and the State Health Insurance Act.

---

20 Section 5, Health Insurance Act (Ravikindlustuse seadus) - RT I 2002, 62, 377, English translation: https://www.riigiteataja.ee/en/eli/524042020006/consolide. Accessed 12 May 2020.

21 Section 5(4) of the Estonian Health Insurance Fund Act (Eesti Haigekassa seadus) - RT I 2000, 57, 374, English translation: https://www.riigiteataja.ee/en/eli/527122019003/consolide. Accessed 12 May 2020.
Persons equal to the insured are:
1) pregnant women whose pregnancy has been identified by a doctor or a midwife;
2) persons under 19 years of age;
3) persons who receive a state pension granted in Estonia;
4) persons who have been found to have partial work ability or no work ability under the Work Ability Allowance Act;
5) persons with up to five years left until attaining the retirement age who are maintained by their spouses who are insured persons;
6) persons acquiring basic or general secondary education, persons acquiring formal vocational education and higher education students who are permanent residents of Estonia and study in an educational institution in Estonia founded and operating on the basis of legislation or in an equivalent educational institution abroad, except for doctoral candidates that receive the doctoral allowance;
7) a monk or a nun who is a member of a cloister registered in the register of religious associations.

Pursuant to Section 3 (1) of the Unemployment Insurance Act[22], the following persons are deemed to be protected by unemployment insurance: employees, officials, natural persons providing services on the basis of a contract under the law of obligations, public conciliators, members of a rural municipality or city government, rural municipality or city district elders, a non-working spouse accompanying an official on a long-term assignment abroad, and a non-working spouse accompanying an official serving in a foreign mission of the Republic of Estonia. All persons mentioned must have paid the unemployment insurance contributions on the basis of and pursuant to the procedure provided in the Unemployment Insurance Act. In addition to the type of activity, a fact that is also relevant is that a person covered by unemployment insurance must have paid unemployment insurance contributions. Without contribution payments, the insured person will not have completed the unemployment insurance period, and in the absence of the unemployment insurance period, the unemployed person will not be able to receive the unemployment insurance benefits prescribed by law.

The above types of insurance are public. The state pension insurance is administered by the Social Insurance Board, an agency under the Ministry of Social Affairs. The Estonian Health Insurance Fund[23] is responsible for state health insurance. The Estonian Health Insurance Fund is a legal person in public law. This status means that it is a public body, but not a state agency. The activities of the Estonian Health Insurance Fund are administered by the management board and supervisory board. At the same time, the supervisory board of the Estonian Health Insurance Fund operates on the basis of the tripartite principle. The supervisory board of the Estonian Health Insurance Fund includes representatives of employees, employers and the state. There is only one health insurance fund in Estonia. The Estonian Unemployment Insurance Fund is also a legal person in public law. It is not a state agency and the Estonian Unemployment Insurance Fund is not subordinate to any ministry. The activities of the Estonian Unemployment Insurance Fund are also managed by the Management Board and the Supervisory Board. The Supervisory Board consists of representatives of

---

22 Unemployment Insurance Act (Töötuskindlustuse seadus) - RT I 2001, 59, 359, English translation: https://www.riigiteataja.ee/en/eli/530042020008/consolide. Accessed 12 May 2020.

23 Section 5 of the Estonian Health Insurance Fund Act (Eesti Haigekassa seadus) - RT I 2000, 57, 374, English translation: https://www.riigiteataja.ee/en/eli/5271220 19003/consolide. Accessed 12 May 2020.

employers, employees and the state. In Estonia there is one unemployment insurance fund.

The last type of social protection that is relevant in the context of this chapter is the mandatory funded pension.[24] The mandatory funded pension is also called the second pillar of the pension system. Due to its general objectives, the mandatory funded pension is supplementary to the state pension insurance, and one of the main goals of this pension is to provide additional income for individuals of retirement age. With its initial purpose, the mandatory funded pension is supported by a state-guaranteed retirement pension. Mandatory funded pension funds are, by their nature, private equity funds. The state does not directly intervene in the activities of pension funds. The state only determines the rules where and to what extent pension funds may invest the finances raised by them. There are several mandatory funded pension funds in Estonia and a person has the opportunity to change the pension fund.[25]

In the light of the above, it can be concluded that three of the four aforementioned benefits are linked to the obligation to pay social tax (either through the beneficiary himself, e.g. in the case of a self-employed person; or on behalf of the insured person, usually through an employer or – in the case of civil servants – the authority which has employed the official). In the case of unemployment insurance only, the insurance coverage is not linked to the obligation to pay social tax.

3. *Taxes and Contributions Foreseen for Financing Social Protection*

As can be seen from the above, *social tax* forms an important part of the financing of Estonian social protection benefits. The social tax was one of the first taxes to be introduced as early as 1990, and from the outset it

---

24 Section 40 of the Funded Pensions Act (Kogumispensionide seadus) - RT I 2004, 37, 252, English translation: https://www.riigiteataja.ee/en/eli/521012019010/consolide. Accessed 12 May 2020.

25 In 2021, the mandatory funded pension system will change. Under this amendment, individuals will get the right to decide whether they want to withdraw money from pension funds or whether they decide to continue with a mandatory funded pension. Due to this principle, the mandatory funded pension will become more flexible. See: https://www.riigikogu.ee/tegevus/eelnoud/eelnou/9c420335-4f28-43eb-b733-5a56c68daaf8/Kogumispensionide%20seaduse%20ja%20sellega%20seonduvalt%20teiste%20seaduste%20muutmise%20seadus%20(kohustusliku%20kogumispensioni%20reform). Accessed 12 May 2020.

sought to finance state-guaranteed health insurance and state pension insurance. Payment of the social tax is an employer's obligation and it has to be paid from the gross salary. It amounts to 33 percent of the gross sum. The sum is divided into two: 20 percent is accrued in the budget of the state pension insurance, while 13 percent is accrued in the budget of the health insurance.[26] The employee does not pay the social tax and the sum is not reflected in his salary.

In general, and also taking into account the topic of this chapter, the social tax is levied under the following circumstances:

(1) on wages and other remuneration paid to employees in money;
(2) on wages and other remuneration paid to officials according to the Public Service Act;
(3) on remuneration paid to members of the management or controlling bodies of legal persons or the trustee in bankruptcy and members of the bankruptcy committee in the bankruptcy proceedings of a natural person;
(4) on the business income of a self-employed person, after deductions relating to enterprise and permitted in the Income Tax Act have been made;
(5) on remuneration paid to natural persons on the basis of contracts for services, authorisation agreements or contracts under the law of obligations entered into for the provision of other services;
(6) on fringe benefits within the meaning of the Income Tax Act, expressed in monetary terms, and on income tax payable on fringe benefits;
(7) on benefits paid on the basis of the Unemployment Insurance Act.

The minimum rate for the payment of social tax is approved annually by the state budget. There is no upper limit on social tax. It all depends on the payments made by a particular person.

Here, attention needs also to be paid to self-employed persons. A genuine self-employed person (or FIE) is a natural person who is engaged in business.[27] Any natural person can be self-employed, including minors of

26 Section 7 of the Social Tax Act (Sotsiaalmaksuseadus) - RT I 2000, 102, 675, English translation: https://www.riigiteataja.ee/en/eli/527042020012/consolide. Accessed 12 May 2020.

27 The number of self-employed persons is decreasing. In 2010, there were 30,308, and in 2018 there were 22,874 self-employed persons, see Statistics Estonia, http://andmebaas.stat.ee/Index.aspx?lang=et&DataSetCode=EM81. Accessed 12 May 2020.

at least 15 years of age to whom consent has been given by the parent, or whose active legal capacity to engage in economic activity has been extended by the court.[28] Being self-employed does not preclude working for an employer. As a self-employed person and a natural person are one and the same person, a natural person can earn income in several ways (e.g. wage income, income from the transfer of securities, income from business, etc.), but in such cases it must be distinguished between different types of income in a natural person's income tax return. The self-employed person pays social tax on the income received from his or her business, from which the deductions related to entrepreneurship permitted by the Income Tax Act have been made, taking into account limits established in the Social Tax Act. The period of taxation of the self-employed with social tax is one calendar year, because the taxable income is determined on the basis of the income tax return once a year.

The *unemployment insurance contribution* is divided into two parts, of which 0.8 percent is paid by the employer and 1.6 percent by the insured person or the employee. The main aim is to ensure the financing of the unemployment insurance benefits based on the indicated sum.[29] According to the Unemployment Insurance Act, it is possible to use the part paid by both the employer and the insured person for financing the services provided by the Unemployment Insurance Fund. The share paid by the insured person cannot be used to pay benefits in the event of the insolvency of the employer, nor to pay benefits in the event of collective redundancies. According to the principles of the unemployment insurance scheme, an unemployed person receives unemployment benefit only if the required insurance period has been completed. According to the Unemployment Insurance Act, the insured person is required to have had at least 12 months of insurance within the last 36 months. This principle is based on the assumption that if the employee works on the basis of an employment contract for at least four months per year, then within three years the insured person will be able to gain the necessary insurance period. To gain the insurance period, it is necessary that the unemployment insurance contribution is received every month. According to the current practice of the Supreme Court, an employee cannot suffer damage in a situation if the

28 Sections 9 to 11 of the General Part of the Civil Code Act (Tsiviilseadustiku üldosa seadus) - RT I 2002, 35, 216, English translation: https://www.riigiteataja.ee/en/eli/528052020001/consolide. Accessed 12 May 2020.

29 Sections 40 ff. of the Unemployment Insurance Act (Töötuskindlustuse seadus) - RT I 2001, 59, 359, English translation: https://www.riigiteataja.ee/en/eli/530042020008/consolide. Accessed 12 May 2020.

employer has not fulfilled his obligation and has not transferred the necessary amounts to the Unemployment Insurance Fund.[30] The employee cannot transfer the corresponding amounts to the unemployment fund himself. The obligation to withhold and transfer unemployment insurance contributions is the obligation of the employer.

The third special payment relates to a *mandatory funded pension*. Employees regularly pay 2 percent of their salary to a pension fund freely chosen by them. As this is a mandatory funded pension, it means that all persons who have reached the age of 18 years are obliged to join some pension fund and, when they receive a salary, they are obliged to pay a funded pension contribution from that salary. Mandatory funded pension payment does not have to be transferred by the insured persons themselves, such obligation generally lies with the employer. A direct obligation to pay a mandatory funded pension payment rests solely with self-employed persons who pay the said contribution once a year, not monthly. Persons from whose remuneration the employer is obliged to pay social tax are bound to pay the mandatory funded pension contribution.[31]

There are no more special-purpose taxes or payments established in the Estonian legal system. The rest of the possible social benefits are paid directly from the state budget and in case of these benefits it is not important whether the person is subject to a dependent employment relationship or not.

When an employee works on the basis of an employment contract, the above-mentioned taxes/contributions are mandatory. The social tax is paid by the employer on the basis of the employee's gross wages. The payment

30 Estonian Supreme Court, Case 3-3-1-58-14, E.T vers Eesti Töötukassa, 18 November 2014, https://www.riigikohus.ee/et/lahendid/marksonastik?asjaNr=3-3-1-58-14. Accessed 12 May 2020. In case of pension insurance there is no relevant case law, but the same principle could also be applied here.

31 The specifics of the financing of the mandatory funded pension must be referred to here: according to the general scheme, the budget of the state pension insurance (20 percent of the social tax paid by the employer) is also financed on the basis of the social tax. If the person has also joined the mandatory funded pension, in addition to the above-mentioned 2 percent, the state contributes 4 percent of the 20 percent of the social tax to the mandatory funded pension. Thus, if a person is related to both the state pension insurance and the mandatory funded pension, the tax burden is divided as follows: 2 percent plus 4 percent of the social tax that goes to financing the second pillar and 16 percent of the social tax pension insurance part that is entered in the state pension insurance budget. See: https://www.pensionikeskus.ee/en/ii-pillar/mandatory-funded-pension-ii-pillar/. Accessed 12 May 2020.

of the unemployment insurance premium is divided between the employee and the employer, while the mandatory pension fund is paid by the employee on the basis of his gross wages. When the worker does not work on the basis of a definitely established contract, e.g. an employment contract or some other kind of contract, then the nature of the remuneration received is of a different kind and no social tax and unemployment insurance contribution must be paid. Therefore, a substantial risk occurs that persons working via a platform and providing a service are not entitled to either – state pension insurance or health insurance. Hence, the allowances and benefits ensured by the Estonian social protection system are of a limited nature: not all people receiving some kind of income must pay established taxes and payments for the financing of social benefits. For instance, if a person rents out his dwelling via airbnb, the periodical income is subject to income tax. Concurrently, according to the Social Tax Act the income from the rental of one's dwelling is not regarded as income, which would give the host an opportunity to receive social benefits. Based on the above, not any activity or any kind of income is of a nature which gives people the required social insurance protection.

IV. New "Workers" Outside of Social Protection[32]

1. General Tendencies of Development of Social Protection

Analysing possible future perspectives and labour market developments until 2035, different development scenarios have been elaborated for Estonia, as well as possible changes in social protection and its financing.[33]

(1) Diversification of employment forms and fragmentation of income is likely. In the case of intermittent employment and income, longer accounting periods for the accumulation of necessary seniority and income, as well as individual savings accounts, would help to improve

32 Also: *Tavits, Gaabriel,* Social Security Protection and New Forms of Employment: Case of Estonia. In: Проблеми Реалізації Прав Громадян у сфері Праці та Соціального Забезпечення, Harkiv: Pravo 2019, pp. 494-497.

33 Social Protection Models and their Suitability to Alternative Scenarios Reflecting Cchanges in the Labour Market and Employment Rlations in Estonia (Tööga seotud sotsiaalkaitse mudelid ja nende sobivus alternatiivsete tööturuarengute korral Eestis), Praxis 2018 (in Estonian), http://www.praxis.ee/wp-content/uploads/2018/02/tooga_seotud_sotsiaalkaitsemudelid_raport_pdf. Accessed 12 May 2020.

the coverage of social security schemes. The said perspective applies to all the types of social protection mentioned above.

(2) Given the longer-term future trends in forms of work and risks of financing social protection, it is also necessary to consider the introduction of new possible sources of financing. It must therefore be decided whether to increase the rates of taxes and payments (social tax, unemployment insurance contributions) used for financing within the current system or to use other sources of central state revenue.

(3) In the case of long-term structural unemployment and underemployment, coverage should be improved through the introduction of employment and work-independent minimum protection schemes. Speaking of future work, the possibility of introducing a citizen's salary, i.e. an unconditional minimum income protection, has also been discussed here, although it is not a realistic measure to replace the social protection system as a whole today or in the near future.

(4) Inequality may increase due to the polarization of skills and labour market opportunities: better-skilled workers earn significantly more in high-value-adding jobs than those engaged in routine and medium-skilled jobs. Discussions on future work forms indicate the possibility of introducing, in addition to more progressive income taxation, a negative income tax, in which the state pays households a benefit linked to the income tax rate if the declared income is below a certain level.

2. *Shortcomings in Health Insurance Cover*

Occasionally, the sustainability and shortcomings of the Estonian health insurance system have been analysed. Both legal and substantive issues have been addressed. In 2018, a study was commissioned by the Ministry of Social Affairs to find out how it would be realisable to ensure the most universal feasible protection for persons insured in Estonia. This study highlights the main topical areas of the Estonian health insurance system.[34]

34 Health Insurance Protection to Everyone or for the Chosen – How to Resolve Gaps in the Estonian Health Insurance System? (Ravikindlustus valitutele või ravikaitse kõigile — kuidas täita lüngad Eesti ravikindlustuses?), Praxis 2018, http://www.praxis.ee/wp-content/uploads/2017/09/Ravikindlustus.pdf. Accessed 12 May 2020.

There are approximately 120,000 people of working age[35] in Estonia who do not have permanent health insurance. The vast majority of people without health insurance have intermittent insurance coverage. This discontinuity is also due to the discontinuity of income and employment. The reasons for the interruption or lack of insurance cover are found both in the labour market and in the social security system. Health insurance is often lacking due to irregular income or the nature of a person's job. The current Estonian health insurance system is not flexible with regard to different forms of work. Therefore, as one of the policy changes in Estonia, it has been proposed to consider the possibility of taking into account the receipt of social tax for the last 12 calendar months in order to validate health insurance, which would help to smooth out insurance disruptions arising from irregular employment and income. There is no such waiting period under the current health insurance system. Rather, it is based on the amount of social tax paid. The only condition where a certain waiting period is expected is related to the employment on the basis of an employment contract. Under the Health Insurance Act, health insurance cover arises only after the employment relationship has lasted for at least one month. There are no specific requirements for the length of the social tax collection period. One alternative to increase health insurance coverage is to move towards a universal health care system. Given the situation in Estonia, it would mean a fundamental change as in order to access the state health care system people would not have to make contributions from their salaries (to buy so-called health insurance), but the right to state health care services could automatically be accompanied by resident status. The creation of an inclusive health protection system requires fundamental changes in the financing of health care and in the state tax system. At present, no such discussions are taking place, and the idea of creating universal treatment protection is not relevant.

In view of the above situation, the health insurance system and access to it currently point to the fact that people who earn income from short-term platform work or whose income is below the minimum amount of social tax to be paid appear to be excluded from any health insurance coverage.

---

35 This makes approx. 14 percent of the whole working age population or less than 10 percent of the whole population of Estonia. See: Health Insurance Protection to Everyone or for the Chosen – How to Resolve Gaps in the Estonian Health Insurance System? (Ravikindlustus valitutele või ravikaitse kõigile — kuidas täita lüngad Eesti ravikindlustuses?), pp. 13-14, Praxis 2018, http://www.praxis.ee/wp-content/uploads/2017/09/Ravikindlustus.pdf. Accessed 12 May 2020.

Being excluded from health insurance coverage means that these persons have no access to either primary care or specialist care. The main opportunity for these persons to receive health care services is through emergency medical care only.

3. *Unemployment Benefits – Access for the Privileged*

The Unemployment Insurance Act in force in Estonia does not allow for those engaged in new forms of employment to receive unemployment insurance benefits, and such additional activities are also equated with work, regardless of the size of income of a particular employee. According to the law in force in Estonia, a person is registered as unemployed if he or she does not have a job or activity that is considered to be an activity equivalent to work on the basis of law. Due to the health insurance system, if a person is registered as unemployed, he or she also has the right to receive health insurance cover through the Estonian Unemployment Insurance Fund. If a person provides a small-scale service through a platform, he or she cannot be registered as unemployed, and, on the other hand, there is no guarantee that he or she will receive sufficient income to pay the social security contributions required to obtain health insurance cover. In a study conducted in 2018, it has been found that the problem of unemployment in Estonia correlates with insufficient social protection:[36] benefit rates are low and only a small part of the unemployed receive benefits or support, so these measures fail to prevent people from falling into poverty.

Another problem is that the Unemployment Insurance Act is outdated and the labour market has changed a lot since 2002 when the Act was adopted. The current law provides social security for a traditional employment relationship. Both the employee and the employer pay unemployment insurance contributions. When the employment relationship ends and the person registers as unemployed, the person receives compensation from the unemployment insurance fund according to the length of gainful activity. Many new forms of employment do not currently provide unemployment insurance protection. For example, the Bolt car-sharing service is not the driver's employer, but only an intermediary service. Thus, the driv-

36 Analyses of Principles of the Unemployment Insurance in order to avoid situations of need and support participation in the employment market (Töötuskindlustuse põhimõtete analüüs vaesuse ennetamiseks ja tööturul osalemise toetamiseks), Praxis 2019, http://www.praxis.ee/wp-content/uploads/2018/09/T%C3%B6%C3%B6tush%C3%BCvitis30.05.2019.pdf. Accessed 12 May 2020.

er is not a Bolt employee, but a business partner. As a self-employed person, these hours are not taken into account when calculating the unemployment insurance period or unemployment benefits when driving with Bolt. In addition to drivers, couriers and board members, there is the same problem with others, such as choirmasters, babysitters, beauty professionals, and so on. In other words, the circle of persons who work either through the platform or perform rather short-term work tasks (work gigs) currently remain outside the main and important areas of social protection. This, in turn, leads to a situation where short-term employment as well as irregular incomes do not guarantee protection against the social risks listed in § 28 of the Constitution of the Republic of Estonia.[37]

V. Entrepreneur Account – a New Opportunity

1. What is an Entrepreneur Account?

An entrepreneur account is intended to simplify the tax liability for payments received for the provision of services from one natural person to another natural person or for the sale of goods to a natural or legal person.[38] It is not allowed to transfer to the entrepreneur account the funds earned from providing a service or selling goods during the period when the entrepreneur account holder is socially insured in another European Economic Area country[39] or in a social security agreement country[40] where this income is subject to social security contributions. A person who has

---

37 At the time of completion of this chapter, the Ministry of Social Affairs has drafted the Unemployment Insurance Act with the intention of making the unemployment insurance system more flexible. Among other things, the changes allow for small-scale work. It means that the requirement that a person registered as unemployed has no job at all will be waived. See: http://eelnoud.valitsus.ee/main/mount/docList/f580df2f-4096-4828-9849-bbc859af99a6#TyHGsaPR. Accessed 12 May 2020.

38 Simplified Business Income Taxation Act (Ettevõtlustulu lihtsustatud maksustamise seadus), English translation: https://www.riigiteataja.ee/akt/107072017002. Accessed 12 May 2020. As of the end of 2019, there were 1,702 active entrepreneur accounts in Estonia. During the year, EUR 2,060,000 were received in entrepreneur accounts, of which EUR 418,000 in taxes were paid. See https://arileht.delfi.ee/news/uudised/on-seda-siis-palju-voi-vahe-ettevotluskontodele-laekus-esimese-aastaga-ule-kahe-miljoni-euro?id=88806367. Accessed 12 May 2020.

39 The EU Member States, Norway, Liechtenstein, Switzerland.

40 Canada, Ukraine, Australia, Belarus.

opened an entrepreneur account is not obliged to register as an entrepreneur and to calculate revenues and expenses. The owner of the entrepreneur account cannot be a VAT payer or be acting as a self-employed person in the same or similar area of activity.

The entrepreneur account creates a new simple and affordable way of doing business. Accounting and tax reports are not required when using an entrepreneur account because the tax liability is calculated on the basis of the payments to the entrepreneur account. An entrepreneur account owner does not issue invoices because he or she is not an entrepreneur or accounting entity. An entrepreneur account owner can provide services or sell goods by verbal contract. However, if necessary he or she can also conclude a simple written contract containing relevant data on providing the services or selling the goods.

An entrepreneur account is useful for any person who provides services to other natural persons in areas of activity that do not involve any direct expenses, or for a person who sells self-produced goods or handicraft goods or goods with low material or acquisition costs. Examples include baby-sitting, housekeeping, gardening, repair or construction services that do not involve direct costs or in which a customer pays for the costs. An example would be that a customer orders the repair or construction service and has bought the tools and materials for the repair him- or herself. Another example would be the sale of self-produced goods to natural persons as well as to legal persons if the cost of the raw material or source material is low compared to the selling price of the goods, such as is the case with the sale of handicraft and art, or the sale of food, plants etc. grown or produced by the natural person. An entrepreneur account is also an appropriate solution for new forms of entrepreneurship, such as payments received from the provision of services from one natural person to another natural person through ride-sharing service platforms, e.g., Uber, Bolt, etc.

Since the total amount received on the entrepreneur account (not only the profit from the provision of the services or the sale of the goods) is taxed with business income tax, it is not possible to deduct costs or expenses. Therefore, in the areas of activity that involve direct or high costs, it is more beneficial to operate as a self-employed person or through a company. For example, it is important to deduct the acquisition costs of the goods from the income when selling goods or providing intermediation.

There is only one bank that offers such a possibility to open an entrepreneur account. A natural person can open an entrepreneur account with LHV Pank (hereinafter Bank). By signing the agreement, the entrepreneur account owner will arrange for Bank to reserve business income tax from the total amounts received on the entrepreneur account and transfer the business income tax to the Estonian Tax and Customs Board. Bank informs the Estonian Tax and Customs Board of the details of the person who has opened or closed the entrepreneur account and of the entrepreneur account number, and immediately transfers the business income tax reserved from the total amounts received on the account within a calendar month to the Estonian Tax and Customs Board. The free money on the entrepreneur account can be used by the account owner in the same way as money on a regular current account.

The Estonian Tax and Customs Board must carry out the following tasks:

- transfer the taxpayer's data received from Bank upon the conclusion of the agreement of opening the entrepreneur account into the register of taxable persons and delete the taxpayer's data from the register upon the end of the term of the entrepreneur account agreement;
- distribute the received business income tax if the taxpayer is an obligated person required to make contributions to a mandatory funded pension:
  - an income tax rate of 20/55 of the business income tax rate,
  - a social tax rate of 33/55 of the business income tax rate,
  - a mandatory funded pension contribution rate of 2/55 of the business income tax rate;
- distribute the received business income tax if the taxpayer is not an obligated person required to make contributions to a mandatory funded pension:
  - an income tax rate of 20/53 of the business income tax rate,
  - a social tax rate of 33/53 of the business income tax rate;
- forward the data of the mandatory funded pension contribution to the registrar of the pension register and the social tax data to the Estonian Health Insurance Fund and the Estonian Social Insurance Board.

The business income tax rate is 20 percent of the total amount received on the entrepreneur account if the amount does not exceed EUR 25,000 per calendar year and 40 percent of the amount exceeding EUR 25,000 received on the entrepreneur account per calendar year. If the amount received on the entrepreneur account exceeds EUR 40,000 per calendar year, the natural person is obligated to register as self-employed (FIE) or to establish a company (e.g. limited company or GmbH – in Estonian: OÜ) in the Commercial Register and as a person liable to value added tax in the Estonian Tax and Customs Board. The entrepreneur is required to keep accounts for taxation purposes.

2. *Necessary Social Security Protection (Example: Health Insurance)*

The important question is: Does a natural person get health insurance if he or she is using an entrepreneur account (e.g. working via platform)? An entrepreneur account owner has the right to receive health insurance benefits if the received social tax in a calendar month is to the extent of at least the minimum social tax requirement. In 2020, the monthly rate of social tax is EUR 540 and the minimum social tax obligation is EUR 178.20 per month (540 × 33%). In order to get health insurance, social tax to the extent of the minimum social tax requirement for the previous calendar month has to be received for the natural person. Health insurance begins on the day following the receipt of social tax (10th day) and stops after one month if the minimum social tax obligation is not fulfilled by the 10th of the following month. Data on the person for whom the minimum social tax liability has been received, is to be submitted by the Estonian Tax and Customs Board to the Estonian Health Insurance Fund.

To illustrate this situation, two examples shall be given.

Example 1
If a person is operating only through an entrepreneur account to get health insurance, he or she must receive at least EUR 1,485 per calendar month for the provision of services or for the sale of goods, from which the business income tax is EUR 297 (1485 × 20%) and of which social tax is EUR 165 (297 × 33/55 for an obligated person required to make contributions to a mandatory funded pension). If the minimum social tax obligation is fulfilled, the person has the right to receive the health insurance benefits.[41]

Example 2
In February 2020, a natural person earned EUR 400 under a service agreement (concluded with a legal person) and the legal person paid a social tax of EUR 132 (400 × 33%). In February, the natural person also received EUR 800 on the entrepreneur account, of which the business income tax was EUR 160 (800 × 20%) and social tax was EUR 96 (160 × 33/55). Thus, in February a total of EUR 228 (132 + 96) of social tax was collected from the natural person. In this case the natural person's minimum social tax

---

41 The minimum wage in Estonia is EUR 584 gross, the average in 2019 was EUR 1,407, see https://www.stat.ee/et/avasta-statistikat/valdkonnad/tooelu/palk-ja-toojoukulu/keskmine-brutokuupalk. Accessed 12 May 2020.

obligation is fulfilled in February and he will get health insurance from 11 March.

Deductions in a natural person's income tax return from the revenue received on the entrepreneur account cannot be made (for example, tax-free income, mortgage interests, training costs). Also the income tax part of the business income tax is not included as paid or withheld income tax in the income tax return of a natural person. At the same time, it is important to take into account that the sums received on the entrepreneur account, from which the social tax part has been deducted, are taken into account as the annual income of the natural person and thus affect the amount of tax-free income of the natural person.

An entrepreneur account owner can provide services and sell goods to both private persons as well as to companies, non-profit associations, foundations, legal persons in public law, state and local government authorities and other persons. When providing a service to a resident company, non-profit association, foundation and religious association which is a legal person, it is only necessary to take into account the fact that these persons will be subject to additional income tax (rate 20/80), which equates the tax burden with the tax burden of a regular employment relationship. The additional tax liability of a legal person is intended to prevent the routine transfer of employment relationship to a more favourable entrepreneur account.

Therefore, in case of the service fee transferred to the entrepreneur account, it must be assessed who has received the service provided by the entrepreneur account holder, whether it was the employer (company) or the employee, and whether it may be a case of the employer's compensation of expenses to the employee. When a natural person receives amounts on the entrepreneur account that have been paid to a natural person from a resident company, non-profit association, foundation or religious association which is a legal person (hereinafter also "a payer") for providing services and which are subject to taxation on the basis of the Simplified Business Income Taxation Act, these persons will be subject to additional income tax (rate 20/80) from expenses unrelated to business.

An entrepreneur account owner is obligated to inform the payer of the fact that he or she provides the service through an entrepreneur account and that the service is taxable under the Simplified Business Income Taxation Act.[42] If the entrepreneur account owner does not report that he or she is providing the service through an entrepreneur account, the payer is obligated to tax the payment made to a natural person for the service with all labour (salary) taxes.

3. Entrepreneur Account – Sufficient for Social Protection?

The creation and operation of an entrepreneur account is one of the measures that enables new workers to earn an income and to pay all the necessary contributions and taxes from this income in order to receive social protection. In essence, it can be argued that opening an entrepreneur account is a new alternative to operating as a self-employed person or setting up a single-member private limited company. Although the establishment of a private limited company has been made quite simple in Estonian conditions, the establishment of a private limited company and the existence of its activities require special knowledge of accounting and timely payment of taxes. Therefore, it also takes quite a lot of time to administer the activities of a private limited company. Creating an entrepreneur account and owning it provides an opportunity to ensure the necessary social security protection in a simplified manner in the case of small-scale income. On the other hand, it is important that also in the case of an entrepreneur account, a person's income must be higher than the average salary. Otherwise, it is possible to receive income and pay the necessary insurance premiums from this income, but the necessary and required social security protection (in the form of health insurance) is still not guaranteed.

The entrepreneur account and the income received in it indicate that the person has an activity equivalent to work. If the amount received through the entrepreneur account is not equal to at least the average salary granted in Estonia, the owner of the entrepreneur account does not receive health insurance cover and he or she cannot register as unemployed either.

The possibility of opening an entrepreneur account must be seen as one of the important measures to bring new workers closer to possible social protection and still give certain new workers access to social protection in two important areas: pension insurance and health insurance. At the same time, the entrepreneur account does not solve important problems related

42 Simplified Business Income Taxation Act (Ettevõtlustulu lihtsustatud maksustamise seadus), English translation: https://www.riigiteataja.ee/akt/107072017002. Accessed 12 May 2020.

to social protection, but is part of ensuring the necessary social protection for new employees.

VI. Conclusion

The social protection rights are mainly targeted at people who are involved in performing work in dependent employment, i.e. who work on the basis of an employment contract or in the civil service. When a person is working on the basis of an employment contract, the main responsibility for health insurance and the state pension fund lies with the employer, who has to pay the insurance taxes/contributions established by the Estonian legislation. The Estonian Social Tax Act also foresees an option that a self-employed person must pay social tax, but for this he has to register in the Commercial Register and also has the obligation to submit an annual report of the economic activity.

The owner of the entrepreneur account does not have to register in the Commercial Register; concurrently, there is no obligation to submit an annual report of the economic activity. The implementation of the entrepreneur account gives the person short-term work assignments and when the income per month is over the average gross wages of the state, it is possible to ensure minimal social security protection (health insurance and the state pension insurance). However, an important condition is established saying that the turnover of the entrepreneur account must not be bigger than EUR 40,000 per year. Otherwise, the obligation of paying VAT applies. The obligation of paying VAT requires a different kind of bookkeeping and accounting system, and due to that different forms of entrepreneurship are required.

An entrepreneur account is a simple but effective system for those who work with platforms. The employee only has to open a special entrepreneur account with the bank, and transfer the income from his/her business to it. Other formalities are done for him/her in cooperation with the bank and the Tax and Customs Board. While the number of ordinary self-employed persons shows a declining trend, the number of entrepreneur account openers shows an increasing trend. The Tax and Customs Board plays an important part in the administration of the amounts received in the entrepreneur account, and distributes the corresponding amounts among the necessary types of social protection schemes.

The entrepreneur account can be considered a positive and necessary tool, as it frees the platform worker from complicated accounting and reduces potential tax errors as well as the risk of the platform worker being deprived of social protection. The only important factor to be aware of is the amount received in the entrepreneur account. Only working for the minimum wage does not guarantee the minimum social protection, as the income earned must definitely be higher than the average wage in the country. Since the entrepreneur account was created only a year ago, it is possible to review its usefulness and necessity after a while.

Part IV:
Transborder Perspective: The Future Role of the European Union

Chapter 12
Building Up and Implementing the European Standards for Platform Workers

Paul Schoukens

I. Introduction

Is platform work changing the way in which we organise our work? If so, to what extent does this have an impact on organising social protection in our national social security systems? Is the EU – on the basis of its policy monitoring procedures and, in particular, through its European Pillar of Social Rights – saying anything on how to organise social protection for platform workers? If so, is this enough in terms of concerted European action or do we need additional (legal) measures coming from the EU? These are the main questions that are put forward in this contribution addressing the overall theme of the future role of the EU in a transborder perspective, one of the major topics that came to the fore at the conference held at the Max Planck Institute for Social Law and Social Policy in Munich on 12 and13 December 2019.

Platform work essentially refers to the organisation of professional activities through the mediation of a (digital) platform where supply of work and demand for work can be exchanged (against remuneration). The facilitation of work through the means of an intermediary agent is not new; a vast industry related to agency work emerged from it in the past. The novelty now lies more in the digitalisation of these intermediary platforms; as they are now internet-based and/or driven by an IT app(lication), quite some opportunities have been created for a faster and more global work organisation. Labour and services can thus easily be exchanges at a global level though the "World Wide Web"; work can be performed from a distance and is not necessarily bound to the premises of the employer. It can be performed at home, and depending on the complexity of the job, can be done without too big an amount of instructions; the fact that the job can be done almost instantly is considered as yet another asset, as the restrictions stemming from regular work-time patterns are avoided. Platform work can be done on a free-lance basis (by self-employed persons), which has potential with a view to cost reduction. In order to facilitate this global approach to labour exchange, work activities are increasingly divided into a series of sub-tasks which can be easily contracted out to an endless number of platform workers. Platform work is indeed often related to “gigs” or “small tasks” which do not always require major skills and hence there is a large pool of candidates who can perform the work. Platform work challenges the more traditional organisation of work and its underlying regulatory frameworks, in particular social security.

In this contribution, we will focus on the European Union and how the EU institutions address the challenge of organising social security for platform workers. Knowing that the main competence to organise social security remains at Member State level (Article 153 of the Treaty on the Functioning of the European Union, TFEU), it may seem awkward to raise this question from the outset. The EU can, however, intervene to provide support (Article 6 TFEU). All the more so when the Member States are confronted with similar problems for which a solution is hard to find. With the European Pillar of Social Rights (EPSR) of 2016 the EU set itself a common framework to monitor the social policies of its Member States in terms of their social outcomes. One of the major goals of this Pillar is to safeguard (enough) access to social protection for all workers and self-employed workers (principle 12). To that purpose, the Recommendation was launched, inviting all Member States to provide to all professionally active persons access to an adequate level of social protection. The Recommendation is considered to be an answer to the growing groups of non-standard workers and self-employed persons that face exclusion from social security because of their irregular work patterns, low levels of income or their autonomous way of working.

For this contribution we address the question as to what extent the Recommendation responds to the challenges that platform work generates for the organisation of social security. Since platform work did not really emerge fully until after the EPSR and the Recommendation had (already) been launched, in essence we are trying to figure out whether the Recommendation is still relevant for the latest evolutions in work organisation. In order to do so, we will first define the concept of platform work and subsequently indicate where it deviates from standard work forms. After this definition, the major typical features of platform work that pose challenges to our traditional social security will be assessed based on the provisions set out in the Recommendation; finally, we will try to indicate where the Recommendation (and its underlying EU vision on access to social protection) may fall short and what kind of action is (still) to be expected. After this definition, we will have the major typical features of platform work that cause challenges to our traditional social security assessed against the provisions of the Recommendation.

In a final section we shall address the question of whether the legal standards developed by the Recommendation are sufficient. And complementary to this question, what kind of EU legal action in the field of social security could still be relevant. The section takes up the discussion again in a broader perspective and will by definition go beyond the strict set of problems surrounding platform work and its impact on the organisation of social security. That being said, platform work is to be considered as yet another development in work organisation that urges the EU to develop clearer rules in order to safeguard fair competition (i.e. an equal-level playing field) on the internal market. Organising social security has an impact on labour costs; this is true as well for platform work, even if only in the sense that this new work form is often (falsely) used for legitimising a reduction in production costs and hence improving its competitive position at the detriment of the worker. Common standards at EU level are needed. In the final section, we call for more EU attention to the financing of social security rather than to the benefits side.

II. Platform Work as a New Non-Standard Work Form

1. Platform Work

Platform workers can be defined[1] as persons selected online from a pool of workers through the intermediation of a platform to perform personally[2] on-demand short-term tasks for different persons or companies in exchange for income. It is evident that we restrict ourselves to platform activities that have a (potential) relation to professional work, leaving out plat-

1 As defined previously by us: *Barrio, Alberto/Montebovi, Saskia/Schoukens, Paul*, The EU Social Pillar: An Answer to the Challenge of the Social Protection of Platform Workers?, in: European Journal of Social Security, 20 (2018) 3, pp. 219-241.

2 Our focus is thus on persons who personally deliver the service and are not in a position to have it carried out by another person. This means that the platform worker is required to create a personal profile, to which reviews may be linked. In some cases, this feature is expressly mentioned by the platform in its terms of service. See *Prassl, Jeremias/Risak, Martin*, Uber, Taskrabbit, & Co: Platforms as Employers? Rethinking the Legal Analysis of Crowdwork: in: Comparative Labour Law & Policy Journal, 37 (2016) 3, p. 30. In other cases, it might be evident from the personal character of the ratings.

forms that are based exclusively in the non-profit sharing of property or knowledge. The online character of platforms is one of the major defining features, facilitating access and reducing transaction costs.[3] Furthermore, the fact that the platform acts as an intermediary between the person who receives the service and the person who performs it means that, in its role, the platform typically:

(1) possesses essential information about the relationship (e.g. the nature of the tasks performed, remuneration, the identity of the parties, etc.),
(2) has a monopoly over the contact between the two parties in the relationship (i.e. the person performing the work and the person receiving it may only contact each other through the platform),
(3) provides rules concerning the behaviour of both parties,
(4) may monitor compliance with such rules, and
(5) may sanction the lack of compliance with such rules by stopping temporarily or permanently an individual from accessing the platform.

Finally, in the definition the on-demand[4] nature of platform work is essential too. It means that the performance of a task is offered when and if a person requests it, without any obligation by the platform to ensure that a minimum amount of work is performed by the workers registered in it. It goes without saying that significant periods of unremunerated time will often exist, when a worker waits between tasks, for instance. This shows what the fragmentation of work (assignments) can cause with regard to the total working time (all tasks added), the irregularity of work time (tasks can be done at whatever time of day and workers are thus not confined to the traditional 9-to-5 time schedule) and the intermittency of work (tasks do not always succeed one another without any transition, meaning that persons are often confronted with non-remunerated waiting periods between assignments).

3 For some examples on the importance of the online character (which results, among other things, in the use of apps), see *Valenduc, Gerard/Vendramin, Patricia*, Work in the Digital Economy: Sorting the Old from the New, ETUI, Brussels, 2017, https://www.etui.org/publications/working-papers/work-in-the-digital-economy-sorting-the-old-from-the-new. Accessed 18 June 2020.

4 *Kittur, Aniket/Nickerson, Jeffrey/Bernstein, Michael/Gerber, Elizabeth/Shaw, Aaron/Zimmerman, John/Lease, Matt/Horton, John*, The Future of Crowd Work, in: CSCW 2013 – Proceedings of the 2013 ACM Conference on Computer Supported Cooperative Work, 2013, pp. 1301-1307, https://doi.org/10.1145/2441776.2441923. Accessed 18 June 2020.

2. *Platform Work Compared to Standard Work*

Its definition makes clear that platform work deviates from normal (standard) work that traditionally forms the basis for labour regulations and (work-related) social security schemes. In general terms, standard work is understood to be subordinated, full-time work of an indefinite duration. More specifically, it may be defined as the "stable, open-ended and direct arrangement between dependent, full-time employees and their unitary employer". This definition not only contains the traditional elements[5] of the employment relationship but also refers to the outcomes of this traditional labour relationship, this being job security[6] and income security[7].

Atypical work deviates from one or more of these characteristics of the standard work relationship. Originally, deviations could occur in relation to one of the following (three) components:

(1) The subordinated relationship between worker and employer: the absence of such a relationship refers traditionally to autonomous (or self-employed) work; the self-employed are mainly characterised by the freedom to organise their work and their work time. Since they work for various commissioners they can also spread their economic dependency. Contrary to the full-time worker, their income is derived from various clients.

(2) Full-time work: part-time work arrangements challenge in particular the income security that normally originates from standard work. Consequently, part-time work will create problems for traditional social security schemes that guarantee income security on the basis of income replacement of labour income (wage). Part-time work often results in lower income, so the income replacement guaranteed by social security is at risk of falling below minimum subsistence levels. Part-time work (and covering part-time work in social security) often be-

5 This being the presence of personal subordination, the bilateral character of the relationship, and hence mutuality of obligations as a consequence, the wage as (main) source of income that is provided in return to the offered labour, the economic dependency as the worker depends fully for this income on the employer, and a fixed workplace where the work is done, normally at the premises of the employer.

6 Labour contracts are concluded for an indefinite period and relate to full-time occupation.

7 The wage may be the only source of income but is guaranteed at a certain (minimum) level and in case of loss of the position, income replacement is guaranteed through the means of social security.

comes an issue of poverty alleviation (combating poverty and social exclusion). This is especially true for persons living alone or persons who are head of the family. Part-time work will often demand that systems provide corrective (supportive) income support.

(3) Indefinite work: contracts for specific fixed-time periods challenge work security. Work is only guaranteed for the contracted time period, which is by definition restricted in time (short). The workers risk intermittent periods of (no) work (and consequently no income). As a result, social security will often function as a bridge covering intermittent periods (of no work) by providing income replacement (see e.g. schemes of temporary unemployment).

These major categories aside (part-time, fixed time or self-employed work), we have recently been observing an increase of new kinds of atypical work forms, such as on-call work, zero-hour contracts, solo self-employment, internships, self-employed workers active within management companies, student work, interim work, agency work, crowd work, portfolio work etc., with platform work being one of them. When we take a closer look at these new forms[8] we notice however that they are a further development (to the extremes) of the traditional atypical work categories (part-time work, fixed-time work or self-employment), sometimes even applied in combination and including some new elements that deviate from standard work (no remuneration, the triangular contractual relations, etc.). In some situations, typical of work forms seen on platforms such as crowd work and portfolio, hardly any of the traditional elements present in the standard work relationship are seen. It should not come as a surprise that this in turn creates challenges for traditional (work-related) social insurance schemes.

III. Platform Work as a Challenge for Organising Social Security

Platform work creates some challenges for the organisation of social security systems. We shall enumerate a selection of some major challenges, based on previous research work[9]:

---

8 *Barrio, Alberto/Schoukens, Paul*, The Changing Concept of Work, in: European Labour Law Journal, 8 (2017) 4, pp. 306-332.

9 *Barrio, Alberto/Schoukens, Paul*, The Changing Concept of Work (fn. 8), pp. 306-332; *Barrio, Alberto/Montebovi, Saskia/Schoukens, Paul*, The EU Social Pillar: An Answer to the Challenge of the Social Protection of Platform Workers? (fn. 1), pp.

1. *What is "Work"?*

The main aim of income replacement schemes, addressing risks such as old age, unemployment and work incapacity, is to compensate the loss of income when persons are no longer in a position to work. For these schemes it is therefore rather crucial to have the concept of work well-defined, since income originating from work is the main element around which the eventual protection is organised. This is true for schemes with both a Bismarck and Beveridge signature, even if in Bismarckian social security schemes the work-related income has even more relevance for financing purposes (employee and employer contributions levied on wages).

Which activities are now considered to be work? Normally, two main elements are taken into account for the application of social security: the regularity of the activity and the intention to earn one's living from the performed activities. Most of the social security schemes are still based on the assumption that the activity should be of a regular and repetitive nature in order for it to be considered as a genuine work activity; this applied at least for the default case reflecting standard work in subordination (the "9-to-5" job).

When applied to platform work, it is not always easy in reality to find out which of the activities can be considered as labour-related activities and which cannot. This might be due to the fact that the scope of the activity (the gigs) is too marginal in nature to be considered as genuine work; or it may be due to the fact that the generated income can only be indirectly related to the platform activity (e.g. sponsorship granted to influencers). In some cases, the activity may generate enough financial means but the underlying activity cannot be considered as work (lack of regularity).

A second issue refers to the relationship between work and income: what should be done when income is less work-related and based more on returns from goods such as capital or property? It is currently already hard to make the division between professional income and return from (invested) capital for the self-employed, and the latter kind of income source is traditionally left out of social security financing.[10] In many non-standard

---

219-241; *Barrio, Alberto/Montebovi, Saskia/Schoukens, Paul*, The EU Social Pillar: An Answer to the Challenge of the Social Protection of Platform Workers?, in: Devolder, Bram (ed.), The Platform Economy. Unravelling the Legal Status of Online Intermediaries, Cambridge – Antwerp – Chicago: Intersentia 2018, pp. 227-258.

10 *Schoukens, Paul*, Adequacy and Financing. Thematic Discussion Paper. Report for European Commission, Brussels, 2020 (publication online to follow).

work forms, the distinction between work-related income and other income sources is becoming blurred, especially in the case of the prosumers, platform workers, employee shareholders, self-employed shareholders also performing professional activities within the ambit of the company in which they are shareholders, etc. Work-related social security schemes face problems in addressing income that is not strictly related to work, both from the financing side (income as basis for the levy of contributions) and from the income replacement side (previously earned income as basis for the calculation of benefits). Income sources that are not strictly work-related (such as income in nature, return on investment, income from movable or immovable property) disqualify as a source for social security purposes. But is this not somewhat unrealistic as in reality people may live on these income sources and hence may risk losing them when confronted with certain types of social risks?

2. *Who is the Employer?*

Determining the (main) employer is a key aspect for social security, in order to identify who is responsible for paying contributions (financing), deciding on redundancy (unemployment) and for granting the income replacement (work incapacity). Nevertheless, this is not always straightforward for several non-standard forms of work. Temporary agency work is a field in which a great deal of effort has been put into overcoming this problem, mostly through ensuring that agency companies remain responsible for satisfying the obligations of the employer with regard to contributions. However, this challenge reappeared with significant force in the situation of platform work. Whether these workers are employed by the users of the platform or the platform itself is an on-going discussion, the outcome of which will have different consequences (employer responsibilities for social security). Finally, it should be noted that, in the case of forms of work as flexible as platform work, the same person is often active on several platforms almost simultaneously (while, at the same time, the person is not necessarily active on all the platforms he is registered with), and these platforms may be based in different countries, making it extremely difficult to track employers and work that has been performed (see also below).

3. Irregular Work Patterns

This problem is particularly clear in the case of thresholds to access certain social insurance schemes, i.e. the requirement of having paid contributions for a certain time within a specific period. As a consequence, persons in atypical work forms are pushed out of social insurance schemes, as even though they may end up accumulating a multitude of fixed-/part-time work assignments, each of these assignments is too small to be taken into account for social insurance purposes.

Again, regulations on temporary agency work have pioneered in tackling this issue, and in some European countries employers, agencies and trade unions have collaborated to create particular provisions to compensate for some of the periods of inactivity which characterises the fragmented careers of temporary agency workers. Another approach is to considerably lower the threshold for accessing social insurance schemes such as the unemployment scheme.[11] Labour instability may also hinder the tracking of periods of employment, as in some cases the person may perform work for a few hours in a row with one employer, after which long periods of inactivity may follow. Social security schemes should be redesigned to accommodate these irregular work patterns where active periods followed by periods of inactivity and/or work periods generating low income alternate with high-income work assignments. Otherwise, schemes may miss out on a large group of work activities that do not coincide with the traditional work organisation characterised by full-time work assignments within a fixed working time period (9-to-5 jobs).

4. Virtual Mobility of Platform Workers

In a similar manner, the discussion on the geographical aspect of work will increase. New work forms applied in e.g. telework and platform work are becoming more virtual. Most of our (work-related) social insurance schemes start from a very physical concept of work: it is required that the work is physically performed on a particular territory in order to be made subject to a certain social security system. The EU coordination rules (in particular Title II of Regulation (EC) 883/2004) follow this logic closely us-

11 *Barrio, Alberto/Montebovi, Saskia/Schoukens, Paul*, The EU Social Pillar: An Answer to the Challenge of the Social Protection of Platform Workers? (fn. 9), pp. 227-258.

ing the *lex loci laboris* principle as a basis to indicate the competent state in case of cross-border activities: ultimately, the physical place where the person is working determines the Member State competent for social security, such as in the *Partena*-case.[12] But also in national social security law it is often required that work is performed on the territory where an employer is based in order to have it taken into account for social security.

Can this still be upheld as a basic assumption now, in a world where people organise their work in an increasingly virtual manner? Virtual work as often applied in platform work makes long-distance work relations possible, where employers and employees are well-connected online but remain geographically very distant from each other. Moreover, due to IT tools it is now much easier to carry out (parts of) the work at home. The "geographical" relationship between employees, self-employed persons and employers on the one hand, and the Member States on other hand will become more virtual and hence will further complicate the applicable law rules in their application.[13] Persons do not necessarily organise their work anymore in a given place.

IV. The EU Recommendation on Access to Social Protection

1. The Recommendation as a Concrete Outcome of the European Pillar of Social Rights

With the idea of socially counterbalancing the economic financing of the monitoring procedures applied by the EU in the European Stability Pact[14], the EU Commission launched the European Pillar of Social Rights under

---

12 ECJ of 27 September 2012, Case C-137/11, Partena vzw v Les Tartes de Chaumont-Gistoux *SA*, ECLI:EU:C:2012:593; see also: *Schoukens, Paul*, Social Security Coordination and Non-Standard Forms of (Self-)Employment, in: Revue belge de Sécurité sociale, (2019) 2, pp. 81-112.

13 For some examples, see the conference Employment, Social Policy, Health and Consumer Affairs Council (EPSCO), The Future of Work, Making it E-Easy, Tallinn, Estonian Presidency, 13-14 September 2017, https://www.eurofound.europa.eu/sr/events/future-of-work-making-it-e-easy-eu-presidency-estonia. Accessed 18 June 2020.

14 *Beke, Joris/Schoukens, Paul*, Fighting Social Exclusion under EU Horizon 2020. Enhancing the Legal Enforceability of Social Inclusion Recommendations?, in: European Journal of Social Security, 16 (2014) 1, pp. 51-72 and *Schoukens, Paul*, EU Social Security Law: The Hidden "Social" Model. Inaugural Address, Tilburg: Tilburg University 2016.

the Presidency of Juncker. The programme, which should serve as a reference framework for assessing national social policies, contains a series of fundamental social rights that will undergo further development via concrete European actions. In the end, The European Pillar of Social Rights[15] was jointly announced by the European Parliament, the Council and the Commission in November 2017; it set out 20 principles and rights to support fair and well-functioning labour markets and welfare systems.

Principle 12 of the Pillar states that "regardless of the type and duration of their employment relationship, workers, and, under comparable conditions, the self-employed have the right to adequate social protection". In order to have this principle further developed, a proposal for a Council Recommendation was launched by the European Commission on access to social protection for workers and the self-employed,[16] finally adopted in November 2019.[17]

Interestingly, the Recommendation addresses all atypical forms of work, and calls for proper social protection for different types of work, even though they may be organised in a different way than traditional standard work. An essential principle in the proposal for a Recommendation is the neutral character of the labour status of the worker or self-employed worker: the basic principles shaping social security are equal for all professionally active persons, whatever the kind of work or work status; yet at the same time, social security should in its application respect as much as possible the specific working circumstances under which the work is carried out. In a way, it applied the general principle of equal treatment (underlying Union citizenship as per Article 18 TFEU) to work-related social security: the same rules should apply to groups of persons that are comparable; however, by the same token, in situations where groups are different, the rules need to be adapted in order not to apply one and the same rule to different groups. The Recommendation, which seeks to ensure minimum standards in the field of social protection of workers and the self-employed, applies to all traditional social insurance schemes related to labour (i.e. unemployment benefits, sickness and health care benefits, maternity

---

15 European Commission, Proposal for an Interinstitutional Proclamation on the European Pillar of Social Rights, COM (2017) 251.

16 European Commission, Proposal for a Council Recommendation on Access to Social Protection for Workers and the Self-Employed, COM (2018)132.

17 Council Recommendation (EU) of 8 November 2019 on Access to Social Protection for Workers and the Self-Employed (Recommendation Access Social protection), OJ C 387/1, 15 November 2019.

and equivalent paternity benefits, invalidity benefits, old-age benefits, and benefits in respect of accidents at work and occupational diseases).[18]

2. *Access to Social Protection*

The Recommendation regulates access across four main angles: formal access and effective access; adequacy of benefits and transparency. The Recommendation makes thus a clear distinction between formal and effective coverage, the first referring to the elements conditioning the personal scope of (work-related) social insurance, the latter mainly targeting entitlement conditions to benefits. Formal coverage stems from existing legislation or collective agreements setting out that the workers are entitled to participate in a social protection scheme in a specific branch.[19] Effective coverage refers to real protection in cases where workers and self-employed persons have the opportunity to accrue adequate benefits and the ability, in the case of the materialisation of the corresponding risk, to access a given level of benefits.[20]

a) Formal Access

In its final version that was accepted by all Member States the requirements regarding formal access have been levelled down for the self-employed. As some Member States had difficulties with the idea of a mandatory coverage for the self-employed for the eventuality of work incapacity and work accidents, it has been decided to provide at least a voluntary coverage for this group of workers. However, this creates a somewhat unbalanced approach by the Recommendation from the outset: it is difficult to strive towards a comparable protection for all professionally active people, yet at the same time accept that for the self-employed, access to social protection can be organised on a voluntary basis. This is especially problematic for the group of platform workers, as the issue of legal qualification – are they wage-earners or self-employed – is still strongly disputed in the

18 But not family benefits; Article 3.2 of Recommendation (fn. 17). Not directly linked to work-related protection, social assistance has been left out as well from the scope.
19 Article 7, Sub. e of Recommendation (fn. 17).
20 Article 7, Sub. f of Recommendation (fn. 17).

majority of Member States. The reason for this is the limited protection the self-employed "enjoy"[21] and hence the reduced cost of hiring them as self-employed on platforms. Hiring platform workers as self-employed freelancers is part of a deliberate business policy as (some major commercial players in the) platforms want to cut labour costs as much as possible. Asking now from Member States to make access to social protection available on a voluntary basis will not change much in this respect as the majority of low-income (and high-income) self-employed do in the end not take out social insurance when they are given the freedom to do so.[22] The original objective to create an equal-level playing field for all workers is thus seriously undercut in the Recommendation.

b) Effective Access

Of particular interest for platform workers are the provisions dealing with effective coverage (Articles 9-10). The Recommendation establishes that rules governing contributions and entitlements should not hinder the possibility of accruing and accessing benefits due to the type of employment relationship or labour market status; and, moreover, that differences in the rules governing the schemes between labour market statuses or types of employment relationship should be proportionate and reflect the specific situation of beneficiaries. Platform work is characterised by specific work patterns, often leading to intermittent work periods (see above). Minimum qualifying periods and minimum working periods may prove to be problematic to opening entitlement to benefits for these workers.

However, the Recommendation states that such minimum conditions should not impede the effective building-up of social protection for per-

---

21 *Spasova, Slavina/Bouget, Denis/Ghailani, Dalila*, Self-Employment and Social Protection: Understanding Variations between Welfare Regimes, in: Journal of Poverty and Social Justice, 27 (2019) 2, pp. 157-175 and *Spasova, Slanina/Bouget, Denis/Ghailani, Dalila/Vanhercke, Bart*, Access to Social Protection for People Working on Non-Standard Contracts and as Self-Employed in Europe. A Study of National Policies, European Social Policy Network (ESPN), Brussels: European Commission, 2017.

22 European Commission, Behavioural Study on the Effects of an Extension of Access to Social Protection for People in All Forms of Employment, Luxembourg: Publications Office of the European Union, 2018 and *Schoukens, Paul*, Extending Formal Coverage. Thematic Discussion Paper. Report for European Commission, Brussels, 2019, https://ec.europa.eu/social/BlobServlet?docId=21913&langId=en. Accessed 18 June 2020.

sons with an irregularly built up insurance record (Article 9, Para. 1, Sub. a); the rules should be justified by a clear objective (e.g. financial sustainability, insurance logics such as the respect of equivalence and/or the combat of abuse); the reason for their introduction should thus be unrelated to the labour status of the worker.

Consequently, time periods for the definition of qualifying periods or waiting periods (full-time work equivalents per day or per week) may for example be better reformulated in smaller time units (working hours), under the condition that the total result of the smaller time units reflects the same overall volume as that required for standard work. Similarly, the reference period during which the work time or income has to be earned can be stipulated in a more extensive way as long as a comparable average in workload or income is reached (e.g. work hours per year instead of per day, week or month: e.g. at least X euros earned on average on a monthly or yearly basis instead of per week or per month).

c) Adequate Benefits

The Recommendation calls for an adequate level of protection (Article 11). What constitutes adequate protection? And how can adequate benefits levels be guaranteed if at the financing side the income that serves as a basis for the benefits calculation was anything but adequate? The Recommendation remains vague about the level of benefits as no clear figures or references are to be found in the document: what is an "appropriate income replacement" or "a decent standard of living"? What is the minimum? The prior observation (17) in the Recommendation provides further guidance indicating what benefits adequacy could mean: "… [s]ocial protection is considered to be adequate when it allows individuals to uphold a decent standard of living, replace their income loss in a reasonable manner and live with dignity, and prevents them from falling into poverty while contributing, where appropriate, to activation and facilitating the return to work".

Although general in its wording, the Recommendation nevertheless refers to some protection levels that must be respected by the systems. The bottom line is that workers and the self-employed, when on benefits, should be kept out of poverty. Benefits levels should not fall below minimum subsistence levels as applied in the social assistance schemes. Likewise, the minimum social pension for a person having worked a full career should, for example, not fall below the minimum subsistence applied in social assistance.

The starting principle for standard work is a reasonable income protection so that the beneficiary can live in dignity. In this way, the Recommendation strongly reflects the basic philosophy behind our European social security systems, in which social insurance schemes and social assistance schemes overlap when it comes to income protection. The latter schemes are designed to provide residual protection against poverty if labour market (policies) and social insurance fail to do so. Consequently, social protection schemes must do more than (only) protect against poverty: they must guarantee reasonable protection against loss of income (from work). Of course, with no concrete indications of the requested minimum income replacement ratios (such as we e.g. could see in the minimum standard conventions), the condition to guarantee adequate benefits remains difficult to monitor. And although the Recommendation calls for an approach to lower the financial burden on workers and the self-employed with a low income, the fundamental question remains what kind of social protection is to be guaranteed to persons with a structural low income. Providing decent levels of social protection may work well when the vast majority of the professionally active population work in standard work relationships. It becomes more challenging though when a growing number of workers or self-employed workers are on low incomes or do not have regular work.

d) Transparent Access

The condition of transparency refers first and foremost to clear rules that are openly communicated to the citizens. Yet, it refers as well to the design of the schemes; these should not be made too complicated or too costly to be applied by the workers and the self-employed. Especially in relation to the latter group, there should be enough transparency in design, with not too many complicated conditions to comply with. Especially for freelancers with limited income or platform workers who earn small incomes on an irregular basis, applying complicated contribution assessments will in the end be detrimental to system compliance; [23] by the same token, the underlying logic of benefits accrual should be kept simple for persons who bear the responsibility of contribution payment themselves, reflecting the idea of benefits equivalence: entitlements of the self-employed should re-

23 *Schoukens, Paul*, Adequacy and Financing (fn. 10).

flect their actual earnings (adequacy of benefits).[24] Moreover, the Recommendation states that Member States should ensure that entitlements are accumulated, preserved and transferable across all types of employment and self-employment statuses and across economic sectors (transferability of entitlements).[25] In a society where persons are increasingly starting to combine (professional) activities the design of the social protection system should be kept transparent allowing a gradual and integrated benefits accrual across the various income sources.

V. *The EU Recommendation: Are the Needs of Platform Work Sufficiently Addressed?*

The Recommendation regarding access to social protection was not designed specifically with platform work in mind. Platform work came only recently to full exploitation after some major companies saw the "commercial" potential of the sharing economy. The preparatory works for the Recommendation were already too advanced in their development to incorporate this emerging new atypical work form in its regulations. But as the Recommendation had from the outset the ambition to address all different work forms this was probably not necessary; its design should make it versatile enough to incorporate new developments in work organisation, such as all kinds of platform work. Platform work does challenge the Recommendation in some aspects, three of which will be given further attention: the difference between self-employment and wage-earnership when it comes to formal access; adequacy and low-income workers; and finally, the lack of definition of work.

1. *Platform Work: Self-Employment or Wage-Earnership?*

Compared to the proposal in which the option of voluntary access was restricted to the risk of unemployment, the final adopted version levelled down the condition on formal access for the group of self-employed workers. Article 8 now calls upon Member States to improve the formal coverage and have it extended to all workers, regardless of the type of employment relationship, on a mandatory basis; for the self-employed though, the

---

24 Article 14 of Recommendation (fn. 17).
25 Article 10 of Recommendation (fn. 17).

extension should be at least on a voluntary basis and, where appropriate, on a mandatory basis. Even though one can interpret the Recommendation in an extensive way to mean that mandatory coverage is the standard approach for having social protection organised for all professionally active workers[26], there remains a legal distinction in place between the groups of wage-earners and the self-employed. This distinction goes against the fundamental philosophy of the Recommendation which aims at an equal approach towards social protection for all working groups; distinctions are still accepted but should be restricted to the application of the principles, which can be adapted to the specific working circumstances of the working groups at stake (see above). Choosing between mandatory and voluntary coverage is not in line with this; it goes against the very essence of social protection, which is to be organised on a mandatory basis in order to generate enough redistribution between the groups (of workers).

When applied to platform work, we can see that the distinction between protection levels across the self-employed and wage-earners is one of the major problems at stake. The legal discussion in social law on platform work is still largely focused on the legal qualification of the work activities[27]: are they wage-earners or are they to be considered as self-employed? The vast majority of platforms try to have them contracted as self-employed workers, essentially to keep the labour costs as low as possible. For some platforms, contracting cheap labour is the cornerstone upon which their business is based.

In relation to the Recommendation, a potential weakness could be the differentiation between workers and the self-employed when it comes to guaranteeing social protection. Apart from the idea of equal protection, the Recommendation also aspires to an equal-level playing field across work groups; ultimately, it should not matter for (the cost of) social protection whether one contracts a worker or a self-employed person. The reality of platform work shows that, in reality, it does matter very much indeed. The fact that the self-employed have the choice to be protected (voluntary protection) will have the effect that in the end they will not be protected at all.[28] The Recommendation is running short here: distinguishing

26 *Schoukens, Paul*, Extending Formal Coverage (fn. 22).

27 *Rocca, Marco*, Perspective internationale: les Juges face aux Plateformes, in: Lamine, Auriane/Wattecamps, Céline (eds.), Quel Droit social pour les Travailleurs de Plateformes?, Brussels: Anthemis 2019.

28 European Commission, Behavioural Study on the Effects of an Extension of Access to Social Protection for People in All Forms of Employment (fn. 22) and *Schoukens, Paul*, Extending Formal Coverage (fn. 22).

the self-employed from workers from the outset with regard to the formal coverage risks undermining the very objectives for which the Recommendations stands: equal levels of protection and the safeguarding of an equal-level playing field for all workers. To limit the potential damage caused by this voluntary protection clause, this clause must be interpreted strictly: it is to be restricted to situations where the organisation of coverage against particular social risks is too challenging for the group of self-employed persons (such as might be the case for work accidents or unemployment).[29] For the other eventualities, mandatory coverage is the key principle to be followed, also by the self-employed.

2. *Low-Income Groups Covered by the Guarantee of Adequate Benefits?*

Another major challenge for platform work is low income and how to take this into account for the organisation of social protection. The Recommendation focuses mainly on the work-related social protection risks. From a point of view of sustainability, it is challenging to guarantee adequate (minimum) benefits that are structurally of a higher level than the income on which contributions were paid in the past. This is rather problematic. Platform work is known to have amid the groups a strong proportion of persons earning a low to very low income. And even though some of these workers engage in platform work in terms of a second job, the question remains of how to take into account these low-income levels for the organisation of work-related social protection schemes. The national approaches diverge in their answers, although we notice a strong resurrection of all kinds of minimum thresholds excluding platform workers from (effective access to) social protection.[30]

The Recommendation calls now for guaranteeing an effective social protection and thus for organising the system so that scattered insurance records should not be disproportionally sanctioned in social protection systems. However, it remains silent as to what should be guaranteed in terms of decent levels of social protection; similarly, it remains silent about what kind of decent protection „should be guaranteed if the previous (underlying) income basis (of the worker) was too low during his/her working life to justify a (decent) minimum protection.

29 *Schoukens, Paul*, Extending Formal Coverage (fn. 22).
30 *Schoukens, Paul*, Adequacy and Financing (fn. 10).

Overall, Article 11 of the Recommendation calls for making sure that (non-standard) workers and the self-employed should not end up in poverty. Article 11 refers to the overall social protection system and the national circumstances that have to be taken into account in that respect. By doing so, it acknowledges that work-related social protection cannot address this problematic issue on its own; when shaping redistribution these systems are still bound by other principles, such as sustainability and equivalence, principles that limit the levels of redistribution that can be put into the system. It is thus an invitation to have a further look beyond the social protection schemes (in the narrow sense) and to see the interplay with other social schemes, such as social assistance, (health) care, family policies and social housing. In order to keep these references to other protection schemes manageable, it would be helpful to make them somewhat more concrete in the monitoring of the Recommendation. First, it would be recommendable to state what is understood by benefits adequacy (and thus indirectly what is expected from the other schemes not targeted by the Recommendation to achieve this). The fact that the EU, but also other international organisations such as the ILO and the Council of Europe, have already developed a substantial arsenal of social indicators enabling the monitoring of social outcomes is promising in this regard. The Recommendation could use a coherent measurement framework with regard to adequacy and in that way Article 11 can be seen as an invitation to coherently bring together these indicators in order to provide some guidance on benefits adequacy and on the positioning of social protection benefits, minimum benefits and social assistance schemes when it comes to providing social protection. Secondly, in order to reach the goal of adequacy, social insurance protection schemes will have to be aligned well with schemes such as social assistance and family benefits.

3. *What is a Professional Activity and What is Not?*

The Recommendation does not define what is considered to be work or what a professional activity must consist of, nor does it provide its own definitions of workers and the self-employed. There is indeed something to be said about keeping these concepts open and having them gradually defined over the years on the basis of national reporting. After all, the Recommendation is mainly targeting an approach whereby national systems are monitored; using strict legal definitions from the outset does not work very well with this approach.

The case of platform work does, however, immediately show some limits of this approach: what is to be considered as work and professional income becomes increasingly blurred. If social protection systems do not start to recalibrate their scope of application (and thus the underlying concepts, such as work and income, that fall within this scope) they may lose out on the new and evolving realities of work. Already with regard to self-employment we notice that it is difficult to delimit precisely which income sources are work-related and which are related to capital. This is also the case with platform work. Platform work itself is possibly the exponent of a societal evolution where people's main concern is, in the first place, to earn sufficient income to earn a living. This can be on the basis of a regular standard job (as had for many decades been the main tool for earning sufficient income), but it can also be through other means in place of or in combination with a job. Taking into account the latest evolutions in non-standard work (platform work), increasing emphasis is put on income protection rather than on the protection of labour income.[31] More than ever before, persons tend to combine a series of activities and/or live from various income sources (from movable and immovable property). Social protection should develop alongside this evolution and incorporate these various income sources both into the financing of social protection and the payment of benefits. Some systems have already started to move in this direction, hence it is a call for the Recommendation to incorporate this evolution as well and to apply a broad definition of work and income in order to do what it had originally intended to do: monitor the design of proper social protection systems where all workers are treated equally in the protection of their social needs, regardless their source of professional income.

VI. An Alternative to Benefits Harmonisation: Towards an EU Financing Fork?

The Recommendation can be considered as a positive evolution in the standard-setting history of the EU, be it because from a legal point of view

31 *Barrio, Alberto/Schoukens, Paul*, The Changing Concept of Work (fn. 8), p. 221 ff; European Commission, Commission Staff Working Document Impact Assessment Accompanying the Document Proposal for a Council Recommendation on Access to Social Protection for Workers and the Self-Employed, Strasbourg, 13 March 2018, p. 32 ff.

nothing considerably happened since 1992.[32] However, at the same time some criticism arose, most often referring to the weak legal character of the Recommendation. This is especially true knowing that originally the Recommendation was conceived as an EU directive, which as an instrument could have had a stronger legal impact than the Recommendation, where ultimately any sanctioning is restricted to naming and blaming the Member States which do not follow the Recommendation. Moreover, the fact that the Recommendation weakened the formulation in relation to the formal access conditions for the self-employed has also been strongly criticised, as well as the too general wording in relation to benefits adequacy; the trade unions expected a clearer stipulation of what is considered to be the minimum income replacement for social protection benefits that Member States have to respect (somewhat in the style in which the minimum standard-setting instruments such as ILO Convention 102 and the European Code of Social Security do so).[33]

As mentioned earlier, another point of criticism is the fact that no clear definitions have been developed for the description of the professional groups for which standards have been set: workers, self-employed, and non-standard workers.[34] Consequently, the Recommendation does not add very much in the ongoing legal fight on whether platform workers are to be considered to belong within the group of wage-earners or that of the self-employed. Similarly, the Recommendation does not give much direction as to the protection to be guaranteed for the emerging group of in-between workers that has been identified by quite some Member States, as a mid-group of sorts between wage-earners and the self-employed (such as the "*parasubordinati*" in Italy and the "*trabajador autónomo economicamente dependiente*" (*TRADE*) in Spain); some see this third group to be representative of the growing group of platform workers. From a perspective of the Recommendation, it is however not clear which standards are to be respected for these "in-between" workers; at least voluntary protection such

32 The year during which were enacted: Council Recommendation (EEC) 92/441 of 24 June 1992 on common criteria concerning sufficient resources and social assistance in social protection systems, OJ L 245, 26 August 1992 and Council Recommendation (EEC) 92/442 of 27 July 1992 on the convergence of social protection objectives and policies, OJ L 245, 26 August 1992.

33 *Schoukens, Paul*, Extending Formal Coverage (fn. 22).

34 *Barrio, Alberto/Montebovi, Saskia/Schoukens, Paul*, The EU Social Pillar: An Answer to the Challenge of the Social Protection of Platform Workers? (fn. 1), pp. 219-241.

as for the self-employed, or mandatory protection for all contingencies as is applicable for wage-earners should be introduced (see also above).

However, one should not lose sight of the fact that the Recommendation and, more specifically, its application will be monitored, and as has been mentioned before, the strength (or the weakness) of the application of this instrument will also depend on how additional contents and follow-up will be given on the occasion of this control process of monitoring. In case some of the country recommendations made by the EU are picked up for the annual semester monitoring, the legal impact may become even stronger than originally foreseen by the designers of the Recommendation on access to social protection.[35]

For possible future initiatives the EU might think of an instrument that targets, in the first place, the financing of social security, indicating at once the minimum investments but also the limits of the contributions to be made for social protection schemes. Recently we have pleaded for this (rather new) approach after we came to the conclusion that both in international and European law not much attention has been paid to the financing side of social security.[36] In short, we can summarise this idea as the concept of the financing fork. We will explore this concept more profoundly in the following paragraphs.

So far, lawyers have mainly focused on the benefits side, if only with little impact. On the other hand, the financial side of social security has been the focus of the monitoring of systems at European level from a fiscal-financial view (addressing the national budgets and inevitably looking at social security mainly as a cost). Perhaps the time has come now for the financial side to become the object of legal harmonising measures that deal with the concerns which from the start called for the wide diversity of national social security schemes to be addressed. In other words, rather than trying to overcome (only) the differences in the benefits side of social security, we should try to develop some harmonising standards with regard to the financing of national social security schemes. This would optimally respect the national competence to define a state's social security system (see above), yet at the same time take into account the concern about the socioeconomic and financial impact of social security on the budgets. It also allows for a direct address of the main arguments that the EU had raised

35 *Beke, Joris/Schoukens, Paul*, Fighting Social Exclusion under EU Horizon 2020. Enhancing the Legal Enforceability of Social Inclusion Recommendations? (fn. 14), pp. 51-72.

36 *Pieters, Danny/Schoukens, Paul*, Harmonising Social Security Financing, in: Van Lancker, Wim, et al., Liber Amicorum Wim Van Oorschot 2020 (forthcoming).

from the very start for the harmonisation of social security: the avoidance of unfair competition through social security; and the combatting of the social dumping phenomena. In relation to emerging platform work, "false competition" between social security systems should be a major concern; as highlighted before, the (reduction of the) employment cost of platform workers definitely plays a major part in many a business model applied by platform providers. Instead of undergoing yet another attempt to undermine the solidarity underlying all of the national social security systems, the EU should urgently call for some fair playing rules in its internal market – and respecting an equal level playing field when it comes to the cost of protecting working persons may be one of them. To that purpose, the financing (rules) of social security should be harmonised within a given bandwidth or fork. Harmonising standards with regard to the financing of social security could indeed best be developed by defining a "fork" or a "bandwidth" within which social security contributions and government subsidies to the social security systems would need to be allocated.

The basic idea is to set a minimum and maximum percentage for social security contributions to be levied on the real professional incomes and a minimum and maximum percentage for the costs of social security to be financed out of the public budget. These minimums and maximums constitute the "fork" or "bandwidth" within which national social security systems can determine the specifics of the social security benefits (e.g. amount payable, eligibility criteria, etc.).

It is obvious that in doing so, the possibilities to (ab)use social security arrangements to falsify competition between (enterprises of) Member States would be considerably reduced; at the same time, the specified fork would guarantee that each Member State allocates an adequate amount of the workers' incomes and of the state budget to social security, thus countering a rush to the bottom.

Such an approach would call for the use of some clearly defined concepts related to work and income out of work. It is expedient that future evolutions, such as we can already see emerge from platform work and the like, be taken into account. First of all, we will have to define clearly what we understand by social security and by social security schemes affected by this financing fork. Which social security schemes are to be taken into account? In an initial approach, we mainly consider the contributory social insurance schemes of the country and, specifically, the schemes that today fall under the EU coordination regulations, however excluding the special non-contributory benefits schemes. As for social assistance and special non-contributory benefits, Member States would continue to retain competence to finance these as they wish. As for other social security benefits, they should be financed by the fork-related levy. Perhaps the cost compensating schemes, health care and family allowances could also be excluded, as these have little to do with the social charges on labour, but this would require further examination.

When it comes to social contributions, we would not make any distinction between employer and employee contributions.[37] What matters in the end is the overall social security cost for the employer (nominal wage plus employer's contribution) and what net income the worker receives for his/her work (wage minus employee contribution). We would set the "fork" for the total of the contributions, not considering the specific social risk schemes separately. All kinds of special tariffs (such as financing exemptions) for specific groups or for specific situations would have to be incorporated in the final totals of the eventual set (maximum) level of the fork. This could end up being a rather complex, but in our opinion possible procedure.

A "fork" for the social security contributions levied on the income from work (wages, professional income of the self-employed) would also require a clear definition of what is to be considered "income from work" and thus, ultimately, what is "work". This will inevitably lead to a broader definition of work and income from professional activities compared to the one we are using today (see above). Otherwise, a new danger, namely that of competition falsification, could indeed result from the emerging new patterns of work such as gig work, platform work, etc.

Furthermore, the "fork" for the amount of state subsidies (to the relevant social insurance schemes) could perhaps best be defined in relation to the share of that financing in the total cost of the social insurance schemes concerned; or perhaps, more practically, in relation to the total amount of social contributions. In the latter case the "fork" could be expressed as a fraction (or multiple fractions) of the total amount of social security contributions.

In order to keep the necessary order and structure, the EU should make a clear classification of what should be understood (for the purpose of EU law) as a contribution and what as a state subsidy. National social security levies should then, regardless of their national classification, belong to the one or the other category. Social security levies that are not (clearly) labelled in the country as social security contributions should best be allocated to either the "social contribution" or the "state subsidy" rubric; in order

37 See on this fictitious distinction: *Pieters, Danny*, Social Security: An Introduction to the Basic Principles, Alpen aan den Rijn: Kluwer Law International 2006.

to make that distinction, it could, for example, be useful to fall back on (or at least be inspired by) the labelling as it is applied right now in the existing EU coordination instruments (Regulation (EC) 883/2004). If the levy is considered to be a tax, then the proceeds should be added to the rubric of direct subventions of the state.

The question, of course, remains as to whether it will be feasible to define a minimum and a maximum of social security contributions for all EU Member States. Here too, research on the current financing of national social security schemes would be needed: What is the share of social contributions? What is the share of state subsidies? Simple questions they may seem, but they are, however, very complex to answer, requiring not only legal and social policy knowledge but also macro-economic expertise. Anyhow, let us first explore what for most EU Member States could be a reasonable "fork" of social contributions and of public subsidising of the work-based social insurance schemes.

VII. Conclusion

Platform work is challenging labour and social security law, probably more than any other (new) work form ever. Moreover, due to the fact that it gives many employers a new impetus to hire low cost work that due to its virtual character is intrinsically mobile on the global market, the question for more harmonisation in the field of social protection again comes to the fore. This new emerging form of work thus challenges national and European policy makers, in particular with regard to low-income workers (working poor) and to activities which are not of a professional nature, but from which persons (can) generate (sufficient) income to live on. Low-income work is a challenge to the sustainability of every (work-related) social insurance scheme and will in the future call for a smart co-existence of social insurance, social assistance and other welfare schemes. At the same time, the second form of work calls for the rethinking of our professional social insurances. When generating income is no longer (only) a matter of standard work, but is increasingly accompanied by other types of activities and returns from (movable/immovable) goods, it may be the right time to reconsider the organisation of social security. This may call for a broadening of the income basis for social security financing, but at the same time will demand a rethinking of our social security risks (unemployment and work incapacity in particular) and of a different way of conditioning and calculating our social security benefits. At the European level, it invites policy makers to think beyond the protection of social benefits (social outcomes) but in turn takes interest in developing fair competition rules on the internal market: the financing of social security definitely belongs to the scope of these competition rules – hence our proposal to apply a fork or bandwidth within which Member States have to set their social security contributions. In that way, platform work is not to be considered as a threat to social security but mainly as a strong invitation to finally bring social security into the 21st century ("towards a work-related social security 2.0").

Chapter 13
Social Law 4.0 and the Future of Social Security Coordination

Grega Strban

I. Introduction

The law of social security, or social law in a narrower sense,[1] is among the youngest branches of law. Although, it has evolved into a separate and fully-fledged legal field, some connections to labour law remain and certain connections to other fields of law, like tax law, family law or even criminal law were established.

Moreover, social law cannot remain static in the contemporary dynamic or fluid society.[2] One of the aspects of fluid society is challenging the traditional norms of work, its stability and predictable social security coverage. Traditional patterns of (organising) work and mobility, which used to be considered as a norm (standard), also when shaping social security systems after the Second World War, are changing. According to ILO Convention 102 concerning minimum standards of social security of 1952, the stan-

1 The definitions of social law may vary, e.g. in Belgium *droit social* or *sociaal recht* encompasses labour and social security law (although both fundamental pillars emancipated to a certain extent). *Debaenst, Bruno,* Belgian Social Law and its Journals: A Reflected History, in: C@hiers du CRHIDI. Histoire, Droit, Institutions, Société [En ligne], 37 (2015), https://popups.uliege.be:443/1370-2262/index.php?id=183. Accessed 15 May 2020. Similarly, the European Social Charter (in its initial and revised versions) addresses both fields of law. Conversely, in Germany *Sozialrecht* could more straightforwardly be translated as the law of Social Security, although it may cover some fields of law that are considered to be outside of its scope in some other countries, e.g. social compensation schemes. The latter are, for instance, outside the scope of social security law in Slovenia and within the broader field of social protection law. See *Strban, Grega,* Systematisierung des slowenischen Rechts der sozialen Sicherheit im Vergleich zur Systematisierung des deutschen Sozialrechts, in: Zeitschrift für ausländisches und internationales Arbeits- und Sozialrecht, 24/25 (2010/2011) 4, p. 353.

2 Nowadays, some authors discuss fluid borders, fluid services, work without boundaries, and fluid communications. *Hoencamp, Jeroen,* The Fluid Society, Working Without Boundaries, The Perspective Series, New Insights into the UK Workplace, Circle Research, Vodafone 2014.

dard beneficiary is a man with a wife and two children in a stable (full-time and permanent) employment relationship. Standard social security benefits should suffice for such a standard beneficiary. Nevertheless, work (organisation), movement and social security have become more non-standard or unstable (fluid), especially within the EU.[3]

Societal fluidity may be reflected in new forms of work or, more specifically, organisation of work. Standard employment is being replaced by non-standard forms of employment and new forms of self-employment. Among them are fixed-term contracts, part-time work (either temporary or on a more frequent basis, horizontal or vertical), temporary agency work, telework, traineeships and student work, as well as casual work, including on-demand work (including zero-hour contracts) and platform work (i.e. people working for digital platforms, without having a fixed workplace). Moreover, self-employment, especially involuntary, bogus, dependent, new[4] and part-time self-employment, or other country-specific non-standard contracts (mini-jobs, civil law contracts, etc.) may exist. The distinction between employment and self-employment is blurred to a certain extent also in EU law.[5]

Fluidity may also be associated with the problem of fraudulent forms of undeclared work, especially its grey zone, in the form of under-reporting of wages or hours worked. What is noticeable in the areas of platform work and IT networks is undeclared own-account work, i.e. self-employed work.[6] On many occasions, labour-intensive rather than capital-intensive platforms may not be required to declare the earnings of workers. Al-

3 *Vukorepa, Ivana/Jorens, Yves/Strban, Grega*, Pensions in the Fluid EU Society: Challenges for (Migrant) Workers, in: da Costa Cabral, Nazaré/Cunha Rodrigues, Nuno (eds.), The Future of Pension Plans in the EU Internal Market, Financial and Monetary Policy Studies, 48, Cham: Springer 2019, p. 326.

4 New self-employed persons may fall between the two traditional, standard categories of dependent and subordinated workers (or employees) and independent self-employed persons (entrepreneurs) also in social security law.

5 Article 48, Treaty on the Functioning of the EU - TFEU, OJ C 202, 7 June 2016 (Title IV, Chapter 1 on the free movement of workers) referring to employed and self-employed workers. Such provision is indeed a bit odd, since self-employed persons are usually distinguished from workers and other provisions of EU law might apply to them, such as freedom of establishment and freedom to provide services in the internal market. However, this shows that workers and self-employed persons might no longer be clearly separable categories, especially in social security coordination law.

6 *Reinhard, Hans-Joachim*, Adjusting Old-Age Pensions to Match Employment Biographies – The German Case, in: Hohnerlein, Eva Maria/Hennion, Sylvie/Kaufmann, Otto (eds.), Erwerbsverlauf und sozialer Schutz in Europa, Berlin – Heidel-

though such platforms try to avoid being considered as employers, national courts may classify them as such,[7] which may lead to more comprehensive social security coverage.

Many of the mentioned forms of non-standard work or new, more flexible forms of work organisation are associated with various elements of precariousness. They may range from job insecurity, to employment record discontinuity, and lower earnings.[8] Moreover, they may be involuntary for persons performing such work.[9]

As much as it might be thought-provoking, the present paper does not analyse labour law aspects of non-standard forms of employment and self-employment. It rather focusses on the question how social law should follow the changes in social relations in order to provide effective social security to persons requiring it. Although persons performing various kinds of non-standard work or engaged in new forms of self-employment do not present a very homogenous group, they shall be defined as non-standard

---

berg: Springer 2018, p. 577; *Becker, Ulrich,* Die soziale Sicherung Selbständiger in Europa, in: Zeitschrift für europäisches Sozial- und Arbeitsrecht, 17 (2018) 8, p. 307.

7 For instance, Italian Corte di Cassazione, judgment No. 1663 of 24 January 2020 qualifying riders delivering food to be considered as subordinated workers, https://www.lavorodirittieuropa.it/images/Cassazione_Foodora-.pdf. Accessed 15 May 2020. Similarly, French *Cour de Cassation* qualifying an Uber driver as a worker: Arrêt No. 374 du 4 mars 2020 (19-13.316) - *Cour de Cassation - Chambre Sociale,* FR:CCAS:2020:SO00374, https://www.courdecassation.fr/jurisprudence_2/chambre_sociale_576/374_4_44522.html, or in English: https://www.courdecassation.fr/IMG/20200304_arret_uber_english.pdf. Both accessed 15 May 2020.

8 *Schoukens, Paul/Barrio, Alberto,* The Changing Concept of Work: When does Typical Work Become Atypical?, in: European Labour Law Journal, 8 (2017) 4, p. 306; Kresal Šoltes, Katarina/Strban, Grega/Domadenik, Polona (eds.), Prekarno delo: Multidisciplinarna analiza (precarious work: multidisciplinary analysis), Ljubljana: University of Ljubljana, Faculty of Law and Faculty of Economics 2020; also: *Mandl, Irene/Biletta, Isabella,* Overview of New Forms of Employment – 2018 update, Eurofound, Luxembourg: Publications Office of the European Union 2018, doi: 10.2806/09266.

9 In 2017, one in three among the economically dependent self-employed wished to work as an employee. Hence, economically dependent self-employed persons most particularly wish to work as employees (32.6 percent). The corresponding percentage for the independent self-employed without employees is 17.4 percent, and for the self-employed with employees 10.5 percent. These results show that a strong relation exists between self-employed status and the willingness to change. See Eurostat, Self-Employment Statistics, November 2018, https://ec.europa.eu/eurostat/statistics-explained/index.php/Self-employment_statistics. Accessed 15 May 2020.

workers (unless a specific group would require specific mentioning) for the purpose of the present article.

It might be recalled that also during its establishment and over the course of history, social security had to be modified in order to fulfil its function, i.e. provide (income) security to people. Basically, it has always followed the industrial revolutions.[10] The response to the Industrial Revolution 4.0 has to be modernised social law, hence designated as Social Law 4.0.

Even though Member States have transferred the execution of certain sovereignty rights to a supranational organisation, such as the EU, they remain exclusively competent to determine the substance of their national law of social security. They should find their own solution and shape Social Law 4.0, whereby they might be supported by the EU.[11] National solutions are bound to be distinctive. They always reflect various historically conditioned and rather distinctive structural (e.g. educational, living and working conditions) and cultural elements (e.g. powers of trade unions or civil movements)[12] and policy preferences of each Member State. Today, the courts of law might remind the legislature that the rule of law de-

10 The first one presenting manufacturing and focusing on a more optimised form of labour performed through the use of water- and steam-powered engines and other types of machine tools. Industrialisation and urbanisation led to the establishment of social security schemes. The second industrial revolution introduced steel and the use of electricity in factories, enabling mass production on the assembly lines. In the third one, electronic and eventually computer technology was introduced in factories, moving from analogue to digital technology and automation software. The fourth industrial revolution is based on the interconnectivity through the Internet of Things, access to real-time data, and the introduction of cyber-physical systems, i.e. connecting physical with digital, allowing for better collaboration and access across departments, partners, vendors, products, and people. See EPICOR, What is Industry 4.0 – the Industrial Internet of Things (IIoT), https://www.epicor.com/en-ae/resource-center/articles/what-is-industry-4-0/. Accessed 15 May 2020.

11 See e.g. The European Pillar of Social Rights, Principle 12 on Social Protection, emphasising that regardless of the type and duration of their employment relationship, workers, and, under comparable conditions, the self-employed, have the right to adequate social protection, https://ec.europa.eu/commission/sites/beta-political/files/social-summit-european-pillar-social-rights-booklet_en.pdf. Accessed on 25 May 2020; Also *Schoukens, Paul/Barrio, Alberto/Montebovi, Saskia*, The EU Social Pillar: An Answer to the Challenge of the Social Protection of Platform Workers?, in: European Journal of Social Security, 20 (2018) 3, p. 219.

12 *Berghman, Jos*, The Invisible Social Security, in: Van Oorschot, Wim/Peeters, Hans/Boos, Kees (eds.), Invisible Social Security Revisited, Essays in Honour of Jos Berghman, Tielt: Lannoo 2014, p. 37.

mands of them to follow the changes in social relations with its normative action.[13] Hence, the law of social security is not only one of the youngest, but is also bound to be one of the most rapidly changing areas of law.

In the present article, one additional element is added when considering the most appropriate modifications of social law, or when discussing Social Law 4.0, namely the element of cross-border movement. Fluidity within EU society is reflected also in the changing trends of mobility. Patterns of mobility of (non-standard) workers have become more diverse. The traditional long-term mobility of moving from home Member State to host Member State and working there for a longer period of time has been partially replaced or supplemented by mobility characterised by multiple shorter-term movements to other Member States.[14]

Therefore, the research question is: How should the coordination of national social security systems be modified in order to follow the development of non-standard forms of employment and self-employment? This includes higher digitalisation and ITC-supported work patterns, which might be boosted even more by the recent pandemic[15] with a higher ratio of home office work and telework and remote (or blended) schooling,[16] which is not occurring only within one Member State, but is bound to entail a cross-border element in certain cases.

---

13 E.g. Decision of the Slovenian Constitutional Court U-I-69/03, 20 October 2005, OdlUS XIV, 75; *Strban, Grega*, Country Report on Slovenia, in: Becker, Ulrich/ Pieters, Danny/Ross, Friso/Schoukens, Paul (eds.), Security: A General Principle of Social Security Law in Europe, Groningen: Europa Law Publishing 2010, p. 412.

14 *Fries-Tersch, Elena/Jones, Matthew/Böök, Birte/de Keyser, Linda/Tugran, Tugce*, 2019 Annual Report on Intra-EU Labour Mobility, European Commission 2020, p. 13.

15 The WHO declared the outbreak of the new coronavirus Covid-19 (caused by SARS-CoV-2 virus) a pandemic in Europe on 12 March 2020, http://www.euro.who.int/en/health-topics/health-emergencies/coronavirus-covid-19/news/news/2020/3/who-announces-covid-19-outbreak-a-pandemic. Accessed 15 May 2020.

16 See the outcome of the European Institute of Social Security, Blended Courses in Social Security, https://www.eiss.be/training%20and%20education/blended%20courses.html. Accessed 25 May 2020.

II. Coordination of Social Security Systems

1. The Objective

In highly mobile societies,[17] where movements are more frequent, last shorter and include various destinations, the reminiscence of the principle of territoriality can hardly be justified.[18] One of the major objectives of the EU, which should enable the functioning of the internal market, is the promotion of free movement of EU citizens, and all kinds of professionally active persons and workers in particular. Without an effective, uniform social security coordination mechanism, such free movement could be seriously hampered. Nevertheless, Member States are still free to shape the substance of their social security systems, i.e. to determine the scope of entitled persons, kind and scope of benefits and conditions for their entitlement. However, the shaping of national social security is not an island outside of EU law. The latter must still be taken into account, e.g. when treating national and Union citizens alike in national social security systems. The Court of Justice of the EU (CJEU) tries to construe the secondary legislation as a whole in order to achieve the desired result[19] and uphold the fundamental values of the EU.

As already noted above, the social security system is first and foremost regulated by national law. The more similar national social security systems are, the easier their coordination might be. However, it seems that national social security systems are growing apart, making their coordination more complex. In order to guarantee the free movement of workers (Article 45 of the Treaty on the Functioning of the European Union, TFEU) and Union citizens in general (Article 21 TFEU) social security systems have to be legally and administratively connected, interlinked, coordinated. Similar to national social law, EU social security coordination law has to be adapted to the new and more fluid 4.0 social relations, based on digitalised and non-standard forms of employment and self-employment.

---

17 Notwithstanding temporary restrictions to contain the pandemic in 2020.

18 For instance, ILO Social Security (Minimum Standards) Convention No. 102 of 1952 foresees that a benefit to which a person protected would otherwise be entitled may be suspended for as long as the person concerned is absent from the territory of the Member State (Article 69). Also, the European Court of Human Rights ruled that such restrictions can no longer be justified, ECHR of 07 February 2014, Application No. 10441/06, Case of Pichkur v Ukraine.

19 E.g. one of the latest decisions: CJEU of 2 April 2020, Case C-802/18, Caisse pour l'avenir des enfants v. FV and GW, ECLI:EU:C:2020:269.

2. *Two Paradoxes*

It is correct that EU law does not unify national social security systems. However, paradoxically, their coordination is achieved through a regulation, which is by itself a unifying measure. It is generally and directly applicable and binding in its entirety in all Member States.[20] The attribute of direct applicability is linked to the doctrine of supremacy. In principle, it is not open to Member States to interfere with the direct application of a regulation in the national legal order. However, social security systems are not unified, at least not in their substance. Rather, the part of formal social security law, governing the application of the substantive social security law in transnational situations is unified among all the Member States.[21]

Historically, the text on linking or coordinating social security systems of the six EU founding Member States[22] was agreed upon in the form of an international convention. However, it was decided to make the coordination rules operational as soon as possible to avoid the time-consuming procedure of ratification. Hence, already agreed rules were passed in the form of a regulation. In fact, this was done in the form of the third regulation ever adopted by the (current) EU, i.e. Regulation (EEC) No. 3 concerning social security for migrant workers.[23] It was the first real legal instrument in the EU.[24] Regulation (EEC) 4/58 was the Implementing Regulation, mainly containing rules of behaviour of the institution responsible for social security coordination.[25]

Choosing a regulation over the traditional international convention has important implications. It gives the CJEU the possibility to interpret secondary legislation and establish its conformity with the Treaties,[26] or in fact apply the Treaties directly to the situations under the material scope of EU law. Later on, the initial Social Security Coordination Regulations

---

20 Article 288 TFEU.

21 *Strban, Grega*, Social Rights of Migrants in the European Union, in: Malfliet, K./ Abdullin, A. I./Shaikhutdinova, G. R./Davletgildeev, R. Sh. et al. (eds.), Regional Aspects of Integration: European Union and Eurasian Space, Moscow: Statut 2019, p. 73.

22 The founding Member States were Belgium, France, Germany, Italy, Luxembourg and The Netherlands.

23 OJ L 30/561, 16 December 1958.

24 Regulations No. 1 and 2 dealt with the use of languages and the form of the *laisser passer* to the Members of the European Parliament, respectively.

25 Both Regulations 3 and 4/58/EEC became applicable as of 1 January 1959.

26 Treaty on EU (TEU) and TFEU, both published as consolidated versions in OJ C 202, 7 June 2016.

were replaced by Regulation (EEC) 1408/71 and its Implementing Regulation (EEC) 574/72. Interestingly enough, the currently applicable Regulation (EC) 883/2004 was passed only a couple of days before the largest enlargement of the EU so far. The 15 Member States agreed on the wording of the Regulation on 29 April 2004.[27] The 10 States joined the EU on 1 May 2004 and the unanimity of 25 (and later 27) Member States would be required.[28] The Implementing Regulation was passed only in 2009, in the form of Regulation (EC) 987/2009,[29] which shows the resistance of the Member States to give more competence in the field of social security to the EU and difficulties on agreeing on a complex social security coordination mechanism within the EU.

Another paradox of a regulation might be detected when comparing it to a directive. The latter has to be transposed into national law,[30] whereas a regulation applies directly. Hence, the reader of national law might be readily aware of the directive rules, but not of the regulation rules, since they have to be studied in addition to national law. This is very much evident also in the field of social security coordination, more specifically in the law of cross-border healthcare. The rules of Directive 2011/24/EU on the application of patients' rights in cross-border healthcare[31] had to be transposed into national law (in 2013), whereas the Regulation (EC)

27 OJ L 166, 30 April 2004.

28 After the Lisbon Treaty came into force in December 2009 (OJ C 306, 17 December 2007) the unanimity requirement was mitigated, but not completely abolished. According to the ordinary legislative procedure votes of a qualified majority in the Council as a rule suffice for the legislative act to be passed (Articles 48 and 294 of the TFEU). However, a so-called "alarm procedure" or "brake procedure" has been installed in the TFEU. In case the Commission proposal affects important aspects of its social security system (including its scope, cost or financial structure) or affects the financial balance of that system, the Member State may refer the matter to the European Council. In this case, the ordinary legislative procedure is suspended and the European Council may accept or reject the proposal. Nevertheless, the European Council as a rule adopts the decisions unanimously. The right of Member States to a veto has not been completely abolished, it has merely been modified. Moreover, if no decision is taken in four months, it is deemed that the act originally proposed has not been adopted.

29 Regulation (EC) 883/2004, OJ L 284, 30 October 2009. The latest proposal for the revision of the Coordination Regulations was presented in December 2016: European Commission, Proposal for a Regulation of the European Parliament and of the Council, COM (2016) 815 final.

30 A directive is binding, as to the result to be achieved, upon each Member State at which it is addressed, but leaves to the national authorities the choice of form and methods (Article 288 TFEU).

31 OJ L 88/45, 4 April 2011.

833/2004 has been directly applicable since May 2010. Yet, the discussion was much more vivid when the Directive was transposed into national law and a very limited discussion (if any) was noticeable when the new social security Coordination Regulation became applicable.[32]

Some principles of the EU social security coordination law can be deduced already from primary law (the Treaties),[33] others from the secondary law – most notably from the Coordination Regulations. These principles are the principles of equal treatment, unity of applicable legislation, protection of the rights in course of acquisition (by aggregating all relevant periods), the protection of acquired rights (by the export of benefits) and good and sincere administrative cooperation.[34]

III. Distinctive Definitions

One of the core problems related to social security of moving non-standard workers might be their distinctive treatment in various Member States. The concept of worker may be defined either by national or by EU law. It constitutes an autonomous concept specific to EU law, unless the EU instrument in question makes express reference to definitions under national law (at the same time attributing the EU meaning to such concept).[35]

There is a distinction in EU law between a free movement definition of a worker, and a social security definition.[36] According to settled CJEU case

32 *Strban, Grega*, The Right to Health in the EU, in: Brameshuber, Elisabeth/Friedrich, Michael/Karl, Beatrix (eds.), Festschrift Franz Marhold, Wien: Manz 2020, p. 843.

33 Articles 18, 21, 45 and 48 TFEU.

34 The present article is too limited in scope to analyse all the facets of administrative cooperation among the Member States. Suffice it to note that a huge project on the electronic exchange of social security information (EESSI) is under way and the first electronic documents were exchanged between Slovenia and Austria in 2019. See General Secretariat of the Council of the European Union, Electronic Exchange of Social Security Information (EESSI): state of play – Information from the Commission, 28 February 2019, 6986/19, p. 3, https://data.consilium.europa.eu/doc/document/ST-6986-2019-INIT/en/pdf. Accessed on 19 June 2020.

35 See: CJEU of 19 March 1964, Case C-75/63, Unger v Bestuur der Bedrijfsvereniging voor Detailhandel en Ambachten of Nijenoord 1 a, ECLI:EU:C:1964:19.

36 For instance, in the Coordination Regulations there is a reference to insurance under national social security systems, disregarding nationality (Regulation (EU) No. 1231/2010). However, according to the free movement perspective, the migrant worker concept is only applied to EU nationals. See also CJEU of 14 October 2010, C-428/09, Union syndicale Solidaires Isère v Premier Ministre, Min-

law, there is an autonomous EU concept of migrant worker linked to free movement[37] that follows a factual perspective, i.e. services must be performed for and under the direction of another person in exchange for remuneration.[38] Such definition explicitly excludes persons who do not perform activities considered genuine and effective, but perform them on such a small scale as for them to be considered marginal and ancillary.[39]

Conversely, Regulation (EC) 883/2004 does not provide a definition of worker or of a self-employed person.[40] It refers to national law when activities of employed and self-employed persons have to be determined.[41] Such EU definition in the form of referral to national law is relevant, especially with respect to non-standard workers, since national legislatures are free to determine the conditions under which non-standard workers are covered by their respective social security law.[42]

---

istère du Travail, ECLI:EU:C:2010:612. For more on the concept of worker in labour law and social security law, see: *Lhernould, Jean-Philippe/Strban, Grega/Van der Mei, Anne Pieter/Vukorepa, Ivana,* The Interrelation between Social Security Coordination Law and Labour Law, FreSsco Analytical Report 2017, European Commission 2017, p. 15.

37 See e.g. CJEU of 3 July 1986, Case C-66/85, Lawrie-Blum v Land Baden-Württemberg, ECLI:EU:C:1986:284; CJEU of 23 March 1982, Case C-53/81, Levin v Staatssecretaris van Justitie, EU:C:1982:105.

38 See also CJEU of 17 July 2008, Case C-94/07, Raccanelli v Max-Planck-Gesellschaft, ECLI:EU:C:2008:425.

39 On the scope of these undefined terms (marginal and ancillary) in the Member States see *O'Brien, Charlotte/Spaventa, Eleanor/De Coninck, Joyce,* The Concept of Worker under Article 45 TFEU and Certain Non-Standard Forms of Employment, FreSsco Comparative Report 2015, European Commission 2016.

40 Which avoids complex annexes with specifications of these definitions. See Annex I of previous Regulation (EEC) No. 1408/17; *Jorens, Yves/Van Overmeiren, Filip,* General Principles of Coordination Regulation 883/2004, in: European Journal of Social Security, 11 (2009) 1-2, p. 55.

41 Article 1(a) defines "activity as an employed person" as any activity or equivalent situation treated as such for the purposes of the social security legislation of the Member State in which such activity or equivalent situation exists. See e.g. CJEU of 3 May 1990, Case C-2/89, Kits van Heijningen v Bestuur van de Sociale Verzekeringsbank, ECLI:EU:C:1990:183; CJEU of 30 January 1997, Case C-221/95, Hervein v Inasti, EU:C:1997:47; CJEU of 30 January 1997, Case C-340/94, De Jaeck v Staatssecretaris van Financiën, ECLI:EU:C:1997:43.

42 Of course respecting the EU Law at the same time. See cases CJEU of 12 July 1979, Case C-266/78, Brunori v Landesversicherungsanstalt Rheinprovinz, ECLI:EU:C:1979:200; CJEU of 24 April 1980, Case C-110/79, Coonan v The Insurance Officer, ECLI:EU:C:1980:112; CJEU of 30 January 1997, Case C-340/94, De Jaeck v Staatssecretaris van Financiën, E ECLI:U:C:1997:43.

For historical reasons, the best social security coverage and hence all social security coordination rules apply to persons who are defined as or are equivalent to full-time workers under national law. If persons are excluded from such national definition, due to work being considered as marginal or merely ancillary, they are also not subject to any social security coordination for workers. They might be covered as non-actives, if they are covered at all by the national social security law. If covered as non-actives, distinctive social security coordination rules would apply to them as compared to those of workers. Alternatively, if a national social security system covers all residents, the problems of classification of economic activity might not be as pertinent.

Although the number of cases across Europe (re)qualifying platform workers as employees for the application of their social insurance schemes has risen,[43] it is hard to tell under which status these workers eventually fall. Depending on the concrete organisation of their work, they might be considered either as employed or as (dependent) self-employed persons. However, what is clear though is that a multitude of these workers are formally hired as self-employed yet in reality work as wage-earners (bogus self-employed).[44] In some Member States platform work as such is not regulated yet and it does not offer social security coverage due to the ample use of minimum (insurance) thresholds.[45]

Hence, problems that may cause difficulties for coordinating distinctive social security systems for non-standard mobile workers might be related to distinct classifications in various Member States. Moreover, classification in one Member State may not be recognised in another Member State. Especially thresholds related to certain income levels or working hours, for being covered by the social security system and subject to (traditional) coordination rules may cause problems for non-standard workers.

---

43 *Strban, Grega/Carrascosa Bermejo, Dolores/Schoukens, Paul/Vukorepa, Ivana*, Social Security Coordination and Non-Standard Forms of Employment and Self-Employment: Interrelation, Challenges and Prospects, MoveS Analytical Report 2018, European Commission 2020, p. 25, https://ec.europa.eu/social/main.jsp?catId=1098&langId=en, Accessed 15 July 2020. And recent judgments of e.g. Italian and French courts, as mentioned above.

44 See e.g. an example of massive requalification to wage-earner in Spain: https://elpais.com/economia/2019/07/28/actualidad/1564322291_541124.html. Accessed 15 May 2020.

45 *Strban, Grega/Carrascosa Bermejo, Dolores/Schoukens Paul/Vukorepa, Ivana,* Social Security Coordination and Non-Standard Forms of Employment and Self-Employment: Interrelation, Challenges and Prospects (fn. 43), p. 25.

Therefore, social security coordination law, adjusted to the Social Law 4.0, should disregard the thresholds concerning the level of income or number of working hours for mobile non-standard workers, since the adding of income or hours worked (e.g. simultaneously) in two or more Member States may de facto present genuine and effective activities, and not only marginal and ancillary ones. Moreover, the distinction between activities as a worker and as a self-employed person might be abolished and a person's entire income or duration of work should be considered in its entirety. In order to achieve this, information should be readily exchanged among the Member States involved, e.g. for a person who is simultaneously self-employed in two or more Member States and works part-time for one or more platforms.

Moreover, a classification of economic activities might be essential for determining which Member State's legislation should be applicable to a non-standard worker.

IV. Applicable Legislation

The rules on applicable legislation, designated also as collision or conflict rules, differ between working and non-working groups and between employees, self-employed persons and civil servants. Consequently, Title II of Regulation (EC) 883/2004 on the rules for determining the applicable legislation is not neutral concerning the eventual qualification of activities.

1. Impact of Qualification to Collision Rules

As a rule, each of the Member States on whose territory professional activities are performed by a non-standard worker is competent to determine the nature of these activities. The competent Member State will then be assigned by the social security coordination rules. For instance, a non-standard worker, performing the same activities in two Member States may be qualified as a self-employed person in one and as an employed person in the other. The outcome is that the Member State of employment, which has priority over self-employment, will be competent due to the application of Article 13 (3) of Regulation (EC) 883/2004.[46] Only in the case of

46 Similarly, civil servant activities prevail over employee and self-employed activities, according to Article 13 (4) of Regulation (EC) 883/2004.

posting does the country from where the worker is posted retain its competency to qualify the respective activities.[47]

The question might be whether each of the Member States concerned should remain competent for determining the nature of activities performed on its territory. If the purpose of social security coordination is to avoid negative consequences of the principle of territoriality and improve the legal position of a moving (also non-standard) worker, it could be argued that the Member State solely competent for the social security of such worker should have the sole responsibility for qualifying all activities. In the above case of employment and self-employment, the Member State of employment should have the competence to qualify the person's activities in both Member States as (dependent) employment for social security purposes.

Moreover, due to a larger fluidity and flexibility of work patterns, more people than before are combining different activities, which may also be performed across national borders. It might not always be easy to determine at what point a certain activity becomes an economic or professional activity. Some Member States might not consider very minor activities as work, while others might. It is important in determining the legislation of the respective Member State responsible for social security whether a person is qualified as a worker or as a non-active person. In the first case, the *lex loci laboris* rule becomes applicable, while in the second it is the *lex loci domicilii* rule.[48]

These rules on determining the legislation applicable are based on the geographical aspect of work. This is being emphasised also by the CJEU, which mentions the location of the employed or self-employed activity as a main criterion for social security coordination.[49] However, Social Law 4.0 is based more on digital platforms and remote (i.e. tele-) working (boosted by the Covid-19 pandemic), also from different Member States.[50] Geographical stability between a worker, his/her employer and a Member State is no longer guaranteed in all cases, which might complicate the coordina-

47 Article 12 of Regulation (EC) 883/2004.

48 Article 11 of Regulation (EC) 883/2004.

49 CJEU of 27 September 2012, Case C-137/11, Partena v Les Tartes de Chaumont-Gistoux SA, ECLI:EU:C:2012:593.

50 See in this respect CJEU of 13 September 2017, Case C-570/15, X v Staatssecretaris van Financiën, ECLI:EU:C:2017:674 (also the opinion of Advocate-General Szpunar, ECLI:EU:C:2017:182).

tion of national social security systems.[51] Gainful activity from a distance may no longer be of a merely marginal and ancillary nature.

2. *Rules on Marginal Activity*

Nevertheless, many non-standard workers struggle to earn enough income to survive and the Coordination Regulation itself applies a concept of marginal activities which refers to the limited amount of working time and/or remuneration.[52] However, there is no clear rule on what marginal activity may be. As an indicator the Administrative Commission for the Coordination of Social Security Systems proposes that activities accounting for less than five percent of the worker's regular working time and/or less than five percent of his/her overall remuneration should be regarded as marginal.[53] However, it seems that this rule applies only when activities in two or more Member States are performed simultaneously, not generally in all cases.

Nevertheless, even if applicable only to simultaneous activities,[54] odd results may be produced for non-standard workers. As already discussed, employed activities prevail over self-employed activities, and this might even be the case when a person is only marginally employed (e.g. slightly over five percent)[55] in one Member State and genuinely, effectively and predominately self-employed in another Member State. Does then the closest link to the Member State of employment really exist?

Moreover, when simultaneous employments, which are rather popular in some Member States,[56] are performed in two or more Member States, the one where the non-standard worker resides might be competent if sub-

51 *Strban, Grega/Carrascosa Bermejo, Dolores/Schoukens, Paul/Vukorepa, Ivana*, Social Security Coordination and Non-Standard Forms of Employment and Self-Employment: Interrelation, Challenges and Prospects (fn. 43), p. 31.

52 Article 14 (5) (b), (7) and (8) of Regulation (EC) 987/2009.

53 European Commission, Administrative Commission for the Coordination of Social Security Systems, Practical Guide on the Applicable Legislation, December 2013, p. 27.

54 Article 13 of Regulation (EC) 883/2004 and Articles 14 to 16 of Regulation (EC) 987/2009.

55 In CJEU of 13 September 2017, Case C-570/15, X v Staatssecretaris van Financiën, ECLI:EU:C:2017:674, marginal employment was 6.5 percent.

56 E.g. in 2018, there was a sharp decrease in postings, but at the same time a sharp increase in simultaneous employments in Slovenia. The reason was that the law of cross-border provision of services only regulates posting (among other things

stantial activity is performed in this Member State of residence. However, it might not always be easy to determine the quantitatively substantial part (i.e. at least a quarter) of all activities. Account has to be taken of the working hours and/or remuneration (for employees) and of turnover, working time, number of services and/or income (for the self-employed).[57] Some interpretation issues in determining the substantial part of activities might arise, especially with regard to platform work.[58]

3. *Minimum Coverage for a Legislation to be Applicable?*

Social law coverage for non-standard workers differs among the Member States. Many of them exempt non-standard workers from social security schemes, or reduce coverage to certain basic insurances.[59] As a rule, social security coverage depends on the social law arrangements of the Member State of work. In cross-border situations decisions of the CJEU have to be taken into account. Following the Petroni principle (or principle of

requiring for all taxes and other duties to be paid, before A1 form can be issued), but not simultaneous activities.

57 Article 14 (8) of Regulation (EC) 987/2009.

58 Leaving aside the question of determining residence. For non-standard workers another question might be raised due to salary thresholds, i.e. would they be considered as workers or would they have to satisfy the sufficient resources and comprehensive health coverage conditions of the Free Movement Directive, i.e. Directive 2004/38/EC on the Right of Citizens of the Union and their Family Members to Move and Reside freely within the Territory of the Member States, OJ L 158, 30 April 2004.

59 For instance, so-called "Mini-Jobs" in Germany and in Austria are excluded from the scope of the social security system. In the UK, if a person is employed, but earns less than £116 a week, the latter will not be eligible for social security. In some Member States non-standard workers are not covered against accidents at work: in the Netherlands self-employed persons are not entitled to employee insurance, as there is no separate scheme for accidents at work and occupational diseases; the same situation can be found in Norway (however, freelancers are covered), Portugal, Iceland, Malta, Sweden and Austria. In Spain, insurance against accidents at work and occupational diseases is compulsory for TRADEs and voluntary for other self-employed persons. *Strban, Grega/Carrascosa Bermejo, Dolores/ Schoukens, Paul/ Vukorepa, Ivana*, Social Security Coordination and Non-Standard Forms of Employment and Self-Employment: Interrelation, Challenges and Prospects (fn. 43), p. 39.

favourability),[60] the CJEU reduced the exclusive and binding effect of the applicable law rules.[61] From the *Bosmann* case[62] onwards,[63] the Court has been allowing an insured person to fall back on the social security system of the Member State of residence, in case the applicable legislation of the Member State of work does not provide certain social security benefits or when these benefits are too limited.[64]

Contrary to its previous case law,[65] the CJEU seems to be no longer upholding the rule on one single legislation applicable for a moving person at the same time, in order to avoid positive and negative conflicts of national laws. Deviations are allowed, at least if it is *in favorem laboratoris*. Moreover, it seems that social security systems are no longer perceived in their entirety, but rather that specific social security schemes, such as family benefits or pensions,[66] are being compared.

Nevertheless, the CJEU seems to insist on the *lex loci laboris* rule, even when it does not provide comprehensive social security coverage *ratione materiae*. In the *Franzen* case[67] the CJEU recalled that the general principle of *lex loci laboris* means that a resident of a Member State who works for several days per month on the basis of an on-call contract in the territory of another Member State, is subject to the legislation of the Member State of employment both on the days on which he performs the employed ac-

60 In CJEU of 21 October 1975, Case C-24/75, Petroni v Office national des Pensions, ECLI:EU:C:1975:129, the CJEU argued that workers moving in the EU should not be worse-off than those who are not moving.

61 Legislation of a single Member State only shall apply despite any territorial conditions of national systems.

62 CJEU of 20 May 2008, Case C-352/06, Bosmann v Bundesagentur für Arbeit, ECLI:EU:C:2008:290.

63 See also the following cases: CJEU of 12 June 2012, Case C-611/10, Hudzinski & Wawrzyniak v Agentur für Arbeit, ECLI:EU:C:2012:339; CJEU of 23 April 2015, Case of C-382/13, Franzen v Raad van bestuur, ECLI:EU:C:2015:261; CJEU of 19 September 2019, Case of C-95/18, van den Berg, Giesen and Franzen v Sociale Verzekeringsbank, ECLI:EU:C:2019:767.

64 *Strban, Grega*, Family Benefits in the EU: Is it Still Possible to Coordinate Them?, in: Maastricht Journal of European and Comparative Law, 23 (2016) 5, p. 787.

65 CJEU of 19 June 1980, Case C-41/79, Testa v Bundesanstalt für Arbeit, ECLI:EU:C:1980:163; CJEU of 12 June 1986, Case C-302/84, Ten Holder v. Nieuwe Algemene Bedrijfsvereniging, ECLI:EU:C:1986:242; CJEU of 10 July 1987, Case C-60/85, Luijten v Raad van Arbeid, ECLI:EU:C:1986:307.

66 Apart from the concrete case of Ms Franzen, C-382/13 integrated two other similar (national) cases, i.e. Giesen and van den Berg, where access to the Dutch universal pension scheme (AOW) was under consideration.

67 CJEU of 23 April 2015, Case of C-382/13, Franzen v Raad van bestuur, ECLI:EU:C:2015:261.

tivities and on the days on which he does not. However, due to the irregular and low income earned from her activities, Ms *Franzen* was only covered by one scheme (i.e. accidents at work) in the competent Member State. She was excluded from other parts of social security law, such as child benefits, which she could also not claim in her Member State of residence, since it was not a competent Member State. The CJEU argued that the amount of time devoted to employment, and also the existence of an employment contract and the type of employment, whether partial or casual, were irrelevant for determining the competent Member State.

However, a migrant worker who is subject to the legislation of the Member State of employment is not to be precluded from receiving, by virtue of national legislation of the Member State of residence, social security benefits from the latter State. This seems to be only the case if benefits in the Member State of residence are provided on the mere fact of residing in that country. For contributory social security systems the Court still upholds the competence of a single Member State.[68] Nevertheless, such double designation rule may cause problems in practice. The question is whether it should be verified in each case which benefits are provided to non-standard workers in the Member State of work and which are provided in the Member State of residence. Another question is whether the legal nature of the benefits should be compared, i.e. whether they are residence- or insurance-based.

It might be better to condition the application of the *lex loci laboris rule* on certain minimum standards, meaning that it can only be applied if comprehensive social protection is provided. If not, the Member State of residence might be exclusively competent for non-standard workers, since it also provides social assistance, recourse to which might be necessary for many non-standard workers. Minimum standards are explicitly mentioned in the Recommendation on access to social protection for workers and the self-employed,[69] and non-standard workers (regardless of the form of employment or self-employment) should be covered at least against the social risks of unemployment, sickness, parenthood (maternity and paternity) invalidity, old age, decease, accidents at work and occupational diseases All non-standard workers shall be mandatorily covered. Alternatively, all self-employed persons should have at least voluntary access to such mini-

68 CJEU of 19 September 2019, Case of C-95/18, van den Berg, Giesen and Franzen v Sociale Verzekeringsbank, ECLI:EU:C:2019:767.

69 Point 1.2. of the Recommendation on Access to Social Protection for Workers and the Self-Employed, OJ C 387, 15 November 2019.

mum standard coverage,[70] which brings us to another problem: voluntary insurance.

4. *Only Voluntary Insurance for Non-Standard Workers?*

Some Member States may offer non-standard workers only voluntary access to (certain) social insurance schemes, especially if they receive a rather low remuneration.[71] Voluntary schemes related to social risks covered by the Coordination Regulations[72] do fall under their material scope. Nevertheless, specific rules for such schemes exist.

The general rule stipulates that the applicable law rules[73] are not applicable to voluntary insurance (or optional continued insurance), unless only voluntary insurance for a certain branch exists in a Member State.[74] The question might be whether for non-standard workers to have voluntary access to a certain social security scheme could be argued to be for them the only voluntary insurance for a specific branch. In this case it would be subject to EU social security coordination law and linked to other mandatory schemes. However, if the rule were to be construed as a mandatory scheme for (standard) workers, and hence as not the only scheme for a specific branch, it might not be subject to the social security coordination rules for non-standard workers. The latter interpretation should be avoided in order to provide social security also to cross-border non-standard workers accessing a certain scheme on a voluntary basis.

Moreover, if a non-standard worker is covered by a compulsory scheme in one Member State s/he should not be covered voluntarily against the same social risk in another Member State. However, an exception exists for pensions (or more generally, benefits in respect of invalidity, old-age and decease), where a non-standard worker may be compulsorily and voluntarily insured in two Member States, respectively. Nevertheless, a connection to the previous insurance has to exist in the Member State of voluntary in-

---

70 Point 8 in relation with point 3.2. of the Recommendation.

71 *Strban, Grega/Carrascosa Bermejo, Dolores/Schoukens Paul/ Vukorepa, Ivana*, Social Security Coordination and Non-Standard Forms of Employment and Self-Employment: Interrelation, Challenges and Prospects (fn. 43), p. 40.

72 CJEU of 9 July 1987, Joined Cases of C-82 and 103/86, Laborero and Sabato v OSSOM, ECLI:EU:C:1987:356.

73 Articles 11 to 13 of Regulation (EC) 883/2004.

74 Article 14 Regulation (EC) 883/2004.

surance.[75] However, if in both concerned Member States access to a given scheme is voluntary, a non-standard worker may avoid the coercive (*ius cogens*) rules on applicable legislation and opt for a scheme of his or her choice.[76] Only the interpretation that both schemes, not entire social security systems, should be voluntary would be coherent for the entire article of the Regulation 883/2004 on voluntary insurance.

In cases where the competent Member State provides only for restricted social protection, also the CJEU is tempted to accept additional access to the social security system of the other Member State involved (usually linked to residence) when under its national law this is made possible.[77]

V. *Equality of Treatment*

Rules on applicable legislation are, in principle, neutral and apply to all non-standard workers in that Member State, just as for national workers.[78] Hence, moving to another Member State might provide for more or less advantageous social law for a mobile non-standard worker, but the principle of equal treatment has to apply.

Moreover, if no coverage is provided in the Member State of employment, the equal treatment principle might be applied in the Member State of residence, e.g. in case of family benefits not provided in the Member State of employment.[79] Another situation might be related to the rules on applicable legislation, i.e. to the question in which Member State a non-standard worker, who is teleworking, should be covered and treated the same as other workers. Should it be the Member State of the company s/he is teleworking for or the Member State s/he is residing in? Additionally, should it be verified where such a worker habitually resides and where the

---

75 Article 14, Paragraph 3 Regulation (EC) 883/2004.

76 Article 14, Paragraph 2 Regulation (EC) 883/2004.

77 See cases already mentioned above, i.e. C-352/06, Bosmann, EU:C:2008:290 and following.

78 Article 4 of Regulation (EC) 883/2004. More: *Becker, Ulrich*, Die Bedeutung des gemeinschaftsrechtlichen Diskriminierungsverbots für die Gleichstellung von Sachverhalten im koordinierenden Sozialrecht, in: Vierteljahresschrift für Sozialrecht, 18 (2000) 3, p. 221.

79 See under the previous point mentioned cases C-352/06, Bosmann, EU:C:2008:290; C-382/13, *Franzen*, EU:C:2015:261; and C-95/18, van den Berg and Giesen, EU:C:2019:767.

centre of his or her activities is located?[80] In order to avoid focus on the physical location of work, a special designation rule for applicable legislation might be applied and, in any case, minimum income thresholds for social security coverage should be abolished.

Specific problems might relate to unemployment insurance if a non-standard worker was covered by such a scheme in one Member State, but after moving to another Member State s/he is not covered anymore (either excluded with no possibility to voluntarily join the scheme, or because such possibility was not exploited). Should such non-standard workers be treated equally with national non-standard workers only in the Member State of last employment, hence depriving them of unemployment benefits? Even if this were the case, previous insurance periods from the Member State of previous employment should not be lost. They should either be taken into account as relevant periods in the Member State of last employment, or the competent Member State should be the one, where such insurance periods were completed. In any case, different treatment of the same activities across Member States raises more questions than the Coordination Regulations provide answers for.

However, a solution might be found in the emanations of the equal treatment principle, i.e. equal treatment of benefits, income, facts or events.[81] If certain circumstances occur on the territory of another Member State, they should be taken into account by the competent Member State as though they had taken place on its own territory. The competent Member State should grant access to social security coverage or enable higher social security benefits.[82]

Hence, national social security administrations should also consider income (or benefits) acquired in a different Member State when assessing the status of a non-standard worker. Certain income thresholds applicable to grant worker status in the competent Member State should also include income generated in other Member States. By doing so, non-standard workers might reach the minimum level and be considered as genuine work-

80 Should *corpus* and *animus manendi* be verified? See Article 11 of Regulation (EC) 987/2009, also the Administrative Commission for the Coordination of Social Security Systems, Practical Guide on the Applicable Legislation, Brussels, European Commission, EU 2013, p. 41.

81 Article 5 of Regulation (EC) 883/2004.

82 See also *Pöltl, Manfred/Eichenhofer, Eberhard/Garcia de Cortázar, Carlos*, The Principle of Assimilation of Facts, FreSsco Analytical Report 2016, European Commission 2016.

ers.[83] The CJEU already established that income earned in a different Member State must be considered when calculating benefits.[84] It would be only reasonable to adopt this approach also in the granting of access to social insurance.

Another reason for assimilating conditions might be given if facts or events are alike[85] in both Member States concerned. Provisions do not have to be identical and assimilation has to be applied on a case-by-case basis whenever similarity can be detected.[86] Hence, coverage under unemployment insurance in one Member State should be treated as a like fact also in the competent Member State.[87]

Nevertheless, equal treatment of benefits, income, facts or events has its limits. It must not interfere with the rules on applicable legislation[88] and it cannot lead to objectively unjustified results or to the overlapping of benefits of the same kind for the same period.[89] Moreover, it should be differentiated from the aggregation principle.[90]

---

83 Member States might be obliged to report income on a Structured Electronic Document – SED or Portable Document – PD, which would make assimilation of income more transparent.

84 CJEU of 15 December 2011, Case C-257/10, Bergström v Försäkringskassan, ECLI:EU:C:2011:839 (family benefits); CJEU of 15 December 2016, Case C-256/15, Nemec v. Republika Slovenija, ECLI:EU:C:2016:954 (invalidity pension).

85 Article 5 of Regulation (EC) 883/2204 mentions "like facts or events".

86 On broad interpretation see CJEU of 21 January 2016, Case C-453/14, Knauer v Landeshauptmann von Vorarlberg, ECLI:EU:C:2016:37 and CJEU of 18 December 2014, Case C-523/13, Larcher v Deutsche Rentenversicherung Bayern Süd ECLI:EU:C:2014:2458.

87 Assimilation of income, benefits, facts and events could also turn out to be negative for the non-standard worker, e.g. by landing him or her above the social assistance threshold. See CJEU of 28 June 1978, Case C-1/78, Kenny v Insurance Officer, ECLI:EU:C:1978:140. Due to assimilation of facts, the Slovenian Supreme Court denied the right to a pro-rata old-age pension to a person still insured in Austria, see Case VIII IPS 169/2010, SI:VSRS:2011:VIII.IPS. 169.2010.

88 See Recital 11 of the Preamble to Regulation (EC) 883/2004.

89 See Recital 12 of the Preamble to Regulation (EC) 883/2004.

90 See Recital 10 of the Preamble to Regulation (EC) 883/2004, also Decision H6 by the Administrative Commission for the Coordination of Social Security Systems, OJ C 45, 12 February 2011.

VI. Aggregation of Periods

The social security coordination rules on the aggregation (or totalisation) of periods[91] concern the "legal qualification of facts"[92] and ensure that persons who have used their freedom of movement may access social security benefits under the legislation of the competent Member State. These rules should be differentiated from the rules on the calculation of benefits (especially the *pro rata temporis* rule) which ensure a fair share of payment of benefits between institutions of various Member States, corresponding the time being insured under each of the legislations.[93]

Specific rules might apply to unemployment benefits[94] and non-standard workers might benefit from them. They make a distinction between periods of insurance, employment or self-employment required by a national scheme and provide for aggregation of such periods, to the extent necessary, in order to satisfy the conditions of the legislation of the competent State (usually the Member State of last employment).[95] Hence, if periods of employment or self-employment are considered under the unemployment insurance of the competent Member State, they should be aggregated with equal (employment or self-employment) periods from another Member State, even if in that Member State they would not be leading to unemployment insurance.[96]

Conversely, it should be prevented that periods of unemployment insurance recognised as such in a Member State other than the competent

---

91 See Article 48 TFEU and Article 6 of Regulation (EC) 883/2004.

92 *Pennings, Frans*, European Social Security Law, Cambridge – Antwerp – Chicago: Intersentia 2015, p. 135.

93 *Strban, Grega/Carrascosa Bermejo, Dolores/Schoukens, Paul/Vukorepa, Ivana*, Social Security Coordination and Non-Standard Forms of Employment and Self-Employment: Interrelation, Challenges and Prospects (fn. 43), p. 54.

94 Article 61 of Regulation (EC) 883/2004, Article 54 of Regulation (EC) 987/2009.

95 For more details see *Pennings, Frans*, European Social Security Law (fn. 93), p. 270; Fuchs, Maximilian (ed.), Europäisches Sozialrecht, 7th edition, Baden-Baden: Nomos 2018, p. 461.

96 Article 61 (1) Regulation (EC) 883/2004 specifies that "*when the applicable legislation makes the right to benefits conditional on the completion of periods of insurance, the periods of employment or self-employment completed under the legislation of another Member State shall not be taken into account unless such periods would have been considered to be periods of insurance had they been completed in accordance with the applicable legislation.*" More: *Strban, Grega/Carrascosa Bermejo, Dolores/Schoukens, Paul/Vukorepa, Ivana*, Social Security Coordination and Non-Standard Forms of Employment and Self-Employment: Interrelation, Challenges and Prospects (fn. 43), p. 55.

Member State are disregarded and hence lost. This could be the case when a non-standard worker is covered as a self-employed person in one Member State, but moves to a different, i.e. competent Member State, which does not recognise periods of self-employment under its unemployment insurance. Another case might be that the same activity is recognised as employed activity in one Member State and as self-employed activity in the competent Member State, the latter of which aggregates only periods of equal legal nature (in this case self-employment).

The solution could be mandatory recognition of all periods of insurance, whether in employment or self-employment, by the competent Member State in cases where such periods were already recognised as unemployment insurance periods by the legislation of another Member State. To this end, the social security Coordination Regulations should be amended. The current proposal for amending them in fact envisages the insertion of a new article. It should provide that only the periods which are taken into account under the legislation of the Member State in which they were completed for the purpose of acquiring and retaining the right to unemployment benefits shall be aggregated by the competent Member State.[97] Another problem might lie in the requirement of an uninterrupted period of insurance for a Member State (of the last or penultimate activity) to be competent.[98] It might be more difficult for non-standard workers to satisfy the requirement of an uninterrupted insurance period.

Specific aggregation rules exist also for invalidity benefits and (old-age and "survivors") pensions.[99] Regulation (EC) 883/2004 still contains the special rule that a Member State is not required to provide benefits in respect of periods of less than one year completed under its legislation, if no benefit can be acquired under its legislation for such short period of time.[100] The rule is tuned to longer-term (or professional life-time) mobility from one Member State to another and may cause problems with short-

97 European Commission, Proposal for a Regulation of the European Parliament and of the Council, COM (2016) 815 final.

98 Proposal of the new Article 61 of Regulation (EC) 883/2004; ibid.

99 Articles 45 and 51 of Regulation (EC) 883/2004.

100 Article 57 of Regulation (EC) 883/2004. See also CJEU of 20 November 1975, Case C-49/75, Borella v Landesversicherungsanstalt Schwaben, ECLI:EU:C:1975:158.

term mobility – especially for non-standard workers, who might be more flexible also concerning movements to other Member States.[101]

Periods of less than one year are usually not completely lost, since they are proportionally taken over by Member States, which have to aggregate all periods of insurance or residence in order to calculate a theoretical pension amount and pay a *pro-rata temporis* pension.[102] However, in practice such short periods may be disregarded when a Member State concerned pays only a national pension, a so-called independent benefit[103] (and not a pro-rata one). Still, they would have to be considered in such a case.[104]

The Coordination Regulations provide a solution for many periods shorter than one year. In such cases, the Member State of last employment is solely competent,[105] which can be rather financially burdensome if no reimbursement from other Member States is received. The one-year rule might be abolished altogether even if this increases the administrative burden of the Member States involved.

VII. Export of Benefits

Providing social security benefits in a Member State other than the competent Member State is essential for the protection of already acquired (vested) social security rights. Such export of benefits applies predominately to cash benefits.[106]

---

101 The initial goal seems to be to simplify the administrative procedure and reduce costs related to the payment of very low pensions; *Janda*, *Constanze*, in: Fuchs, Maximilian (ed.), Europäisches Sozialrecht (fn. 95), p. 452.

102 Article 57 (2) refers to Article 52 (1) (b) (i) of Regulation (EC) 883/2004.

103 See Article 52 (1) (a) of Regulation (EC) 883/2004.

104 In CJEU of 18 February 1982, Case C-55/81, Vermaut v Office national des Pensions, ECLI:EU:C:1982:68, it was argued that the national pension institution must take account of periods of insurance of less than a year completed by the worker under the legislation of other Member States even if the right to a pension arises under national legislation alone.

105 Article 57 (3) of Regulation (EC) 883/2004.

106 They are not subject to any reduction, amendment, suspension, withdrawal or confiscation, when the beneficiary or the members of his or her family reside in another Member State. Article 7 Regulation (EC) 883/2004. On specific export and overlapping rules for family benefits: *Strban*, *Grega*, Family Benefits in the EU: Is it Still Possible to Coordinate Them? (fn. 64), p. 792.

However, general social assistance, even when provided in cash, is excluded from the social security coordination rules.[107] Also not exported is the so-called categorical social assistance (special non-contributory cash benefits) for which specific coordination rules apply.[108] The latter might be considered as social assistance also under the Free Movement Directive, i.e. Directive 2004/38/EC and qualified as social advantage under Regulation (EU) 492/2011.[109]

Non-export of special non-contributory cash benefits might prove to be especially troublesome for non-standard workers, who might be paying low social security contributions resulting in low benefits, or who might even have to rely on (general or categorical) social assistance. Therefore, they might not satisfy the residence condition of sufficient means and comprehensive social insurance cover.[110]

Although it might be considered controversial, categorical (and possibly general) social assistance should be provided also outside of the competent Member State.[111] It might be phased out in the former Member State and gradually phased in in the new Member State of residence (according to the "closest link" principle). Alternatively, the approach applied for family benefits could be used, meaning that if the new Member State of residence provides social assistance, the former Member State would have to cover half of it (up to the actual amount of assistance) in the initial several (as a rule five)[112] years of residence. Social assistance and family benefits might have similar characteristics. They are of a non-contributory legal nature, and might be perceived as assistance to (or promotion of) the family (or household) community.[113]

---

107 General social assistance (as well as medical assistance) is excluded from the material scope by Article 3 (5) (a) of Regulation (EC) 883/2004.

108 Article 70 of Regulation (EC) 883/2004.

109 OJ L 141, 27 May 2011.

110 Article 7 Directive 2004/38/EC.

111 See also the Nordic Convention on Social Assistance and Social Services, e.g. https://www.riksdagen.se/sv/dokument-lagar/dokument/svensk-forfattningssamling/lag-1995479-om-nordisk-konvention-om-socialt_sfs-1995-479. Accessed 25 May 2020.

112 Article 16 Directive 2004/38/EC; see CJEU of 19 September 2013, Case C-140/12, Brey v Pensionsversicherungsanstalt, ECLI:EU:C:2013:565 and the following cases.

113 Some German authors call them *Hilfs- und Förderungssysteme*. More: *Von Maydell, Bernd Baron*, Binnenstruktur des Sozialrechts, in: Von Maydell, Bernd Baron/Ruland, Franz/Becker, Ulrich (eds.), Sozialrechtshandbuch (SRH), 5th edition Baden-Baden: Nomos 2012, p. 51.

Moreover, benefits in kind may not be exported as such, but the right to them, e.g. the right to healthcare, may be "exported" and healthcare provided in another Member State at the expense of the competent Member State.[114] The competent Member State should strive to issue to all non-standard workers the European Health Insurance Card (EHIC), regardless of the legal basis they are insured upon.[115] This would enable not only urgent, but necessary healthcare in other Member States.[116]

VIII. Conclusions and Proposals de lege ferenda

To paraphrase Heraclitus, the only constant in society is change. As societal relations evolve, so should social law and consequently its coordination law. For the latter, it might be more difficult to fulfil its function today than it was in the past, since a number of very distinct national social security systems have to be linked. It could be argued that coordination is much easier if social security systems are similar and, in turn, that diversity adds to its complexity. It should be recognised that the single breadwinner is no longer the common model and cannot present the ideal of a standard beneficiary.

Solutions to contemporary challenges could and should be found in order to promote not only freedom of movement of standard, but also of non-standard workers (who in some Member States might already present a new standard). They might include coverage of all mobile (employed and self-employed) workers regardless of the amount of activity, by abolishing income and working time thresholds. Already existing social security coordination rules could be subject to a more dynamic interpretation, e.g. in terms of equal treatment of facts and event, income and benefits from other Member States.

Some other solutions might require a targeted modification of the Coordination Regulations. For instance, rules on applicable legislation

---

114 *Strban, Grega*, The Right to Health in the EU (fn. 32), p. 841.

115 More on EHIC at https://ec.europa.eu/social/main.jsp?catId=559. Accessed 25 May 2020.

116 E.g. EHIC is issued to all self-employed persons in Slovenia, even if contributions are not paid. It has been conceived to provide urgent treatment (to which anyone is always entitled), although all necessary treatment may be provided as well; *Strban, Grega/Carrascosa Bermejo, Dolores/Schoukens, Paul/Vukorepa, Ivana*, Social Security Coordination and Non-Standard Forms of Employment and Self-Employment: Interrelation, Challenges and Prospects (fn. 43), p. 63.

should consider an economically active person as one legal subject, not giving priority to a classification of employed activities over self-employed activities. Moreover, in order to apply the *lex loci laboris* rule, the competent Member State should provide at least a minimum standard of social protection to non-standard workers. Previously recognised periods of insurance or employment should be fixed and recognised in all other Member States in order to avoid losing insured periods and to erase any obstacles to free movement. Social security coordination rules should be rethought and fine-tuned also to the social and legal reality of non-standard workers. Hence, the one-year rule could be abolished and social assistance schemes should be included in the material scope of EU social security coordination law. It would be said too lightly that if a person does not contribute (enough), no benefits are due.

Social Law 4.0 should make use of the technology provided by the Industrial Revolution 4.0, and so should social security coordination law. There should be no obstacle (technical or other) to sharing all the information of a moving non-standard worker. One contribution to this end could be the introduction of a European Social Security Number (ESSN).[117] More competencies on the part of the EU might be required in order to establish a truly uniform internal single market. Some attempts are visible within the European Unemployment Benefits Scheme (EUBS),[118] and the proposal for a separate EU social security system for mobile persons[119] is not new.

We should bear in mind that non-standard workers are gainfully active workers, too, and they should be treated as such and not as inactive persons with all the possible limitations that are linked to such status. They, too, must be able to enjoy the fundamental human right to social security, and this should not be limited solely because they make use of the freedom of movement within the EU.

---

117 See https://ec.europa.eu/info/law/better-regulation/have-your-say/initiatives/1222-European-Social-Security-Number. Accessed 25 May 2020.

118 See https://www.ceps.eu/ceps-publications/legal-and-operational-feasibility-european-unemployment-benefits-scheme-national-level/. Accessed 25 May 2020.

119 Today it could be called the 28th social security system, next to 27 national social security systems. See *Pieters, Danny/Vansteenkiste, Steven*, The Thirteenth State - Towards a European Community Social Insurance Scheme for Intra-Community Migrants, Leuven: Acco 1993.

Chapter 14
Taxation of the Platform Economy: Challenges and Lessons for Social Security

Katerina Pantazatou

I. Introduction

The digital economy encompasses various different business models mediating technology in multi-sided markets (such as social networks, online marketplaces, and *sharing economy platforms*) and highly specialised services in single-sided markets (for example, cloud computing, diagnostics, etc.).[1] The *platform economy* constitutes a sub-area of the *digital economy*. Variously called the platform, sharing, collaborative, gig or "peer-to-peer" (P2P) economy, and sometimes described as collaborative consumption or crowd-based capitalism,[2] all terms intend to describe an economic model in which individuals are able to borrow or rent assets owned by someone else.[3] This contribution aims to shed some light on issues arising from the taxation of the platform economy. While it is rather obvious that the purposes of labour law, social security law and tax law differ, this chapter will attempt to answer the question whether any lessons can be learned for social law from the treatment of platforms and platform workers in tax law.

As will be discussed, tax law, both at an international and EU level, has focused mostly on how to ensure that the profits of the platforms are taxed

1 *Kofler, Georg/Mayer, Gunter/Schlager, Christoph,* Taxation of the Digital Economy: A Pragmatic Approach to Short-Term Measures, in: European Taxation, 58 (2018) 4, p. 123.

2 This term was coined by *Sundararajan, Arun,* The Sharing Economy: The End of Employment and the Rise of Crowd-Based Capitalism, Cambridge: MIT Press 2016, p. 27.

3 *Schneider, Henrique,* Creative Destruction and the Sharing Economy: Uber as Disruptive Innovation, Cheltenham: Edward Elgar Publishing 2018, p. 6. Throughout this chapter, these terms, and in particular the terms "sharing economy" and "platform economy" are used interchangeably.

where they should.[4] Similarly, it is the taxation of the *digital economy*, and not the sub-area of the *platform economy*, that is in the spotlight in the discussions of policy makers. These two facts taken together have contributed to the absence of clear proposals as to the taxation of the platform economy, and more specifically the taxation of "platform workers". While some discussion at policy level has been initiated recently,[5] the approaches and solutions rest with individual countries and are very far from being coordinated.

The present chapter will provide an account of the main problem arising from a tax law perspective in the taxation of platform workers, it will highlight the importance (or lack thereof) of the taxation of the platform, and will examine some solutions put forward in different jurisdictions. It will conclude by attempting to answer whether there is anything for social law to learn from tax law and whether taxation, one of the main sources of financing social protection, is adequately prepared to deal with the platform economy challenges.

II. Platform-Related Issues and International Initiatives

Despite the challenges it poses, the taxation of the platform economy has received little attention in the recent EU and international proposals that focus primarily on the taxation of the *digital economy*. The recent proposals aim to find ways to tax the big multinational corporations operating in the digital economy, like Facebook and Google,[6] which are usually taxed in their place of residence (which is often the US) yet escape taxation in other places where they create profits. It is obvious that the potential of taxing Facebook in other states on the basis, for instance, of its number of users there will bring much more revenue to those states, as opposed to the taxation of the "platform workers".

---

4 The place of the taxation of these profits is a debatable issue in taxation. Several concepts have been put forward to substitute the required physical presence of the platform as a nexus for taxing. One of those is "value creation".

5 See for instance *Milanez, Anna/Bratta, Barbara*, Taxation and the Future of Work: How Tax Systems Influence Choice of Employment Form, in: OECD Taxation Working Papers, No. 41, OECD Publishing, Paris, 2019, https://doi.org/10.1787/20f7164a-en. Accessed 10 July 2020.

6 Note, for instance, the GAFA tax (Google, Apple, Facebook and Amazon) adopted in France in July 2019, which imposes a 3 percent levy on the total annual revenues of the largest technology firms providing services to French consumers.

Placing this in the context of the platform economy, it comes as no surprise that both the OECD and the EU focus on how they can tax the profits of Airbnb and Uber instead of the Airbnb host and the Uber driver.[7] Consequently, it is the taxation of the *platform itself* that has attracted the focus of international proposals and recommendations, and notably the question *where* to tax the profits of the platforms operating in the *digital economy*, in absence of a physical presence in the countries where they operate.[8] But even in this case, a uniform definition of a platform does not exist, as each one of them employs different business models. The question is not merely rhetorical as one common definition encompassing a number of those models would allow for a common tax treatment of the different platforms and platform workers.[9]

EU and international initiatives have focused on how to allow Member States (or third countries) to tax the profits of companies that have no physical presence in the respective country; yet, they certainly contribute to value creation. By allowing for the fiction of the "digital presence" or "significant economic presence evidenced via digital technology and other automated means"[10] and by ensuring that taxation will arise wherever a Multinational Enterprise (MNE) has a "virtual permanent establishment",[11] the recent proposals aimed to thwart the outdated idea that an enterprise needs to be physically present in a country to supply goods or services in that market. However, the proposals as to how to best tackle this

---

7 The different proposals are discussed in the last sections. Among the different solutions put forward is the suggestion to tax the platform's profits where "value is created", that is where the profits arise and where the service is provided, instead of the place of the tax residence of the corporation.

8 See for instance, OECD, Tax Challenges Arising from Digitalisation – Interim Report 2018: Inclusive Framework on BEPS, OECD/G20 Base Erosion and Profit Shifting Project, OECD Publishing, Paris, 2018, (hereinafter "2018 OECD Interim Report") p. 196, http://dx.doi.org/10.1787/9789264293083-en. Accessed 10 July 2020; European Commission, Proposal for a Council Directive laying down rules relating to the corporate taxation of a significant digital presence, COM (2018) 147 final (hereinafter "2018 SDP Directive Proposal").

9 *Pantazatou, Katerina*, The Taxation of the Sharing Economy, in: Haslehner, Werner/Kofler, Georg/Pantazatou, Katerina/Rust, Alexander (eds.), Tax and the Digital Economy: Challenges and Proposals for Reform, Alphen aan den Rijn: Wolters Kluwer 2019, pp. 215-236, at 217.

10 OECD, Addressing the Tax Challenges of the Digitalisation of the Economy. Public Consultation Document. 13 February – 6 March 2019, https://www.oecd.org/tax/beps/public-consultation-document-addressing-the-tax-challenges-of-the-digitalisation-of-the-economy.pdf. Accessed 10 July 2020.

11 OECD, 2018 OECD Interim Report (fn. 8), p. 160.

issue were many, each one of them coming with its own set of problems, such as the allocation of profits across countries.[12] In 2018, the Commission followed the OECD's initiatives and published proposals for two Council Directives on the taxation of the digital economy[13] and one (non-binding) Commission Recommendation relating to the corporate taxation of a significant digital presence (SDP).[14] These proposals have now been put "on hold" in favour of the OECD's suggested "Unified Approach".[15] In 2019, the OECD attempted to find the commonalities among the different proposals and agree on a "Unified Approach" towards the tax challenges raised by the digitalisation of the economy.[16]

In January 2020, the OECD came up with a new proposal on a "Unified Approach" hoping that consensus will be reached among the participating countries regarding the best way to address the challenges arising from the taxation of the digital economy.[17] The proposal focused on the taxation of the platforms and advocated, inter alia, the creation of a new nexus for the taxation of the platforms' profits, not dependent on physical presence but largely based on sales, a profit allocation rule and mechanisms to ensure greater legal certainty.[18]

While the aforementioned reports and proposals have been inadequate in tackling the taxation of the platform workers, the 2018 OECD Interim Report acknowledged that the focus, with regard to the sharing economy, should be placed on the *contractual relationship between the platforms and*

12 These proposals included the "user participation", "marketing intangibles", and "significant economic presence" proposals.

13 European Commission, Proposal for a Council Directive on the Common System of a Digital Services Tax on Revenues resulting from the Provision of Certain Digital Services, COM (2018) 148 final as well as 2018 SDP Directive Proposal (fn. 8).

14 European Commission, European Commission Recommendation of 21 March 2018 relating to the Corporate Taxation of a Significant Digital Presence, COM (2018) 1650 final.

15 OECD, Statement by the OECD/G20 Inclusive Framework on BEPS on the Two-Pillar Approach to Address the Tax Challenges Arising from the Digitalisation of the Economy, January 2020, https://www.oecd.org/tax/beps/statement-by-the-oecd-g20-inclusive-framework-on-beps-january-2020.pdf. Accessed 10 June 2020.

16 OECD, Public Consultation Document: Secretariat Proposal for a "Unified Approach" under Pillar One, November 2019, p. 4, https://www.oecd.org/tax/beps/public-consultation-document-secretariat-proposal-unified-approach-pillar-one.pdf. Accessed 10 July 2020.

17 OECD, Statement by the OECD/G20 Inclusive Framework on BEPS on the Two-Pillar Approach to Address the Tax Challenges Arising from the Digitalisation of the Economy (fn. 15).

18 Ibid.

the service providers, as the grey zones that can be found therein could lead to a minimisation of both tax liability and the tax base.[19] In the context of the platform economy, focusing on the platform worker would indeed make sense, as on average, the "service provider" rather than the platform receives over 85 percent of the transaction value.[20]

Nevertheless, as the sections below will show, the platform and its taxation does play a role in the taxation of the platform workers. One way this may happen is through its classification and placement in the appropriate legal and regulatory environment, which, in turn, may affect the employment relationship between the platform and the platform workers and, thus, their taxation. Another way is by providing tax incentives to the platform to create or opt for a particular work status of its workers (whether this is an employment status or an independent contractor's status). I now turn to explore these two possibilities.

1. *Relationship of Platform and Work Status*

This section will attempt to explain how the classification of the platform may influence the work status of "gig workers" and, in turn, their taxation. As will be argued, the "worker classification" question relates (also) to the classification of the platform. An Uber driver does not necessarily need to be classified for tax purposes in the same way as an Airbnb host or a "BlaBlaCar" driver. The classification, for example, of an Uber driver as an independent contractor, a worker or an employee, cannot be considered independently of the classification of the platform and the nature of the services it requires.[21] Consequently, one would have to start by understanding and classifying the services provided by the platforms in the sharing economy, in an attempt to understand the legal relationship between the platform workers and the platform. Two recent CJEU Grand Chamber non-tax-related judgments aimed to shed some light on this problem, ex-

---

19 OECD, 2018 OECD Interim Report (fn. 8).

20 *Elliot, Carrie Brandon*, Taxation of the Sharing Economy: Recurring Issues, in: Bulletin for International Taxation 72 (2018) 1: Platform revenue models vary significantly, even within the same commercial sector, but most adopt a fixed or variable commission approach, with commissions ranging from 1 percent to 2 percent of transaction value for crowdlending, to as high as 20 percent for ride-sharing.

21 CJEU of 20 December 2017, Case C-434/15, Asociación Profesional Elite Taxi, ECLI:EU:C:2017:981.

amining, inter alia, the types of services provided by the two "flagship" platforms in the sharing economy, Uber and Airbnb.

The CJEU dealt first with the *Uber* case,[22] where it found Uber to be a transportation service provider, instead of a digital platform, as the intermediation service provided by the platform was inherently linked to a transport service.[23] In its recent case *Grand Chamber Airbnb Ireland*[24] the CJEU emphasised that Airbnb was different from Uber. In contrast to Uber, the services provided by Airbnb could be classified as "information society services" within the meaning of Directive 2000/31. In reaching this conclusion, the CJEU considered that even though "the purpose of the intermediation service provided by Airbnb Ireland is to enable the renting of accommodation [...] the nature of the links between those services does not justify departing from the classification of that intermediation service as an "information society service" and therefore the application of Directive 2000/31 to it."[25] However, in the Court's view and unlike its judgment in Uber, in this case, the intermediation service is so strong and essential that it "cannot be separated from the property transaction itself, in that it is intended not only to provide an immediate accommodation service, but also [...] to provide a tool to facilitate the conclusion of contracts concerning future interactions. It is the creation of such a list for the benefit both of the hosts who have accommodation to rent and persons looking for that type of accommodation which constitutes the *essential feature* of the electronic platform managed by Airbnb Ireland." (*emphasis added*).[26]

In reaching this conclusion the Court considered the essential features of each platform, the indispensability of the platform in the delivery of the underlying service as well as the setting or the "capping" of the price to be

22 Ibid.

23 Ibid., para. 48: The services Uber provides "[...] must be interpreted as meaning that an intermediation service such as that at issue in the main proceedings, the purpose of which is to connect, by means of a smartphone application and for remuneration, non-professional drivers using their own vehicle with persons who wish to make urban journeys, *must be regarded as being inherently linked to a transport service* and, accordingly, must be classified as "a service in the field of transport" within the meaning of Article 58 (1) TFEU. Consequently, such a service must be excluded from the scope of Article 56 TFEU, Directive 2006/123 and Directive 2000/31."

24 CJEU of 19 December 2019, Case C-390/18, Airbnb Ireland, ECLI:EU:C:2019:1112.

25 Ibid., para. 52.

26 Ibid., para. 53.

charged to the guests. Under all these criteria, the Court found that Uber and Airbnb were different.[27]

The question of the services (and their ancillary or essential character) provided by each platform is fundamental in the assessment of the taxation of both the platform and the Uber driver or the Airbnb host. With regard to the former point, the nature of the services provided by the platform is relevant for the assessment of the VAT to be paid, notably the definition of the place of supply of the service, which decides, *inter alia*, where the VAT will be paid. This concerns both the B2B relationship between the platform and the "supplier"/platform worker as well as the B2C relationship between the platform and the consumer. In turn, the place of supply of the service at issue "to a taxable person acting as such shall be the place where that person has established his business."[28] For instance, if the service at issue were to be classified as a transport service, then the place of supply (and the place where VAT would be payable) would be where the transportation takes place, pursuant to Article 48 of the VAT Directive.[29]

With regard to the second ramification, the legal framework to which the platform is subject will be defined by its classification. In other words, if Uber is classified as (mainly) a transportation service, then it will be subject to the transport policy-related directives. This categorisation may inform other important features in the systematisation of the work status of the "service-providers" on the platform, such as control (i.e. ensuring that the requisite standards of safety and quality are met) or the influence the employer has to exercise over the service-provider and the quality of the services (s)he provides.[30]

27 For more on the comparison of the two cases see *Beretta, Giorgio,* Airbnb is Not Uber: VAT Reflections on the Airbnb Ireland Case (C-390/18), Blogpost on LinkedIn, 22 December 2019, https://www.linkedin.com/pulse/airbnb-uber-vat-reflections-ireland-case-c-39018-giorgio-beretta/. Accessed 10 July 2020; and *Loquet, Erwan/Karoutis, Dimitrios*, European Union – VAT Considerations on CJEU's Ruling that Airbnb is Not a Real Estate Agent, in: International VAT Monitor, 31 (2020) 4.

28 Article 44, Directive 2006/112/EC on the Common System of Value Added Tax (6th Recast VAT Directive). On the definition of the taxable person, see infra, under IV. 2. B.

29 See *Beretta, Giorgio,* Airbnb is Not Uber: VAT Reflections on the Airbnb Ireland Case (C-390/18) (fn. 27).

30 Indeed, the degree of the influence and control of the platform to the "service providers" was decisive in their classification as an "information society services" platform for Airbnb and as a transportation services platform for Uber. In the words of Advocate General Spzunar: "It should be noted, in that regard, that Uber exercised control over the quality of the vehicles and their drivers and also

2. *Labour-Related Tax Incentives for Platforms*

When looking into the platform economy, one should not overlook that, in general, brick and mortar companies tend to opt for contracting self-employed workers instead of hiring standard employees, because they face lower tax burdens per worker hired. Indeed, tax incentives may play an important role in platforms' preferences as to what kind of contracts they would like to conclude with their workers. Besides not having to pay social security contributions for independent contractors, tax incentives may consist of deductions from Corporate Income Taxes (CIT) or the absence of the obligation to pay certain taxes (such as payroll taxes), or reduced administrative costs for the platforms. Consequently, taxation may be decisive for the preferences of the platforms as to the "work status" they want their workers to have.

For instance, it has been reported that in the Netherlands, the tax cost of hiring an independent contractor is 37 percent lower compared to the cost of hiring a standard employee, reflecting substantial labour cost savings for firms.[31] This is because the employer of an independent contractor is not liable for social contributions for the worker. Similarly, the employer/platform can deduct from its corporate income liability labour-related costs or make use of "labour-related" tax allowances and credits against its total CIT liability.[32] These deductions and allowances obviously vary from country to country and depend on the respective employment. For instance, in Argentina, corporations (and platforms) are allowed to deduct from their CIT base labour costs, including wages, employer social security contributions and employee non-tax compulsory payments (NTCPs) *for*

over the drivers' conduct by reference to the standards that Uber itself had determined. On the other hand, as is apparent from points 27 and 29 of this Opinion, the control exercised by Airbnb Ireland concerns users' compliance with standards defined or, at the very least, chosen by those users. In any event, as regards Uber's activity, the exercise of the power of administrative control was only one of the factors that led to the assertion that that provider exercised decisive influence over the conditions under which the transport services were provided." See CJEU of 19 December 2019, Case C-390/18, Airbnb Ireland, ECLI:EU:C:2019:1112, para. 76.

31 *Milanez, Anna*, Gig Workers and the Tax Web, in: OECD Observer, 319 (2019) Q3, https://oecdobserver.org/news/fullstory.php/aid/6278/Gig_workers_and_the_tax_web.html. Accessed 10 July 2020.

32 Such can be the case, for instance, when an employer hires a person with disabilities.

standard employment contracts.[33] In contrast, in Italy, according to the OECD Working Paper, firms are able to deduct the overall employment cost (gross wage plus profits) both when computing the CIT and the IRAP, also when they "employ" independent contractors.[34]

In the same vein, the contractors are entitled to make certain deductions, which vary from country to country, from their income tax, lowering both their own tax burden and their employer's.[35] When firms/platforms can save a lot on tax-related labour costs by hiring contractors, and when contractors are also in a tax-beneficial position if they are not classified as employees, it is obvious that the tax system at issue promotes demand for independent work.

The recent OECD Working Paper highlights how tax systems may offer tax incentives to both platforms and workers to distort the employment relationship.[36] Taking the Netherlands as one of the case studies, the OECD Working Paper explains how the Dutch tax system entitles unincorporated self-employed workers to two deductions from personal income tax allowing them to pay less tax than employees.[37] Consequently, unincorporated self-employed workers have the lowest payment wedge, both at the average wage but also across the wage spectrum.[38] Indeed, the degree of variation between payment wedges across different employment forms is considerable among the countries studied in the OECD Working Paper.[39] As the authors note, in countries like Hungary, Italy, Sweden and the United States the payment wedges are rather "clustered" reflecting little incentive to shift between employment forms for tax reasons (individual or firm-re-

33 *Milanez, Anna/Bratta, Barbara,* Annex – Taxation and the Future of Work: How Tax Systems Influence Choice of Employment Form, in: OECD Taxation Working Paper Series, 42 (2019), p. 19, https://doi.org/10.1787/6b20cce5-en.

34 Ibid., p. 66. Similarly, for the Netherlands, p. 79: "[E]mployer's labour costs are deductible from the CIT base, irrespective of the type of worker."

35 *Milanez, Anna*, Gig Workers and the Tax Web (fn. 31).

36 *Milanez, Anna/ Bratta, Barbara*, Taxation and the Future of Work: How Tax Systems influence Choice of Employment Form (fn. 5).

37 Ibid., p. 60: "In summary, in the Netherlands, this analysis shows that the tax system provides an incentive for a firm to hire an unincorporated self-employed worker, as by doing so it pays a total employment cost of EUR 40,911 instead of EUR 64,960 for a standard employee or EUR 53,074 for an incorporated self-employed worker".

38 Ibid. The paper defines the average compulsory payment wedge ("payment wedge") as the net amount that government receives as a result of taxing income from work, inclusive of social contributions (SSCs and NTCPs), over the total employment cost of the worker under consideration.

39 Ibid., pp. 55 f.

lated), whereas in countries like the Netherlands and Argentina payment wedges vary greatly, reflecting the opposite outcome.[40] In this latter scenario, "[t]his translates into a tax system incentive for firms to contract labour rather than offer standard employment contracts, potentially misclassifying workers in the process. It also implies a tax system that incentivises individuals to become self-employed."[41]

III. Tax Issues and Employment Relationship: National Responses

The classification of platform workers is crucial not only for social security contribution purposes, but also for tax purposes. When someone qualifies as an employee, it is the employer that has to withhold (at least part) of the taxes from the employee's salary. In contrast, when someone qualifies as self-employed or as an independent contractor, he/she is responsible for declaring his/her income and for paying taxes (and social security contributions) accordingly, saving the company significant administrative costs. There are certainly variations with regard to the applicable tax rates, the minimum taxable income, the deduction of business expenses etc. Usually, in addition to paying income tax, a self-employed person who provides some sort of services is liable to pay VAT.

Thus, the definition of the work status of the service providers/suppliers becomes essential, equally for labour law, social law and tax law. Obviously, such a universal or pan-European allocation of work status in the sharing economy or per platform does not exist, not least because such rules do not even exist even for the traditional forms of work. A lawyer, a plumber and an artist are taxed differently in different countries, depending on how much they work, where they work, whether this is their main or ancillary activity and considering many more factors. Equally, this difference in taxation may be expressed via different applicable tax rates, different tax bases (the income to be taxed) and as such, different allowances and deductions. Things get even more complex when we consider a cross-border scenario, even in the traditional (non-digital) understanding of work.

The context of the collaborative economy makes it even more difficult to answer the crucial questions of who should pay/withhold taxes, where taxes should be paid and what kind of taxes should be paid. There are several reasons for that. 1) The uncertainty as to the qualification of the type

40 Ibid.
41 Ibid., p. 66.

of work performed. For instance, the Uber driver may have a different status in different countries ranging from an employee to an independent contractor. This classification affects not only the direct taxes he will have to pay but also the requirement of VAT registration and payment. Similarly, his status may change if he works for "BlaBlaCar". 2) The nature of services provided in the sharing economy and the lack of reporting standards make it easier for the shadow economy and undeclared work to flourish.[42] 3) The majority of platform workers work in at least one more job, resulting in the fragmentation of their income.[43] For instance, someone may be resident in France, rent out an apartment he has in Portugal via Airbnb and, at the same time, provide online consultancy advice to a company in Belgium. In such a multi-state scenario, it is possible that the person at issue does not even know where to report the income he made from the use of different platforms.

A question that arises frequently is who has the final say in this classification. There is no obvious or clear answer to this question that would allow for a coherent legal framework. Reis and Chand provide for a good account of recent judgments in different countries that found Uber drivers to be either employees or independent contractors, considering a number of (similar) criteria.[44]

---

42 See for instance, OECD, Shining Light on the Shadow Economy: Opportunities and Threats, 2017, p. 19, https://www.oecd.org/tax/crime/shining-light-on-the-shadow-economy-opportunities-and-threats.pdf. Accessed 10 July 2020. Where one of the main issues tax-related to the sharing economy was identified as: "since there is usually no traditional employer, payments received will not generally be visible to the tax administrations in the way, for example, that they are for salaried employees in many countries." I will come back to this point in Section IV. 3.

43 See for instance, OECD, Automation and Independent Work in a Digital Economy, Policy Brief, May 2016, OECD Publishing, Paris, p. 4, https://www.oecd.org/els/emp/Policy%20brief%20-%20Automation%20and%20Independent%20Work%20in%20a%20Digital%20Economy.pdf. Accessed 10 July 2020: "As workers in the "platform economy" are more likely to have multiple jobs and income sources, the role and meaning of traditional labour market institutions are being challenged."

44 *Reis, Ariene/Chand, Vikram,* Uber Drivers: Employees or Independent Contractors?, in: Kluwer International Tax Blog, 3 April 2020, http://kluwertaxblog.com/2020/04/03/uber-drivers-employees-or-independent-contractors/?doing_wp_cron=1591797547.0120589733123779296875. Accessed 10 June 2020.

For example, the UK employment tribunal dealt with a case about the employment status of Uber drivers.[45] That tribunal was asked whether Uber drivers qualified as self-employed/independent contractors or as employees/workers. In defining whether Uber drivers should be treated as contractors, the tribunal looked into whether income tax and UK national insurance were deducted from their pay. Conversely, to determine their tax liability, the "tax test" would have had to look at their holiday pay, sick pay and pension rights.[46] The UK employment tribunal concluded that Uber's drivers were to be classed as workers with access to minimum wage, sick pay and paid holidays, although they treated themselves as self-employed persons for tax purposes.[47] The decision was also upheld by the Employment Appeal Tribunal[48] and the Court of Appeal.[49]

The case highlights the distinction between labour law, social security contributions and tax law in the sharing economy and raises the question of whether there is a need to coordinate these interrelated policy areas. The 2018 OECD Interim Report identified this distinction as one of the thorniest issues in the sharing economy context.[50] As different states provide for different tax incentives or disincentives, depending on the type of labour contract at issue, sharing economy features (and uncertainties) within the tax system could lead to tax revenue losses if there are large shifts in working patterns and taxable status.[51] Another pertinent question is who decides on the qualification of the status of the "worker". For instance, the judgment of the UK employment tribunal seemed to cross-cut between the tax treatment of Uber drivers, which is, in turn, informed by the drivers' access to certain social security benefits. In some countries, it appears that "priority" is given to the designation made by the tax authorities and whether the Uber driver, for instance, falls within the given tax defini-

45 UK Employment Tribunal Judgement of 28 October 2016, Case No. 2202550/2015, Aslam and Farrar and Others v. Uber BV, Uber London Ltd and Uber Britannia Ltd (hereinafter "UK Uber Case").

46 *Sayliss, Leigh,* Be Careful What You Wish for, in: Taxation, 178 (2016) 4579.

47 UK Uber Case (fn. 45), para. 65.

48 UK Employment Appeal Tribunal Judgement of 10 November 2017, Appeal No. UKEAT/0056/17/DA, Aslam and Farrar and Others v. Uber BV, Uber London Ltd and Uber Britannia Ltd.

49 UK The Court of Appeal Judgement of 19 December 2018, Case No. A2/2017/3467, Aslam and Farrar and Others v. Uber BV, Uber London Ltd and Uber Britannia Ltd.

50 OECD, 2018 OECD Interim Report (fn. 8), p. 196.

51 Ibid., p. 196.

tion.[52] The problem is circular in that, if the definition is informed by, for instance, the access to social security benefits, as happened in the Uber UK case, then the different criteria and classifications may lead to contradictory results. What if, for example, one is classified for tax purposes as an employee but his employer does not pay for social security contributions? Which classification will take precedence and how will the classification for labour law purposes be made?

In Switzerland, there seems to be general consensus that Uber drivers should be classified as employees.[53] The French *Cour de Cassation* also agreed that Uber drivers should be characterised as employees on the premise that they do not have independence in fixing their price or building their clientele.[54]

In the US, the classification of "gig workers" has created a lot of tension between platforms and workers, upon the delivery of the famous judgment of the California Supreme Court.[55] The judgment dealt with the applicable standards in determining whether workers should be classified as employees or as independent contractors for purposes of California Wage Orders.[56] Pursuant to the judgment that suggested a new presumption that all workers be employees instead of contractors, unless the employer proves otherwise under the newly adopted "ABC test",[57] the State of California approved, with effect from 1 January 2020, the California Assembly Bill 5 ("AB-5") incorporating the "ABC test".[58] Under this test, for a worker to be classified as a contractor, the employer will have to prove that: (A)

52 Such an example is Denmark.

53 With regard to that see *Reis, Ariene/Chand, Vikram,* Uber Drivers: Employees or Independent Contractors? (fn. 44); the references made there to SUVA, SECO and UNIA and judgments by domestic courts.

54 Arrêt No. 374 du 4 mars 2020 (19-13.316), Cour de Cassation – Chambre Sociale FR:CCAS:2020:SO00374, https://www.courdecassation.fr/jurisprudence_2/chambre_sociale_576/374_4_44522.html, or in English: https://www.courdecassation.fr/IMG/20200304_arret_uber_english.pdf. Both accessed 15 May 2020.

55 *Win, Suzin,* The Bill That Disrupted the Gig Economy: AB-5 and Uber's Troubling Response, in: GGU Law Review Blog, 2 March 2020, https://ggulawreview.com/2020/03/02/the-bill-that-disrupted-the-gig-economy-ab-5-and-ubers-troubling-response/. Accessed 10 June 2020.

56 Supreme Court of California Judgement of 30 April 2018, Dynamex Operations West, Inc. v. Superior Court of Los Angeles, https://law.justia.com/cases/california/supreme-court/2018/s222732.html. Accessed 10 June 2020.

57 Ibid.

58 For the text of the Bill, see California State Legislature, Worker Status: Employees and Independent Contractors, 19 September 2019, https://leginfo.legislature.ca.gov/faces/billNavClient.xhtml?bill_id=201920200AB5. Accessed 13 July 2020.

the worker is free from the control and direction of the hiring entity in connection with the performance of the work, both under the contract for the performance of the work and in fact; (B) the worker performs work that is outside the usual course of the hiring entity's business; and (C) the worker is customarily engaged in an independently established trade, occupation, or business of the same nature as the work performed. The three criteria are cumulative, therefore, if one of the three conditions is not met then an employment relationship between the employee and the worker will be established.

As it appears very likely that an Uber driver (though not an Airbnb host) will not meet the ABC test, and, hence, will be qualified as an employee, the Bill has sparked reactions from Uber and like companies. In the fear that approximately $500 million a year will be added to Uber's labour costs and payroll taxes Uber filed a lawsuit in federal court challenging the constitutionality of AB-5 and sent an email to more than 150,000 California drivers and millions of passengers, notifying a change in the way they conduct the service.[59] These changes consist in giving more freedom to the drivers to select their passengers and destinations to escape condition (A).

Despite these positive changes for gig workers at domestic or regional level, several other institutions and organisations have classified Uber drivers as independent contractors.[60] Among the factors considered towards such a finding, the control of the drivers over their workload (how much, how often, when they can perform their work) was fundamental.

59 *Win, Suzin*, The Bill That Disrupted the Gig Economy: AB-5 and Uber's Troubling Response (fn. 55).

60 According to *Reis, Ariene/Chand, Vikram*, Uber Drivers: Employees or Independent Contractors? (fn. 44) such examples include the District Court of Pennsylvania in the US, United States District Court for the Eastern District of Pennsylvania, Ali Razak, Kenan Sabani and Khaldoun Cherdoud v. Uber Technologies Inc., Civil Action No. 16-573, 11 April 2018; the State of Florida in the US, Third District Court of Appeal of State of Florida, Darrin E. McGillis v. Uber, No. 3D15-2758, Lower Tribunal No. 0026283468-02, 1 February 2017 and the Brazilian Superior Labour Court that pronounced Uber drivers are contractors. In Australia in June 2019, the Fair Work Ombudsman decided to qualify Uber drivers as independent contractors, https://www.fairwork.gov.au/about-us/news-and-media-releases/2019-media-releases/june-2019/20190607-uber-media-release. Accessed 10 June 2020.

IV. What can we Learn from Taxation?

A common definition, or at least a common understanding of what constitutes an employment relationship, would facilitate the taxation of "platform workers". As highlighted, however, such a definition is lacking across countries, or at a supranational level, and even across inter-related sub-disciplines (labour law, tax law, social security contributions). Given the importance of the classification of gig workers either as employees or independent contractors, the lack of common criteria and the complex legal relationships in the platform economy have led to the paradoxical situation that one and the same person, the Uber driver for instance, may for labour law purposes be classified as an independent contractor, whereas for tax law and/or social security law purposes as an employee. The situation is even more complex when driving the Uber car is only an ancillary activity, and the Uber driver's main income is generated through different activities. Similarly, when the Airbnb host is resident in France and he rents out his villa in Portugal for 2 months per year. This section will examine the contribution of taxation in deciphering this complicated relationship in the context of the platform economy.

In a *cross-border scenario*, a worker's income may be taxed in multiple countries, the country/ies where he works (source state(s)) and the country where he resides (residence state). In order to limit or eliminate double taxation, countries usually conclude Double Tax Treaties (DTTs). In a non-cross-border scenario where an employee resides and works in the same place, obviously there would not be much doubt as to where his income from employment should be taxed, although in the context of the platform economy his work may not be visible to the tax authorities. Things get more complex, however, in the case of frontier workers, or posted workers, or people with multiple jobs across the globe. In these cases, usually the DTTs aim, via their distributive rules, to "allocate taxing rights" between the involved states. This allocation does not imply that the DTT creates a taxing right in one state, but it rather suggests that if the income from employment has already been taxed in state A (source state), then state B (the residence state) should refrain from taxing the income again and provide for relief from the double taxation that would otherwise arise.[61] In absence of a DTT, then in principle both the source state and the residence state would have a right to tax.

61 The relief is usually provided either via the exemption method (Article 23A OECD MC) or the credit method (Article 23B OECD MC).

These DTTs usually follow the Organisation for Economic Cooperation and Development Model Convention on Income and Capital (hereinafter OECD MC).[62] Article 15 of the OECD MC provides that when employment is exercised in a country other than the residence country, then salaries, wages and other similar remuneration shall be taxed in the source state, in other words the state where employment is performed. The double taxation that could arise may, thus, be resolved either via the applicable DTTs or in an intra-EU scenario, by resorting to the non-discrimination principle and the fundamental freedoms, provided some other conditions are met.[63]

1. Double Tax Treaties and the OECD MC

In social law, it has already been discussed whether the place of work rule (as a conflict of law rule of Regulation 883/2004) is still apt for social insurance purposes. Other options (based on the location of a platform provider or of a client) would, on the one hand, address the problem that platform providers and clients might try to take advantage of "a planetary labour market" in digital work,[64] where platforms and clients can choose the cheapest platform workers (service providers) and countries without social and tax obligations imposed on platforms or clients. On the other hand, such options are inconsistent with the collection of social contributions at the source.

The underlying problem in both social law and tax law is finding a *nexus* to tax or to collect social security contributions in a digitalised world. It has been widely accepted that the rules defining the legal bases upon which a State may assert its tax jurisdiction over a particular taxpayer or an item of income (nexus rules) will have to be rewritten.[65] The purpose of this section is to provide for an overview of the existing allocation rules

62 Developing countries usually follow the UN Model, which is similar (but not identical) to the OECD MC.

63 There is extensive CJEU case law that requires, inter alia, that resident and non-resident taxpayers are found to be in a comparable situation.

64 *Graham, Mark/Anwar, Mohammad Amir,* The Global Gig Economy: Towards a Planetary Labour Market? in: First Monday, 24 (2019) 4.

65 *Gadzo, Stjepan*, New Nexus for the Digital Economy: An Analysis of Digital, Revenue-Based and User-Based Factors, in: Pistone, Pasquale/Weber, Dennis (eds.), Taxing the Digital Economy: The EU Proposals and other Insights, Amsterdam: IBFD 2019, p. 93.

with regard to income from employment, in order to investigate whether they can provide a) for any useful guidance as to the distinction between independent contractors and employees and b) whether they are still apt for use in the context of the platform economy.

According to the OECD MC, different taxing allocation rules exist depending on the activity of the "worker". Thus, different provisions exist for entertainers and sportspersons whose income may be taxed in the state where they perform (Article 17 OECD MC), pensions that are usually taxable in the state of residence of the recipient (Article 18 OECD MC), government services (Article 19 OECD MC) and students (Article 20 OECD MC). Of relevance for the purposes of taxation of workers and/or self-employed persons are also Article 7 OECD MC on business profits, as well as the definition of what constitutes a Permanent Establishment (hereinafter PE) in Article 5 OECD MC, and when and how profits can be attributed to it. If an enterprise carries out business through a PE, the profits that are attributable to the PE may be taxed in the state of the PE. Such may be the case, for instance, when a company carries out business in another state via a dependent agent.[66]

While the aforementioned provisions will at first appear rather evident as to their application in a cross-border scenario, there are too many variables to be considered in order to answer *where* the particular income will be taxed, and *how* it will be taxed. These variables include factual assessments, such as the frequency with which a frontier worker returns to his "home country" during a fiscal year;[67] as well as interpretative assessments including qualification of the particular income,[68] residence qualification and qualification (or absence thereof) of the "employee" status. This ensuing lack of coordination becomes all the more visible in the context of the digital economy, whereby physical presence is not essential and the type of work provided is uncertain in terms of frequency, ancillary character and legal definition.

66 For more information on the distinction between dependent and independent agent, see paragraph 32 of the OECD MC Commentary on Article 5.

67 See, for instance, Article 15 (2) of the OECD MC.

68 For instance, does the income at issue qualify as income from employment or as business profit? The distinction is not always clear and depends also on the qualification of the person at issue as employed or self-employed.

However, the OECD MC could be of assistance in understanding the *concept of employment* in international tax law. Article 15 (1) and (2) OECD MC read: [69]

> "1. Subject to the provisions of Articles 16, 18 and 19, salaries, wages and other similar remuneration derived by a resident of a Contracting State *in respect of an employment* shall be taxable only in that State unless the employment is exercised in the other Contracting State. If the employment is so exercised, such remuneration as is derived therefrom may be taxed in that other State.
> 2. Notwithstanding the provisions of paragraph 1, remuneration derived by a resident of a Contracting State in respect of an employment exercised in the other Contracting State shall be taxable only in the first-mentioned State if:
> a) the recipient is present in the other State for a period or periods not exceeding in the aggregate 183 days in any twelve month period commencing or ending in the fiscal year concerned, and
> b) the remuneration is paid by, or on behalf of, an employer who is not a resident of the other State, and
> c) the remuneration is not borne by a permanent establishment which the employer has in the other State."

Article 15 OECD MC includes several undefined terms, on which the Commentary attempts to shed some light.[70] However, the concept of employment itself is not analysed in the Commentary. Instead, the Commentary only acknowledges that "[...] the issue of whether or not services are provided in the exercise of an employment may sometimes give rise to difficulties which are discussed in paragraphs 8.1 ff".[71] Yet, one could argue

69 Note the change in the title of Article 15 OECD MC in 2000, from "Dependent Personal Services" to "Employment". The amendment followed the elimination of Article 14 OECD MC which referred to "Independent Personal Services".

70 For a discussion on the many undefined terms, see *Peeters, Bernard,* Article 15 of the OECD Model Convention on "Income from Employment" and its Undefined Terms, in: European Taxation, 44 (2004) 2, pp. 72-82.

71 Commentary on Article 15 (1) OECD MC (2017 version). See also para. 8.1. of the Commentary on Article 15 (1) OECD MC that provides: "It may be difficult, in certain cases, to determine whether the services rendered in a State by an individual resident of another State, and provided to an enterprise of the first State (or that has a permanent establishment in that State), constitute employment services, to which Article 15 applies, or services rendered by a separate enterprise, to which Article 7 applies or, more generally, whether the exception applies."

that from the remaining Commentary some valuable characteristics of what constitutes employment in this particular context could be derived.

Subject to the limit described in paragraph 8.11 and unless the context of a particular convention requires otherwise, it is a *matter of domestic law of the State of source* (i.e. the place where the employment is exercised) to determine whether services rendered by an individual in that State are provided in an employment relationship and that determination will govern how that State applies the Convention.[72] In such cases, the relevant domestic law may ignore the way in which the services are characterised in the formal contracts. It may prefer to focus primarily on the nature of the services rendered by the individual and their integration into the business carried out by the enterprise that acquires the services to conclude that there is an employment relationship between the individual and that enterprise.[73] The Commentary then goes on to give guidance on when a formal contractual employment relationship should be disregarded, taking into account the relevant facts and circumstances.[74] As already mentioned, the distinction between "employment services" and "services rendered under a contract for the provision of services"[75] is important for the application of the relevant DTT article and the allocation of taxing rights between the states.[76] The Commentary encourages the involved states to solve any disagreement as to the qualification of the work relationship having regard to the nature of the services rendered by the individual. In this bid, according to the Commentary, when the services rendered by the individual constitute an integral part of the business of the enterprise to which these services are provided, "it is logical to assume" that an *employee* will be providing such services.[77] For that purpose, a key consideration will be which enterprise bears *the responsibility or risk for the results produced by the individual's work.*

---

72 Para. 8.4. of the Commentary on Article 15 (1) OECD MC (2017 version).

73 Para. 8.7. of the Commentary on Article 15 (1) OECD MC (2017 version).

74 See notably para. 8.11. of the Commentary on Article 15 (1) OECD MC (2017 version): "For instance, a State could not argue that services are deemed, under its domestic law, to constitute employment services where, under the relevant facts and circumstances, it clearly appears that these services are rendered under a contract for the provision of services concluded between two separate enterprises."

75 Similar to the concept of the independent contractor.

76 In the case of the independent contractor, Article 7 OECD MC would apply whereas in the case of employment, Article 15 OECD MC would apply. The two articles allocate in a different manner the taxing rights of the residence and the source state.

77 Para. 8.13. of the Commentary on Article 15 (1) OECD MC (2017 version).

Additional factors and questions to be taken into account when determining the working relationship, include:[78]

- who has the authority to instruct the individual regarding the manner in which the work has to be performed;
- who controls and has responsibility for the place at which the work is performed;
- whether the remuneration of the individual is directly charged by the formal employer to the enterprise to which the services are provided;
- who puts the tools and materials necessary for the work at the individual's disposal;
- who determines the number and qualifications of the individuals performing the work;
- who has the right to select the individual who will perform the work and to terminate the contractual arrangements entered into with that individual for that purpose;
- who has the right to impose disciplinary sanctions related to the work of that individual;
- who determines the holidays and work schedule of that individual.

These *indicative* factors do not provide for any clear solutions as to the qualification of gig workers. As Reis and Chand observe, both indications of employment (some degree of subordination and control by the company) and of independent services (flexibility of the drivers) can be met in the case of Uber drivers.[79] Consequently, while the OECD MC provides for some indicia that could lead to the platform workers' classification, the "hybridity" of many platform models that encompass worker characteristics of both an employee and a contactor cannot be resolved by solely relying on the Commentary. In case of no agreement between the states, the Commentary advises to use, where appropriate, the mutual agreement procedure (MAP) to resolve the tax dispute.

78 The factors as appear in para. 8.14. of the Commentary on Article 15 (1) OECD MC (2017 version). Note that the Commentary suggests that these are "additional factors [that] may be relevant to determine whether this is really the case [i.e. a formal employment relationship or a contract on the provision of services]."

79 *Reis, Ariene/Chand, Vikram*, Uber Drivers: Employees or Independent Contractors? (fn. 44).

2. *Can VAT Provisions be of any Help?*

a) Carrying out Activities "Independently"

The payment of indirect taxes, specifically VAT, may also provide for guidance with respect to the distinction between independent contractor and employee in the context of the platform economy. In general, employees are not required to register for and pay VAT, unlike independent contractors. One of the distinguishing criteria is, once again, the exercise of activities "independently". Article 10 of the EU VAT Directive provides that the requirement of "independent" activity, to qualify as a VAT "taxable person",[80] excludes "employed and other persons from VAT in so far as they are bound to an employer by a contract of employment or by any other legal ties creating the relationship of employer and employee as regards working conditions, remuneration and the employer's liability." Therefore, the concept of independence becomes once again essential in informing the distinction between independent contractor and employee.[81]

In the Court's case law, the three criteria used to determine whether an activity is carried out independently, include: a) whether it is exercised by a person who is not organically integrated into the undertaking; b) whether the person at issue has the appropriate organisational freedom with regard to the human and material resources used in the exercise of the relevant activity; and c) whether the person at issue bears any economic risk when performing the relevant activity.

It is obvious that an evaluation of the aforementioned criteria necessitates an ad hoc factual assessment. The CJEU has provided guidance as to the concept of independence in the context of the VAT Directive in several cases.[82] Applying these criteria in the platform economy, one may note that usually "gig workers" are not organically integrated into the platform,

---

80 For the concept of the "taxable person" in EU VAT law see Article 9 (1) Council Directive 2006/112/EC of 28 November 2006 on the Common System of Value Added Tax (hereinafter EU VAT Directive), https://eur-lex.europa.eu/eli/dir/2006/112/oj. Accessed 14 July 2020; analysed right below.

81 Note, however, that the concept of "employee" is not defined anywhere in the VAT Directive.

82 See for instance, CJEU of 18 October 2007, Case C-355/06, van der Steen, ECLI:EU:C:2007:615, where the CJEU ruled that since the sole director at issue received regularly his salary regardless of the company's financial situation, he could not qualify as independent supplier and, hence, was not a taxable person for VAT purposes. Also, CJEU of 12 October 2016, Case C-340/15, Nigl, ECLI:EU:C:2016:764.

they have sufficient organisational autonomy to decide whether to drive their cars or rent their properties, and that their remuneration is not regular and secured in that it depends on the number of transactions concluded. The "independent activity" criteria, therefore, as enshrined in Article 10 of the EU VAT Directive are usually met. However, this does not suffice to qualify a "gig worker" as a "taxable person" for VAT purposes. Article 9 provides for a number of further conditions, which I turn to examine now.

b) Taxable Person

According to the EU VAT Directive, the definition of a taxable person includes any person or entity "who, independently, carries out in any place any economic activity, whatever the purpose or results of that activity".[83] Hence, employed and other persons bound to an employer by a contract of employment or by any other legal ties creating the relationship of employer and employee as regards working conditions, remuneration and the employer's liability, escape taxability under the VAT Directive.

The test the CJEU usually applied to establish whether a particular activity, including the renting out of property, fulfils Article 9 (1) of the VAT Directive examines whether the activity is carried out for the purpose of obtaining income on a continuing basis.[84] This criterion must be assessed on a case-by-case basis "having regard to all the circumstances of the case, which include, *inter alia*, the nature of the property concerned".[85]

The term "economic activity" has been interpreted by the CJEU in very broad terms, considering the activity per se rather than its purpose or results.[86] Along these lines, the CJEU has repeatedly held that: "[T]he fact

83 Article 9 (1) EU VAT Directive. With regard to the second condition (i.e., independent performance), it may be concluded that in cases where the sharing platform can be recognised as an employer of an individual provider (for the latter, the criteria of the existence of a subordination link, the nature of work and the presence of remuneration should be assessed pursuant to EU law), the individual provider may not be regarded as a taxable person. In such cases, only the sharing platform may be regarded as a taxable person instead – also with regard to underlying supplies of goods and services.

84 CJEU of 19 July 2012, Case C-263/11, Rēdlihs, ECLI:EU:C:2012:497, para. 33; CJEU of 20 June 2013, Case C-219/12, Finanzamt Freistadt Rohrbach Urfahr, ECLI:EU:C:2013:413, para. 19.

85 Ibid., Rēdlihs, para. 29.

86 CJEU of 12 January 2006 Joined Cases C-354/03, C-355/03 and C-484/03, Optigen Ltd, Fulcrum Electronics Ltd, Bond House Systems Ltd v. Comm'n,

that [the] property is suitable only for economic exploitation will normally be sufficient for a finding that its owner is exploiting it for the purposes of economic activities and, consequently, for the purpose of obtaining income on a continuing basis. By contrast, if, by reason of its nature, property is capable of being used for both economic and private purposes, all the circumstances in which it is used will have to be examined in order to determine whether it is *actually being used* for the purpose of obtaining income on a continuing basis (emphasis added)".[87]

Consequently, if the property is, due to its nature, clearly used for purposes of obtaining income on a continuing basis, then it (the economic activity) will be subject to VAT. If the use of the property, as matter of fact, is not clear, then a more complex, factual analysis will be necessary to assess whether the activity is carried out for the purpose of obtaining income on a continuing basis.

Several issues arise with respect to whether "platform workers" are (and should be) subject to VAT. At first sight, the CJEU-made "continuity" condition seems to be rebuttable: for instance, in the case of Airbnb rentals, if one shows that the purpose of renting out the property for a very short period did not aim at "obtaining income *on a continuing basis*", then the activity will not be subject to VAT. Hence, in a strictly literal interpretation of the phrase, it remains unclear whether someone who has rented out his apartment every August for the past five years should be assessed. Recent legislation in some countries has reduced, for non-tax-related reasons, the number of days a service provider can provide short-term rentals of his immovable property.[88]

Article 12 of the VAT Directive attempts to ensure that even these service providers can be made subject to VAT: it stipulates that "Member States *may* regard as a taxable person anyone who carries out, on an *occasional basis*, a transaction relating to the activities referred to in the second subparagraph of Article 9 (1)" (emphasis added). While the CJEU has held that the mere exercise of the right of ownership and the management of

---

ECLI:EU:C:2006:16, para. 43 and CJEU of 26 March 1987, Case C-235/85, Comm'n v. Netherlands, ECLI:EU:C:1987:161, para. 8.

87 CJEU of 19 July 2012, Case C-263/11, Rēdlihs, ECLI:EU:C:2012:497, para. 34; CJEU of 20 June 2013, Case C-219/12, Finanzamt Freistadt Rohrbach Urfahr, ECLI:EU:C:2013:413, para. 20.

88 In Paris, for instance, short-term rentals (Airbnb type) were reduced by law to a maximum of 120 days per year. In Amsterdam, owners will be able to rent out their property through Airbnb only for thirty days per year.

the private property do not constitute economic activity,[89] it has also ruled that if the party has taken active steps to market property by mobilising resources similar to those deployed by producers, traders or persons supplying services within the meaning of Article 4 (2) of the [VAT] Directive, such as, in particular, "the carrying out on that land of preparatory work to make development possible, and the deployment of proven marketing measures," then such initiatives go beyond mere exercise of the management of the private property.[90] In other words, marketing or advertising the property constitutes, in the CJEU's view, the distinctive element that separates the mere management of private property from its economic exploitation.

This very broad, CJEU understanding has led the Commission to suggest that:

> "Given the very wide understanding of the concept of economic activity [...] it can be therefore concluded that the supplies of goods and services made through sharing-economy platforms, such as driving customers to requested destinations or renting out immovable property *may* qualify as an economic activity in the sense of the VAT Directive *irrespective of whether such supplies are delivered with clear continuity or on a more occasional basis*" (emphasis added).[91]

Indeed, under these circumstances, and as the Commission notes, it seems almost impossible for "platform workers" to escape the "taxable person" definition. In the Airbnb and Uber scenarios, therefore, once someone uploads an apartment for rent or avails himself of the opportunity, through the Uber platform, to drive someone to that person's destination, he auto-

89 CJEU of 15 September 2011, Joined Cases C-180/10 & C-181/10, Słaby & Others, ECLI:EU:C:2011:589, para. 36; CJEU of 9 July 2015, Case C-331/14, Trgovina Prizma, ECLI:EU:C:2015:456, para. 23.

90 CJEU of 15 September 2011, Joined Cases C-180/10 & C-181/10, Słaby & Others, ECLI:EU:C:2011:589, para. 39-41; CJEU of 9 July 2015, Case C-331/14, Trgovina Prizma, ECLI:EU:C:2015:456, para. 24.

91 European Commission, Question Concerning the Application of EU VAT Provisions: VAT Treatment of Sharing Economy 6, Value Added Tax Comm., Working Paper No. 878, 22 September 2015, https://circabc.europa.eu/sd/a/878e0591-80c9-4c58-baf3-b9fda1094338/8 78%20-%20VAT%20treatment%20of%20sharing%20economy.pdf. Accessed 14 July 2020.

matically becomes a taxable person for VAT purposes, even if he only does so on an occasional basis.[92]

Beretta lists the following as the main conditions to check whether an individual supplier carries out an economic activity pursuant to Article 9 of the VAT Directive: non-exclusionary membership, organisational autonomy, economic risk, regulatory autonomy, remuneration independence and personal liability.[93] He uses four different platforms to evaluate whether these criteria are met: Airbnb, Uber, HomeExchange and BlaBlaCar and he notes that the assessment varies significantly depending on the platform at issue.[94] Upon carrying out a functional analysis, he concludes that only Uber drivers "*might* eventually be recharacterised as employees of the platform" as long as they tick more than half of the criteria listed.[95]

c) Economic Activity/ Income Definition

Although one would expect that the definition of the type of work precedes the income definition, it is noteworthy to examine the questions that pertain to what kind of income should be taxed. To exemplify the problem, income arising from renting property via Airbnb could be classified as either income from immovable property or income from business.

The distinguishing criterion in answering this question is a thorny issue. The remuneration or "income" the platform worker receives varies widely depending on the platform itself and the worker himself. As the Commission pointed out, such income could range from "recovering costs (e.g.[,] for the personal use of a good such as in ride-sharing/car sharing) to amounts comparable to business/work activities."[96] While the Commission suggests that "tax rules should follow national laws and jurisprudence,

92 The only obvious escape from the application of VAT in such circumstances would be the application of the *de minimis* exemption from VAT reporting. In this vein, some Member States have established a minimum annual turnover for VAT imposition (VAT registration threshold). See subsection below.

93 *Beretta, Giorgio,* European VAT and the Sharing Economy, Alphen aan den Rijn: Wolters Kluwer 2019, p. 99.

94 Ibid.

95 Ibid.

96 European Commission, Communication from the Commission to the European Parliament, the Council, the European Social and Economic Committee and the Committee of the Regions on A European Agenda for Collaborative Economy, COM (2016) 356, p. 41 (hereinafter EU Collaborative Economy Agenda), avail-

which determine from which moment an activity becomes a business activity,"[97] income is not defined in a uniform manner across the Member States. That fact adds to the uncertainty of the definition of what constitutes an economic activity, according to the test the CJEU employs. Accordingly, the same activity may constitute an economic activity for VAT purposes in one Member State and not in another because the remuneration at issue does not qualify as *income*. If one adds to that situation the different thresholds Member States apply by reference to what constitutes a "professional activity" vis-à-vis an "occasional" activity of private individuals, the fulfilment of the aforementioned definitions becomes even more segregated.

Another interpretation difficulty across the different Member States relates to the exemption of "small businesses" (i.e., businesses with low annual turnover) from VAT registration.[98] This special exemption scheme is applied in most EU Member States, but it is not compulsory. Unfortunately, the VAT Directive does not specify whether "small taxable persons" who participate in the sharing economy (e.g., somebody who occasionally rents out his apartment) can benefit from such exemption schemes. One (administratively burdensome!) option would be to treat them all as "full-blown taxable persons" based on "tax points".[99] The other option would be to extend the special rules for small businesses to the "small taxpayers" in the context of the sharing economy.[100]

As a yardstick for measuring the level of business activity, a person's annual turnover, exclusive of VAT, is generally used.[101] However, registration thresholds vary consistently among Member States. Some Member States set very high thresholds before a person incurs VAT payment obligations. Italy for instance, sets a registration threshold at EUR 65,000, whereas Fin-

---

able at https://ec.europa.eu/transparency/regdoc/rep/1/2016/EN/1-2016-356-EN-F 1-1.PDF. Accessed 10 June 2020.

97 Ibid.

98 Articles 284-287, EU VAT Directive. Member States are allowed to exempt small businesses from VAT registration up to a given threshold.

99 *Kogels, Han/van Hilten, Markien*, Never a Dull Moment, in: International VAT Monitor, 28 (2017) 2, p. 121. Tax points (or "time of supply") for a transaction is the date the transaction takes place for VAT purposes. Tax points can be, for instance, the date of invoice or the day the supply took place.

100 Ibid., p. 122.

101 *Beretta, Giorgio*, VAT and the Sharing Economy, in: World Tax Journal, 10 (2018) 3, pp. 381, 414.

land and Greece do so at only EUR 10,000.[102] It is doubtful how many Airbnb hosts would reach the Italian threshold, and how much the market would be distorted due to these differences.[103] Some other Member States, such as Greece, grant service providers an exemption from VAT as long as the host does not provide any services similar to the ones offered by hotels, such as regular cleaning and linen changes.[104]

A remedy against potential tax evasion that could arise from the non-payment of VAT by platform workers is the collection of such VAT by the relevant platform (in addition to any other taxes they collect), provided, however, that the hosts have exceeded the threshold for VAT registration. This would presuppose an updated and informed reporting system between the platform and the platform worker. This way, all relevant details that would define the amount to be paid by the taxpayer would already be available to the platform and the risk of tax evasion would be minimised.

3. *Enforcement and Collection*

An additional problem that is created by blurring the boundaries between employment and self-employment in the platform economy is the difficulty for the authorities to "follow the money".[105] The lack of visibility of the activity and the inability to identify potential taxpayers and their taxable income has cost the tax authorities billions of tax revenue.[106] This obviously poses obstacles to effective taxation and collection of taxes. The solutions

---

102 For VAT registration thresholds, see https://www.avalara.com/vatlive/en/eu-vat-rules/eu-vat-number-registration/vat-registration-threshold.html. Accessed 14 July 2020.

103 *Houlder, Vanessa*, Airbnb's Edge on Room Prices Depends on Tax Advantages, Financial Times, 2 January 2017, https://www.ft.com/content/73102c20-c60e-11e6-9043-7e34c07b46ef, reported that: "When you book an Airbnb room in London, around a third of the USD 100 saving you make over the price of an average hotel room is due to tax advantages that favour Airbnb's business model." Accessed 13 July 2020.

104 Article 111 (4) of Law 4446/2016 as amended by Law 4472/2017.

105 *Mineva, Daniela/Stefanov, Ruslan*, Evasion of Taxes and Social Security Contributions. September 2018, European Platform Undeclared Work.

106 While estimates of lost tax revenue per country do not exist, this is a recurring theme. See for instance, OECD, Shining Light on the Shadow Economy: Opportunities and Threats (see fn. 42); *Migai, Clement Okello/de Jong, Julia/Owens, Jeffrey*, The Sharing Economy: Turning Challenges into Compliance Opportunities for Tax Administrations, in: eJournal of Tax Research, 16 (2018) 1, https://www.business.unsw.edu.au/About-Site/Schools-Site/Taxation-Business-Law-Site/Docu

for effectively taxing the sharing economy, in the OECD's view, should focus on improving the effective taxation of activities facilitated by online platforms through improving taxpayer education and facilitating self-reporting.[107] Effective taxation becomes, hence, a matter of collaboration between the platform and the taxpayer. This recommendation has been implemented by some Member States that have attempted to incentivise the service providers to include their income from the sharing economy when completing their tax returns through simplified procedures or automated, pre-prepared tax declarations available to the service providers directly through the platforms. In France, for example, as of July 2016, collaborative platforms have been legally obliged to communicate to each individual providing services in the sharing economy an annual summary of their tax situation, mentioning how to do their tax declaration and how much they have to declare to the tax authorities.[108]

Other countries, like Belgium, provide tax incentives to platform workers if the latter enrol with a platform and register their activities.[109] Reduced taxation applies to platform workers who provide services up to a EUR 6,000 exemption threshold per year.[110] The platform must share the income of the platform worker with the tax administration. If the income exceeds the EUR 6,000 cap, then the platform worker must register as self-employed and be affiliated with the mandatory social security system for the self-employed.

A commonly used example of a successful strategy for simplifying and streamlining tax collection is Estonia. Upon working together with Uber, the Estonian Tax and Customs Board developed a (voluntary) income data reporting system that would simplify the tax declaration process for Uber drivers. The main idea was to minimise bureaucracy and facilitate automatic tax reporting for businesses and entrepreneurs. Consequently, transactions between the driver and the customer are registered by the collaborative platform, which then only sends the data that is relevant for taxation purposes to the authorities, who in turn will then pre-prepare the taxpay-

---

ments/The-sharing-economy-turning-challenges-into-compliance-CM-JdJ-JO.pdf. Accessed 14 July 2020.

107 OECD, 2018 OECD Interim Report (fn. 8), p. 198.

108 EU Collaborative Economy Agenda (fn. 96), p. 43.

109 In order for the platform worker to benefit from the tax exemption, the platform needs to be formally recognised by the Belgian authorities.

110 OECD, OECD Economic Surveys: Belgium, February 2020, p. 115, https://www.oecd.org/economy/surveys/Belgium-2020-OECD-economic-survey-overview.pdf. Accessed 14 July 2020.

er's tax forms. The main idea is to help taxpayers fulfil their tax obligations effectively and with minimal effort. The voluntary income reporting system has been operational since the 2017 tax year and it is not limited to the ride sharing sector; all platform operators can use the system if they wish. However, it remains an "opt-in" system – if the platform decides not to join, then reporting relies on the "good will" of the platform worker.[111]

Denmark has also developed an automated income reporting system that could be used by all platforms. Currently, Denmark is testing the "technical pilot" in several platforms in order to investigate the technical feasibility of having an automated reporting scheme and a technology to support platforms and taxation.[112] This reporting system necessitated a change in the Danish law in December 2018 stating that digital platforms that facilitate the letting of property (homes, cars, etc.) should report all income earned by users of the platforms to the Danish tax authorities.[113]

Mexico is another example of successful cooperation between the tax authorities, the platform and the service providers. By using data recording technologies that drivers of a particular ride-for-hire service are able to use, the platform's own systems file and send invoices to the customers and to the Mexican Tax Administration (Servicio de Administración Tributaria (SAT)), as well as download them for record-keeping purposes.[114]

In Australia, a consultation paper by the Treasury suggested that the reporting "burden" should be placed either at the platform level or at the financial institutions' level.[115] Operators of sharing economy platforms should be required to collect and report to the Australian Taxation Office (ATO) key information such as identity details and income received by their sellers based in Australia. Some platforms may already provide transaction information on a regular basis to their sellers, which assists them to meet their tax or other obligations and can be used by the ATO to match

---

111 See also *Ogembo, Daisy/Lehdonvirta, Vili,* Taxing Earnings from the Platform Economy: An EU Digital Single Window for Income Data?, in: British Tax Review, 82 (2020) 1, pp. 92-93.

112 Ibid., p. 89.

113 Ibid. The authors also note that "[g]ig work platforms were also considered but excluded from the scope of this initial legislation because of Denmark's complex social security legislation."

114 OECD, 2018 OECD Interim Report (fn. 8), p. 201. Drivers are obliged to register with the particular recording system of the platform.

115 The Australian Government Treasury, Tackling the Black Economy: A Sharing Economy Reporting Regime – A Consultation Paper in Response to the Black Economy Taskforce Final Report, January 2019, https://apo.org.au/node/216381. Accessed 10 June 2020.

and potentially to pre-fill in tax returns. This will contribute to reducing the compliance burden on taxpayers.[116] Alternatively, the financial institution or the payment processors, who would be required to report the transaction data to the tax authorities, could incur the reporting burden. Such an "opt-in" model – with variations – already exists in Estonia.[117]

In July 2020, the OECD released a new global tax reporting framework, the Model Rules for Reporting by Platform Operators with respect to Sellers in the Sharing and Gig Economy ("MRDP").[118] Under the MRDP, digital platforms are required to collect information on the income realised by those offering accommodation, transport and personal services through platforms and to report the information to tax authorities. While the model reporting rules included in the MRDP are not compulsory for "interested jurisdictions", they constitute a first consolidated effort by the OECD to codify on a uniform basis information collection and information reporting by specific platforms. This way, automatic exchange agreements between such interested jurisdictions will be facilitated, and the proliferation of different domestic reporting requirements will be contained.

V. Conclusion

Upon analysing the several problems and solutions provided from a tax perspective, the question remains: how can taxation be of use for social law? The first takeaway relates to the taxation of the platform. If platforms are tax-incentivised to "hire" contractors, then obviously, they will resist any change in the work relationship between them and the platform workers, as the Uber example in California demonstrates. By contrast, if platforms receive adequate tax deductions and credits that could set off the social security contributions they pay for employees, then a formal employment contract would be an option for both parties.

The second question relates to the issue as to who should identify the work relationship and under which criteria. While it is widely acknowl-

116 Ibid.

117 For details on the "small business account", see Chapter 11, Section V, pp. 299 et seq.

118 OECD, Model Rules for Reporting by Platform Operators with respect to Sellers in the Sharing and Gig Economy, OECD, Paris, 2020, https://www.oecd.org/tax/exchange-of-tax-information/model-rules-for-reporting-by-platform-operators-with-respect-to-sellers-in-the-sharing-and-gig-economy.htm. Accessed 10 September 2020.

edged that labour law, social law and tax law serve different purposes, and that the same person may be classified differently for social law or tax law purposes respectively, it appears that the criteria of dependence, subordination and freedom in the way to provide services are pertinent across jurisdictions and different legal areas, including within taxation (VAT and OECD MC). Even though, indeed, an *ad hoc* assessment will have to be performed each time, it is possible that the existing case law from these three interrelated areas may result in convergence towards one, uniformly applicable test. Such a coordinated approach would prevent resorting to circular arguments including the platform worker's *tax* treatment for *labour* law classification purposes, which may lead to contradictory results.

Finally, the discussion at policy level appears to be slowly including the taxation of platform workers and the revenue lost due to the platform shadow economy. Platform workers, even when they fall under the "independent contractor" status should be facilitated and encouraged to declare their income. A series of reporting measures has been proposed by several countries that often requires the cooperation of the platform, the worker and the tax authorities. Laudably, the OECD published very recently its Model Rules for Reporting by Platform Operators that aim to provide (in a consistent and uniform manner) guidance to jurisdictions as to the reporting rules to be adopted and applied to platforms. A combination of the right tax incentives at both platform and platform workers' level, together with a simplified reporting system would contribute to ensuring both adequate revenue to finance social security schemes as well as a framework that would assist in fighting bogus self-employment.